I0881078

Hanna Temkin

MY INVOLUNTARY JOURNEYS

A Memoir

Hanna Temkin

My Involuntary Journeys

A Memoir

יד ושם
YAD VASHEM
THE WORLD HOLOCAUST REMEMBRANCE CENTER
THE INTERNATIONAL INSTITUTE FOR HOLOCAUST RESEARCH

Hanna Temkin
My Involuntary Journeys
A Memoir

Academic Editor: Eliyana R. Adler
Language Editor: Adina Mendelsohn
Production Editor: Enno Raschke

© 2023 All rights reserved to Yad Vashem
P.O.B. 3477, Jerusalem 9103401, Israel
publications.marketing@yadvashem.org.il

The publisher has made every effort to trace the copyright holders and to obtain permission to reproduce copyrighted material included in this book. Any inadvertent errors or omissions will be rectified at the earliest opportunity.

This book may not be reproduced, in whole or in part, in any form, without written permission from the publisher.

Responsibility for the opinions expressed in this publication is solely that of the author.

ISBN 978-965-308-681-4

Typesetting: Ronit Gilad

Printed in Israel by Ayalon Amit and Raffi Ltd.

To Gabriel, with love for the life we shared,
and to our children Henryk and Helena.
For my family that was,
and for the generations that follow.

CONTENTS

FOREWORD

A CHILD OF HER TIME AND PLACE OF BIRTH[1]

The "journeys" in the title of Hanna Temkin's (1921–2019) memoir, *My Involuntary Journeys*, are both literal and metaphorical. Temkin had to relocate—and reinvent herself in a new country and culture—multiple times during her long and productive life. As she writes,

> As a child of my time and place of birth, who was caught in the web of the war, survived the Holocaust unleashed by Nazi Germany on Eastern Europe, as well as the tumultuous years after the war, I knew but one way to save my life: to run for it. I did, and I survived. I am the lucky one. Millions perished.

1 Readers interested in learning more about Hanna Temkin, her husband, Gabriel, and their experiences might also wish to read his memoir about his time in the Red Army: *My Just War: The Memoir of a Jewish Red Army Soldier in World War II* (Novato: Presidio, 1998). Both Temkins also recorded video testimonies. See Hanna Temkin interview, January 5, 1996, Florida, USA, USC Shoah Foundation Visual History Archive (VHA), 13826; and Gabriel Temkin interview, January 5, 1996, VHA, 13827.

Hers is the story of a life journey through some of the most difficult episodes of the twentieth century. Through it all, Temkin is a judicious guide with an outsider/insider perspective and an abiding interest in how ordinary people responded to the circumstances dealt to them by fate. The reader gets a sense of Temkin's wide-ranging intellect, fascination with the human condition, and adaptability.

Beyond her unique voice and compelling storytelling, Temkin's book also introduces readers to a number of important and unfamiliar settings in the literature in English on Polish Jews in the twentieth century. Temkin spent her first eighteen years in the provincial city of Łódź, neither the metropolis of Warsaw nor a picturesque shtetl. At the outbreak of World War II, unlike the majority of Polish Jews, she fled eastward into Soviet territory. She thus escaped the German occupation and had to contend with dislocation, hunger, and an entirely foreign political and social system. After the war, she returned to Poland, and instead of emigrating, along with most other surviving Polish Jews, she stayed there until the political upheavals of 1968.

All of these factors make her memoir particularly valuable to students of the Holocaust, regarding Jewish life in Poland, the wartime Soviet Union, and the sweep of modern Jewish history. Temkin's memoir is rich in insights and characters from her dramatic and mobile life. This introduction seeks to provide historical context for these lesser-known twentieth-century Jewish journeys.

Interwar Łódź

Hanna Temkin, née Rabinowicz, was born into a traditional and working-class Jewish family in Łódź, the declining industrial center and second-largest city in interwar Poland. She describes her family and life there with appreciation, but also with a clear-eyed perspective on the political and economic struggles faced by so many during that period. Although her narrative includes information about the deaths of these same relatives in the Holocaust, this does not preclude her from rendering them as complex and fully human.

Temkin's book is not the first to describe Jewish life in prewar Łódź. In addition to numerous Holocaust memoirs, English readers also have access to Chava Rosenfarb's semi-fictional work.[2] Yet Temkin devotes more space to the city and her early life than many of these other texts. Hers is not just a war story but a life story. As such, it describes her family's decline from working class to barely surviving. Although the particulars are unique to her parents, the general trend was fairly common.

The Second Polish Republic, which emerged out of the ruins of the pre-World War I Russian and Austrian empires, was built on shaky economic and political ground despite its great promise from a patriotic perspective. In recognition of the Polish contribution to the war and long-suffering cause, the powers in Versailles granted them a large country. Polish leaders celebrated their national rebirth, while also being aware that the war-torn landscape and population, including the national minorities, which constituted 20 percent, would make it challenging to forge a strong and unified nation.[3]

The new country struggled to meet its citizens' needs but also, particularly in its first decade, proved to be a dynamic democracy where Jews, about 10 percent of the population, could take an active role in political and cultural life. In the latter half of the interwar period, with

2 Chava Rosenfarb, *The Tree of Life: A Trilogy of Life in the Lodz Ghetto* (Madison: University of Wisconsin Press, 2004). Some of the memoirs of survivors of the Holocaust and of Soviet exile in English include: Sara Zyskin, *Stolen Years* (Minneapolis: Lerner Publications, 1981); Sara Selver-Urbach, *Through the Window of My Home: Recollections from the Lodz Ghetto* (Jerusalem: Yad Vashem Press, 1986); Ben Abraham, *And the World Remained Silent* (New York: Vantage Press, 1996); Manny Drukier, *Carved in Stone: Holocaust Years—A Boy's Tale* (Toronto: University of Toronto Press, 1996); Israel Ignac Feldman, *The Lost Dream* (Toronto: Lorne Miller and Associates, 2007); and Ann Szedlecki, *Album of My Life* (Toronto: The Azrieli Foundation, 2010).

3 Much has been written about Polish history in the modern era in English. See, for example, the second volume of Norman Davies's classic *God's Playground: A History of Poland*, 2 vols. (New York: Columbia University, 1982). For a useful summary of the interwar period, see Halik Kochanski, *The Eagle Unbowed: Poland and the Poles in the Second World War* (Cambridge: Harvard University Press, 2012).

the death of Poland's founding father and under the conditions of the Great Depression, economic despair deepened, and antisemitism was increasingly mobilized as a political tool not only of marginal groups but even in governing circles. The largest Jewish community in Europe faced the paradox of burgeoning Jewish cultural and religious life combined with crushing poverty and growing hatred.[4]

While these circumstances prevailed throughout the country, Łódź had its own challenges. Having emerged as a textile boomtown in the Russian Empire, it had been allowed to develop haphazardly, with enormous inequality. State-of-the-art factories and the palatial homes of their owners stood alongside workers' neighborhoods that lacked basic amenities. The collapse of the manufacturing center during World War I left the largely proletarian city without plumbing, electricity, or even sidewalks in most of the residential areas.[5] Throughout the interwar period, city leaders struggled to redefine the former industrial capital and build basic services but with little success.[6]

Łódź differed from other Polish cities not only in its industrial decline but also in its uniquely mixed population. Germans and Jews, originally welcomed for their manufacturing know-how, had held prominent positions in the city. Even as their numbers and influence waned in the interwar period, some important families remained there. Whereas Jews represented approximately 10 percent of the overall

4 See Ezra Mendelsohn, "Interwar Poland: Good for the Jews or Bad for the Jews?" in Chimen Abramsky, Maciej Jachimczyk and Antony Polonsky, eds., *The Jews of Poland* (Oxford: Basil Blackwell, 1986). For an overview of the Jewish experience in interwar Poland, see volume three of Antony Polonsky, *The Jews in Poland and Russia* (Oxford: Littman Library, 2013).

5 Wiesław Puś, "The Development of the City of Łódź (1820–1939)," *Polin: A Journal of Polish–Jewish Studies*, vol. 6 (1991), pp. 10–11.

6 Kamil Piskała, "The Interwar: Democratic Politics and Modern City between Two World Wars 1918–1923," Agata Zysiak, Kamil Śmiechowski, Kamil Piskała, Wiktor Marzec, Kaja Kaźmierska, Jacek Burski, eds., *From Cotton and Smoke: Łódź—Industrial City and Discourses of Asynchronous Modernity 1897–1994* (Łódź: Kraków, 2018).

population of the Second Polish Republic, according to the 1921 census, Jews constituted 31 percent of the population of Łódź.[7]

Most of these Jews had come as workers, rather than textile magnates, and lived in the poor and overwhelmingly Jewish part of the city known as Bałuty. This area would also later serve as the location of the second-largest ghetto in Poland. The workers of Bałuty faced the same economic downturn and loss of jobs as those in the rest of the city. Along with the rest of Poland, they weathered the challenges of a new country recovering from war and buffeted by economic and political upheaval. At the same time, the Jews were often blamed for these difficulties.

Temkin spent her early years in an apartment outside the Jewish neighborhood. A year or so before the war, the Rabinowiczes had to relocate to the family "compound" in Bałuty. In telling her own story, and that of her family members, Temkin embodies the paradox of interwar Poland, and especially Łódź. The threats of interethnic antagonism and financial woes take place in tandem with the joys and opportunities of youth. Despite her academic success and passion, and even support from teachers, high school tuition was beyond her family's means and private schools and scholarships were not accessible to Jews. However, she eventually found great purpose, as well as serious intellectual engagement, in the Young Communist League. As she writes about her intense reading of Marxist literature,

> Anyway, trying to find an answer to my questions, I realized that I did not envy these girls anymore for having what I wanted and never got—access to formal education. I had found my informal way to the sources of knowledge and was taking full advantage of these rich, endless sources.

Temkin's description of her involvement in political education and activism is masterful and reflects the central role of youth movements

7 Ibid, p. 152.

in interwar Polish–Jewish life noted by scholars.[8] Her romance with the Communist Party, with the other activists, and especially with Gabriel Temkin, plays out against the backdrop of growing tensions in the world and incipient questions about Soviet power and policies. She manages to depict the naivete and ardor of youth with dignity and understanding,

> Worshipping the Soviet Union was not incompatible with having some doubts about this or that, even if "this or that" was no small horror. Despite everything, the Soviet Union remained the beacon of hope for working people all over the world, as the phrase went, and it was so for me.

Throughout this period, Temkin also introduces the international and local events leading up to the war.

Indeed, the Holocaust shadows Temkin's description of her family and her youth. Many individuals are depicted not only as she knew them in the 1930s, but also in terms of what she later learned about their deaths. The dispersion of her family, and their survival rates, are fairly representative. Two of Temkin's older siblings, Rachel and Mayer, left to pursue opportunities abroad. As the situation in Poland worsened, the combination of the Great Depression and the rise of Nazism in Germany made it increasingly difficult to find refuge. Fortunately, Rachel and Mayer joined their aunts in Belgium in the early 1930s. Whereas some of their relatives who stayed in Belgium were able to hide and survive, almost all of Temkin's extensive family and group of friends in Poland died in the death camp of Chełmno, established near Łódź to murder its large Jewish community, or other Holocaust sites of suffering and death.

8 See, for example, Ido Bassok, "Jewish Youth Movements in Poland between the Wars as Heirs of the *Kehilah*," *Polin: Studies in Polish Jewry*, vol. 30 (2018); and Emma Zohar, "Feeling Communists: Communism, Emotions, and Gender in Interwar Polish Jewry," *Journal of Modern Jewish Studies* (2020).

Polish–Jewish Refugees in the USSR

Temkin herself avoided almost certain death because of a difficult decision, although no one at the time could have predicted its results. Along with well over 100,000 other Polish Jews, and some of their own relatives, Hanna and her boyfriend, Gabriel, fled east in 1939. Young and impressionable, Hanna spent the next six years largely on her own, wandering around the USSR. She held a variety of jobs, attended several educational institutions, and lived in different regions of the vast and diverse Soviet Union. At each stop along the way, Hanna made friends, while also observing the lives and choices of her colleagues and the Soviet system closely. Her account of this period offers a grassroots-level exploration of life in the USSR during the war and after, as she kept in touch with many of her friends long afterward.

By the time she wrote her memoir, Temkin was well aware of the Holocaust that she narrowly escaped. Indeed, it proves impossible for any of the Polish Jews who survived the war in the unoccupied regions of the USSR to write or speak about their own wartime experiences without referencing the alternative. The genocide that destroyed their families and communities swept through Poland with such force that—at least in retrospect—their trials and tribulations in Soviet exile pale in comparison. Temkin uses a unique and effective metaphor to convey this,

> When I look back at those first months of my life in Gomel, the enormous mass of impressions, the emotions of setting up "a household," of working a full-time job, of getting used to new surroundings, and new people, it makes for a rather blurred picture. In addition, I see all this as if on a small screen on the background of a larger one, something like the picture-in-picture feature some TV sets now have built in. On the larger picture is the war, the German invasion, and events of the recent past—our leaving Łódź, saying goodbye to my parents and sisters.

Portraying her personal struggles as if displayed in the little box overlaid on the larger televised image of the war provides a powerful image of the marginalization of survival in the USSR. The anachronism of contemporary TV technology also neatly points to the backward gaze.

The Soviet invasion of Poland on September 17, 1939, following on the heels of the German invasion on September 1, was initially seen by some leftists as the promise of help. However, even as it became clear that the Soviet Union had come to take its share, for many Jews Soviet occupation was, to use Dov Levin's memorable formulation, the lesser of two evils.[9] While devastated by the rapid fall of their country, they also recognized that the German occupation would undoubtedly bring increased antisemitism, even if they could not yet imagine its dimensions. On the other hand, staying home, with one's social support, local knowledge, and access to resources, is a natural human predilection. Furthermore, many Orthodox Jews, wealthy property owners, and political activists had good reason to fear Soviet retribution. Due to all of these factors, most Polish Jews in the German-held areas remained in their homes; only a relatively small number took their chances by crossing the new border into Soviet-occupied Poland.[10]

For Hanna Rabinowicz and Gabriel Temkin, young Jewish workers with a belief in the promise of the USSR, the hardest part was leaving their families. Her description of crossing the border, and of the crowds and confusion in the new Soviet territory, fits in well with other memoirs of the period. Where her narrative begins to diverge is in their choice to accept the Soviet offer of labor in the interior. Even as the authorities embarked on a process of rapid Sovietization in the formerly Polish areas that they annexed as Western Ukraine and Western Belarus, they also began to pay attention to the population of refugees. Crowded in the cities near the border, the refugees were seen as obstacles to a smooth transition.

9 Dov Levin, *The Lesser of Two Evils: Eastern European Jewry under Soviet Rule, 1939–1941* (Philadelphia: Jewish Publication Society, 1995).

10 On this decision, see Eliyana R. Adler, "Hrubieszów at the Crossroads: Polish Jews Navigate the German and Soviet Occupations," *Holocaust and Genocide Studies* 28:1 (Spring 2014), pp. 1–30; and Eliyana R. Adler and Natalia Aleksiun, "Seeking Relative Safety: The Flight of Polish Jews to the East in the Autumn of 1939," *Yad Vashem Studies* 46:1 (2018), pp. 41–71.

The Polish–Jewish refugees in the new Soviet territories upset the new authorities by continually crossing back and forth across the new border. Some brought other family members with them, while others engaged in black-market smuggling. Additionally, the residents of the annexed areas received automatic Soviet citizenship and had to conform to Soviet laws and mores. However, the refugees operated outside of the system, and Soviet authorities began to blame them not only for speculation but also for engaging in forbidden political organizing and religious activities.[11]

Beginning in November 1939 and lasting until February 1940, the Soviet state launched an effort to solve the refugee problem at the same time as addressing labor shortages in certain industries. Refugees in the newly annexed territories were offered guaranteed jobs, in return for moving where they were needed. Often, the offers included promises of comfortable living quarters, good working conditions, and high pay. In the event, most of the promises remained unfulfilled as the manufacturing and mining centers were not given the advance warning or supplies required to absorb the new workers. The Polish–Jewish volunteers were shocked by the living and working conditions and many, including Hanna and Gabriel, ended up leaving.[12]

One of the unforeseen consequences of opting for labor in the interior was that Hanna and Gabriel avoided the deportation that characterized the experience of the majority of the Polish–Jewish refugees. Those who did not accept either labor in the interior, or a subsequent offer of Soviet citizenship, were rounded up in June 1940 and deported to special settlements in Siberia, the Arctic, the Urals, and Northern Kazakhstan. These labor installations, under the authority of the NKVD, were generally isolated and closed off.[13]

11 See Adler, *Survival on the Margins*, pp. 80–81.

12 Sara Bender, *The Jews of Białystok during World War II and the Holocaust* (Waltham: Brandeis University Press, 2008), pp. 57–58 and Eliyana R. Adler, *Survival on the Margins: Polish Jewish Refugees in the Wartime Soviet Union* (Cambridge: Harvard University Press, 2020), pp. 85–90.

13 Yosef Litvak, "Jewish Refugees from Poland in the USSR, 1939–1944," in Zvi Gittelman, ed., *Bitter Legacy: Confronting the Holocaust in the USSR*

By contrast, although Hanna, Gabriel, and the other refugees who volunteered for labor in the interior also faced difficult working conditions, they had more freedom of movement and possibilities for interaction with Soviet citizens. As a result of these freedoms, Hanna and Gabriel decided to leave the mine in the Urals where they had been working and relocate further west to Gomel. This move offered them greater professional and educational opportunities, a more comfortable climate, and access to people more like themselves. However, it also placed them closer to the border.

Whether deported or working in areas distant from the border, most of the Polish–Jewish refugees had the ambiguous good fortune to evade the fate of the Jewish residents of the new Soviet territories and the small number of refugees who had opted to take Soviet citizenship. These communities were largely overrun by the June 22, 1941, German invasion, and the escalation of the Holocaust that accompanied it.

Located in Gomel, within the pre-1939 borders of the USSR, Hanna and Gabriel had a few extra weeks to escape, yet the German advance was swift. By mid-July, the Axis forces were approaching, and Gabriel had been drafted into the Red Army. Hanna evacuated by train with some relatives and acquaintances, all Jewish women and children. And thus began her period of wandering in the USSR.

Over the next several years, Hanna, only just barely an adult, took on all the responsibilities of adulthood in the midst of war. She became proficient in Russian, developed her clerical skills, supported herself, made new friends, and learned to live in the Soviet Union. Perhaps most impressively, Hanna made important decisions about her life. While remaining in contact with Gabriel and other relations, she lived independently and moved jobs and locations as she saw fit.

In addition to all the informal education involved in adapting to her new environment, work, and social mores, Temkin elected to pursue formal education with all of her considerable energy. Unlike in Poland, where both class and ethnicity mitigated against the pursuit of her educational dreams, the Soviet Union offered tremendous educational

(Bloomington and Indianapolis: Indiana University Press, 1997), pp. 130–131; and Adler, *Survival on the Margins*, pp. 101–147.

opportunities to those willing to work hard. Temkin managed to complete her high school equivalency while working full-time. She then applied for university admittance and moved to Saratov and then Leningrad in pursuit of her degree. Eventually, after the war ended, Gabriel would join her at Leningrad University.

Temkin's depiction of her time in the USSR combines the dread and suffering of war with the joy of friendship and the complexities of life under Stalin. The voluminous literature on the Soviet Union during World War II includes descriptions of the tactical relaxation of certain strictures to rouse public opinion and raise funds and of the overcrowding and lack of resources in evacuation centers.[14] Yet, there are relatively few firsthand testimonies and even fewer by equally astute observers.

At various points, and especially as a student, Hanna lived a meager existence, with barely enough food and warm clothing to survive. She also feared greatly for her family in Poland and for Gabriel in the military. At the same time, she threw herself into her friendships and studies, forming deep and meaningful relationships and taking full advantage of the excellent professors and books at her disposal.

This ambivalence, and the willingness to show diverse perspectives, provide the reader with a multifaceted picture of life in the USSR. It also made it difficult for Hanna and Gabriel to decide whether to stay in the Soviet Union to complete their studies, or to return to a Poland wrecked by war and bereft of their relatives. Finally, after hearing about the tragic life of one of their colleagues, they understood that their place was elsewhere,

> And overwhelmed suddenly by a painful, acute, nostalgic feeling as if stung by those needles, I half-stated, half-asked Gabriel that very same evening, "We are going home, aren't we?" He nodded affirmatively as if he was simply waiting for me to ask the question.

14 See, for example, Shimon Redlich, *Propaganda and Nationalism in Wartime Russia: The Jewish Antifascist Committee in the USSR, 1941–1948* (USA: East European Monographs, 1982); and Rebecca Manley, *To the Tashkent Station: Evacuation and Survival in the Soviet Union at War* (Ithaca: Cornell University Press, 2009).

And so, among all this, my pregnancy, morning sickness, torn by contradictory feelings, we suddenly knew what we had to do: we are going home, we are returning to Poland.

Postwar Poland

In 1946, Gabriel and a pregnant Hanna married and joined the stream of 150,000 or so Polish Jews returning to Poland from the USSR.[15] However, unlike the majority of survivors and repatriates, the Temkins elected to stay and build their family and professions in communist Poland.[16] Although exact numbers are difficult to ascertain, there is general agreement that the postwar high of just under 250,000 Jews in Poland, of whom the majority repatriated from the Soviet Union, diminished to 100,000 by early 1947, when emigration became more difficult. A brief opening of borders in the mid-1950s saw a smaller wave of repatriates from the USSR and a new emigration resulting in perhaps 40,000 Jews remaining in Poland by the end of the decade. Approximately half of this group left as a result of state-sponsored antisemitism at the end of the 1960s.[17]

15 Mark Edele and Wanda Warlik, "Saved by Stalin? Trajectories of Polish Jews in the Soviet Second World War," in Mark Edele, Sheila Fitzpatrick, and Atina Grossmann, eds., *Shelter from the Holocaust: Rethinking Jewish Survival in the Soviet Union* (Detroit: Wayne State University Press, 2015), p. 118.

16 A number of recent books deal with Jewish life and migration in postwar Poland. See, for example, Karen Auerbach, *The House at Ujazdowskie 16: Jewish Families in Warsaw after the Holocaust* (Bloomington: Indiana University Press, 2013); Feliks Tych and Monika Adamczyk-Garbowska, eds., *Presence in Absence: The Aftermath of the Holocaust in Poland, 1944–2010* (Jerusalem: Yad Vashem Publishers, 2014); Anna Cichopek-Gajraj, *Beyond Violence: Jewish Survivors in Poland and Slovakia, 1944–1948* (Cambridge: Cambridge University Press, 2014); Monika Rice, *What! Still Alive?! Jewish Survivors in Poland and Israel Remember Homecoming* (Syracuse: Syracuse University Press, 2017); and Lukasz Krzyzanowski, *Ghost Citizens: Jewish Return to a Postwar City* (Cambridge: Harvard University Press, 2020).

17 Albert Stankowski, "How Many Polish Jews Survived the Holocaust," in Tych and Adamczyk-Garbowska, *Presence in Absence,* pp. 205–217; and Edyta Gawron,

Perhaps surprisingly, although antisemitism appears throughout Temkin's memoir, it is not a major theme. She relates some antisemitic encounters before the war, as well as the rise in harassment of Jews in the USSR during the war. She also notes anxiety about returning to Poland in view of the violent antisemitism there after the war as well as popular and state-sponsored waves of antisemitism in Poland in the 1950s and 1960s. These are part of the narrative, but unlike in other Jewish memoirs, they rarely drive the plot. The July 1946 pogrom in Kielce, for example, cited as a primary rationale for leaving Poland by many Polish–Jewish survivors of the war, is mentioned only in passing by Temkin. Antisemitism was rarely the only reason that Jews decided to leave Poland after the war, yet Kielce became a retrospective turning point.[18] It stands to reason that it would be less significant for someone who chose to remain.

In this decision, Temkin's memoir diverges from other stories of Polish Jews after the war.[19] She offers a multifaceted view of life in the Polish People's Republic. The reader sees Hanna and Gabriel raising their two children, pursuing their educational dreams, and finding success and fulfillment in their academic careers. At the same time, colleagues and friends are raised high or brought low by ideology and politics and emigration to the West is a frequent topic of conversation. Throughout her narrative, Temkin shows the variable nature of life in postwar Poland.

The changing political winds and ambivalence of living as Jews in the early years of the Polish People's Republic are neatly illustrated in her anecdote about naming children in the late 1940s. Even as she and Gabriel struggled with how to honor their deceased fathers in naming their son, a neighbor weighed political factors. "Gabriel wanted to name our son Chaim, after both our fathers," she writes, "but how

"Post-War Emigration of Jews from Poland: The Case of Kraków," in Tych and Adamczyk-Garbowska, *Presence in Absence*, pp. 473–501.

18 Adler, *Survival on the Margins*, pp. 256–257.

19 Exceptions in English include Janina Bauman, *A Dream of Belonging: My Years in Postwar Poland* (London: Vigaro Press, 1988); and Włodzimierz Szer, *To Our Children: Memoirs of Displacement. A Jewish Journey of Survival in Twentieth-Century Poland and Beyond* (Boston: Academic Studies Press, 2016).

could you do this to a child who had to grow up and live in Poland, go to school there? It seemed to deliberately invite problems for the child." Meanwhile, an ambitious non-Jewish neighbor sought advice about how to provide his son with a name that curried political favor without risking trouble as various Polish communist leaders jockeyed for positions. In the end, Hanna and Gabriel chose the solid Polish name of Henryk for their son, and their neighbor gratefully took Hanna's suggestion to bypass internal Polish conflicts and follow the safe path of naming his son after Lenin.

Temkin narrates her family's growth and development alongside that of her country. Readers unfamiliar with the vicissitudes of Polish politics will come across many new names and situations. A series of communist leaders in Poland believed that it would be possible to carve out a state under the Soviet umbrella while also uniquely Polish in character. Describing her tempered optimism in returning to Poland, Temkin wrote, "And there would be a socialist system in Poland, too, it seemed certain now, yes, but it need not repeat the same pattern, with all its drawbacks. Perhaps it will be a better one, a kinder one?"

Against the background of political and social transformation, the Temkins lived a relatively stable and comfortable life. During a bout of political upheaval and increased antisemitism in 1956, some of their friends left Poland, but they decided once again to remain,

> Ten years of hard, intensive work had brought us to a point from where we could see a clear way of doing what we liked to do most and what we could do best, and to leave now, when we had only just started, was just unthinkable and scary, too. And our main tool of work was the Polish language, the only one we felt comfortable in, the one we had learned to express ourselves in.

In the next decade, their decision seemed justified. Both Hanna and Gabriel had success in their fields and were among the privileged few allowed to travel abroad for work and to visit relatives. They accustomed themselves to the peculiarities of their living situation, including that they could leave the country only individually and not with the entire family.

Temkin describes her rise in academia, some of her most colorful colleagues, and her research directions in some detail. She does not pay much attention to questions of gender. It is worth noting, however, that much of the material and moral support that Temkin received in her professional path was due to living in a Communist country. While it is certainly true that the Soviet bloc never achieved the sort of radical equality that Communism seemed to promise, gender norms and universal employment did give women new opportunities. Temkin earned her accolades, but she had the chance to do so at least in part because of living in People's Poland. Indeed, after the family's move to the United States, although Gabriel eventually found an academic post, Hanna was not able to reclaim her previous status.

As in the prewar section of the memoir, where Temkin describes friends and family members of her youth, while also including their wartime fates, the section covering the postwar years highlights her friends' and colleagues' intellectual developments and political dealings in later years. In many ways, these concise biographies depict the political peaks and valleys of postwar Poland even more eloquently than her explanations of party intrigues and changing political directives from Moscow. These stories of individuals and their choices and treatment illustrate what it meant to live in communist Poland. Temkin generally reserves judgment in describing complicated situations, as in her reaction to an acquaintance's apology for having written a denunciation about her, "In the end, things turned out for the better for me. Yet I could not help but wonder what makes a person do such things."

The Temkins' sense of tranquility was eventually disrupted by the upheavals of 1968. Amidst a worldwide movement of student demonstrations, including even within the Soviet bloc, Polish authorities responded to internal dissent by instrumentalizing antisemitism, couched as "anti-Zionism."[20] Hanna's depiction of the unfolding of these events,

20 For more on these events, see Dariusz Stola, "Anti-Zionism as a Multipurpose Policy Instrument: The Anti-Zionist Campaign in Poland, 1967–1968," The Journal of Israeli History 25:1 (2006), pp. 175–201; and "Fighting against the Shadows: The Anti-Zionist Campaign of 1968," in Robert Blobaum, ed., *Antisemitism*

as a spectator and participant, is invaluable. The reader watches how the "anti-Zionist" campaign gradually reached each member of the family, in ways that they could not have imagined previously. In the end, the family elected to leave their homeland together,[21]

> But where to? And how? Into the unknown? Again? Begin anew when you are almost at the peak of your professional career? When you are well over forty?

This brief précis of Hanna Temkin's life passes over many other occurrences along the way and does not do justice to her intellectual achievements or resilience. Nor does it accurately reflect her intense curiosity. It should, however, provide historical framing for some of the major stops on her itinerary. The only way to access her singular style is to read her words on the following pages.

Legacy

In between the time I was asked to edit this text and when I received the manuscript, Hanna Temkin died. She was nearly 100 years old, which, in Polish culture, is the aspiration, as evinced by the ubiquitous birthday song "*sto lat*" (100 years). Although she had not yet approached Jewish culture's higher bar of 120 years, surely it was a long and full life by any measure. According to her daughter, Temkin was active and engaged until the end. While I am genuinely sorry not to have met her in person, Temkin left behind an invaluable legacy in this book.

In our conversations, Helena Temkin-Greener emphasized how important completing this book was to her mother. Although she wrote

and Its Opponents in Modern Poland (Ithaca: Cornell University Press, 2004), pp. 284–300; and Anat Plocker, *The Expulsion of Jews from Communist Poland: Memory Wars and Homeland Anxieties* (Bloomington: Indiana University Press, 2022).

21 Gabriel Temkin's perspective on this same period is available in a powerful essay he wrote soon after the family's arrival in the United States, "Flight from Poland—1968," *Midstream* (April 1969).

it around 2000, her husband Gabriel's subsequent illness and death in 2006, followed by the devastating death of their son in 2009, took much of her energy and attention for the next decade. By the time she came back to finish editing the text and to look for a publisher, her own health was failing. Yet she explained to her doctors that she could not die before seeing the project to fruition.

It is to all of our benefit that Temkin and her family persevered. In a text that is loving, without sentimentality, and honest without self-indulgence, readers have the opportunity to encounter prewar Poland, the wartime Soviet Union, and People's Poland with new eyes. Temkin is a probing yet generous guide to these diverse settings. Her journeys—and her retelling of them—provide readers with invaluable access to crucial, although sometimes overlooked, sites of Jewish life in the twentieth century. Moreover, her humanity and humor, and many of the scenes that she evokes, will stay with us long after we finish reading the book.

***

I am grateful to Ella Florsheim, of Yad Vashem Publications, for inviting me to edit this memoir, and to the other members of staff for their patience and care. Thanks also to Professor Monika Rice for providing comments on a draft of this text and to Helena Temkin-Greener for reading over the introduction, telling me about her mother, and trusting us with this wonderful memoir.

Hanna Temkin was not a native English speaker. This is sometimes reflected in her writing. Since it does not impact readability, we chose to edit the text as little as possible in order to keep her unique voice alive.

Eliyana R. Adler

PREFACE

I came to the United States in the spring of 1969 as a refugee from Poland, then still a Communist country. Harvard University's Russian Research Center kindly awarded me a research fellowship that offered the possibility of returning to a productive life, so crudely interrupted by the forced emigration from my native country.

I was in the United States for the first time. Excited and certainly a bit dazed by the array of impressions, I went to the meeting that traditionally opens the new academic year at the Russian Research Center, my new place of employment. I went with great anticipation, eager to make the acquaintance of my new American colleagues, whom I knew hitherto only from their writings. Unfortunately, I have not retained many memories of that first meeting.

However, a rather odd incident occurred that has stuck in my mind. Amidst the meeting's chatter, an eminent professor's wife approached me. She wanted to know how I, as a Jew, managed to survive the war years in Poland. She was also Jewish, so I understood her interest and was glad to oblige. In brief, I explained that I had escaped the Nazis, fled my native city, Łódź, then traveled to the Soviet Union where I stayed until the war ended and I returned to Poland. Yet twenty years later, I had to emigrate again. She listened attentively, nodded, and said, "Yes, I see you like to travel!"

I took her remark as well intended, as it no doubt was, but I was at a loss for an answer. I admitted rather meekly that yes, I do indeed like to travel. Yet I kept wondering: should I not have also said how much I wished that I hadn't had to make any of those "journeys," this last one included? As a child of my time and place of birth, who was caught in the web of the war, survived the Holocaust unleashed by Nazi Germany on Eastern Europe, as well as the tumultuous years after the war, I knew but one way to save my life: to run for it. I did, and I survived. I am the lucky one. Millions perished.

Years have passed since that first meeting at the Harvard Russian Research Center, but that odd exchange kept coming back to me. It provided me with a rather amusing anecdote. People reacted with understanding smiles to the account of my wartime wanderings as a result of my love for traveling. Some would also urge me to write a "travelogue," and publish it, adding that it should be "interesting" and "educational." I hesitated for a long time. It did not seem right to write about myself. It was somehow "too close for comfort." In my analytical writings, I did as does anyone who writes about conceptual, abstract problems; I hid behind the subject, the problems. However, when writing an autobiography, I would become the subject. To write a kind of "confession," to write about myself without being forced to do so seemed to be beyond me. However, upon reflection, it occurred to me that this would not only be about myself. It would be, first of all, about the impossible, often horrible times that had befallen me, which I managed, despite so many odds, to survive. There's a curse that says, "May you live in interesting times." I, who was cursed by fate and circumstances to live through those "interesting" times, now suddenly felt something akin to an obligation to recount everything. It would also be about people, my loved ones, my family, my peers, people who loved me, people whom I loved, about the world that was and is no longer. And this, too, suddenly felt like a kind of obligation. To bring them back from oblivion! They deserve it! Yes, I decided to try while the images of the places, the events, and the faces had not yet faded away.

This is how this manuscript came into being. Will it ever become a book that a reader will take into his hands and read? This I cannot know, but I hope it will. Will the bygone world, as perceived by me then and as I see it from a distance now, and my feelings experienced then, which I have tried to recapture here, tell the reader something relevant for the present times? Again, I cannot know this, but I continue to hope that it will.

Hanna Temkin
Sarasota, Florida, 2001

Photo of the Rabinowicz family, taken ca. 1930. From left to right: Ajgla Rabinowicz, née Sznurman (1890–1942), the author's mother; Helcia (Helena), Hanna's younger sister (1924–1945); Sala, the older sister (1914–1942); Hanna (Hanka), the author (1921–2019); and the father, Chaim Moshe Rabinowicz (1884–1944). Helcia and Hanna are holding photos of sister Rachel (1908–1925) and brother Mayer (1910–2004), both living in Brussels, Belgium at the time.

CHAPTER ONE

CHILDHOOD

I'm browsing through the old family album. Yes, here it is, the old family portrait! Taken by a professional photographer in Łódź, in the early 1930s, the name of the studio, "Parisian," is proudly displayed in the lower right-hand corner. With a name like this, it must have been a well-known and rather expensive studio, and the occasion for which the photo was taken was considered to be a suitably important one.

Yes, I remember that it was quite an event. My parents, my two sisters, and I all went to be photographed for this family portrait. My parents wanted to send it to our family members, Rachel and Mayer, our older siblings, who at that time lived in Brussels, Belgium, having recently emigrated from Poland in search of a better life and future than Poland could provide or promise.

Over time, the photograph has turned dark brown, but the images of the people have remained clear and unfaded. Here they are: my parents, Ajgla Sznurman and Chaim Moshe Rabinowicz, and the three girls between them, from left to right: my baby sister, Helcia, my sister, Sala, and myself. The missing members of the family are included on the snapshots which Helcia and I are holding. With their snapshots in the portrait, too, a kind of magic act was accomplished, and the family was complete and whole again! This seemed to be the real reason for which the portrait was taken. It was to reassure the two absent family members, as well as all of us, that the family was doing fine, and remained intact.

Now I look at the old portrait, the images of my loved ones imprisoned within that photograph, unchanged by the passing years, motionless, while I by some miraculous, inexplicable outcome have stepped out of that frame into life and am looking at them from the outside, still wondering, always wondering: How? Why?

My Parents

My parents were both born in Łódź, and so were all their children. They had six children in total, four daughters and two sons, and I was my mother's fifth child. One of the boys died as a toddler, long before my time. My father told me about him. His name was Usher, and one could not keep him away from the constantly dripping water pipe in the yard. The water was very cold and the days at the peak of summer were very hot. This made the child sick, Father explained, and little Usher died that summer.

In 1940, the Germans renamed Łódź to Litzmannstadt, after some crummy general of theirs, and the Jews were herded into what has since become known as the Łódź ghetto. My parents both died there. Mother died on August 24, 1942. She was just fifty. According to the *Chronicle of the Łódź Ghetto*, it was the hottest day of that summer and so many people had died on that particular day that the gravediggers could hardly keep up with their job.[22]

When, after the war, I tried to find my parents' graves to put a stone on them, the cemetery manager could not be sure that the place he

22 One branch of the Łódź ghetto bureaucracy was charged with keeping a chronological report of occurrences and conditions within the ghetto. It remains an invaluable source for historians and others searching for information about life in the Łódź ghetto. For the English translation, see Lucjan Dobroszycki, ed., *The Chronicle of the Łódź Ghetto, 1941–1944* (New Haven: Yale University Press, 1984), p. 243.

indicated, according to his books, was actually my mother's grave. His advice was to put the stone commemorating the whole family on my father's grave, the location of which he claimed to know with certainty.

Father died in 1944, on March 19, a memorable date for me for another reason, too: exactly twenty-five years later, on March 19, 1969, I came with my family to the United States. The last day of my father's life became the first day of my new life here! Two intense feelings became forever entwined for me on that date: sadness and hope.

When I arrived in the U.S., I was greeted by a nice Baltimore man, a dentist who was volunteering for the Baltimore chapter of the Hebrew Immigrant Aid Society (HIAS). He asked me, "Are you happy, Mrs. Temkin, to have arrived in America?" He picked us up at the airport and drove us to a motel for an overnight stay. We were to be met there the next day by a HIAS social worker. It would have made my father very happy to know that my family and I had arrived in America. But I was at a loss for an answer to this question. Did I really arrive? Will I ever really arrive? I was terribly tired at that moment, exhausted from the long trip and the emotions of the travel to this unknown place, and I already anticipated that we would all have a long way to go and a lot of very difficult moments, perhaps more than moments, to overcome before we would be able to see some hope. And hope was slow in coming, not only because I was impatient. The fact is, to start anew when you have already passed more than the halfway mark of your life, is just hard.

The parents: Ajgla Rabinowicz, née Sznurman, and Chaim Moshe Rabinowicz.

Lucky Were Those Who Died in Their Beds

My many friends, survivors of the Łódź ghetto, told me more than once that my parents were both "lucky." They both died in their own beds, thus avoiding deportation to the camps or the trip in the cramped train cars that sometimes arrived at their final destination with half their human cargo dead. It seemed that they had somehow cheated death. Jews who were too old to be kept alive to work were gassed in the camps upon arrival, according to German policy. By the same token, one might perhaps say that my mother was even "luckier" than my father: she died two years before him and was thus spared some of the excruciating pain of starvation that he had to suffer for longer. He was not a powerfully built man, yet strong enough to endure the hunger and all the deprivations of life in the ghetto for over four years. He lived to the age of sixty.

Sala Sztrubel, née Rabinowicz, Hanna's older sister.

My Sister Sala

Sala was a very beautiful girl. Her features and big, light-brown eyes made heads turn. The image in the family portrait taken when she was no more than thirteen does not do her justice. In 1938, Moniek (Moshe Joseph) Sztrubel, my sister Rachel's brother-in-law and a very handsome young man, came from Będzin, a city in southern Poland, to Łódź, to see his brother's in-law's family and fell in love with Sala. She was enchanted, and they were soon married.

A year later, at the time the war broke out, Sala was in advanced pregnancy and an escape to the Soviet side, under the circumstances, seemed to be out of the question. Of course, not everybody was overly eager to go to the Soviet side, to jump into the unknown and go to the part of Poland which had been taken or liberated, depending on one's thoughts about the Soviets. Besides, Sala's husband, who sympathized with the Zionists and those on the far right of the spectrum of the Zionist ideology, distrusted and abhorred the Communists, Bolsheviks,

Sala with her husband Moniek (Moshe Joseph) Sztrubel.

and such, and refused even to consider such a move. In the face of the incoming harsh winter, they decided not to risk a trip bristling with dangerous prospects, and they stayed where they were. My sister Sala perished in a camp, most probably in Chełmno,[23] to which the Germans began deporting people from the Łódź ghetto as early as 1942. Her child, a boy born in early 1940, "pretty like a cherry" as she described in a postcard that reached me in Russia in 1941, died soon after birth. I tried hard to find out when and how Sala died, but to no avail. Checking the registry of inhabitants of Łódź available from Yad Vashem,[24] I concluded that she was most probably deported in 1942 because her name did not appear on the registry after that year. As for her husband, Moniek Sztrubel: survivors of the camps whom I met by coincidence after the war, told me that he had been seen as late as spring 1945 during one of the death marches from some camps in the eastern part of Germany to another one in the west. He must have perished on that horrible *Golgotha* or in one of their far too many camps. Either way, he did not survive, this healthy, very good-looking young man, forever in his late twenties.

My Sister Helcia

My dear, sweet baby sister, Helcia, perished in Stutthof,[25] most probably during the evacuation of that camp almost at the war's end. I got this information from survivors of Stutthof, friends of hers who settled after the war in Israel. Dora Francuz-Zorek was with Helcia almost to the very end. They were good friends from the time the Łódź ghetto was

23 The Germans established the first death camp in the Polish village of Chełmno, called Kulmhoff in German, in December 1941 in order to be near the large Jewish population in Łódź. Approximately 77,000 Jews and 4,300 Roma from the Łódź ghetto were murdered in Chełmno.

24 Based on information that the Judenrat kept, Yad Vashem and the Organization of Former Residents of Łódź in Israel were able to publish *Łódź-Names: List of the Ghetto Inhabitants, 1940–1944*, 5 volumes (Jerusalem: Yad Vashem, 1994).

25 Stutthof was a large concentration camp near the Baltic Sea to which many Jewish and non-Jewish Poles were deported.

Hanna's sister Rachel Rabinowicz (1908–1985), on the left, with a friend in Brussels.

established, and Dora also knew and remembered my parents. At the time of the liquidation of the Stutthof camp, Dora happened to be sick with typhus and, ironically, this saved her life. The Germans, afraid of the infectious disease, left the prisoners in the infected barracks to their deaths, while Helcia, who was healthy, was evacuated. The Stutthof evacuation has been described many times. As horrible as the other stories of the death marches are, this is even more so. Prisoners were loaded onto barges and taken out to the cold Baltic Sea. Dora's eyes filled with tears while recalling her last days in Stutthof. I reminded her of Helcia. "You look so much like her," she kept repeating. Years later, I would still sometimes wake up at night, my heart aching, because I had left my little sister with my mother and father, and she was forced to see them die, only to perish herself afterward, while I went away, and survived.

Rachel, Our Family in Belgium

Although emigration or going abroad for economic reasons had not been a very novel notion in our extended family, Rachel was the first in our immediate family to do so, and she was barely eighteen at the time. She did well for herself in Brussels. There were many small Jewish businesses there and she got a job working for a clothing manufacturer. Her two aunts, my mother's two sisters, had already settled in Belgium, and even though they were only recent immigrants to the country, they became a substitute family of sorts. Rachel soon found a husband, a handsome young man called Chaim Sztrubel. He was a tailor and, like herself, a newcomer to Brussels from Poland. Chaim Sztrubel turned out to be entrepreneurial, and soon they were owners of a store, "Men's Clothing Tailor-Made and Ready-Made" in a good location in the city. They prospered and, until the German invasion of Belgium, lived there happily with their son, Joseph, who was born in 1933.

Rachel came home to Łódź to visit us twice before the war. She came for the first time after a three-year absence to ask for her parents' blessings for her marriage. I remember the visit clearly. Everything was so exciting: the trip to the train station, the train rolling into the station when the hands on the big clock showed exactly one minute after ten, exactly as the train schedule had called for. Trains in prewar Poland were famous for being very punctual! And I especially remember the ride from the station to our home. It was my first ever taxi ride and I can still see myself standing between my father's knees (there was not enough space for everybody to sit) with a chocolate bar in my hand, a gift that my sister had brought from Belgium. The second visit was some five years later. She came with her young son, a beautiful little boy of three, and naturally, everybody was crazy about him. A very bright child, and like many little boys, seemingly afraid of nothing. He was terrified though by the sound of planes. We didn't live very far from an airport then and as the planes approached with the intensifying noise of their engines, he would hide behind his mother or anybody else around. My sister maintained that the child had not paid any attention to planes before. He seemed to have discovered them only there and then. Their roar scared him as if he could hear in it something the grown-ups were unable to; a foreboding of the roars that would soon fill the skies over Europe bringing destruction and death during the war.

Rachel Rabinowicz with her husband, Chaim Sztrubel, in Brussels, Belgium.

Rachel and her family survived the war and the Holocaust in Belgium. Close to the end of the war, when they were still in hiding, her second child, a daughter, Genevieve/Gitele was born. We call her Ginette. Rachel gave birth at a small hospital run by a convent, not far from Brussels, with the help of the convent's nuns. Rachel and her husband both passed away in 1985 in Brussels. Their son, Joseph, a gifted medical student, died in 1958, a victim of the polio epidemic that gripped Europe and the United States in the fifties. Ginette, a very beautiful and talented cardiologist, married Maurizio Mayer, son of a prominent, rich Jewish–Italian family. They first lived in Milan, Italy, and then in Brussels, but a few years ago, they moved with their three children and grandchildren to Israel.

Rachel's visit to Lodz, 1936. From left to right: Mayer (brother), Ajgla (mother), Rachel and her son, Joseph Sztrubel (1933–1958), Moniek (brother-in-law), and Sala (sister).

Mayer Rabinowicz, Rachel Rabinowicz Sztrubel, and two of Hanna's aunts (her mother's sisters), in Brussels, Belgium, early 1930s.

Mayer, Our Other Connection to Belgium

My older brother, Mayer, did not initially stay in Belgium. Not able to make it there, he returned to Poland in the early 1930s. On the way back, he got a taste of the turmoil that was going on in Germany around the time Hitler was coming to power. It must have been quite a scary trip even though he was only passing through Germany by train. The atmosphere was filled with palpable hatred, and what he had witnessed along the way left a deep impression on him. He was a young man of only twenty then, but the impressions and the memory of that trip later (almost ten years later) played a certain role in his decision to leave Poland as soon as the Nazis took over the country.

After returning home, Mayer was conscripted into the Polish army and served out his term. He did quite well afterward, eventually becoming a sales clerk at a large lumberyard. He married shortly before the outbreak of the war, and after the Germans took over Poland, he went with his wife, Dora, over to the Soviet side, and he went, as I remember, without any hesitation. His move was not politically motivated or inspired by political sympathies toward Socialism. From the very beginning of the German takeover, it became quite clear that for Polish Jews, to live and work in Poland under the German occupation would be very difficult if not outright impossible. Though the Holocaust as the "Final Solution" was then perhaps only in the imagination of its perpetrators (and it is not quite sure if they knew already then what they were going to unleash on the Jews), for many, the problem "to stay or to go" became the foremost problem on the agenda rather early on.

Mayer Rabinowicz (on the right) in the Polish army uniform (early 1930s).

In Mayer's case, the Jewish-owned lumberyard where he was a salesman, and where he was expected to become a partner that year right before the war broke out, was taken over by the Germans. Not seeing any possibility to be gainfully employed, he decided to move, and on my parents' urging, take me along. He and his wife survived in the Soviet Union, but their child, a girl, who was born in Soviet Russia in 1941, died in Uzbekistan the same year. After the war, Mayer went to Belgium again. He and his wife, Dora, settled there, and Mayer still lives in Brussels. Their son Maurice was born in Brussels in 1947. He is an artist, a moviemaker, TV producer, and lives in Paris.

The Rabinowiczes

Rosa, the half-crazy Holocaust survivor, depicted by Cynthia Ozick in her heartbreaking tale *The Shawl,* recalled with horror her family being pushed into the squalid ghetto accommodation,

> Three families, including all their children and old folks, into one apartment. Can you imagine a family like us—my father who had been the director-general of the Bank of Warsaw, my sheltered mother, almost Japanese in her shyness and refinement, my two young brothers, my older brother, and me—all of us, who had lived in a tall house with four floors... Imagine confining *us* with teeming Moszkowiczes and **Rabinowiczes** and Perskys and Finkelsteins, with all their bad smelling grandfathers and their hordes of feeble children!...we were furious because we had to be billeted with such a class, with these old Jew peasants worn out from their rituals and superstitions…[26]

It is rather well known that memoirs are all too often written to endow the authors and their families with qualities they did not enjoy in real life and that memoirs are often written with the purpose of hiding the truth rather than uncovering it. I think to a certain degree, this is also the case for many of the Holocaust memoirs. Only very few seem to remember that the poor and the deprived made up the majority of the Jewish population in Poland. Certainly, it is more pleasing to think about one's father as having been director-general of the Bank Polski, than a simple poor Jew, a Rabinowicz like Rosa's object of contempt.

26 Cynthia Ozick, "Rosa," *The Shawl: A Story and Novella* (New York: Alfred A. Knopf, 1989), pp. 66–67. Emphasis added by Hanna Temkin.

Well, I happened to be a Rabinowicz. "Of which Rabinowiczes?" someone asked me once while I was visiting Israel and attending one of those meetings of ghetto survivors. People with name tags on their chests mingled around in the huge kibbutz dining room that also doubled as a convention hall. "From the best, of course, the very best," my quick-witted husband answered for me. Rabinowicz was a rather common name in Poland. It indicated that the family was somehow connected to the rabbinical world; that there might have been a known or even famous rabbi in the family, or that the family originated from the northern parts of Poland; more precisely, from the Lithuanian territories. There, people were given names ending with an "icz"—Rabinowicz, Aronowicz, Abramowicz, Moszkowicz, Mickiewicz—yes, Mickiewicz too, much to the embarrassment of those who seemed to be pained by the thought that the national poet-prophet, Adam Mickiewicz, also had some tainted Jewish blood.

Grandfather Mendel, Who Almost Went to America

So, from which Rabinowiczes did I descend? I am not sure myself, but not from the rich, not from the affluent, and not from the famous rabbis either, because I would have known something about it. My daughter, Helenka, who has a Ph.D. in anthropology with an interest in genealogy, traced our family tree. On my mother's side, she came up with data going back to 1769. Unfortunately, when she conducted her research, the Mormons had not yet collected the appropriate data for Łódź,[27] and I have no family tree on my father's side.

My memory does not go further than my father's father, my grandfather Mendel, a tall, bony man, a widower for as long as I can remember. I have a vivid picture of him in my memory as he sat behind

27 The data collection by members of the Church of Jesus Christ of Latter-day Saints, commonly known as the Mormons, has been a controversial topic over the years, since the data was, and allegedly still is, used to perform posthumous proxy-baptisms, including baptisms of Orthodox Jews who were murdered in the Holocaust.

his enormous (as it then looked to me) loom, weaving with a steady, repetitious movement of his arms. To avoid serving in the tsarist army, one of his sons emigrated to the United States around the turn of the century, settled somewhere in Chicago, and raised a family there. Maybe some Rabinowiczes of that area have something to do with him. A second son, Shiya, joined his brother in America, but after a while, when the family was able to scrabble together enough money to "bail him out" of military service, he returned to Łódź. I am not sure what the meaning of this "bailing out" was. Perhaps it meant gathering enough money to hire a substitute lawyer, a so-called "fixer," or *macher* to get the draftee off the hook, to arrange whatever was needed with the authorities, which sometimes meant finding a reasonable excuse, sometimes to bribe whoever had a say in these matters, or even both.

The first son, having had a hard time in Chicago, was cross with the family for not bringing him home as well but later, when he got used to the new country, he forgave them and even tried to help out by sending money home to Poland. But Shiya, who went back to Łódź, perished many years later in the Holocaust, with all the others. Shiya was married, but childless. In my memory, I have a very vague picture of his wife, Aunt Yenta, and it certainly was *nomen est omen* in this case. A tall, skinny woman, she used to ask me if I would like a cookie when I visited with my father, and I, a child brought up to be modest, would usually say "No, thanks, I don't want any," and so I did not get any which I resented, evidently strongly enough to remember it.

My Father's Sisters

There were also my father's two sisters. One of them, Edith Feldman, was a widow earning a meager living as a shirtmaker, with a son, Elie. He was in his late teens at the outbreak of the war and went over to the Russian side. He perhaps survived, but his mother, who stayed behind in Łódź, did not. My father's other sister married someone called Zajaczkowski; they lived in Kielce and had two sons. One was a very gifted singer, a real prodigy with a promising future. Many years after the war, I was talking with a man from Kielce when I mentioned that I had relatives there. The man told me, "There were two families by that name there. One was pretty well-off, kept stalls selling fabrics of all kinds in the marketplace." "These were not my relatives," I laughed. "The other family, they were *kaptzunem,*[28] the man continued, "but they were well known for their very talented boy endowed with a wonderful voice." These were my relatives!

I vaguely remember Uncle Zajaczkowski. He was a stout man and when he came to visit once, my mother bought very pretty and expensive pears to honor our guest. Those pears were put in a dish used only for special occasions. It was a somewhat stiff, almost solemn atmosphere, and I, a very young child looking from the corner of the room, was impressed, though it's difficult to say what impressed me more; the unknown uncle who gave me candy or the unusual beauty of the pears, for we usually had a different kind of pear, the so-called *ulęgałki* in Polish or wild pears, the kind that shrinks and mellows on the ground, that taste good but aren't such a pretty sight!

The Prodigy Singer and the Flunked Matura

My Kielce cousins also came to visit, but this must have been much later. My older cousin told us that he had failed his *matura* (high school graduation exam) and he was quite upset and frustrated because of that. When I asked him what had caused this failure, he told me that the question was "Explain the meaning of the notion 'nature.'" "And you did not know the answer to such a simple question?" I wondered. I was twelve years old then and dreamed about going to high school which I would start at the age of thirteen, if I were lucky enough to be allowed to enroll. School beyond the basic seven grades was expensive and I doubted that my family would be able to afford it. It seemed offensive to me that someone with the opportunity to go to high school would flunk it. Of course, my remark managed to antagonize my cousin, an

28 A Yiddish term for poor people, also spelled *kabsonim*, based on the Hebrew *kabtsan*, or beggar.

almost grown man of eighteen, dressed in a proper jacket and tie and looking quite mature to me, despite the flunked exam.

The visit of my younger cousin, approximately at the same time, was more memorable because he had sung for us (or perhaps it was for himself?). I will always remember this boy of thirteen or fourteen sitting on the windowsill and singing. His voice was strong and beautiful, and his song was unusual. It was music of a kind I had never heard before. He had stopped giving concerts professionally at this time because his voice was changing, but he was still taking lessons, the means for which were provided by some wealthy sponsor.

The Kielce Zajaczkowski family did not survive the Holocaust. Although as far as my older cousin is concerned, I have some hope that he nevertheless did. On a visit to Israel in the early sixties, my sister Rachel lost a string of pearls on a Tel Aviv bus. She had never taken them off and wondered how this could have happened. Was it an accident or a robbery? Whether someone unclasped it without her noticing it and stole it, she could not say, but she anyway decided to call the police. She was interviewed by a pleasant police officer in his forties who spoke Polish with her, and whose name was Zajaczkowski. She later regretted that she failed to ask him whether they were relatives and if he was the cousin from Kielce. "Never mind the pearls. He might have been our cousin, and I did nothing to find out," she told me with regret.

She Slapped My Father's Face

I do not remember my Kielce aunt, my father's sister. Perhaps I had never seen her, but I do remember a story my father told me, which had to do with her. When my sister Rachel, as a very young girl no older than eighteen, left for Belgium, my aunt was so angry with my father for letting his young daughter leave home and go abroad alone, that in the fervor of her reproaches she slapped his face. My father did not hold it against her. He was apparently troubled as well by his feelings of guilt for letting his beloved first child, a young and pretty girl, leave home and go alone to face this unknown country. It must have pained him then and it was still painful when he recounted it to me, despite the successful turn in Rachel's fortune. He told me that he understood his sister's feelings and didn't hold that slap in the face against her. But the story did not sit well with me. I could still see my gentle father's face reddened by the hand of that aggressive woman. It was, and still is, painful to remember.

My Father

He was a gentle, good-natured man who would never raise his voice, not to say a hand, against anyone. When my mother urged him to "do something" about the unruly me, he would twist a towel in preparation, giving me time to take cover under a chair. He would urge me to come out for the spanking which I, of course, was not in any hurry to do.

He was a hardworking man; to feed his five children, he had to work hard. There was a period before my time when he was manufacturing some textiles on his own, but the inflation after World War I ruined him, and, as far back as I can remember, he was working as a spinner in a textile factory. As a child, I used to spend hours there, especially on Sundays, when my father was the only person working in the large hall (he did not work on the Sabbath). I used to play with the big wooden spools, building fences around imagined houses built of the same spools, and so on, while my father was busy with his work, turning the frame of the spinner and humming something quietly. It was a Jewish-owned factory and the supervisor, a big, red-bearded man, and my father were the only Jews working there. The weavers, about forty or so of them, were Poles, and they were all union members, including my father. However, when the depression came, the factory was moved to a smaller place, outside the city, and my father lost his job.

My father was a very religious man. He prayed a lot; twice every day at home and on Sabbaths and holidays in the *shtibel,* a small congregation that held services in a semi-private home. He was not Hasidic, and he had no rabbi he would adhere to, but he was traditional, wearing the customary Eastern European Jewish garb. He had a role in his *shtibel,* and it was a role he was proud of: he was a *balkoire* whose task it was to read aloud the fragment of the Torah for any given Sabbath to the congregation. He didn't have much formal education besides Judaic subjects. He spoke Polish but did not have enough knowledge of the language to write a letter in it, so he would write to me in Yiddish. To make it easy for me to read, he used Latin letters, embellishing the capital letters in Gothic style. He devoted his free time to the study of religious books, both old and leather bound, as well as smaller, newer siddurs.[29] He also very much enjoyed discussing theological and philosophical questions with whoever was there to discuss them with him. For some time, our new neighbor's two sons, former yeshiva students, were visiting him, and I remember all three of them engaged in a lively debate. Soon, however, the young men lost interest in those discussions. The younger of them, a short fellow whose round face, rosy cheeks, and laughing eyes I remember well, became a Communist, while the other, taller, lanky, his face dry, and always wearing an expression of determination on it, became an anarchist.

I remember my father praying; there was a remarkable intensity and sincerity in it. Standing in a corner of the room, swaying lightly and moving his lips, he would say his prayers. I "saw" him like that for the last time when I was in the Ural Mountains in Russia in 1942. It was a hot summer and I was sitting in the office at my typewriter. I must have dozed off for a moment when I "saw" him, just there in the corner of the office, praying silently. The image was so vivid that it kept coming back to me, as only a real-life phenomenon could. Years later, when I found out from the *Chronicle of the Łódź Ghetto* that August 24, 1942, the day my mother died, was "the hottest day of the year," that moment came back to me instantly, and a thought popped into my head: it must have been then when I "saw" my father praying.

29 Prayer books.

My Mother

In her younger years, she wore a *sheitel* (a wig), as was customary for a married woman, but she gave it up later. I only know this from an old picture. She had little formal education from when she attended a Russian school for some time, and I remember her reciting, just for fun, what she recalled from those school years. She remembered all the titles of the Russian tsars, the kings of Poland, and so on; the list was long. She married very young. Born in 1890, she had her first child in 1908. During the first seven years of her married life, she gave birth to four children, one of whom died as a toddler (as I mentioned earlier). These were the pre-World War I years. Two more girls (the youngest, Helcia, and I) were born after that war. Mother did not expect to have any more children by then, so the old crib was not only put away, it was given away to younger relatives (this I have heard repeated many times). Mother was thirty-four when her youngest child was born. Father was forty, and somewhat embarrassed about this, as he once told me. Forty—an old man! It was kind of unbecoming! I did not quite understand then what he meant by this.

The financial means of the growing family were very limited, to say the least. Father was the only wage earner and to make ends meet must have been quite an achievement. The only moment of "prosperity" in the family came around the time I was born. Mother could even afford to hire a young non-Jewish girl to help her with the everyday tasks of caring for everything, a small child, and all the normal household chores, but the "good times" were short-lived, and cut short by the lasting postwar inflation.

Shopping with Mother

I remember going with Mother to the grocery store on a Friday. It was a small store packed with merchandise and buyers who were mainly housewives like my mom. I liked that place; it smelled nicely of cinnamon and other condiments, and the barrels filled with flour, barley, dried beans of all kinds, and sugar, were full of promise. The store was quite a distance from our home, but because the prices there were lower, it was favored by lots of housewives, who often came from afar. There was no problem with lugging the merchandise home; this was not buying in bulk. Flour, kasha, or beans were bought in small quantities, and sugar in even smaller quantities. I still see the attentive, worrisome expression on my mother's face, comparing prices and adding the small sums, careful to stretch her few zlotys to allow her to buy whatever was necessary to prepare a decent Sabbath, with the challah and the *putter-kuchen*[30] that she would bake for the whole family to enjoy. On a Sunday morning, Father would serve us, the two youngest, a piece of that *kuchen* with a cup of milk to have in bed. It was so good!

Of course, Mother kept a kosher household, but in other matters of religion, she became increasingly lax and even skeptical over time. She worried a lot about her children, about those who had emigrated and about those who were still around, about the ones who were already married, and about the ones who were still in her charge. She would sometimes take us, her two youngest, to the movies. To this day, I remember that this must have been my first visit to the movies; the elevated screen in the dark movie theater, and the large numbers projected onto it, chronologically, just like the years of our lives following one after the other, and the pictures turning like the pages of a book. I remember my mother sighing, "So turns the book of life, so are our years passing by!" These were unusual words, not everyday language, and there was such special sadness in her voice.

The Sznurmans

As mentioned before, thanks to my daughter's interest in genealogy and the data collected by the Mormons, I know the family tree on my mother's side. It goes back to 1769 when Abraham Sznurman was born in a small town called Błaszki, in the western part of Poland. He was the father of Hersz (1807), who was the father of David (1836). It goes on almost like in the Bible, who begot who. David married a girl

30 A butter cake made by Jews and Germans in the region.

named Sulka Matysiak, who became my great-grandmother. Matysiak is a proverbially Polish name. A soap opera by the name *Matysiakowie* (Family Matysiak) ran on Polish radio in the fifties and later, on TV, as well. They would not have come up with a name like that if it was not a proper, "kosher" Polish name. This was an enormously popular show, and when I learned that this was also my great-grandmother Sulka's maiden name, it made me laugh. So much for "what's in a name?" If I would let my imagination run wild, I might have come up with a story about a non-Jewish girl converting in secret to marry my great-grandfather, and so on. It would have perhaps made my story more interesting by adding such a romantic touch to it, but there was nothing of the kind there. Sulka, Sulamit?—what a beautiful name!—was, of course, Jewish, and she was the mother of my grandfather Shoel Sznurman (b. 1872), whom I remember well: he died in the early 1930s.

I remember sitting on his lap as a child and plaiting his gray beard into tiny braids. He would sometimes give me five groszy to buy candy. And he would also take my side when my aunts pestered me to recite some children's rhymes, a *wierszyk*, which they loved to hear. I would often refuse, annoyed or maybe I was just playing hard to get, and he would encourage me not to recite anything, knowing very well that because of my contrariness, I would finally end up reciting all the rhymes I knew. He too liked to listen.

As the documents show, the Sznurmans were producers of textiles, fabrics, lace, ribbons, and ropes. The family surname perhaps stems from this; *sznur* means rope in Polish, indicating the occupation of the name's owner.

My Mother's Mother: Bubbe Estera

My grandmother Estera, née Brombart, lived to see the war. I found out quite recently that she too was "lucky" to die in her bed, after surviving her oldest daughter, my mother, for more than a year. She had six children—five daughters and one son, Benjamin. He in his turn had five children. He did not survive the Holocaust, and I do not know if any of his children did either. Bubbe Estera was, exactly as a Jewish *bubbe* (a grandmother) should be: a tiny, round woman and her face had the shape and color of a dried apple. She was energetic, kept her family firmly together, and her word, especially after Grandfather Shoel passed away, was final. She was admired as being wise and just. Many years after the war, people who had known her during those prewar years, asked me if I knew how wise and just a woman my grandmother was. She adhered to the Jewish tradition, but the times she lived in were not conducive to strictly upholding it and the younger generation was increasingly moving away. She was not, however, excessively rhetorical about it. To my sister Rachel, who was her oldest grandchild, Bubbe Estera gave a pair of old, bronze candlesticks as a wedding gift, remarking, "You will have them, so you will perhaps also use them." I admired those candlesticks in Brussels many years later.

Once, when I was perhaps seven, I had a bad falling out with my grandmother. I said something to her that I should not have said. Yet, she did not rebuke me. Instead, she reproached my mother, and I, seeing my mother's embarrassment, felt ashamed, too. A talkative child, I would hear more than once from my *bubbe* that it is not good to talk too much. She would explain, "Every person is allotted from Above a certain quantity of words. If you use up your allotment now as a child, you will have very little left to say when you're grown up!" And how right she was!

She was seventy-four when she died in 1943 in the ghetto, in her own home which she shared with her youngest daughter, Sheindl, and her family, since Grandfather Shoel's death. Yet, she was alone at the time of her death. The registry of the Łódź ghetto, listed Sheindl and her child as deported in 1942. The Germans began deporting little children from the Łódź ghetto, with or without their mothers, at a very early stage. The first such big *Szpera* took place in the summer of 1942.[31]

31 In September 1942, a mass deportation action targeting those who could not work rounded up over 15,000 children, elderly, and ill Jews, shocking the ghetto population. Based on the euphemistic German *Allgemeine Gehsperre* (general curfew), the ghetto inhabitants referred to this event as the "*Sperre*" or—in Polish—as the "*Szpera*."

Rumkowski,[32] the ghetto tsar, gave up about 10,000 children to "save the others," as a kind of payment or offering to satisfy the Nazi god's lust for blood. Removed from the ghetto, those children were then sent to their death. A survivor who witnessed the public meeting on the Balut Market, called on that occasion by Rumkowski to inform the ghetto inhabitants about his decision to consent to the German demand to deport the children, recounted to me the Dantean scenes of that deportation's execution. Children were thrown from windows right into the waiting vans and children were pulled out from unimaginable and most ingenious hiding places.

Bubbe Estera remained in her apartment, while her young daughter and grandchild were deported. The Germans seemed to have no firm rules about who goes first. There was only one rule; that all the ghetto inhabitants were to die, but when and how was up to the will and calculations of the "death master" alone.

André the Priest: My Grandmother's Great-nephew

Here I feel compelled to add a story pertinent to my grandmother, though it surfaced only recently, over sixty years after my grandmother Estera's death in the Łódź ghetto. Some time ago, my daughter, Helenka, following her interest in genealogy, put together our family tree and published it on the internet. A few months ago, someone called André Brombart contacted us. He lives in Belgium, where he was born in 1942, and he is a Catholic priest! A most dramatic story because Brombart was my grandmother's maiden name! It seems that André, the priest, is indeed a relative, possibly a son of a nephew of Bubbe Estera's, the son of a Brombart from Błaszki, the small shtetl in Poland of my grandmother's birthplace, who came to Belgium in 1929 to pursue medical studies there. He graduated from the University of Brussels and became a doctor in a small town in Belgium where he married a local Christian woman, had several children with her, and survived the

32 Mordechai Chaim Rumkowski (1877–1944), the chairman of the Judenrat in Łódź, had an outsized personality and power and remains a controversial figure.

war, all the time careful to hide his Jewish origins while Belgium was under German occupation. This was not very difficult to do there, André explained, as the surname, Brombart sounded Flemish enough, and nobody bothered him. Shortly before André's father passed, however, in the late 1990s, he wrote down the information about himself and the members of his family left behind in Błaszki who had perished there during the Holocaust.

André's connection with my grandmother seemed to be beyond doubt. I remembered that among other family anecdotes, there was talk about a Brombart, a relative of Bubbe's, who went to Belgium to study medicine. I was so impressed with the fact that someone in the wider family was pursuing higher education that this information stuck in my mind. I had a relative who went to another country to become a doctor! He was talked about in the family, sometimes with pride, but mostly with derision or irony. "A doctor? Hair will sooner grow on my palm than this would happen," one of those disbelievers would smirk. "He must be crazy to work so hard, ironing trousers for some clothmaker all day long to make a living and pay his tuition and studying in the evenings and late into the night," someone else would add. I must have heard similar comments often enough. Such aspirations were well beyond most people in the family, and the irony or derision I could hear in the opinions voiced on the subject reeked of jealousy. I often wondered why nobody seemed to understand that this man deserved admiration for working so hard to achieve his goal.

André's father had provided him with a list of names of his close relatives from Błaszki who had perished during the Holocaust in Poland. And when I looked at that list, I found names that, though rather uncommon in general, were quite common in our family, for example, my mother's name, Ajgla, is a clear indication of some common ancestors in both our families. I was struck by this fact. What else can I say, it was a very interesting, unusual, unexpected turn, one of life's twists. Who would have expected that a great-grandson of my Jewish grandmother, Estera Brombart-Sznurman, would turn out to be a Catholic priest? That the son of her nephew who went off to Belgium in 1929 to study medicine would become a founder of a whole new branch of non-Jewish Brombarts in Western Europe? We all welcome Father André with open hearts, even more so, as someone remarked, in these uncertain times, his connections in the "highest places," combined with those we have in our own right, should make us feel much safer and isn't this something to cherish in today's troubled, tumultuous world?

The Sznurman Daughters

Of the five of my grandmother's daughters, only one survived the Holocaust; Rachel Lea married to Mendel Kropka or Krupka. Mendel was small, a dot of a man and in fact, *kropka* in Polish means just that, a dot. He was, however, a very energetic and enterprising man. Having no formal education or special skills, he did many things to eke out a living for himself and his family. From the many family anecdotes, I remember that for a certain time he was a traveling salesman, making deals along the way as if he was a character out of a Sholem Aleichem book. Once he bought a truckload of broken glass, expecting to make a killing, but lost whatever money he had put into the transaction. Unable to find a buyer for the breakage, he had to pay for the right to dispose of it in the city dump, which turned out to be quite costly. In one of his seasonal occupations during the last months of his life in Poland, I, as a child, had a special interest.

He was busy making little houses out of colored waffle sheets which people used as Christmas tree decorations. These little houses were of very simple design; four walls, the front wall with three openings marking two windows and the entrance door, and all this standing on a flat "floor" and covered by a steep roof with a shiny star or a little angel glued on to the top. The walls were usually one color: red, pink, or green, and the roof of another contrasting color. They were very nice, those little Christmas tree houses. My uncle the architect, I could have said, only I did not know the word then! I spent a lot of time at my aunt's tiny apartment, which later on became ours, watching these creations come to life from my uncle's deft hands, but also, and perhaps mostly so, waiting for the leftover scraps of the building material, the waffles, which, though they had no taste at all, were nevertheless quite a tempting treat.

Finally, after trying his luck at all possible and impossible tasks, my uncle with his wife and two little daughters emigrated to Belgium. This was in the very late twenties. He didn't do badly there, first peddling bananas and oranges from a pushcart, then some cheap shirts and other articles of clothing. Again, as the family story goes, he put considerable energy, even panache, into hawking his wares. "*Menyje, heng'ach on a shneer*," he shouted, calling the customers' attention to his goods. In Yiddish, his call approximately means, "Mister, hang yourself on a rope." But to him, it had sounded sufficiently Flemish, especially because "*menyje*" (mister) rhymed so nicely with "*shneer*" (rope). Of course, I am not certain that Uncle Mendel was the only and the original subject of the story. Perhaps similar ones were told about many other poor Jewish immigrants trying hard to find their way in any one of those new countries to which circumstance was pushing them. Though life in Belgium was not easy, it nevertheless was easier for him to make a living there than it was in Poland. But, as the family tale with the abundance of anecdotes about this particular uncle goes, one day, having declared that he got "fed up with all that stinking Europe," he decided to look for an even better opportunity across the ocean. Shortly before the outbreak of World War II, Uncle Mendel moved to Argentina where he started anew, from scratch. He managed to bring over his wife and two children from Belgium just before the outbreak of the war, and the family survived in Argentina. I have a rather foggy memory of the girls, especially the older one, named Royzele, who must have been close to my age. According to my sister Rachel, who kept in touch with Aunt Rachel Lea until the end of this aunt's life, Royzele married an Israeli pilot who worked for El Al flying planes between Tel Aviv and Buenos Aires, but whether she lived in Argentina after marrying or moved to Israel, I don't know.

The "Prettiest of Them All"

The one that was the "prettiest of them all," of all my mother's sisters, was Aunt Sala. She was married to Izaak Fajtlowicz and they had two children, Adela and Henryk. The Fajtlowicz family also immigrated to Belgium in the late twenties but returned to Poland a few years before the start of the war. Aunt Sala's jealous husband, as another family tale goes, insisted on returning to Poland. He would not have his wife working as a hostess in a delicatessen where she would be seen by other people, by men. He would not take this. I remember their homecoming. After the years abroad, even if those years were not so great, they all looked somewhat different, foreign. Aunt Sala looked majestic in a fur coat, and Adela and Henryk were also dressed up, looking "holidayish," and they spoke French which struck me as almost supernatural! Aunt Sala and her children perished in the Holocaust, but her husband supposedly saved himself in Russia, though I do not know that for sure.

The Markels

Aunt Hendel was married to Shiya Markel, a printer, and they had one child, a girl named Hindele. Shiya was the only one with skills and some education; almost a learned man, considered as such in the family and treated with great respect. He had a job in some Jewish newspaper, but it must not have been anything permanent or steady which would explain their immigration to Belgium in the very early thirties. He started in the new country from scratch, as they say, as a floor sweeper at some chemist's workshop, but in no time mastered not only the language (to the amazement of the other members of the family) but also the intricacies of whatever they were producing at that enterprise, without having any prior knowledge of chemistry. Soon, he was managing the whole business. I got this information recently from my brother, Mayer, who was still in awe of Shiya Markel's achievements, an awe that had not diminished as time passed. When the Germans invaded Belgium, the Markels escaped to France. There they registered as refugees and were later rounded up by the French government as Jews and non-French nationals and deported to Auschwitz where they perished. Shiya's brother, Jankel Markel, a talented painter, survived Auschwitz and lived in Paris after the war, where, as I have heard, he achieved some success as an artist.

The Youngest Daughter

My mother's youngest sister, Sheindl, was also married and had a child, a girl, born a few years before the war. Sheindl, along with her child, perished in the Holocaust. I remember the child well, a little girl with soft blonde curls. I can still see her in my mind from when I saw her, perhaps, for the last time, shortly before the outbreak of the war, a child of about three. She was holding a banana in her little hand, eating it with evident relish, and gave me a suspicious look when I tried to approach her, as if afraid that I might take it away from her. As for Sheindl's husband, he was drafted into the Polish army at the outbreak of the war, and never returned home. Killed? Missing in action? Poor Sheindl tried hard to get any information about his fate, but with the war lost and the Polish state dismantled there was not much she could do.

The Sznurman "Compound"

The Sznurmans lived on 52 Dworska. This was their "family nest." It was a family dwelling, shared by my grandfather and his sisters. When and how it was acquired, I do not know, but I remember the place very well. A wooden fence separated the "compound" from the street, and a brick wall separated it from the neighbor at the other end. Close to that wall grew an old tree, a tall lilac tree that somehow miraculously bloomed year after year. Its heavy, fragrant and rich clusters of flowers were so out of place there!

On the right, there was a three-story brick edifice containing five separate two-room apartments. Across from it was a smaller, only two-story, A-frame house. This one was in much worse shape, almost a ruin. I wondered how the renters (because it was rented out for income) could live there. The wooden stairs leading to the upper floor were half broken and one needed almost acrobatic skills to reach the second floor safely, even though the renters were old Jews and anything but acrobats. During the last two years before the war, a family with two grown boys moved in there, and they became my friends.

There was one more edifice in the "compound"; a small, freestanding outhouse with two cubicles. This wasn't, of course, anything unusual in these parts of the city; a city sewage system was a long time in coming, as was running water in the apartments. In 1939, only 16 percent of properties in Łódź were connected to the water and sewage system. From this point of view, Łódź was rated as the worst city in Poland.

The Compound's Inhabitants: Aunt Miriam

My grandfather's sister was living on the first floor of the brick house. A large woman, tall and shapely built, a widow, with clear evidence of past beauty on her face and in her figure. Aunt Miriam kept a student as a renter, though I cannot say where he studied. There was no university in Łódź at that time, but there were some other schools of higher learning in the city and he, perhaps, was training to become a teacher. Anyway, he must have been a poor (in terms of money) student, since he came to live so far away from the center of the city where educated people were easier to come by. I remember him well; a grown man yet still a student, and this was unusual. There was only one member of the family, Grandmother Estera's nephew, who, as I mentioned earlier, went to Belgium to study to become a doctor, and he was talked about, sometimes with pride, but mostly with derision or irony.

There were two other things that made Aunt Miriam's apartment remarkable; one was the cellar in her kitchen, a deep dugout in the ground, right beneath the wooden floor, masked by a wooden trapdoor. The cellar was cool and dry, and she kept her provisions, like home-baked cookies, there. I knew that she always had some at hand and that she would never ask if I wanted one but would just give me one when I happened to come by. The second remarkable thing about Aunt Miriam's place was a piano, a shiny, black, big-like-an-elephant instrument. I saw a piano for the first time in my life at her place. It did not belong to her, and she would not have known how to use it. The piano was tucked away in her place by the Szwarcmans, my grandfather's other sister's family that occupied the upstairs apartment, right over that of my grandparents, on the third floor. The Szwarcmans (or rather their two sons who became furriers and lived in the better part of the city) were not doing so well at the time, having fallen behind with the payments of their taxes or had otherwise gotten into debt. They had to hide what valuables they possessed from the watchful tax or debt collectors. I remember very little of the Szwarcmans and their sons, the two tall, well-built men, in contrast to most members of the extended family who were rather short and slightly built. For that reason alone, they aroused a good deal of jealousy in the rest of the family and were often gossiped about. The boys, it was often said, grew so tall and strong just on the lima beans which they were fed on the Sabbath, cold to boot, since there was no fire under the stove on a Sabbath day.

My Grandparents' Apartment

The apartment on the second floor, above Aunt Miriam's, belonged to my grandparents. I visited there very often as a child and remember it very clearly; the furniture, dark and shiny, the green velvet cover on the two beds that took up a lot of space in the room, the heavy velvet —also green—curtains on the windows, and even the green, leafy cactuses my grandmother liked to keep. After Grandfather's death, Grandmother took in her youngest daughter with her husband and their child, who was expected to arrive soon. This stirred up some resentment in the family since it meant the youngest would probably become the inheritor of the family dwelling.

Across from my grandparents', there was a similar apartment inhabited by the Lewkowicz family. I do not know how Aunt Lewkowicz was related to my grandparents; I remember though that she was a very sick person. It was something incurable that had caused her to suffer, long and terribly, and about which the family talked only in whispers. In hindsight, it seems that it was cancer, unrecognized and, perhaps, untreated. The Lewkowiczes had two sons, my cousins, who were close to my age. The younger, Motl, went over to the Soviet side at the end of 1939 and returned from there with a Russian wife and a child born in Russia only in the mid-fifties, with the second wave of returnees. His brother, the older one, Szymek, survived the ghetto and the concentration camps. I remember him well as he used to play *Hatikva*, the *Internationale*, and many other tunes on Aunt Miriam's piano, using just one finger and without any knowledge of the notes—he just had a good ear. We met briefly in Łódź after the war, but he soon immigrated to the West, and I lost track of him. My poor aunt, his mother, died just before the war. Her husband, a stout, heavyset man, always presentably dressed in a jacket and tie, who, as the family gossip had it, was perennially unemployed, perished during the Holocaust.

Marczewska, the Yard Keeper

Leaning on the brick house, as if cuddled up to it, was a wooden extension. There were two rooms there. In the one downstairs, lived Marczewska with her two daughters. She was a non-Jewish woman of uncertain age, tall and skinny, as if all dried up, with a face blackened by hard life and worries, and matching straight black hair. The room was assigned to her as payment for her services around the house: sweeping the yard, locking up the entrance wicket in the fence at night, and keeping the outhouse more or less clean. On the Sabbath, in the morning, she would also light the fire in the stove of Bubbe Estera's kitchens, as well as the other dwellers' kitchens. A Jewish "compound" like that could not have been maintained without a *Sabbath goy*, a non-Jew who helped with those tasks Jews could not perform on the day of rest.

I was about ten or eleven years old when the older Marczewska daughter, Maria, had a child out of wedlock. The grownups talked about this in hushed voices, and sometimes with smirks which made me very interested and intrigued and provided me with "food for thought." Why are they talking about this in such a way? Why the secrecy? She is going to have a child, but she is not married? How can this be? Someone said that such things only happen to "*shiksas,*" others just laughed, while my mother would say, and she would repeat this many times on certain other occasions, "*s'ydiltzech, a soy vi s'christltzech*" (What happens to Christians, can happen also to Jews). This was the time before sex education in school, if not kindergarten, and before TV, and these thoughts which are generally not easy for a young child to deal with, left me confused. Yet, this was something to ponder. With time, my mother's saying came back to me, on different occasions, taking on a new significance, mostly as an expression of the principle of tolerance: People, Christians or Jews, are the same, anything that afflicts "them" can afflict also "us," and vice versa. This was still before the Holocaust, and this conclusion seemed obvious to me then.

Our Tenure in the "Compound"

A year before the war, when the economic circumstances of our family had worsened to such a degree that we could not afford to pay rent, my parents with their two youngest children, Helcia and myself, moved into the room over the Marczewska's place, the same room that was occupied by Uncle Mendel and his family some time ago but had been incorporated into my grandparents' apartment after they immigrated to Belgium. Now, the door between both places was closed again, and we moved in. I could not grasp it then, being too young or too self-absorbed in problems of my own, what a setback this must have been for my parents, and especially for my mother, to "come home" to her old, widowed mother like that.

It was a very poor place to live; small, crowded, and taken up almost entirely by my parents' double bed. I had my separate place to sleep though, a so-called *kozetka* (a settee). It stood along the wall, its headboard reaching the window. The streetlamp, just outside the window, provided enough light for me to read when everybody else in the room was already asleep. And what did I read then? Among others, the *Red Banner*, the illegal weekly distributed for free by the Polish Communist Party.[33]

At the family compound. Front, from left to right: Ajgla (mother), Chaim Moshe (father); second row from left: Helcia (sister), Hanka; top row, from left: Mayer Rabinowicz (brother, 1910–2004); Joseph Sztrubel, and Rachel Rabinowicz Sztrubel. Picture taken in 1936 during Rachel's visit from Brussels.

33 The Komunistyczna Partia Polskii (KPP, Polish Communist Party) was illegal in the interwar Polish state.

Where I Grew Up

I was born and grew up in a non-Jewish neighborhood, on 134 Limanowski Street, a thoroughfare, going from the Bałucki Market to the outskirts of the city. It was previously called Aleksandrowska Street since it led out of the city to a small town called Aleksandrów. The part closer to the Bałucki Market as well as many of the side streets constituted the so-called Bałuty, a neighborhood inhabited mostly by Jews and mostly poor ones. Later, it became the heart of the ghetto. Beginning with Sierakowski Street or so, the neighborhood turned into Żubardź, another part of the city, and it was predominantly non-Jewish.

Ours was a rather large tenement on the corner of Limanowski and Konopnicka Street, named respectively for a Socialist writer and thinker and a popular poetess. It was a corner brick building, five stories high, with at least forty units, inhabited mostly by factory workers, but also elementary school teachers, clerks, and others. For many years, we were the only Jewish family in the building. Later on, at the beginning of the 1930s, other Jews moved in. They were newcomers from the small towns around Łódź, looking for more opportunities in the big city.

We had running water in our two-room apartment and there was electricity. I have a vague memory of it being installed to replace the kerosene lamps. And that was the end of the "luxuries." Of course, there was no inside plumbing, and a bathroom was unheard of.

Neighborhood Relations between Jews and non-Jews

There was an outhouse in the courtyard, a separate structure divided into many cubicles. Tenants had keys to the cubicles, but one was open for everybody's use, and our family used that one. I would sometimes steal a glance into one of those assigned to the other tenants and I liked what I saw: the sitting boards were of gleaming yellowish wood and the floor was always dusted with fresh white sand. Why did we not have the use of one of those? Perhaps, the very thought that the non-Jews would share such an intimate place with us, Jews, seemed strange even to us, as it was indeed unacceptable to "them." I do not remember any talk or complaints about the subject on our part. This was just a fact of life! So much for neighborly relations; this was Jewish–Polish relations at the very grassroots level.

In general, however, we were tolerated and lived peacefully with our neighbors. As a small child I played with other children in the yard, usually on an equal footing, without being excessively reminded that I was what I was; a Jewess, *Żydówka*. But around Passover, and I recall this vividly, I was truly wanted by the other kids in the yard because I was expected to bring them *matzos*, a desired and welcome treat.

An Outbreak of Hostility

During those fifteen years or so that our family lived in that building, my parents had only once suffered from an outbreak of open hostility. Occasionally, the word *Żyd* (Jew) used commonly as an epithet in Poland was hurled at them, especially by a new tenant, expressing derision at their different way of life, their different code of dress, or their poor Polish. Sometimes it was caused more by jealousy than anything else, Mother maintained. The smell of the challah or *putter-kuchen* that she baked regularly for the Sabbath, made "them" (the neighbors) jealous again and again, she would say, giving a piece of advice, "Let them drink less vodka, then they too would have enough for a *kuchen*." "After all," she would sometimes sigh, "God knows, we are not better off than most of them."

The open outbreak of hostility came with the growing tide of antisemitism in the mid-thirties. Late one evening, my parents together with Aunt Edith were followed to the entrance of the building and beaten by a band of hooligans, among whom my parents recognized some of their neighbors. They were returning from the train station, after seeing off my sister Rachel upon her return to Belgium, and my parents were convinced that the whole incident was caused mostly by envy on the part of those neighbors toward Rachel. She came home on a visit from Belgium elegantly dressed; I especially remember the silver fox that she wore on her black jacket as it impressed me greatly. Though my parents were happy that Rachel was doing well in Belgium, they were still not quite certain that she had not overdone it a bit, showing it off in this not-very well-to-do neighborhood. Years later, chatting with me, Rachel still remembered and recalled the impression she had made then: the neighbors could not help but be jealous, and she had heard remarks like "Look how she has dolled herself up, that *Żydówka.*" Interestingly, there was still an undertone of pride in her voice when she recounted this old story.

Unpleasant as the whole incident was, my parents did not make much of it. They played it down. This was, after all, the time when elsewhere in Poland, pogroms were taking place. In the early 1930s, these were not yet endemic, but sometime later there were many such outbreaks, of which the most well-known was the pogrom in Przytyk in 1936. So, were we not lucky, considering? They got scared but not badly hurt, and they did not complain much. The only one complaining bitterly was Aunt Edith. Her index finger was injured, and she was unable to unbend it. She protested about how she couldn't work now as it might take weeks for her hand to mend. But since there was no visible wound or swelling, others refused to believe her, making fun of her grouching, and that's why the story perhaps stuck in my mind. But surely her pain must have been real, even though she was unable to explain what the problem was, and because she used Polish terms to describe it, she would mangle these terms in a way that made the whole thing sound improbable and thus funny. Aunt Edith was famous in the family for the problems she had learning Polish. She would often repeat that forty-something *farkakte*[34] years of living in this country, where she was born, was not that much, and anyway not enough to master that strange language.

134 Limanowski Street

When I close my eyes, I can even now, so many decades later, describe some of the furniture in our household in great detail, as well as many

34 Yiddish, meaning "crappy."

other things in our apartment, including their location and what they looked like. I remember that first home of my childhood better than any other place I lived in during my lifetime. At the entrance to the kitchen stood a small wooden box in which coal was kept. The big, round, white pot on the kitchen sideboard reminded me of the potbelly of my brother's rich boss, Mr. Zalzman, owner of the lumberyard. That pot was always filled with roasted black barley coffee, my brother's favorite drink that would be waiting for him on his return from his bicycle rides. And that humble pot became ingrained in my memory with one more of my mother's edifying thoughts: Mr. Zalzman had diabetes, so we should not begrudge him his riches, or his fat belly! How vivid are these details in my mind!

I do not remember many of the neighbors' names, but retained the name of the building's owner, Mr. Kaźmierczak, a slightly built, very well-dressed, still young-looking gentleman with a mustache. I was once in the landlord's apartment, and ever since then, this is how I picture what a truly big and elegant place to live should look like; a long entrance hall and tall white doors leading to separate rooms on both sides of it. Sometimes, my mother took my little sister Helcia, while she was still a toddler, to the landlord's family. The beautiful, blue-eyed, golden-haired child was invited to play with that family's young child. Mother considered those invitations as something of an honor. She would cover Helcia with her shawl when taking her there as if to protect her from the evil eye on the way. It was, perhaps, on one of those occasions that I got to see this apartment.

Another neighbor's name has come back to me: Leokadia, a young, blonde woman living on the first floor. The two windows of her place overlooking the yard were usually covered by blinds that looked like two blind eyes, similar to Leokadia's own eyes darkened by her drunken husband's fists. I tasted on my tongue and my teeth that fancy name, Leokadia. "*Gotenyu*" ("dear heavens!") my mother would sigh, "he battered her again," but my sister Sala once said—and it was strange to hear this coming from her as she was always so nice, so gentle—"She deserves it, she is no better than him." As Leokadia screamed taking the beating, the children in the yard would scream even louder, imitating her, and then, laughing, would start mock fistfights.

First and Secondhand Memories

One of my first memories goes back to the time when I was less than three years old; to the time when my baby sister, Helcia, was born. I see myself, a little child, standing in the doorway from the kitchen to the "room," holding on to the doorframe. There is some commotion around; people are coming and going, and I do not remember anybody telling me that I had a little sister, but I knew it anyway. Even now I know that this was when Helcia was born and that I was that little girl clinging to the doorframe. The large kerosene lamp, held by four metal straps in the middle of a wide metal ring, hanging down from the ceiling was lit and this was unusual, too. I was looking at the lamp's flickering light. It was lit for special occasions only, and this was a special occasion. Shortly afterward, the kerosene lamp would be gone, replaced by an electric bulb hanging sad and lonely from the ceiling on an electrical cord.

Some of my early memories are genuine memories of events directly experienced and remembered, while others are secondhand memories, someone else's memories about us, heard many times, and retold by us. My secondhand memories, or derivative memories, include one of the family stories told and retold many times about how I was "miraculously" cured of a serious illness. At the age of about four, I got sick with influenza. One particular influenza wave, the Spanish flu epidemic, killed millions of people in the years just following World War I. This was later, though, in the mid-twenties. The disease had already lost its strength, but I got sick anyway and nearly died. Almost all hope was lost. But I was not ready to die yet, and one morning, as the story goes, I suddenly stood up on my bed, and cried out, "I don't want to be sick anymore, I don't want to!" Then, I collapsed and fell asleep. When I woke up the next morning, the fever was gone, and I was on the way to recovery.

Another early memory and this is not secondhand, brings me back to our next-door neighbor. Pani Lenartowicz was a part-time schoolteacher, and her husband was a uniformed policeman. That uniform filled me with awe. I hardly ever met the man, always, perhaps, hiding somewhere whenever I would spot him approaching. The couple was childless, and "Pani" was kind to me, allowing me into her home, which held a special fascination for me. I was always anxious to be let in. I can see myself, a little girl, perhaps of three or four, knocking on her door. "Who is there?" she would ask, certainly knowing who it was. "Me, Hanka," I would answer. "What Hanka?" She would ask again, "Hanka, silly banka?" "Yes," I would admit obediently, knowing that it was the rule of the game, and only when I would repeat "Hanka, banka" she would open the door. What was so interesting for me, to be in the neighbors' apartment? Perhaps, the fascination came just from the fact that it was different from our own home, it had more color, and most importantly, it was unknown. And the lady of the house would teach me little verses and strange words. One of those was a very long one: abstryfitykultykiewiczowna. No meaning, but what an intriguing sound. "Try to pronounce this very fast but be careful, it can break your tongue," Pani would say. But when it did not seem to break my tongue, the lady was surprised. "*Mała małpka*" (little monkey), she would say with a mixture of admiration and something else that was not flattering at all, and I, repeating with laughter the long word, again and again, left the apartment in joyous leaps. I still remember that strange tongue twister.

Childhood Fears

Some memories we would like to forget, and the harder we try the more they seem to insist on coming back. Colored by feelings, by things or events that accompanied them, pervaded with feelings of joy or sadness, hope or helplessness they have caused us in the past, those feelings just come back. At some point in your life, a fear of death comes with the realization that death does happen, that it irreversibly takes away not only your loved ones, leaving you alone in the scary world, but it also makes you aware that you are mortal. I remember the terrible fear I felt at the sight of the hearse. I feared, however, the Jewish hearse, that plain, unvarnished black wagon that seemed to ride on its own, speeding through the streets with a horrible noise made by its unbalanced iron wheels and the horse's shoes, clacking on the cobbled street. As a child, I had not seen it very often; there were not that many Jews in my neighborhood. The other hearse, the one that would carry dead non-Jews, was a more familiar sight, but it didn't instill in me such dreadful terror, if any at all. This "carriage of death" was majestic and solemn, always moving slowly, with dignity. The carvings adorning its top looked like lace drapes on a window, and the pallbearer, his shiny top hat, and the big silvery buttons on his livery added solemnity or even a certain splendor to the whole occasion. But most importantly, it was not coming for "us."

A Happy Childhood

All in all, I had a happy childhood. My parents were loving and caring and so were my older siblings, and I had a younger sister to play with. I was bilingual at the earliest age and liked to make up words by mixing both languages. I do not remember it myself, but my older siblings have told me this many times. Asking for bread with butter, I would say, I want "*chleb z putaskiem*" instead of saying "*chleb z masłkiem.*" I was adding the Polish grammatical suffix to the mangled Yiddish word and came up with the hybrid "*putaskiem.*" It made the grown-ups laugh because "*putaskiem*" rhymes with "*kutaskiem,*" which in Polish has more than one meaning, and among others, it is used as a diminutive form of a popular expletive. I spoke Yiddish with my parents and Polish with my siblings and everybody else, not unlike immigrant children in this country speaking their native tongue with their parents and the language learned in school with everybody else. I learned to read and write Yiddish from a *melamed* (tutor) who taught me for a short time one summer when I was eight or nine. I learned enough to write a short letter in Yiddish, but soon forgot it all. Polish was more interesting, Polish was culture, and Polish was knowledge, while Yiddish was only good for *bubbe-meises* (grandmother's tales).

Starting School

I went to school at the age of seven as was then customary and obligatory in Poland. When I was admitted to first grade, my sister Sala was already graduating from the same grade school. She was fourteen and would start working soon. It was customary that children after elementary school, at fourteen, would work full-time in stores, small enterprises, and so on. But factories had different rules and she was too young for a job in the factory. An opportunity came along, however, in the same factory where Father worked, though to arrange it the rules had to be bent a bit. My father got the ginger-bearded manager to agree that Sala would do her work at home. He would bring home a roll of fabric—I can still see it, the gray silky alpaca—and Sala would look over the roll carefully and check it for defects, and whenever she spotted one, she would put a red tag on the edge of the fabric. Quality control, one might say! I can still see her sitting on a low milking stool, pulling the fabric over a large frame and checking it diligently and attentively. She liked her job, was proud of the money she earned and did not even mind the kickback for the factory's manager who gave her the job and could also take it away without notice.

Hooked on Reading

I did not know my ABCs before starting school, and the *Elementarz*, the first reader from which children of my generation and many others learned to read, impressed me enormously. It was also the first children's book that I had ever held in my hands. The pictures, the colors! My sister Sala bought it for me and tried to teach me the letters to prepare me for my new life as a school pupil. "This is an 'A' and this is an 'L' and here again you have the same letter 'A' and together it says ALA; this is the name of the girl in the picture, right here." I didn't get it. "How do you know that this is the name of the girl in the picture?" "Because it says so here, read it." I still could not overcome my wonderment and my sister lost patience with me, so I went to school completely illiterate. It did not take me long though to catch up and the miracle through which, by putting letters together into meaningful words, a child becomes a reader, happened to me fairly quickly. One day, my teacher called me into the teachers' room, a sanctuary, where children were not often allowed, opened a book, and asked me to read, and I did. "Will you read the rest of it if I let you take it home?" she asked. "Yes, yes!" I assured her eagerly. "Take it then and bring it back tomorrow. If you can tell me then what you have read, you will get another one," she added. I ran home with my treasure, hooked for life.

All the children in my school were Jewish, so I could say that my school was segregated, even though segregation was not the official policy. The teachers in our school were also Jewish and only later on did we get some non-Jewish teachers, but not because the authorities were trying to end this "segregation." With unemployment among teachers on the rise, non-Jewish teachers were given preference. The language of instruction was Polish, and the Jewishness of my school meant there was no school on Saturday; instead, we attended classes on Sunday. Also, the "Jewish" schools had much poorer accommodation in general than the non-Jewish or "Polish" schools, as was the case with my school and others I knew. Jewish schools were often accommodated in regular rental tenements, on a floor or two, not in buildings specifically built for the purpose. And we did not have any special workshops, labs for science classes, or physical education facilities. Sometimes science classes were held for us in a "Polish" school in the vicinity.

My Favorite Subjects

Like in any other school as well as ours, religion was a mandatory subject. But it was taught here in the context of Jewish biblical history rather than as a doctrine, and by a regular teacher, not a clergyman. The Bible was treated as a history of the Jewish people; Jewish kings and prophets were portrayed as kinds of Jewish saints, and history became religion and religion became history.

I liked those classes. The names of the ancient Jewish sects sounded exotic, and I surprised my father when I babbled about the

Sadducees, Pharisees, and Essenes. The stories were fascinating; the story of the little shepherd who became King David and the monstrous Goliath whom he had defeated not only by being brave but also clever, and also of the wise King Solomon who knew how to tell the real mother from the false one, the heroic deeds of the Maccabees, and the miracle of Hanukkah, and that brave woman Esther who saved the Jews from that horrible Haman! These stories were not only very interesting, they were inspiring. Certainly, it was at least as interesting as the legends that Polish history narrated; of Prince Popiel, who was eaten by mice, or of the Princess Kinga, who threw her ring with such success that on the place it had fallen, the Wieliczka salt mines came into existence, and the story of the three brothers Lech, Chekh, and Russ, who founded the future Slavic states.

History, language, and geography were my favorite subjects, but in the last two years of school, I also enjoyed science, especially the experiments for which we were using the labs at the "Polish" school. I had no special love for math, and at twelve wrote a little play with the title *Ah, That Math!* which was successfully staged at our school. Performances, in which many children participated, were very popular and well attended by parents and children. I, too, liked to perform and I might say that I was always eager to get on the stage. At ten or eleven years old, I was not shy at all; on the contrary, I was pretty pushy. I remember a very large, cavernous hall, and an actress or teacher on the stage reciting some poetry and then asking if any of the children would like to recite a piece written by them. Some children raced to the stage (I was among them) and I was perhaps faster than the others because the person on the stage invited me to recite my poem, a rather long and very patriotic one of which I only remember the title, *On the Shores of the Polish Sea.* I saw that sea, the Baltic, for the first time in my life, only fifteen years later.

Sometimes our teachers would take us to a real theater. The first performance I ever saw in such a "real" theater made an unforgettable impression on me. The play was *In the Jungle and in the Wilderness*, based on the book by Henryk Sienkiewicz. Genuinely upset when Stash lost his glove in the desert, unwittingly leaving a clue that would lead the Bedouins, the bad people, to his and Nell's hiding place, I jumped on my chair and warned the actor yelling in full voice, "The glove, the glove, pick it up!"

My Classmates

I recall very little of my classmates. Some names have stuck in my mind, but not too many and, for some reason, most of those sounded Polish, not Jewish: Piwnik, Gawronska, Samborska, Chlebowska. For some time, I was good friends with a girl, Zosia, who lived in an orphanage. I would sometimes invite her—with my mother's permission—to share a meal with us. I guess compassion was the basis of my feelings toward her; she was an orphan, and the very thought of being an orphan caused me pain. Later, I lost touch with her and all the other girls, and never met any of them again, which is no wonder since in the meantime there was the Holocaust.

One of the girls I remember better was Rywcia. She was the girl next door, or almost next door, and a classmate. Rywcia and her family lived on our street, some two blocks closer to our school. I remember the whole family very well. They were all big, fat people; mama bear, papa bear, and four not-so-little baby bears. The most interesting person in the family was, for me, the grandmother; she was so old, and the oldest person I had seen in my childhood. Always sitting in an armchair, motionless, she did not speak, she looked with her round, unblinking, small, dark eyes, but seemed not to see anything. She was obviously well cared for, fed, and always clean, a helpless, scary epitome of old age.

Rywcia's father was a roofer and ran his small business with the help of his two sons. Once, they were fixing the roof of our tenement, covering it with new tar paper. Shlomo, his son, was cooking the tar in an enormous metal drum in the yard, sending buckets of it on a rope up to his father. All that, the fire under the drum, the heat and smoke, and the smell made for a great show for us children, and long after the whole job was done, we used to play roofers, yelling "Shlomo, send up the tar, Shlomooo, the taaar!"

Shlomo had a nickname: Shlomo-soup. An untidy fat boy, his school notebooks were always stained with grease, and when he, by way of explanation, confessed to the teacher that he had spilled his soup on them, the merciless teacher gave him that nickname that stuck. There were many stories about that family. As they were all fat, they obviously must have been big eaters, and as the standard story had it, one day when they complained that someone had broken into their place and taken away all the food that the lady of the house had prepared for the Sabbath, nobody believed them, saying that they, one after another, had most probably gotten up during the night and helped themselves to a bite or two, ate it all up, and then blamed it on a robber.

On the way to school, I would stop at Rywcia's place and we would walk the rest of the way together. She was the youngest in the family, also very fat, a gentle child, a little slow, and a poor student. Her happiest time in school would usually come at the end of class. She always greeted the moment when the teacher dismissed the class with a loud, happy sigh of relief which made the whole class laugh. Whenever I hear someone sighing with relief at the end of a difficult or tedious task, I think about Rywcia. After the war, I met one of her much older brothers who survived the Holocaust in Łódź. Rywcia, he told me, had survived the ghetto and the camp, but died in the first week after liberation. "You know," he told me with a guilty smile, "she threw herself on the food..." The rest of the family perished in the Holocaust.

Where We Played after School

Later, not yet in my teens but almost there, I had different friends. By then there were more Jewish families in the neighborhood and their children, feeling rather isolated in their yards, took to congregating in a different place. They found a large empty lot, about a block from our place, where there was once, a long time ago, an orchard, now abandoned. It was all overgrown with weeds, high grass, and a few apple trees gone wild. Here, not afraid of abuse or being disturbed by hooligans, we could get together, play, and make up games. Also here, I was initiated into games that boys and girls play everywhere, games with a sexual undertone. On the wall of the building adjacent to the lot, large chalk-written signs would show up declaring "Abramek kissed Basia" or "Mania loves Szlomek." These would be quickly erased only to be written again soon after, or be replaced by other similar announcements. The girls, most of them a year or two older than I, whispered and giggled and sometimes sighed in a special way with a mixture of admiration and desire about one boy, whom I was never lucky enough to even see, having to return home early in the evening. His name was Heniek Stern, and I remember his name for some inexplicable or perhaps not-so-inexplicable reason. He was the true idol of all the girls, not unlike a matinee movie idol, if not more so; after all, he was real and the feelings of my friends somehow rubbed off on me, and I too was "in love" with their idol.

Our Worsening Financial Situation

In the meantime, things took a turn for the worse in our family. As I mentioned, the factory, where my father worked, moved, for economic reasons, to Aleksandrów, a little town outside Łódź. At the same time, the owners decided to modernize and made my father's job redundant, among others; his hand-driven spinner was replaced by a machine. Father, already over fifty, was considered too old to learn how to service the machine and had almost no hope of finding another job. We moved out of the place that had been our home for the last fifteen years, and from the meager savings my parents were able to accumulate during those years, they opened a small store selling milk, bread, and not much more. It was a poor store, catering to poor people in a poor neighborhood and it did not work. The unsold milk would curdle and the bread would go stale.

New words such as "*sequestrate*" (tax collector), entered our vocabulary. One day, he came and glued a notice onto my mother's beautiful wardrobe, sequestering it for taxes we could not pay. This was the only piece of furniture of some value in the household, bought a few years back at the peak of the family's prosperous times, when the three older children were already working and helping out, contributing part of their earnings to the family budget. That wardrobe had then replaced the old one, heavy and dark and almost falling apart, which my parents had owned since the beginning of their marriage. Owners of sequestered objects, mostly pieces of furniture, would often damage them, thus, to prevent them from being taken away; damaged goods were worthless. A neighbor of ours cut a big hole in her sequestered sofa and was overjoyed and triumphant when the tax collector had to leave it in place. I would have gladly scratched the golden birchwood wardrobe, but a policeman was guarding it. Mother was terribly upset, and I was old enough to understand the injustice being done to her and to feel her pain, but I was too young to help.

High School Is Not an Option

What else became quite obvious to me at that time was that I would have to forget my dream of continuing school; of going to high school, the coveted gymnasium. I was in sixth grade at the time and from here, you either go to the first year of high school for another four years of learning or to the seventh and last grade of basic school, thus concluding your education. Seven years of it was all I could get, despite my acutely felt need for more and a burning desire to learn. High school cost money and we did not have any to spare.

My teachers, and among them especially Pani (Mrs.) Manelanka who was teaching us Polish tried their best to find a place for me in a high school that would cost less or even be tuition-free, but there were obstacles somehow impossible to overcome. There were not too many such schools in Łódź; I checked this later and there were thirty-two in all for a population of about 750,000. Most were private schools and very expensive, and only four were state-run and thus free of tuition. But for a Jewish child to get into one of those at that time was almost impossible. No matter how hard my teachers tried, they did not succeed. Pani Manelanka was very sorry for telling me this, all the more so because she always encouraged me to read, to study, and to "have aspirations." Sometimes she would even become preachy, telling me again and again how important it is to "reach higher," not to "waste the inborn abilities," etc. I had a special relationship with her; she provided me with books to read and often talked about them with me. From time to time, she would give me extra assignments, such as to write a letter in the name of all the children of our school to some other school on some special occasion, or to write a speech to be read in celebration of a state holiday, or the new school year, or the last day of school, and so on. I got her last assignment when I was in the seventh grade. It was to prepare a speech to commemorate the death of Marshal Piłsudski, Poland's ruler. I remember this assignment well because it was rather unusual. "Do not dwell too much on the facts," she instructed me. "Just try to make it nice, you know what I mean?" I understood her, though I wondered why she asked me to treat the subject in such a shallow way. Did she not like the "*Dziadek*" (grandfather), as the deceased marshal was affectionately known in Poland? I did not ask but just did what she asked me to do, and she liked my speech.

She truly tried to do something for me, but when her efforts failed, she at least did not attempt to console me as some others did by trying to convince me that it doesn't matter whether I go or don't go to high school, that it did not make much sense to stay in school for four more years, because what would you do with your *matura* (certificate of maturity or high school diploma) when you graduate? With unemployment rampant, you will have to learn a trade then anyway, because you know what's going on with the universities; the numerus clausus, ghetto benches, Falanga members, those hooligans sporting the sign of joint sabers in their lapels and knives up their sleeves, beating up Jewish students, so do not have any regrets![35]

There certainly was a lot of truth in all this. I knew the misery unemployment brings, I knew what it did to my unemployed father and

35 With the deepening international Depression and the death of the uniting figure, Marshal Jósef Piłsudski, a hero of World War I and of the Polish–Soviet War, considered the father of the modern Polish state, Poland turned increasingly toward right-wing nationalism and antisemitism in the latter 1930s. On a day-to-day level, this included legal limits on Jewish participation in education and professions, socially enforced segregation such as the so-called "ghetto benches" in university classrooms, and the threat of violence from outlawed groups such as the Obóz Narodowo-Radykalny Falanga, known colloquially as the Falanga (phalanx).

our whole family, and I had also experienced antisemitism firsthand since early childhood, so all this was not new to me. Quite recently, we had one of those especially stinging antisemitic encounters when our teachers took the whole class on an excursion to Kraków. We enthusiastically took in the wonders of that historic city and visited its rich museums. I can still see the pearl-covered veil of Queen Jadwiga exhibited among other relics of Poland's royal past that impressed me so; we oohed and aahed in the Smocza Jama (the Dragon's Cave), almost expecting to spot the dragon in there, and admired the Wawel, the seat of Poland's kings, not without a certain feeling of patriotism and pride for Poland's great history with which we, us Jewish girls, were instilled with by our schools, if not by our homes. All this was truly unforgettable.

Żydówki, Get Lost!

At the old Jagellonian University's courtyard, we were admiring the Renaissance galleries running around the main university building, our eyes wide open, when a rather large group of students hissed at us "*Żydówki*, get lost!" We were children, twelve and thirteen years old, and they were university students who looked, at least to us, like grown men. This too was unforgettable. Yes, I did know the hostility Jews could encounter in places like these, but it made a big difference to me whether I would or would not continue school, and I did regret that I would not.

My parents knew how much I desired it, and they wished me to succeed, but at the same time they could not help having rather ambivalent feelings about the whole thing. The family was facing abject poverty at that time and my parents were hoping, or at least had a right to hope, that I would soon, in a year or two at the most, somehow be able to contribute to the family's income. Also, to my father, a deeply religious and observant Jew, it would not be easy to reconcile himself to my attending school on Saturdays, had I gotten a place in a state-run school, but he was ready to take "my sin," as he would say, on his soul. My mother had reservations too, though of a different kind. My "aspirations," which my teacher held so highly, rather scared her. She was convinced such aspirations would not bring anything but trouble for her child's future. An educated girl would not want a tailor or a carpenter for a husband, yet a doctor would not take her, she reasoned, and one has to grant that there was some logic in such reasoning. After all, I was good with books and as she sometimes complained, I was good "with nothing and for nothing" but books, and she would not argue if the opportunity came my way. Poor mother, what would and should bring joy to parents under more favorable circumstances was only a source of additional worry for her. But all this, her worries, reservations, and problems were "solved" pretty soon when it was decided that I would not be going to high school and my dream was over.

So where to now? Asking the question was in itself a sign of change, of growing up. My childhood was over, adolescence was looming, and it was not looking very bright or happy. I was certainly not a rich girl, and I would not be an educated girl; would I at least be a pretty girl, I asked myself, and not without trepidation. I was growing and changing physically, and naturally, I was thrilled with the signs of change, observing them with awe. The monthly bleeding, though expected, came as a shock, but mercifully without painful cramps, and all of a sudden, I felt the need to wear a bra. I did buy one in great secrecy, hiding it even from Mother. One change, however, gave me great pleasure: my hair was getting much fuller and shinier, and more manageable. It used to be straight and rather disorderly but now I could roll up a strand of hair on my finger to turn it into a curl. Tied by a silky brown ribbon at the nape of the neck, my hair turned into a ponytail, swishing right and left as I walked, and I liked that. Saddened and disappointed by the general condition of my life which made me sometimes cry, I still laughed a lot, and seemingly for no reason at all. Despite all the pitfalls, everything was so interesting, everything seemed like an adventure. Curious about what the next day would bring and hoping that it would be something good, I was a rather happy girl in my early teens and behaved accordingly.

Tribute to Łódź

Julian Tuwim, the great Jewish–Polish poet was a native of Łódź and he conveyed in his poetry his special feelings of love for the city. Let the future generations not argue about his place of birth, he wrote tongue in cheek, "For I myself declare my town is Łódź, it is my childhood home. Let other poets sing the praises of Ganges, Sorrento, Crimea. Give me Łódź. Her dirt and smoke are happiness and joy to me."[36]

I am sorry to say that I cannot share the poet's enthusiastic feelings for the "dirt and smoke" of my native city as well as for that city in general. But though I have lived in and seen many cities certainly greater and more praiseworthy than Łódź, with the passing of time the images of all those great, wonderful places, have become blurred in my memory, and I keep forgetting them, increasingly seeing them only as if through a deep haze. Łódź, however, has stayed in my memory with almost total clarity. No matter how much I wished it were the other way around, Łódź remains, regrettably, the only city I cannot forget.

Sometimes when I have these dreams, now often called "Kafkaesque," dreams of wandering through places full of rubble, half-destroyed buildings, and ruins without end which I never saw in real life, I know that I am in Łódź. Moreover, searching in my dream for a place that I knew I would never find, I know as well that this place was in Łódź. And no matter how much I would like to forget it all, Łódź with its "dirt and smoke," its cobbled streets, its foul-smelling yards, poverty, and ugliness of its crowded quarters, would be with me and would follow me forever.

36 Julian Tuwim, "Łódź," *Jarmark rymów* (Warsaw: Czytelnik, 1991), p. 152, translated in Antony Polonsky, "Julian Tuwim, the Polish Heine," 24, *The American Association for Polish–Jewish Studies* http://www.aapjstudies.org/index.php?id=115 (accessed August 1, 2022).

CHAPTER TWO

ADOLESCENCE

As I look back to that faraway time, to the first few months when school was over, all I see is a black hole. There is nothing I can remember about it; there is nothing there to be retrieved from my memory. I stayed home, helping Mother with the household chores and with running that little store which was my parents' main occupation and the only source of income, a very meager income to be sure. I lost contact with my schoolmates and had no desire or opportunity to make new friends. I lived in a kind of limbo, sad and depressed.

What Is My "Future" Going to Be?

After a while, however, my sister Sala took notice. She was now a grown-up, a beautiful girl, working at one of the Łódź textile factories. "There is no future for a girl sitting home like that," she said one day to Mother, and that very afternoon we went, hand in hand, to find a "future" for me. It would be nice if I would learn to become a hatmaker, a milliner, she proposed, and I rather liked the idea. At least it did not seem to be as boring as learning to become a seamstress.

There were many little milliner shops around. A window dressed with a few hats and the owner, sometimes with a helper but mostly alone, catering to the occasional customer. Yet, the demand was evidently there, because at those times it was considered "not proper" for a woman to go outside of her home without something covering her head, a kerchief for the simple folk, a hat or beret for those of "higher standing." Thus, we decided that there was, perhaps, a future for me in that trade.

"Yes, she would teach me the secrets of the trade," said the first of the owners of a small milliner shop that we had approached. The remuneration for her instruction would be eighty zlotys and she would not pay me anything for half a year. And she could not make any promises to employ me after that initial period. These were harsh conditions. The payment for instruction was very steep and hardly affordable for us. After having inquired at many similar shops and having heard the same message repeated by all the other lady owners of those shops, it looked like we would have to give it all up. Finally, however, despite the initial disappointment, I did get a job. It was close to where we lived, a rather large store called, "Hats for Men and Ladies," and the owners were a young couple, husband and wife. The man had no interest in hats for ladies; his wife, who used to run that part of the business, had just recently become a mother and needed a helper in the store. Here's where I came in. I would learn the trade, helping out in the store, and the woman they employed part-time, would teach me. If I turned out to be able to learn and be helpful, I would get a place, of course without pay and any promises for the months ahead, but also without having to pay for the apprenticeship.

"Hats for Men and Ladies"

I learned the secrets of the trade pretty fast. There was not much to learn there, anyway. The felt hats, which "our" store was selling were not prepared on the premises. We bought the felt forms, as did most other small millinery shops, from much larger and mechanized, specialized workshops, and by adding some finishing touches to them, we would turn the half-raw product into the hats the customers desired. Soon, I got to know these workshops and I would visit them to place orders for hats and bring them back to our store when they were ready. I remember well one of these workshops located on Piotrkowska Street, the city's most famous avenue, but it was hidden inside a large yard, and it wasn't visible from the front.

I liked this part of my duties. It allowed me to see downtown, to see Piotrkowska Street with its glamorous buildings, some embellished with gilded adornments, residences of the very rich industrialists, banks, seats of the big corporations, elegant stores with their beautifully arranged windows. All that was so different from my neighborhood! I liked to experience the noise, the traffic, and the commotion of big city life.

The workshop where the hats were made was also something to be seen. The hats were formed under the pressure of hot steam. The main workshop room was noisy, hot, and full of steam, and the men (the hatmakers), bare down to the waist, were moving around in the clouds of steam like ghosts. They worked on the raw material, shaping it into various forms and designs. Later, in "our" store I would learn, under the supervision of the part-time employee, to work on finishing these half-raw forms, turning them into real hats. Ribbons would be sewn inside the hats, some adornments would be added, a flower, or a feather or a ribbon, or sometimes a short see-through veil made of tulle or a silky delicate mesh peppered with embroidered black spots, as was fashionable at the time. I learned to do this as well and I liked it. It let me use my imagination. And when there was nobody around in the store, I would try on these hats, one after another. Standing in front of a mirror I would make faces at the girl in there, and she seemed to be changing each time I put on a different hat. I liked the round trundle-shaped hats best; raised in the front and sloped at the back with a pinned-on, short mesh veil. The veil, punctuated by embroidered black spots, "beauty marks," would cover more than half my face, and my eyes would shine through it as if they were carrying a secret message. I saw myself as a mysterious woman, in high heels and a long dress, so different from what I was in reality, and this was fun.

And that fun, I might say, was all I got as wages. Despite the long hours I put in, day in and day out, I never got a penny for my efforts from the owners of the store. Nevertheless, making and selling hats would have perhaps become my future, if it hadn't been for a change in my family's situation. After the disastrous end of the store my mother had been running, my brother came to our rescue. By now, he had a job with one of the largest lumberyards in the city, located on its outskirts, close to where the Jewish cemetery was on Brzezińska Street. He set us up in a store that catered to his customers selling tar paper, nails, cement, and similar basic building materials for the construction of the houses for which he provided the lumber. This time my father was to run the store and I was needed as a helper. An old barn adjacent to the lumberyard was rented and this was where the new business got started. In the beginning, it looked quite promising. My brother was doing most of the selling, bringing in his customers; agents from hardware wholesale companies came in, always ready to take commissions and deliver promptly, and the seller's profit, though modest, provided the family with some income.

Goodbye to Hat-making

Thus, I said goodbye to my future in hat-making, and I did it with no regrets. Mysteries covered up by veils, high heels, long dresses, and whatever else a girl supposedly dreams of while changing "from a bud into flower," as quoted in a then-popular song, had no overwhelming hold on me. No, I was not coveting fancy hats or dresses. The most beautiful outfit for me would have been the dark blue uniform of a gymnasium student. There were not many children in my neighborhood who attended high school, but I quite often saw one such lucky girl on my street. And how I envied her! It was what I really wanted, what I dreamed of and regretted not having. Almost two years after leaving school, I would still dream about going to school again and still wanted an education more than anything else. The need to know, to learn, to read, an intellectual hunger, which can be as real and painful as physical hunger, was still with me. It was not fading away; on the contrary, it was growing ever stronger. Once, when still in school, I found a forgotten book in a drawer that had no beginning or end, rather a pitiful remnant of a book. It had no title or author, and only much later did I understand that it must have been a history of literature. It was a wonderful and unusual book, a book about books and about characters who live only in books but are more real than real-life characters could be. I read it back and forth and looked for other such books, but access to libraries was limited for a youngster who was not in school or the workforce and had no money to subscribe to a privately owned library.

Yentl of Singer's Story

To cut a long story short, I would say that there was something in me of Yentl, the girl Singer described so vividly in one of his stories.[37] Yentl, of course, personified all those Jewish girls of my times and place—and there were many—who had a great love for books and learning but were not given the chance to fulfill those aspirations. I, too, dreamed about living in a study house, with books, in pursuit of knowledge as Yentl did. I, too, was a girl that seemed to be "good for nothing but books" for which my chagrined mother, worried about my future, sometimes reproached me. Was I also the "Heaven's mistake," as Yentl was according to her father? Never did I hear this from my father, and as for me, I do not remember regretting that I was born a girl and not a boy. And it never occurred to me to try to achieve my goal the way Yentl had chosen for herself. Yentl used a ruse. She pretended to be a man, and as Singer tries to convince us, she was able to get away with her deception. She kind of looked like a man, as she was "tall, bony with narrow hips and small breasts." There was even, Singer tells us, "a slight down on her upper lip," all this making it easier for her to successfully get away with the deception and join a yeshiva. Later, the story gets complicated, which is, of course, to be expected. But without going into

37 Isaac Bashevis Singer published his short story, "Yentl, the Yeshiva Boy," in the September 1962 issue of *Commentary*.

the vicissitudes, I would like to stress here one very interesting point: Yentl was forced to make many painful sacrifices to pursue her goal and she went as far as humanly possible, giving up not only the pleasures of family, love, etc., but also her eternal life. Knowing that by the precepts of her faith, the way she had chosen was considered sinful, she was nevertheless ready to persevere and take that sin on her soul, risking losing her eternal life. "Would you rather lose your share in the world to come?" she was asked at one point, and she answered, "Perhaps," not unlike Faust,[38] ready to sell, lose, and jeopardize her immortal soul, not for eternal youth, but to quench her thirst for knowledge, for a life with books, and a study house! Yentl knew her priorities, even when confused about her desires, she remained clear about what she wanted most: to pursue knowledge.

Yentl's Faustian Pact

Yes, there was something of that Yentl in me. I too would have perhaps been ready to pay the highest price for the same chance, and I too would have perhaps not hesitated to give the answer Yentl gave. Nobody, however, tried to "buy my soul." Fortunately, Yentl's ways were not for me anyway. To begin with, I would not look like a boy, regardless of how I dressed; I was not "tall and bony" and there was no "down on my upper lip." Neither was I interested in the kind of knowledge Yentl was pursuing; yeshivas and Judaic matters were something too exotic for me. What I was after was secular knowledge, and general culture and to achieve this, I would look to other ways and directions.

38 A reference to Johann Wolfgang von Goethe's most iconic piece, *Faust*, in which the main character by the same name sells his soul to the devil in exchange for a short episode of joy on earth.

Self-education

I found those ways, or rather I must say a substitute way, rather soon. With formal education out of my reach, I found a new way: self-education. Sure, one pays a certain price for self-education. Self-education is always somehow uneven, a search in the dark, and in my case, since it was coming mainly through political and organizational channels, it was accompanied by a rather heavy dose of indoctrination. Here one buys what's offered, lock, stock, and barrel, and it takes time to learn to separate the wheat from the chaff, and perhaps even more time and intellectual effort to unlearn. And isn't there in it an element akin to those Faustian pacts we have to make, willingly or not, consciously, deliberately, or unintentionally when trying to achieve some of our most desired goals?

The Youth Section of the Trade Union

Soon I found a way to those organizations. There was a lot of political activity going on around me. Zionists of all persuasions, Socialists from the most moderate to the most radical, and so on. Some of the most active, and those to which I was most inclined, were the leftist organizations. One day, I found my way to the Youth Section of the Union of Trade, Commerce, and Office Employees, and here I met other young girls and boys belonging to the Communist Youth League. I was now employed in the building materials store run by my father. But since Father was in debt to the Polish state for the unpaid taxes remaining from my parents' first failed business venture and the fact that Mother's wardrobe was taken away by the *sequestrate* was not enough to cover that debt, Father could not get a license to run the new store in his name. My sister Sala, now already married but still working in the factory, took out a license in her name, and I became formally employed by her, though without pay. Since Sala did not possess anything, not even a decent wardrobe to be taken away from her in case of a tax debt accrued by the new business venture, she was safe. This was logical, prudent thinking because the new business indeed did not last long and was again a failure. For the time being, I was however employed, even if by my sister, and even if not gainfully. I had the right to be a member of a trade union, which I would not have had, perhaps, as the daughter of a storeowner. This was a trade union, and the class principles had to be respected.

Youth Organizations, the Communist League, and the Zukunft

The Youth Section was an interesting place. I used to visit there quite often, my eyes wide open, listening to the talks and the discussions, looking for new friends. A bunch of young people, the majority made up of boys, used to come here for the same purpose: to have fun, clown around, exchange jokes, or show off a bit. All political persuasions were represented here, but the two largest groups were the Zukunft, the Bund's youth organization,[39] and the Youth Communist League. The discussions between members of both factions were always lively, to say the least, and sometimes, when arguments were lacking or temperaments were out of control, discussions turned into fistfights. I remember one such fight, though I do not recall what the cause of the disagreement was. One moment we were sitting properly in our chairs, listening to the speaker, and in another moment, things became so heated that there was evidently no other resolution to the crisis but a fistfight. The boys went at each other and I was in the middle, holding onto my chair and perhaps, a bit scared, when one of the young men from the Zukunft, quite aware that my political sympathies were not on his side, picked me up in the air and got me out of the crowd to safety. I often naively wondered then why we had to fight. Didn't we have the same aim? Didn't we want to achieve the same good, Socialism? The main difference, the bottom line, had seemed to me to be in the timing;

39 Zukunft (Future) was the youth group of the socialist Algemeyner Yidisher Arbeyter Bund (The General Jewish Workers' Union), known as the Bund. It was among the largest Jewish political parties in interwar Poland.

they, the Socialists, were not in a hurry while I wanted CHANGE to come not tomorrow, but today. I had no time.

Libraries and Public Reading Rooms

From the youth section, I found a way to libraries and reading rooms and was getting deep into reading. As if to make up for lost time, I read whatever I could get my hands on, but mostly literature, history, and social ideas. I had more time for reading now, using some spare time while sitting in the store which was perhaps to the detriment of the business but good for my education, and importantly, a source of wonderful pleasure. Literature from all over the world was translated into Polish, and books by German, French, English, and American writers became accessible to me, as well as lots of Russian and Soviet writers.

Appetite grows with eating, and I was becoming a voracious, addicted reader—if something was written, I had to read it. I loved thick novels with social content and [Theodore] Dreiser and [Upton] Sinclair were my favorites. I also read books by journalists sharing their impressions of their travels, especially to the Soviet Union, discovering the pluses and sometimes also the minuses of the "socialist experiment," which would only strengthen the air of objectivity of their works; their veracity was not only interesting to read but also very helpful in converting (if this was still needed) such young "seekers" like myself to the socialist/communist cause.

The name of an Austrian or German journalist, Egon Erwin Kisch (I wonder who else remembers him now?)[40] sticks in my mind. His report on the Asian Soviet Republics must have made a great impression on me, mainly because of that air of objectivity. And the list of Soviet writers which—a few years later—would become a list of Stalin's victims—Boris Pilnyak, Aleksandr Avdeyenko, Bruno Jasieński, Karl Radek, and many others! Then came Lenin, a lot of

40 Egon Erwin Kisch, known as the *"rasende Reporter"* (racing reporter) was an Austro–Czechoslovakian Jewish writer and journalist.

Lenin. There was the book with a title that reminded you of a dance, a tango—*One Step Forward, Two Steps Back*, and then *"Left-Wing" Communism: An Infantile Disorder*. And, of course, the most important one, which asked the eternal question of all who were ever critical of the world as it is and determined to redo it: *What Is to Be Done?* After that—or perhaps simultaneously—came Alexander Bogdanov and Nikolai Bukharin, whose popular books on Marxian economics and philosophy have served so many as an introduction to more serious studies of the subjects. And to make the picture complete, I recall the thrill of reading Stalin's *On Leninism* printed on very thin cigarette paper, the way illegal literature should perhaps be printed and read. This was distributed for free by the Polish Communist Party and I read it at night by the light of the streetlamp, as such "dynamite" perhaps should be read. Later came Karl Marx himself.

I was pushing all this into my head, poor girl. Should I not have rather been reading lyrical poetry instead? I read, and with reading, I learned to read, to tell good from not-so-good writing. At first, I was mostly concerned with the ideas these books were promoting, with the social content, totally disregarding or rather failing to notice the aesthetic side. The appreciation of the quality of writing, of the beauty of the words forming a phrase, came later, developing slowly; in a way not unlike taste buds develop with eating, turning an ordinary consumer of food into a gourmet.

"What Is To Be Done?"

I kept reading and studying not only because it interested me, not purely in pursuit of knowledge, or out of intellectual curiosity that once awakened would not let up, but also as if the world depended on it. And why not? My books taught me and convinced me that the world, indeed, depends on it—or at least it depends on it a great deal. In a sense, studying was my answer to the question "What is to be done?" or more precisely, what should I be doing?

One of my favorite books became Friedrich Engels's *The Development of Socialism from Utopia into Science*. I memorized whole pages of it and could recite them as if it were indeed lyrical poetry. It became my bible of sorts. Socialism, Engels taught me, which used to be only a beautiful but unreachable dream, became a science with Marx's discoveries. We would no longer just have to dream about Socialism, about the good and just society that does not know the divisions into haves and have-nots, into poor and rich. Now, we know that the existing unjust society must eventually give way and inevitably be replaced by the new and better one. We know why. Only when private ownership of the means of production, the main root of all evil, would be replaced by common, socialistic ownership, a society of equality and justice for all would come into being. In that new society, there would be a place for everyone, nobody willing to work would be jobless, and education would be accessible to everybody willing to learn. And who would not want to live in such a society? Of course, I would. And this ideal society was not just something desirable, as it should be, but it would inevitably come true.

Historical Inevitability

Engels taught me that history develops in stages and according to its laws, and with Capitalism, history had reached the last, pre-socialist stage. In the very depth of the capitalist society, which is riddled with contradictions, tensions, and struggles, the new society is developing, and when it ripens the old society will give way to the new one. Socialism will become a reality. The new society is historically necessary and thus inevitable.

But, if the forces of history are inevitably driving society toward Socialism what was there left to do about it? Watch and do not miss the moment of Socialism's coming? To hasten the arrival of Socialism? How can one hasten or postpone the occurrence of a process that is "inevitable"? Is there any possibility to influence the eclipse of the moon in one way or another? I had heard those questions and criticisms then, but my books also had answers to these doubts. They were teaching me, quite convincingly, that I had much to contribute indeed. Socialism, although inevitable, nevertheless needs help. As the birth of a child needs the help of a midwife, so the birth of a new society needs people to actively participate in the process and facilitate the coming of the revolution. History does not play itself out over people's heads, independently of them and their ideas. By joining the movement, by learning and studying, we raise our consciousness and through it the consciousness of the masses that would eventually be able to oppose those who would like to hinder or put a stop to this process of historical development. But this, those "dark forces" would not achieve. The laws of science cannot be bent or ignored, and neither can the laws of history. We use the laws of the physical world for our benefit and similarly, we can use the laws of history. Those who would go against them would be doomed to land on the "garbage heap of history." So, I enthusiastically believed in this, and these were happy, reassuring thoughts.

Historical Inevitability Is on My Side

Inevitability—that coin, of course, also has another side. If you like and desire what the historical process is inevitably bringing then that's fine, you win! You have a powerful ally in the very process of history. But what if you do not particularly like what history is promising? Then inevitability becomes a curse. It grows iron claws and jaws, as an old critic noted, that would tear you to pieces if you stand in its way. To go against it is futile, like banging your head against a brick wall, but to bow to it, to accept it, when it goes against one's desires, turns one into a slave. That's why the ancient Epicure would rather resign himself to the mercy of gods as rulers of the world than accept the Democritean necessity: gods may change their sentencing and may show you mercy while there is no mercy in the iron laws of the deterministic order.

Of course, I was not interested in that other side of the coin, and those other implications about the notion of inevitability. I doubt that I even guessed then that another such side existed. For now, this was a fine, neat theory, as if made for me, a theory that makes the weak feel stronger. It felt good to have the historical laws driving in the direction which I desired, to have them on my side. On the coattails of that force, I will reach my goal! And I had learned to believe in Socialism's inevitability, not unlike my father's belief in the coming of the Messiah. My father prayed to facilitate his coming or to make him hurry up a bit and was clasping his hands while praying which would make a sound as if he was catching something. "He tries to catch the angels," my mother remarked once, and there was more than a touch of irony in her voice.

While studying, I was also trying to "catch" or "catch onto" something important to me, the historical inevitability. The theories I studied convinced me sufficiently that this is the case when our actions may influence the otherwise inevitable course of history positively. Marxist dialectics taught that everything is interconnected; it's not unlike the ripple effect, you know, your deeds leave a trace, influence others, and so on. I did not have to believe that Socialism would eventually come—I knew it would and that I could do something to help facilitate its coming.

Gabriel, Love Forever

I was not alone in these pursuits. At the Youth Section, I met Gabriel. A short boy (and girls supposedly don't look twice at short boys), not yet seventeen, I did not even notice that he kept looking in my direction. But when we started talking to each other, it turned out that he was not only much more interesting than all the other boys but also great fun to be with. And wasn't he handsome, too? Definitely the nicest boy around! Suddenly, I had a boyfriend, the best ever. He grew on me, and soon we became almost inseparable.

As it turned out, he was also the "leader," and an important person (!) of the first "cell"; the group of five, two girls and three boys, with whom we were meeting as part of our organization. We had a lot in common; first of all, a passion for reading, and he was so much brighter and smarter than I was. He was better, more inquisitive, and critical.

We were not dating much—poor kids, too busy with studying and our organization—but we saw each other very often anyway. Once, he invited me to a theater performance—he had two tickets—and he asked me through a cousin of mine who lived nearby (we had no telephones and to let me know by mail would have taken a week) "Would I like to come?" I was glad to go.

The theater was the Universal (Powszechny), but what was the performance? I don't remember. I had a good time, it felt good to be with him, and attending a theater performance was in itself an exciting event. During the intermission, while babbling some nonsense or other, I unexpectedly caught his gaze fixed so intently on me as if it was glued to me. This was new—no boy had ever before looked at me in this way. He was taking me in and though it was not offensive or unpleasant, it made me somehow angry, not uncomfortable, but angry. I saw those big blue, blue eyes of his, shining with joy, gazing at me with an expression that I was not yet quite able to read, but would never forget either. And something changed between us from then.

New Year's Party, 1938

To celebrate the coming New Year of 1938, we had a party. It was my first all-night or late-into-the-night party, and there was great excitement because of that very fact. Some twelve young people, girls, and boys got together at Mala's place; her parents had left the apartment to us to attend a New Year's party of their own elsewhere. I do not remember the boys that were there—girls were in the majority.

It was all very sober. We had a few bottles of beer, less than one between two, and five altogether to be exact because Gabriel, who provided the beer, lost one bottle when we were waiting for the building's manager to let us in. It was already after eleven and according to the city laws, the gates of the buildings had to be closed at eleven.

Gabriel and another boy were standing at the entrance behind me, and, as he told me only much, much later, he wanted so much to touch me that when he tried to reach out to me, he was fiddling with the bottles and one slipped out of his hand, fell to the ground with a bang, and broke. So, we only had five bottles of beer, but since most of us had never tried beer anyway, it was enough. There was perhaps some food and we had nuts, and this I remember well because I brought them. So, we spent hours cracking nuts, sipping beer, and chatting. There was some singing, though nobody among us could boast a good voice. There was some revolutionary poetry recitation and a lot of joking around; it was all very proper, and it was even a bit boring at the end until the time came to go home.

I had the impression that Gabriel was rather avoiding me, sitting in the other corner of the room all the time, but when the time came to leave, he suddenly winked at me from across the room—and some wink this was!—a true cockeyed wink, a "Persian eye" as it was popularly called. Before I had time to react, Zoska, one of the girls, noticed the wink and clapped her hands with joy, "They will be a couple!" she cried out. "They will be a couple!" Zoska had either an astigmatic eye or a slight limp, or both, and even though I truly liked her, I do not remember the nature of her affliction. With all the cruelty or directness of youth, we called her either *ślepa* (blind) or *kulawa* (limping) Zoska. She was a warm, caring girl, just over twenty, and a fiery devoted revolutionary, but matchmaking was no sin from the revolutionary point of view, and she was happy to be a witness, as she believed, to the birth of a new love, a union of her two younger comrades. And, not so amazingly, her prophecy came true. We became "a couple," got married with children and grandchildren to follow, and it has been a good long life together.

Less than two years after that New Year's party, our world would be turned upside down. The war and the Holocaust were upon us. When Gabriel and I, having spent the wartime far away in the Soviet Union, eventually returned to our city, to Łódź, we did not find any of those old first friends of our youth. None of them had survived the Holocaust...

Mala

We shared our interest in studying Marxism and related topics with Mala, my and Gabriel's best friend. She was a lively girl, fair-haired with good, intelligent, attentive dark eyes, a short, slightly upturned nose, a Slavic face, nothing Semitic one would say, a *shiksa.*[41] We became very

41 A derogatory term for a non-Jewish woman.

close, and I still see her clearly in my mind. She was a couple of years older than us, very bright and well-read, and by then had a much better general education, having almost graduated from the gymnasium which was so coveted by me. She was an only child, and her parents, both employed, could afford to send her to a good school. However, the good school had expelled her almost on the eve of her graduation for reading books that were not exactly on the school's reading list—some Marxist literature. Her dream of going to university had to be postponed, at least for the time being. Instead, she learned shorthand, and taking advantage of what the school had given her—basic knowledge of the three main European languages—she got a job. When Gabriel and I came to know her some three years later, she was freelancing as a translator, working for firms trading with foreign partners. I was deeply impressed by her, and I truly loved her and wanted to be like her. She was a pleasure to be around and to talk to, always so natural and good-natured, always ready to help you, to share with you, and there was not a trace of putting on airs, as if in defiance of that slightly upturned nose of hers.

The friendship that developed between the three of us was based on common interests in reading and learning, and a shared belief in a cause and an ideology that were truly important to us then. Later, when it became obvious that Gabriel and I were more than just friends when our friendship turned to love, nothing changed between the three of us. We remained good friends to the end, until we left Łódź after the Germans took the city and the Russians opened their border to refugees from Poland. I saw Mala for the last time when I was already set to go over to the Soviet side. Gabriel and I, and some other people whom I do not remember, were sitting at Mala's and discussing with her and her parents the question "What's to be done?" which at this time had a very concrete meaning; to go over to the Russians or stay put in the city. I was set to go: my brother and his wife were leaving in a few days and the decision in my family was that I was to go with them. Gabriel was still hesitating. Where to, he was asking. To Białystok, overcrowded with refugees? Where to sleep there, what to eat, where to work? "Even to pee one would have to wait there in a long line," he quipped at one moment, and everybody laughed. Mala's parents, still young, in their mid-forties at most, were against going and Mala was staying with them. I knew that for Gabriel, the decision to go would not be easy—he still had a job, on which his family depended to a great measure, but he would make up his mind to go anyway at the last minute. But more about that later.

All They Talk About Is Karla Marla, Marla Karla

We would often get together, sometimes at Gabriel's, sometimes at Mala's, to talk or to exchange views on something we were reading or studying at that moment. Gabriel's little brother, Ignas, mocked us, "All you talk about is Karla Marla, Marla Karla," he would say. He was then ten years old at most, a sweet little boy with laughing eyes and he liked to tease us.

Well, it was certainly not all we spoke about, but Marx's own profound literary culture was a good school. We learned to find beauty and poetry in Marx, too. His rich and often dramatic descriptions of historical processes, like the primitive accumulation of capital, for example, to mention at least one, were inspiring. Sometimes when trying to examine a question in more detail, we would spend hours debating a most abstract issue, for example, what is the worker selling to the capitalist, his labor, or his capacity to work? What's the difference? In the Marxian theory, it turned out, there was a big one. If the worker sells his labor, then how is he exploited? He exchanges it on the market for something of equal value. But if the worker sells his capacity to work, the capitalist derives from it the surplus value, and here you put your finger on what Capitalism consists of, you see? Exploitation!

It seemed to be not only an abstract question but also a highly esoteric one, comparable to the kind of questioning a Talmudic student lives by, but for us, seemingly so far removed from Talmudic interests, it was alive and important. And the feeling of victory, of understanding something, of getting to the bottom of a problem, as it then seemed to us! One does not ask for what purpose, because knowledge is the purpose in itself!

Sometimes, however, one may even show off the acquired knowledge, and this is also tremendously satisfying and something I had once experienced with that very issue and why I remember it so well. I dropped in at my Youth Section just for a moment and inadvertently got into a big discussion about the nature of capitalist exploitation. When one of the speakers used the phrase "the worker sells his labor," I was ready and jumped in, explaining why it is not right to formulate it this way and what the right formula is and why, and what Marx had in mind—of course, I knew it exactly!—and so on, and I was ever so eloquent!

My grandmother was certainly right, cautioning me not to use up the stock of words allotted to me from Above in vain, because I might find myself unable to speak up in much more important circumstances. And indeed, I do not remember another case when I spoke in public, uninvited, and with such conviction and fervor.

Five Flights of Stairs

We often met at Gabriel's place in the evenings, after work. He started working when he was fourteen and a half and his working hours were long, from eight in the morning till almost seven in the evening. I sometimes met him at the corner of Sierpnia and Piotrkowska, as his place of work was nearby. He started working with a salary of seven zlotys per week, and after three years on the job he was getting twenty-five a week, and his family's existence was then almost entirely based on this salary. His father was out of a steady job, often ill, and there were two younger brothers at home, still in school.

While I was "pure proletarian," despite my parents' ill-fated attempts to break into the "business class," Gabriel was the son of a former capitalist, a *fabricant* (an owner of a factory) as his birth certificate indicated. Indeed, Gabriel's father co-owned a rather prosperous medium-sized factory producing stockings, and Gabriel was born into a large seven-room apartment in the center of the city. Later, his father lost his share of the factory due to some actions of his dishonest business partner (was not that partner a very close relative?).

At the time Gabriel and I first met, his family, though still living in the center of the city, had found accommodation on the fifth (top) floor of a large building, in a garret with two tiny windows right under the roof. However, living on the fifth floor did not bother him. A young man of seventeen, he could get up and down the stairs in no time. When I started visiting that place later, however, and he would see me off, it would take much longer to get up or down those stairs—we kissed on each step or every second step, and neither one of us minded that it would take a bit longer.

Political Activities

The League was not only encouraging us to study and to read, but it also often provided the reading material and helped arrange access to libraries. I remember the little library called Eisenschlos on Piotrkowska Street, a small place, with just a few rooms packed with books, each one a treasure, a source of emotion and joy, not to mention food for thought.

The Young Communist League was, however, foremost a political organization affiliated closely with the Communist Party, not just a union of scholars, and there were certain other duties, too. These were tumultuous times, only two years before the start of the war. Fascism was on the move, and Hitler's voice was roaring on the radio. In Spain, Franco, supported by Hitler and Mussolini, fought the duly elected left-wing government and a civil war was raging. Some of the older comrades (which means those already in their early twenties) were talking about going to Spain to join the Republican forces there, and some people I knew had left.

Political meetings in support of the Republicans were organized in the city and were well attended; the United Front policies of the leftist organizations added life to all those activities. The fiery *La Passionaria*, Dolores Ibarruri, the leader of the Spanish Communists, was a popular role model for the Communist youth, and her "*¡No pasarán!*" was a loud and moving call for support of the Republican cause. I was, of course, with all my heart on the side of the Republic and one of my duties was to collect money by selling stamps to help the Republicans. Alas, I was not a great fundraiser as the people from my social circles could not contribute much. Still, I certainly put a lot of heart into it, and I was able to collect some change.

My "Cell" Meeting at Guta's

We, the members of my "cell" in the League, met rather regularly, once a month at least, to discuss organizational matters or just to increase "consciousness" and to raise political awareness. Yet, altogether, there were not many of those meetings; after all, my whole "political activity" lasted less than a year but some of those meetings I remember well. Once or twice, we met at Guta's. She was a slim, willowy blonde, with a pleasant, delicately featured face. I remember her as a cheerful girl with a nice smile, though once, when she confided in me her thoughts about her boyfriend, she did not smile, and she was sad. He's nice, she told me, and she liked him, but they would sometimes spend hours taking walks and he would not utter a single word and she does not know what his thoughts are and what to think of it. Should she do the talking? Should she ask him why he's not talking?

Guta's father was a cobbler and they lived in a basement, a walk-in or rather a walk-down, pretty deep in the ground. The entrance to the place was directly from the street, five or six steps leading down to a rather large but almost dark room divided into two parts. In the front, close to the little window high up under the ceiling, the only source of daylight, was her father's workbench. The rest of the room made up the family's living space which Guta shared with her parents and her younger sister.

I was certainly not used to luxury, but how that family lived and functioned in such conditions was beyond even my comprehension. When we, the five girls who at that time made up our cell, met there, Guta's parents were not home, and we had the whole space to ourselves. I remember distinctly that we sat there once, debating the pros and cons of the United Front policies which the Party was promoting.[42] Nacia, the oldest among us, shared with us her thoughts, complaining that these

42 In the late 1930s, the Polish Communist Party sought to form alliances with the

policies needed some reform. It must have been one of my first such meetings because I was overwhelmed by the very fact of considering and debating such serious, important, and lofty subjects.

Meeting at Lolka's

Another meeting was at Lolka's place. Her father was a well-known textile merchant in Łódź, and the family lived in a large apartment in the center of the city. Lolka had a room of her own, and just to be there in that lovely room with nice intelligent girls, all older than me, and to talk with them and learn from them was exciting. I do vividly recall that meeting, though I have no recollection of the subject, perhaps because during the whole event I was absorbed by something very different. We were sitting on a long couch and there was nowhere to hide my feet, and my shoes were utterly worn, and they were almost falling apart. I had never been so self-conscious of what I was wearing than right then and I was embarrassed. Everybody was looking at my shoes, or so it seemed to me, and this was the only thought in my head, all the important, serious questions were pushed out of my mind and were far away. The embarrassment I felt was acute. I tried to convince myself that this was not or should not be a cause for embarrassment, that I should rather wear my poverty like a badge of honor, because aren't we after all fighting for the have-nots, fighting for the have-nots' cause? Don't we consider poverty a virtue? And what can be more proletarian than not being able to afford a pair of good shoes? Anyway, I had a whole new problem to think of and the questions connected with it were mounting. What made it worse still was that I could not bring myself to share them with anybody.

Peasant and Workers' Parties as a united front. Neither the other parties nor the Soviet Comintern supported this endeavor.

Spreading Ideas

I remember yet another meeting. This I attended just out of curiosity or perhaps also just to keep Gabriel company. He got an assignment to meet with a cell of "ours" organized in one of the city's gymnasiums. The girls there wanted someone to discuss with them some notions of the historical process. They also wanted to know why the revolution was inevitable. They did not teach such subjects in their school. I remember the group of girls, our age or perhaps a year younger, listening with great attention to Gabriel, the born teacher, explaining to them the intricate interrelations of abstract processes as he had learned about them not so long ago from his Marxist books.

The girls were all clearly from well-to-do families which was indicated to me by the mere fact that they could afford to attend the expensive high school and by the nice, well-appointed room somewhere in a good neighborhood in the center of the city where we had gathered. This made me think that these girls, by looking for knowledge not approved of by their school, and by being involved with an illegal political organization, had motives that were nobler than mine; they were altruistic while I had a personal stake, a personal interest in society's change. Yet, all my books worshiped the proletariat, the workers, a class with a mission, the historical mission of the proletariat, the mission of putting Capitalism to its grave and thus bringing about the coveted Socialism, and wasn't this in the self-interest of the proletariat? Anyway, trying to find an answer to my questions, I realized that I did not envy these girls anymore for having what I wanted and never got—access to formal education. I had found my informal way to the sources of knowledge and was taking full advantage of these rich, endless sources.

Boys in the League: David

From what I have said until now, I might have given the impression that the organization was some girls-only club. This wasn't the case. On the contrary, boys made up the majority. Let me recall some of them: David, for example, a pudgy young man, big and thoughtful. We nicknamed him "the farsighted," not just because he wore thick glasses, but because he liked to ask and deliberate on "farsighted" questions. What will come after Socialism's full victory? His reply: When all the issues of the capitalist society would be resolved, he would worry about that. In response, we would just laugh.

And yet, that question was not invented by David and was quite "legitimate" in the framework of the Marxist orthodoxy. One can cite perhaps a whole body of literature written on that specific question. It was on young Marx's mind when he pondered on man's return to his "proper nature" with the end of alienation caused by the divisions inherent in the capitalist society and thus bringing society to a stage indicating the end of history.

Bakunin, the anarchist apostle of destruction, also had an answer to the same question, and it was rather a simple one: he would tear down what was built and start all over again! Eighteenth-century utopians, like the French monk Dom Deshamp, for example, who also wanted to bring man back into harmony with his "proper nature" also envisioned a society beyond history or historical development. The notion of the "end of history" kept coming back, as it has quite recently come back with a bang of sorts, as the "newest" invention and answer to the changes brought about by the fall of Communism and the emergence of the "new world order." Suffice to recall the very lively recent debates caused by the writing on that subject by the philosopher [Francis] Fukuyama.

David remained in Łódź after the Germans took the city, and, as survivors of the Łódź ghetto told me, he died in one of the German concentration camps.

Salek

Salek was another young man with clear leadership ambitions. Impatient, he wanted to start right away and once caused something of a riot, threatening to "unseat" Gabriel from the "high" position of the group's leadership. "I will pull that chair from under you," he exclaimed rather dramatically on one occasion, causing a lot of laughter. Eventually, everything settled to everybody's contentment, and we remained good friends for life. Salek survived the war in the Soviet Union and moved to Israel where he lived with his family until he died in 2003. We maintained contact with him the whole time, during war and emigration, and still remember him fondly. Some early friendships can endure forever.

I recall that instance of a "power struggle" because it made us realize then that "power struggle" is not just an abstract notion; that if it may occur at the lowest organizational levels, taking on in this instance a rather comical form, it may also perhaps play a role somewhere up in the higher or even the highest party echelons. And certainly there, on that level, it would not be funny. It would turn into something rather sinister. Since these were the times of the great Moscow trials when many of the oldest, legendary leaders were accused of awful, mind-boggling crimes, were tried, found guilty, and executed; to have such suspicions would seem only natural, at least to some of us. It was difficult to believe that all those old leaders had turned into German, British, and whatnot spies who had sold out on the idea of Socialism and had become traitors. But to harbor such awful thoughts or doubts was scary and to share them with others—was unthinkable. The organization demanded that the "traitors" be condemned, and for expressing such doubts or reservation, one could be branded a "Trotskyite" and this was anathema. It was enough to be expelled from the organization.

On the Subject of Power Struggle

Gabriel, Mala, and I would talk a lot about these events among ourselves, reading whatever there was in the papers on the subject. And there was quite a lot in the "bourgeois" Polish press that we did not trust, but that press also printed facts (true or not) that would hit one in the face. One such fact has stuck in my mind; the case of Krestinsky, one of the defendants in the Bukharin Trial.[43] After admitting during the

43 In 1938, at the height of the Great Purges in the USSR, the so-called Trial of the Twenty-One, against a group of formerly prominent Bolsheviks now accused

investigation to have committed all the crimes that he was accused of, he suddenly retracted it all during an open session of the court. This caused a worldwide sensation; Krestinsky was the only one of the accused who had done so, but the next day, he was back in court, and he had retracted his retraction again publicly, admitting to having perpetrated all those horrible deeds of which he was accused. No wonder we were searching for explanations and could not blindly believe what we were given to believe and so, we talked and talked.

"Where Is Marshal Blueher?"

Gabriel took it especially hard; his inquisitive mind was rebelling against the platitudinous answers, such as "he who hampers the train (Socialism) in full motion toward its goal must be thrown off," meaning that all those criticizing or opposing the Party's leadership are traitors to the cause of Socialism and therefore have to be gotten rid of. By accusing them of heinous crimes and shooting them? Gabriel could not take this for an answer and as a matter of fact, we both (Mala and I) could not reconcile ourselves to this either, but I think that he felt much stronger about it. He could not believe that so many of the leaders, people with glorious names were just "imperialist agents" and traitors. He kept a count of sorts of the prominent people in the Soviet Union leadership who were already sentenced and executed according to what the Polish press was telling us, and the list was growing very fast. But not all of the sentenced and executed were mentioned in the press; some of those well-known people would simply disappear, as was the case, for example, with Marshal Blueher. So, Gabriel kept asking, "Where is Marshal Blueher?"[44] And the search for Marshal Blueher became an almost obsession for him. "Where is Marshal Blueher?" he lamented.

of Trotskyist deviations, included Nikolai Bukharin (1888–1938) and Nikolai Krestinsky (1883–1938).

44 Vasily Blyukher (1889–1938), marshal of the Soviet Union, was one of many high-ranking military commanders to disappear in the Great Purges.

He would also continue that search a year and a half later when we became refugees in the Soviet Union, directing the same question to anybody willing to listen until he finally realized that one should not ask such questions in the Soviet Union because this might be dangerous to one's health.

Reservations and Doubts

Once, during one of such discussions, I cried out in jest, "Watch out, you'll end up against the *stienka!*" which meant you'll be put against the wall as an "enemy of the people" to be shot. I picked up that Russian expression from our "bourgeois" Polish newspapers; *stienka* is Russian for the wall against which those sentenced to death were lined up for execution. The expression would come up quite often in the daily reports about the trials in Moscow, even if the condemned people were shot somewhere in the basement of the NKVD and not necessarily against a *stienka.*[45] And we all laughed at my joke! We were so young and easily given to laughter, but even though we laughed, the joking gave way to our deep-down doubts and our ideal no longer seemed so holy, so beyond reproach.

Did this change our attitude toward the Soviet Union? Looking back, I have to say that perhaps it did a little, but only a little. Worshipping the Soviet Union was not incompatible with having some doubts about this or that, even if "this or that" was no small horror. Despite everything, the Soviet Union remained the beacon of hope for working people all over the world, as the phrase went, and it was so for me. It was still the country building Socialism, a system I firmly believed was based on equality, a country of full employment and access to education for everybody. *Rabfak,* another Russian, or rather a Soviet word, *rabochyi fakultet*, schools for those who did not have the opportunity to get a normal education; this was about me! There, one

45 The *Narodnyy komissariat vnutrennikh del* (People's Commissariat for Internal Affairs, NKVD) was the powerful secret police in the USSR, a precursor to the KGB.

may attend evening university classes while working and this was what I dreamed about! *Rabfak* was the magic word for me and that let me suppress my doubts. Whatever the shortcomings, they will all eventually pass and go away; they are temporary while the achievements are everlasting. And the books I was reading were all set to keep that still half-childish enthusiasm intact. Even those describing the Soviet penal system seemed to present it as the last word in progressive pedagogical theory, not mentioning anything about the terror and the concentration camps which had become part of the Soviet "experiment" right from the beginning.

More about Political Activities

Sometimes, we great conspirators held meetings just on the street. Punctuality was a matter of discipline. It was against the rules to be late and thus endanger others forced to wait needlessly. We would walk, never more than in twos, carefully looking out for spies of the *Defensywa*, the undercover policemen of the Security Police; not that there were so many of them there, but just in case. These meetings were called *podpunkt* (sub-points). While walking, the person from the Regional Committee of the organization would join us, talking first with two of the members of the group and then with the others, conveying whatever messages he (in my experience it was always a man) had to convey.

To one of those meetings came Alter whom I already knew as Nacia's boyfriend, but here he was in his official capacity representing the local branch of the leadership. He gave us an assignment. The Nazis were preparing to march against Czechoslovakia and the Polish government had decided to take advantage and to get a "piece of the action," annexing Zaolzie.[46] Polish nationalists went rampant. I remember a demonstration in Łódź, a crowd of people marching with slogans, "We want colonies!" The colonial system would fall apart a

46 Meaning the area beyond the Olza River, which had been contested since a 1920 border agreement.

few years later, but for now, rabid nationalists went crazy with a desire to make Poland an "empire," from sea to sea, from the Baltic Sea to the Black Sea. That's what Great Poland used to be once upon a time, if only for a short while, but since it was rather impossible right then to regain the territories on the Black Sea, they belonged to the Soviet Union: a colony or two in Africa would do! The demonstration looked ludicrous, and surrealistic, even to the eyes of a girl not yet sixteen as I was then. But not to the government, since even in the face of great and real danger coming from the imperial aspirations and the drive of the German Fascists, it went along trying to get at least Zaolzie.[47]

Protesting Poland's Annexation of Zaolzie

Poland's participation in the attack against its peaceful neighbor was a shameless deed, and my organization reacted by protesting against it in any way that was at its disposal. One of the elements of that protest was the assignment Alter had come to explain to us. We had to prepare leaflets and distribute them, he said. We had no means to prepare leaflets—all we could do was to prepare some small stickers to be glued wherever possible. I was to prepare my share of stickers and bring them to the meeting point in the street the next day. For a few groszy, I bought fifty stickers, the same kind I used to use in school to mark my copybooks, and diligently wrote on them "Hands off Czechoslovakia," "Down with the Fascist aggression," and maybe something else, I do not remember. What I do however remember is that I signed each one of my little slogans with the letters KZMP, Communist Youth League of Poland. I liked what I was doing, thought it to be the right thing to do, and was with all my heart for poor Czechoslovakia and against the German Fascists who, in cahoots with the Polish government, wanted to tear her to pieces. Proud that my organization fought against that evil, I gave credit where it belonged.

The next day, Alter approved my work and told me where to take

47 Poland annexed this contested region in October 1938.

my stickers. Lolka, who had also come to the meeting point but did not have any stickers prepared since she was not present the day before, decided on the spur of the moment that she would go with me, and so we went straight ahead on Kiliński Street together, excited as if it were some school outing. We were sticking up our little slogans on the walls of the buildings which was easy to do because my stickers were adhesive, so we licked them and stuck them on like postage stamps. It was already evening so there were not many people on the street and in our excitement, we had forgotten to behave as conspirators should have, according to what the situation demanded. Instead of going straight ahead on a long open street, we should have taken to the side alleys, changed direction, and so on, so as not to be easily traced or followed. Instead, we marched on and on, even after having glued on the last of our stickers and did not even notice the woman that was steadfastly following us. Suddenly, a policeman showed up, walking slowly in our direction. He was not, however, paying any attention to us and he might not have noticed anything, were it not for the woman who, on spotting the policeman, started yelling, "Get them, get them." In a moment, a blow of a whistle was heard, two other policemen showed up immediately from nowhere, and we were arrested. After all, this was to be expected, because following the instruction to go "straight-ahead," we had almost reached the seat of the Security Police at 152 Kiliński Street. I could not stop wondering about that poor woman who drew the policeman's attention to us. And poor she was, judging from her dress and demeanor, a true proletarian woman, but why was she against us? Did she too, want a piece of Zaolzie? In my naiveté, I had a hard time reconciling her class status with her sympathies for the police and the aggressive deeds of the government.

In Police Detention

I spent the night in a cell at the detention center at the address mentioned above. After a search and some preliminary questioning, I was led into a large cell, already occupied by another woman. The cell, lit only by a faint light coming from the hallway through the still-open door, was dark, and all I could see was that the woman was rather large and not young. It was late evening or even night already, and as it always is at this time of year, it was generally still cold, so the cell was very cold, too. There was only one wooden bunk in the cell, but a wide one. Though the woman took up half of it, there was still enough space and I lay down. "What did they bring you here for?" the woman asked and I, the conspirator, now knew better after my experience, having suddenly recalled how to behave according to the principles of conspiracy, said, "I don't know, they just took me from the street."

It was not easy, however, to fall asleep. I was, of course, scared, and it was unpleasant, to say the least, to think of my parents worrying about me not coming home for the night. Certainly, I knew that something like this might happen to me someday sooner or later, but until then it was only theory while this now was real, a whole new experience, and this made a huge difference. And what will they, the police, do with me? Will they let me go tomorrow? This was trouble and it was very cold in the cell to boot. Suddenly, the woman on the bunk next to me, as if feeling my turmoil, put the half-torn rag of a blanket provided by the jailer around me and moved a little closer to me. Warmed by the blanket and the warmth of her body, I fell asleep.

I woke up early in the morning and looked around, trying to take in the prison cell, to make sure I would remember the thick gray walls, and the tiny, barred window high under the ceiling. My neighbor, now also awake, looked at me and asked more of a statement than a question, "You political?" and added not waiting for an answer, "Thought so, even at night, though at first I wondered because you said they took you from the street, so I thought maybe you were "ours." But no, you are not. No, it must be political, must be political." So, I was proclaimed to be a "political" person, a prisoner of conscience by a Łódź prostitute, who also happened to be Jewish and, of course, had a heart of gold.

The Interrogation

A few hours later, I was called to the interrogator. My parents were waiting in the hallway at the entrance to his office. My sister Sala was there, too. To my surprise, they all smiled at me reassuringly and nobody was mad at me as I had expected they would be. I was not scared anymore; I was reassured and I came to believe that I would be allowed to go home. The interrogator, a thin, sickly, and tired-looking man, asked me some questions. It was a routine procedure, I believe, and as a minor, I was released into my parents' custody. Poor Father, poor Mother! They signed a declaration, stating that they would make sure I would come if called by the interrogator for further questioning during the investigation which was to follow. They indeed called me again, once or twice; the investigator wanted to know who gave me the stickers and tried to check whether I understood their meaning. He also asked me to copy one of them which, as I understood, was to check the handwriting. I did not admit to having done anything, to knowing or understanding anything, and I was not called again.

Lolka Is Sentenced

Lolka, however, did not get off so easily. This was not her first encounter with the police, as she had been apprehended already once before for participating in some anti-government political demonstration and had spent twenty-four hours at the police station then. In addition, she was twenty-one, a grown-up, and she would be brought to trial. In the meantime, I was free after twenty-four hours of detention, as was customary in such cases, while Lolka was still detained, waiting for her trial. Her father asked me once to come and see him, as he wanted to talk with me, perhaps in connection with the preparation of his troublesome daughter's defense. I felt very sorry for Lolka but did not have much to tell her father. I went anyway and it turned out to be a good talk.

Her father and her brother, Ignas, who was also present, were both Bund activists; Ignas was very active in my Youth Section, and it was he who had gotten me to safety from the middle of that squabble, in which I had once inadvertently found myself. Now Ignas was doing the talking while his father was just looking on sadly. They both understood that our protest was prompted by a shameful act of the Polish government and, as such, it was just a way to show well-deserved support, he told me. Taking advantage of Hitler's aggression against Czechoslovakia and joining him in hostilities against Poland's neighbor was not only shameful but also shortsighted. He stressed the point as if to convince me that he and his father were on my side and had nothing against me personally. "But why did you have to sign your proclamations KZMP? Why did you have to give the address?" he asked. I understood then that this might aggravate Lolka's case. But though I was very sorry for her, I could not bring myself to admit that "giving the address" was unnecessary; after all, I was proud that my organization had protested and it had made me participate in that protest. Someone had to protest and I wanted to see that the credit would go where it rightly belonged, to my organization, to the Communists. Little did I know then that only a little over a year later, the Soviet Union would conclude a pact of mutual assistance and collaboration with the very same Fascists I so abhorred: the infamous Molotov–Ribbentrop Pact.

Nevertheless, looking back at those times from today's perspective, I must say that I am still a bit proud of what I was able to do then in my early youth, to be moved by a cause, to do what I had done and, maybe, one day Mr. Havel, the Czech Republic's first president, will give me the medal he still, no doubt, owes me.

Weddings in the Family

Summer 1938. Things in the family were going a bit better and everybody was rather optimistic which was a big and welcome change. My parents did not make much fuss about my political exploits and I was happy about it. They treated it, I would say, as a childhood disease that I would soon overcome. But my sister Sala was not so certain that this would be the case; she looked at those thick books I kept shlepping home, and was rather skeptical, though she did not argue.

We had two weddings in the family at that time. First, Sala got married and then a few months later was Mayer's wedding. To mark these happy family occasions or perhaps just because things were going a bit better for a while, a place was rented in the countryside in the vicinity of Łódź, two rooms with a veranda and the use of a small garden. Mother and Helcia spent most of the summer there and the whole family would get together for the weekends. For a week or so, I was there with Helcia alone while Mother was in Łódź and we were happy to be on our own for a while. My little sister had just finished the obligatory seven-grade school. She wanted to become a pharmacist as she kept saying since she had learned to pronounce the word, but instead, she would start an apprenticeship with a seamstress. She did not mind, she was a sweet, loving, and lovely girl, adroit with her hands, she would master the art of sewing in no time and she would be good at it. And indeed, it would not take long before I, in awe, would watch her making a skirt for me. She put a piece of fabric on the table and cut it with a pair of scissors in a swift motion, turning the fabric into six pieces in a moment. A few hours later I had a beautiful skirt. If I had known what history had in store for us, I might have kept that skirt forever as a precious memento.

Hanna and Gabriel, 1938.

Suburban Summer

One Sunday in August, I had guests at our summer house: Gabriel and Mala came to visit and spend the day in the countryside. I do not remember much of that day but I somehow saved the snapshots we had taken with a Kodak camera, a small black box that my sister Rachel had left for me and Helcia while she was visiting us two years earlier. Here we are in those snapshots: Mala and Gabriel, Mala and I, Gabriel and I; we are smiling and looking happy on that sunny summer day.

Gabriel with Mala, 1938.

The next Sunday, Gabriel came by himself. I took him home to say hello to my parents. My father liked him, a nice young man, he told me smiling, approvingly. They exchanged a few words and father suddenly became interested in the bone structure of Gabriel's forehead.

A skinny face of a youngster, not yet eighteen, with clearly showing even slightly protruding forehead bones. I remember he touched those bones on both sides of Gabriel's forehead. Did the structure of his forehead signify some special characteristics of his personality? According to the German eighteenth-century phrenologist, Franz Gall, there was perhaps something to it, but was there something about it in my father's books too, I wondered? This was the only time Gabriel met my father. In hindsight, the "examination," the memory of which I cherish to this day, took on a special meaning for me. However, at the time, it made me impatient and we ran out for a walk shortly after.

First Kiss

We walked, holding hands. I was happy and proud that he had come to see me. There was no worry, no thought in our minds, just two happy youngsters on a sunny summer afternoon, when suddenly, out of nowhere, three other youngsters appeared, boys approximately our age, and they were almost immediately on top of us. "Beat the Jews!" we heard and then a command from the one that seemed to be their leader, "Leave the girl out!" Some gentleman! I yelled, we both yelled, trying to get away from them when as suddenly as the whole thing had begun, the attack stopped. Some passersby showed up, and this perhaps was the reason the hooligans left us alone. This was Poland, not that things like that would happen all the time, but this was nothing out of the ordinary either. This time, it was only a nuisance, something to spoil our mood for a few moments. Soon, we continued our walk until we reached the nearby woods. Here, under the cover of the trees, or rather the thin brushwood that we called the forest, we embraced and kissed. My heart was thumping. Was it because this was my first kiss ever, or because I still had not yet quite regained my breath after running from the hooligans? Whatever the reason, I knew, without ever thinking about it, or wasting words on it, that we loved each other and that this, believe it or not, would be forever.

Hanna and Mala, 1938.

The Dissolution of the Polish Communist Party

In the fall of the same year, 1938, the Polish Communist Party ceased to exist, and with it came the dissolution of the Youth League. We, the members of the organization, were told that the Comintern came to this decision because the Polish Communist Party was infiltrated by the police, corrupted, and demoralized to such a degree that all its activities had to be brought to a stop. The party leaders were arrested in Moscow, tried for treason, and shot. This was a severe blow to us, the young and trusting followers. A kind of spy mania came over people; close friends, and comrades, began looking at each other with suspicion. It was hard to accept, and it was very sad. I remember the acute feeling of loss as if something very close and dear had suddenly gone from my life; an important goal, hope.

The Comintern's decision resulted in a wide-ranging campaign aimed at eradicating all organized forms of Communist activity in Poland and this must have been a very thorough campaign since even just getting together in groups was considered improper for former members of the league. We did not know then how widespread the distrust of the Soviet authorities was toward the Polish Communists, and how many of those residing in the Soviet Union at that time were arrested, sentenced, and executed. We did not know that all members of the highest party ranks, the Politburo and the Secretariat as well as thirty out of the thirty-seven members of the Central Committee elected in 1932, were executed. Ironically, those who survived owed their lives to the fact that they were imprisoned in Poland at the time and thus out of reach of the Soviet terror apparatus. Only after the war, I got to know some family members of those who perished in the Soviet prisons and camps as well as many of those who had survived those camps and returned to Poland. Only one of the returnees known to me—and I was told that he was an exception—had managed to avoid imprisonment by outfoxing the NKVD. He simply left Moscow as soon as the arrests started and hid somewhere in the immense scope of the Soviet Union, somewhere in the provinces. A learned man, Bronisław Krauze eventually brought back his library with him and was very helpful in lending me the rare books I needed when I was preparing my book on Bakunin.

This turn of events brought a feeling of loss and sadness to me and my friends but perhaps also a certain degree of relief. To belong to an illegal political organization was dangerous; they put you in prison for it. While my spell with the Polish police passed without consequences for me, Lolka paid for it with a year of imprisonment. As for Gabriel, an arrest could also have resulted in the loss of his job and the income on which his family depended. It would have been catastrophic for the whole family. Sad as it was to us, we were now however less busy with "changing the world," and I too had more time to think about what I was going to do with my life. Certainly, I was still dreaming about a "real university," but being seventeen now, the thought of how I would earn my keep crossed my mind more often. It was taking on some urgency even though I was still helping Father in the store. The store itself was still functioning and nobody predicted that its end would come rather soon.

Preparing for a Clerical Job

I do not remember whose idea it was to take up bookkeeping and typing and prepare myself for a clerical job. In the fall of 1938, I enrolled in a bookkeeping course. It was not really a course but more of a three-month tutoring class. The instructor, an elderly man with a fat face of a sallow complexion, always wearing the same old dark, crumpled, colorless jacket, taught us, a group of five students, the basics of credit and debit in two-hour sessions, twice or three times a week. Among my fellow students I remember only one—was a rather nondescript young man who, when the course came to an end, suddenly and out of the blue proposed to me. "Is your father a very traditional, religious man?" he asked me, and before I had time to ask why he was suddenly interested, he added, "I love you and want to ask him for your hand in marriage." A Christian, a Catholic, he was worried about my father's response. What a shock! We were on the sidewalk of a busy street, and the man stopped, took off his hat, his face very solemn, and asked his question. Utterly confused, yet unable to hold back laughter, I just ran away and never saw him again. A block or perhaps further, around the corner, I met Gabriel and Mala, and still laughing almost hysterically, I told them the story. We shared the laugh for a moment and changed the subject soon after, yet before that, Gabriel said something which I still remember, addressing it to no one, but it was about me, "When she laughs, one hears little bells ringing." Wasn't he the smartest young man ever?

At the same time, I was also taking typewriting lessons. For a small fee, I had access to a typewriter for two hours daily. Someone showed me how to use it and from then on, I was on my own to learn and practice. Here, the students were almost exclusively girls, most of them high school graduates preparing for secretarial jobs. Two elderly ladies were running the course in their private apartment and it was rather well attended. There were always many girls in the large living room that also served as a waiting room. My typewriter was also there in one of the room's nooks. Not many memories remain from those typewriting sessions, but one stands out. Once, among the young girls in the living room, there was also a young man, not a student, and while

I was pounding away on my typewriter, he was talking with (or rather to) the girls and I heard some familiar concepts and names he kept using; contradictions of Capitalism, historical process, overpopulation, Malthus, and such. Was it an educational meeting of a cell of "ours" here, almost in the open? I wondered. Or a proselytizing comrade taking advantage of the occasion to raise the consciousness of the future clerical masses and spread the Communist gospel to willing listeners? No, the time for this kind of "activity" had passed. The Party does not exist any longer, I had to remind myself, until it finally dawned on me that this was just a former activist trying to impress the girls and perhaps pick one up, too.

My First Job

In the early spring of 1939, the year the war came upon us, I finally got a job, my first that was supposed to be a paying one, a clerical job. Mala introduced me to a textile manufacturer for whom she was doing some work. She convinced me to wear a little hat, one of her own, to the first meeting to be more presentable and look a bit older. It was a small, green felt hat, its brim raised on one side, a bit too coquettish perhaps, at least for my taste. I don't know if I looked right, more mature, and proper for the job I was aspiring to, but unfortunately, it did not make me feel more self-assured.

The job turned out to be not too demanding and I was rather well prepared for it. Some typing was required and I was quite good with the typewriter by then. Mostly, however, with the help of an abacus, I would be adding long columns of numbers taken from specifications of what was going out and coming in. The office was located at 48 Piotrkowska Street and consisted of three small rooms. My boss was the bookkeeper, a middle-aged, energetic man who ran the whole place. He treated me with some suspicion, or so I thought. I was diligent, did what I was asked to do, and was careful not to make mistakes but somehow, I did not fit in and soon enough, I became quite aware of it. I was from the wrong part of the city, from a different milieu, inexperienced with people, and all this was making me even shyer than I was by nature. Sometimes it also made me feel awkward, if not behave awkwardly, which comes down to the same. I was employed on a trial basis for a month and after this time was over, I was told thank you, but no. The owner of the firm, a rather gentle, elderly man told me this with an expression of regret on his face and asked, since he wanted to compensate me for my effort, what I preferred, a coupon for fabric for a topcoat; or money; I said money. I got twenty-five zlotys, gave my mother twenty, and with the rest, I went to a bookstore and bought myself a new Eckersley, the first two parts of the English-language manual that was very popular then and would be for many decades to come. I had recently started learning English and was working hard on it. Mala was tutoring me and to progress from that point, I needed the manual urgently.

Vacation in the Countryside

Frustrated as I was by the unfortunate turn of events regarding my employment, I was not going to give up yet. I would perhaps find some other place and be made smarter and more confident by the experience of my first try. I would perhaps do much better next time. But I was not feeling well and had apparently been ill for some time already. Some glands on my neck were swelling, I was running a low but constant fever, and the doctor, when I finally went with Mother to see one, said that the glands were infected with TB and that I needed to rest, eat well and regularly, which I had not been doing for quite some time, and have plenty of fresh air. In the face of the family's dire circumstances, the doctor's advice might have sounded like mockery, but fortunately, there was a solution. My brother's wife, Dora, came from a farming family. Her parents were still working that farm, some two hours by bus from Łódź, and I was invited to stay with her there for the summer. Dora herself wanted to spend the summer with her parents and was glad to have me with her. A small group of her acquaintances came along with us for an affordable vacation in the village and at her parents' house.

A Jewish Farm

A Jewish farm with Jewish farmers was something very rare in Poland. Until the 1860s, Jews were barred from owning land. Only the agrarian reforms after the failed 1863 Polish insurrection against the Russian tsar, the reforms freeing the peasants from serfdom, allowed Jews to hold land. Dora's great-grandfather, having made money managing the estate for the village nobleman, bought 200 or so hectares of land from him. After his death, the land was divided among his sons and then again divided among the third generation. Most of the inheritors sold their lots, leaving the village for a life in the city, and doing business elsewhere. In Dora's time, only her parents remained on the land that was left after all the consecutive divisions, and her father, with the help of one of his sons, was still farming. There were two rather large houses on the farm for the two families; Dora's parents and her brother with his large family of his own lived separately but on a Friday evening, all the adults and children came together to celebrate the oncoming Sabbath. With all the visitors present, there was quite a gathering at those dinners. Dora's father, a tall, bony, quiet man, at that time not able to do hard farming work any longer, was mostly occupied with herding his cattle, six or eight cows, and as many sheep. I often saw him sitting in the field, supervising his chewing, munching herd. With a leafless birch twig, he would occasionally swat a bothersome fly or remind a too-individualistic cow, trying to go astray, to go back where she belonged. Dora's mother was a tiny, slow-moving woman with an incredibly wrinkled face—I have never before or since seen an old woman so wrinkled, a proverbial little dried apple—but she always had a good, gentle smile.

The weather of this last peacetime summer of 1939 was beautiful, warm, and sunny. I do not remember one rainy day during those six weeks I spent in the countryside. There was a rather large pond in the village to which the cows came to drink every evening. We spent a lot of time on the shore of that pond, resting, talking, reading, or just frolicking. Plenty of good, fresh air and tasty cottage cheese with sour cream nourished me back to health. In mid-August, it was time to return to Łódź and I was eager to go home. I missed Gabriel, Mala, and my family, too, feeling a bit guilty about this long vacation. Also, there in the countryside, one was almost totally isolated from the outside world and it was like living somehow in limbo. So, goodbye to the good people, to the green grass, warm sun, smells, colors, and sounds of the countryside, and good day to the dust, dirt, smoke, and crowded, bustling streets of Łódź.

With friends at the Jewish farm, 1939.

I did return to that village twice for very short visits, but then the circumstances were different. Only about a year later, it was all over; Dora's parents and her brother with his family were taken to a ghetto in the nearby Minsk Mazowiecki and deported from there to one of the too many German annihilation camps. Which one, we never found out.

Prelude to War

In Łódź, war was on the agenda. Everybody was guessing when, and there seemed to be no doubt that war was coming so the question was only when. Then, by the end of the month, the big news came: the Molotov–Ribbentrop Pact was signed. It was big and unexpected news, very sad and puzzling news. I listened to it with disbelief, utterly confused. The beloved Soviet Union and Fascist Germany together! I still wanted to believe that there was some reason for it but Gabriel was belligerent. What reason could there be? What can explain or justify it? There will be war now, he kept repeating, there will be war soon! We read the papers, listened to the radio, and knew that the long, protracted talks between the Western powers and the Soviet Union on collaboration against the German aggressor had come to nothing. And how we had hoped that the talks would be successful! We knew that the Polish government had not agreed to let the Soviet troops through Polish territory if it would come to it, but we kept refusing to accept what the turn of events had brought.

For us, the young, war was still an abstract concept, a danger we were able to perceive mentally perhaps, but not emotionally, while the older generation, that of our parents, were full of fear. They who had experienced the previous great war, World War I, and had it still fresh in their memory and in their bones, who went through all the deprivations and sufferings that war had brought upon them previously. I remember my mother's reaction to the news about the outbreak of the war, "We have lived too long; we should not have lived to see this. Only twenty years have passed, and now again war, again!" She was shaking her head, the horrors of those previous days when she lost a child, suffered hunger with her family, deprivation that had almost brought them all down, still fresh in her memory. And most people felt similarly, though no one could have imagined then that the new war would be so much worse, that it would be a different war in scope, horror, and consequences.

CHAPTER THREE

THE WAR

The war, though expected, came suddenly. The first two bombs that fell on my neighborhood turned two buildings into rubble. I just happened to be in the backyard and, hearing planes roaring strangely nearby, I looked up at the sky. There they were, two enemy planes. I took cover, and watching from there, saw the first two bombs coming down on Łódź in the afternoon on the first day of September 1939.

The next day, I went to see the results of the bombing. Two medium-sized apartment buildings, one on Brzezińska Street, the other on a side street, were completely destroyed. This first sight of the war's work did not, however, impress on me as something frightening, perhaps because even though people were consoling each other, there were not any human casualties.

But the next day there were more bombs and rumors started spreading that the Germans were advancing very fast, that the Polish army hasn't been able to withstand the Wehrmacht's push, and that the Germans were burning and destroying everything on their way toward us. This caused panic in the city and people began to leave. Whoever had the means of getting away tried to do so.

To the Countryside

My parents decided that we too should not remain in the city under the bombs, that we should leave for the countryside, and take advantage of the fact that we had relatives there. In case our dwellings were bombed, we would at least save our belongings. We would take them to safety, meager as they were, they were all we had, and we would take with us some of the belongings of our older siblings who could not leave the city right away. With this rationale in mind, a driver with a horse-drawn wagon was hired and on the third day of the war, we took off to the village that was about a day's horse ride away.

I vividly recall that ride. The wagon was loaded with bundles of bedding and some suitcases into which the better clothes were packed, and Helcia and I sat on top of those; I, holding my brother's new, silky, gray felt hat. To pack this luxurious head covering into a suitcase would have turned it into a shapeless wrinkled rag.

To avoid bombings, we drove at night. Nobody slept. The road was not very crowded yet, and we were moving rather fast. The night sky as far as the horizon was in flames. The war seemed to be everywhere—it was also in front of us, even though we were going in the opposite direction from where the war was supposed to be coming from. "There is Kalisz," Father pointed in that direction. "The Germans must have reached it already," he said. "They burned that old town and looted and killed so many in the not-so-distant past so what are they going to do there now?" he wondered. Kalisz was near the Polish–German border; in the last war, World War I, the Germans took the city and massacred the population, treating the Jews with special cruelty, and for people of my parent's generation, the memory of those atrocities was still fresh.

We reached the village the next morning. It was still peaceful, serenely basking in the late summer sun. The peaceful quiet did not last long, however. Very soon, as soon as the day after our arrival, hundreds of people, escaping the advancing German army, began flowing into the village, either just passing by on their way somewhere else or seeking temporary refuge right there. My mother took to cooking enormous pots of soup to feed the refugees.

Shortly, disorganized units of soldiers would also show up in the village, some of the soldiers trying to exchange their military garb for civilian clothes, a pair of trousers, and a shirt. Their intent was clear. Convinced that the war was already lost and that they were facing captivity, they were preparing to escape, desert, and go home. They seemed frightened and, most of all, scared of the German tanks.

Driven by curiosity, I went outside the house walking along the usually so quiet unpaved village road that was now full of people, refugees as well as soldiers milling around and stopped not far from where a group of soldiers was resting under the cover of a few trees. I stood there for a while observing the scene. The "Won't you give me a kiss, miss, they might kill me tomorrow?" proposition from one of them, accompanied by the laughter of the others, did not drive me too far away. Their young officer was scanning the environs with his binoculars and spotted a tank emerging from behind a distant hill. The officer cried or rather groaned, more to himself than to his soldiers, "tanks," and they all took off, as if it was a command, and ran toward the nearby forest.

The German army was very fast and soon there were no front lines anymore.

Gallows on Bałucki Market

We returned to Łódź, which was already in German hands. Merely one week had passed, yet the city had visibly changed. Darkened somehow, despite the still strong September sun, and much quieter, toned down. Everybody was talking about the atrocities, the terror that the Germans were instilling in the hearts and minds of the population, and the Jews being singled out for special treatment right from the beginning. The most prominent citizens of the city were taken hostage and their fate was the subject of guessing and rumors.

As one of the first deeds of their reign in Łódź, the Germans blew up the monument of the Polish national hero, Tadeusz Kosciuszko, a well-known and popular symbol of Polish statehood. The tall monument which had adorned the Plac Wolności (Independence Square) for as long as we could remember, was gone, and the three large synagogues in the center of the city on Wolborska, Zachodnia, and Zielona Streets were dynamited and burned to the ground. This was the news that greeted us on the very first day after our return to the city. In addition, someone informed us in a hushed voice that on the Bałucki Market, the Germans had hanged four people. Nobody seemed to know who these people were or for what crime they were punished so horribly.

Bewildered yet driven by curiosity, I ran to the market. Yes, there were gallows there, the grim structure was visible from far enough and there was no need to go closer to see the four shapes, shapes of people hanging by their necks, dangling from the high bar. I did not dare move any closer to the gallows and there was no need to. Frightened and disgusted, I covered my face. I should not have come here to see this at all, I should not have to see this. I kept reproaching myself, now angry with myself for the curiosity that prompted me to come in the first place.

All this was going on in the city and it cast a long shadow of fear on all its inhabitants just by showing what was to be expected from the occupiers, yet it had not touched my neighborhood or my family directly. Here there were no people worth taking as hostages, no rich stores or businesses to be expropriated or looted, or even synagogues worth the Germans effort and the dynamite. Here Jews were praying in small semi-private homes, in *shtibels*, and so far, not much had changed, at least in that respect. However, from the beginning, it became scary to go out on the street, to leave home; the Germans were rounding people up on the streets, taking them away for forced labor, and at the same time making it an opportunity to beat and harass their victims at whim and in any way their imagination would prompt them.

There Is No Bread for Jews

In addition, right from the beginning, Jews became open prey not only for the Germans but also for everybody else, for the Polish population at large. And many, too many of our close neighbors jumped on that bandwagon. Barely a few days after the Germans took the city, I came to experience this harassment and discrimination.

With the beginning of the occupation, bread lines appeared in the city. It quickly became known that if the Jews should even try to join the bread lines, they would be asked to leave. To buy bread "secondhand" was too expensive for us, so I decided once to take my chances and venture into a bread line. It was in my neighborhood, the baker was Jewish, and we used to buy bread there before the war. I did not last long in the line. As soon as the bakery opened and the distribution of bread started, I was told to get out; there was no bread for Jews.

People were pushing and shoving, not in anger, but rather jokingly, playfully. There was no hunger yet in the city, and the whole thing seemed to be treated rather like some kind of new game. A *Volksdeutscher*,[48] a hunchbacked creep with a rifle, was guarding the *Ordnung* [public order] and waved me away. I stepped out of the line but stood there for a few more moments, just observing the people, some of whom knew me well, as they did my parents and grandparents, and I knew them well, too. Then the *Volksdeutsche* reached out his hand and touched the hair I then wore long, held together by a wide bow on my neck. I pushed his hand away with disgust for which he treated me with an angry, dirty look and directed his rifle at me. Would he shoot me for the disrespect shown to him or was it just in jest? I do not know, but the public had a show and reacted with a roar of laughter. I went home empty-handed.

I Do Not Have to Pay You for Your Work, Jew

And there was another case that concerned me greatly and hit me hard. My brother-in-law, Monek, made a pair of slacks for a neighbor of his, a Pole, a guy as poor as he was. Monek was not much of a tailor but

48 *Volksdeutsche* was the word used for ethnic Germans who had resided—often for multiple generations—outside of the German lands. Łódź had a relatively large population of ethnic Germans and there, as well as in other occupied areas, they were given special privileges.

did alterations and sometimes put together a pair of slacks, not shying away from any job that would come his way. On the eve of the war's outbreak, he got a commission from a neighbor of his. As soon as the Germans entered the city barely one week later, his customer, the neighbor, showed up, claimed his trousers, and walked away with them, declaring, "Now, Jew, I don't have to pay you. Go complain if you want, where you want!" It was heartbreaking and scary to listen to and to look at Sala while she was sharing the story with us. We felt helpless, naked in the middle of a jungle.

Gabriel's First Encounter with War

How is Gabriel? I worried about him. I knew that on the sixth day of the war, the Polish authorities had appealed to all male inhabitants of the city from eighteen to fifty-five years of age, to leave the city for Warsaw where on the Vistula, new lines of defense were being organized. Did he go? Did he reach Warsaw? As it turned out, he did heed the appeal but after being overtaken on the way by the much faster-moving German forces, returned home after five days on the road.

Depressed by his first close encounter with war, with burned towns on the way to Warsaw, he was worried now about things to come. He told me about the trepidation his absence had caused his mother, after all her firstborn had gone to war, and then added, "You know, she destroyed our library." "Our library," his and mine, was what he called the books he had started buying and collecting during the previous two years. Poor mother, what a job that was to destroy those mostly hardcover books! She could not burn them as there was no place to do this so she soaked them in her laundry tub for a whole night and then, tearing them to pieces, turned the mass of paper into pulp which she was only able to dispose of then. Anguished about her son out there where the war was raging, she was also worried about what the Germans would do to him once they would take the city and find these books. Don't the Germans burn such books publicly? Don't they put those who own or even read them into their concentration camps? And on top of her anxiety about the war and the Germans taking over the city, was a painful thought about her son's reaction when he would see the destruction of his treasures that she had committed, as she believed, for his good. Would he forgive her?

He did not reproach his mother, I guess he had matured somehow during those first war days—we both had. It was a pity about the books but there were now more serious worries on his mind, and on mine, too. He still had his job, he told me, but the Germans had already taken control of the warehouse where he worked and the Jewish owner had nothing to say about it, he said it would not last, that it was temporary, very temporary. We went together to see Mala and were happy to find her with her parents at their place. They had not left the city and had witnessed the German takeover, frightening and sad as it was. They were safe for now but the outlook was bleak, to say the least.

A Stab in Poland's Back or a Glimmer of Hope?

And then, on September 17, suddenly, out of the blue (at least to us it was out of the blue) came the news that the Soviets had crossed the old Polish–Soviet border and were marching ahead. Are they coming here? Are they going to fight the Germans? But what about the recently agreed Molotov–Ribbentrop Pact? There was no end to talking, guessing, and rumors. Soon, however, the situation would clear up. Warsaw was still defending itself, even if the government had left Poland, and here came the stab into Poland's back from the Soviet Union! Our beloved Soviet Union!

A stab it was, we were fully aware of it, but at the same time, it brought a glimmer of hope to the Jewish population, or at least to a large part of it. Will the Russians also come here to our city? Hope has big eyes. One day my father ventured as far as the Plac Wolności and brought back a fascinating piece of news: there was a red Soviet flag on the City Hall building. Nobody believed it, though we all wished that it were true. The red Nazi flag was flapping in the wind and the swastika adorning it got lost for a moment in the flag's folds, and that was enough to give way to the wildest hope that the Germans would vanish like a bad dream.

Alas, the Germans were here to stay, and as it seemed, they would stay for a long time. Poland was going to be divided anew, with the Russians taking over the eastern Polish territories and annexing them, thus completing a mission of "liberating" what became known as Western Ukraine and Belarus, while the Germans would annex the western part, including the city of Łódź which they—as previously mentioned—would soon rename Litzmannstadt in honor of some Nazi hero, and controlling the rest of the Polish territory, known as the General Government, including Warsaw, till the Bug River.

A new chapter in the history of the war had begun and a new subject of talks, deliberations, and rumors was on the agenda in many homes and families. "To go or not to go!" The old Polish–Soviet border was now in motion, changing almost daily and it became possible to cross it, to go over to Białystok or Lwów, to escape the Germans. News started arriving from people who had made it: it was not easy but it is possible, the Soviets let you in, and to be rid of the Germans was worth the risk involved.

By the end of September, Warsaw had fallen, and Poland was no more. The restrictions the Germans had put on the Jewish population became more stringent. Jews were forced to wear armbands with a Star of David as if we were not marked sufficiently already, and moving around became increasingly difficult. People were losing whatever gainful jobs or occupations they were in, and the prospects were getting worse still.

To Go or Not to Go East?

Soon, larger groups of people started moving east and the question was debated in my family, as it was in many others. My parents would not move. Being around their fifties (Father was fifty-five), they considered themselves too old to undertake the risky trip. Here they at least had a roof over their heads and they also had some provisions stocked up; barley, flour, potatoes, not much but it would somehow see them through the few months of the coming winter. And to think further than that seemed unseemly as everything would certainly change in the spring, everything would be over by then. Why? Nobody asked and no one would have attempted an answer anyway.

My younger sister, Helcia, would stay with our parents; she was now their only help and comfort. Sister Sala would not move either as she was four or five months pregnant and where do you go in such a condition? But my brother and his wife wanted to go and this was wonderful and rather unexpected. Dora's two brothers had already left and sent news and some instructions. Mindful of the incident that had implicated me recently with the Polish police as a "political activist," my family decided that it would be safer for me to leave, too. And so, it was decided that I would join my brother.

We knew all about emigration in the family and we knew that visas and proper papers were required to emigrate safely. This was impossible right now and the hope and belief were that the members of the family who would go now would perhaps be able to arrange for such visas and papers later on and bring the rest of the family over under more favorable conditions, once all this nightmare would end. Perhaps next spring because how could it last longer? It had to vanish in the same way in which it had come upon us.

Left: Bajla Hinda (Helena) Temkin (Bialogorska), Gabriel's mother; right: Chaim Mayer Temkin, Gabriel's father.

And What Will We Be Doing in Białystok?

Gabriel knew that I wanted to go and that I was under pressure from my family to do so. At first, he seemed rather reluctant to make the same decision. Where to and what for? What will he do there? True, that the situation here was getting worse day by day and that all of this was only the beginning, but to take off and go, just like that, move into the unknown? Does this make any sense at all? And it was hard for him to leave his parents and younger brothers, they were relying on him. He did not try, however, to talk me out of doing what I was bent on doing. I understood his reservations but how I wished that he would change his mind! His mother must have been reluctant to let him go, I thought, and I did not know if I should have held it against her then or not.

Thinking about those days many years later, with the advantage of hindsight and myself already a mother, I was able to identify with her, to better understand her motives, and sympathize with them. Would I, under similar circumstances, have reacted differently? Many years after the war, I once asked a friend of mine who happened to be a next-door neighbor of Gabriel's mother during the ghetto years, whether she was angry with me for having "shlepped her son away." Not that I had felt particularly guilty about having done this and I had certainly played a part in his decision to leave, so if she had such feelings, I understood them.

In the beginning, my friend Marysia told me that this was perhaps so, though their mother did not talk about it much. All she told her, she recalled, was that her eldest "went to Russia with a girlfriend" and it would have been easier for her and her two other boys had he stayed with her. Yet later on, when times in the ghetto became what they were, desperately hopeless, and horrible, she was glad that her son was somewhere far away in Russia, a place from where he would eventually come back, she believed, as "their savior." She loved her firstborn son and loved him perhaps more than anything and anybody, and the plan that the family finally came up with was perhaps the measure of that love: Gabriel and his father were both going. Not much was spoken about who was to take care of whom: Gabriel of his father who, being a little over fifty, was an exhausted and not very healthy man; or his father of Gabriel, his eighteen-year-old beloved son. And so, his mother remained in Łódź, alone with her two still young boys, Monek and Ignas, fifteen and eleven respectively, without almost any means of survival, but believing as many others did that her husband and son would eventually secure a way to get the rest of the family over to safety.

Gabriel in 1939.

On Survival in Abnormal Times

These were abnormal times, to say the least, and to cling to old ideas about emigration, formalities, proper papers, and so on, was a terrible misconception that cost many lives. After the war, I read a memoir of a Holocaust survivor, a Jewish doctor from Trawniki, a health resort in southern Poland. He knew all the Jewish doctors, his colleagues, that were practicing medicine there, thirty people altogether. Half of them left with the Russians when the Germans invaded the Soviet Union in 1941, whereas the other half, for one reason or another, stayed behind under the Germans. Of those who left, fourteen returned safely at the end of the war. Of those who stayed under the German occupation, only one survived, the author of that memoir, himself. Those numbers speak for themselves. Whatever was awaiting the refugees in the Soviet Union, there is no comparison to what the Germans did to the Jews. If anybody could have envisioned this, there would have been a mass exodus. We would have all gone, my parents, my sisters, Gabriel's mother, and his brothers, but at that time, nobody was smart enough to have an inkling of what was coming.

Professor Bettelheim, the renowned psychiatrist who wrote extensively on human behavior in extreme situations, tackled the problem of attitudes in the face of danger analyzing, as an example, the fate of Anne Frank's family.[49] "The Frank family's attitude that life could be carried on as usual was glorified precisely because it did lead to their destruction," Bettelheim says.[50] And he went on to comment on what the family should have done under the circumstances to avoid that danger. The Franks, he maintained first of all, went "passively into hiding," while "thousands of other Jews in Holland and elsewhere in Europe were trying to escape to the Free World..."[51] Secondly, he argues that the family had the option "to hide out singly, each with a different family," and that Anne would have had a good chance of survival if she would have "separated from her parents and gone to live with a Dutch family as their own child."[52] And thirdly, he argues that the Franks, "who were able to provide themselves with so much, could have provided themselves with a gun" and "could have shot down at least one or two of the 'green police' who came for them." Bettelheim claims that "they all died anyway except Anne's father" and that they "could have sold their lives dearly instead of walking to their death."[53]

Bettelheim's litany of accusations against the Franks goes on, advancing from strange to ridiculous and to cruelly unjust. To imagine, for example, my father challenging anybody with a gun (which he would not have been able to "afford" anyway), or with a butcher knife," what a ridiculous and cruel notion! As much as I admired some

49 Bruno Bettelheim, "The Ignored Lesson of Anne Frank," *Harper's Magazine* (Nov. 1, 1960), pp. 45–50.

50 See Bettelheim, "The Ignored Lesson," pp. 45–46.

51 Ibid., p. 46.

52 Ibid.

53 Ibid.

of Bettelheim's writings, his *Ignored Lesson of Anne Frank* is simply a misunderstanding, written with the benefit of hindsight.

Perhaps We Should Set Up a Chupe?

Gabriel came early Sunday morning to tell me about his decision. I remember this moment in great detail and it's no wonder because it defined my life. I wondered sometimes later what my life would have been had he not come. Would I have left without him? Would I have tried to return from the other side at the first possibility? Yes, I told myself. I would have gone back to Łódź, or I would have most certainly tried! And how could I have been so light-minded or should I rather say reckless? But he came to say that he already had the train tickets and to make sure that we would meet to board the train together.

I was sitting idly and absentmindedly looking over the few things ready to be packed into my backpack. There wasn't much: a skirt, a sweater, a warm flannel nightgown sewn by Helcia—it is cold in Russia and I would need it, she said—a jacket, and not much more besides the clothes on my back. I looked at those things, but my mind had wandered off, when suddenly I heard steps on the stairs. Gabriel was here, his face pale and drawn, but for me, the world came alive again.

He stayed no more than a few minutes but Mother read into it what a mother's heart could. Her young daughter was going away. She was sending her away into the care of a much older brother, but it seemed now that she was mistaken, that the truth was withheld from her. In reality, her daughter was going with a young man, a friend of hers, a nice young man, to be sure, and yet? Unmarried? "Perhaps we should set up a *chupe?*"[54] she said quietly, rather timidly, when Gabriel left. But I just shrugged it off.

For me, in my defiant youth, marriage was nothing but a ritual, sometimes a ridiculous ritual, walking the bride around the groom seven times, and all those *mazal tovs* and tears, false tears, of course, because what else could they be? Love is what is important and

54 A marriage canopy—in Hebrew, a *hupah*.

sufficient and the rest is meaningless, but how are you going to explain this to a mother, a Jewish mother? My shrugging off her concerns was, of course, sheer cruelty, the innocent cruelty of mindless youth. I was unable to understand then what it was doing to Mother, what I was depriving her of by my disregard and contempt for those "superfluous rituals." Many years later, filled with joy while making arrangements and preparing for my daughter's wedding, I apologized to the memory of my mother.

Crossing the German–Russian Border

A few days later, Mother and Helcia went with me to the train station to see us off. I said goodbye to Father at home. For a Jew, in his traditional Jewish garb, the streets were too dangerous to walk on. Father seemed strangely agitated sending me off. "Go," he said, "Hanele, go, it's time!" He urged me as if he were glad to see me go; as if he knew somehow that he was sending me off to live.

The train from Łódź to Warsaw was packed with Jews going in the same direction—to the East. Mayer and Dora were already at the station and with them were two or three other men, their acquaintances, one of whom I had gotten to know during the recent summer vacation in the village that now seemed so distant as if it were in a different era. Gabriel, his parents, and his brothers were also there. Shortly before the train was supposed to leave, my brother went outside the train station to see our mother and sister to the tramway that would take them home. And there and then, one of the miracles that often happen in Holocaust stories happened. The Germans were hunting for Jews around the train station to do some loading or unloading for them. My brother was stopped but unexplainably managed to somehow convince the officer that his train was leaving in a few minutes and that his wife was in there waiting for him, so the German waved him away. Had he then not returned to the train in time, our trip would have certainly been called off, maybe even for good.

The trip was uneventful. We reached Warsaw late in the afternoon and spent a night in a half-bombed-out building, courtesy of some people, friends of the man who was accompanying my brother. In the morning we boarded the train to Małkinia, the last German post on the new German–Soviet border. Jews were still permitted to travel by train though we all had to wear the hateful yellow armbands. It is not very far from Warsaw to Małkinia, yet the trip seemed endless, though my perception of time, affected by the emotions of the journey, rendered me unable to say how long it took to reach that small border station.

When the train finally stopped, armed, uniformed Germans yelling and barking their orders rushed the passengers out. Right away, we were segregated, Jews separated from non-Jews, who were free to leave. Panic set in instantly, people were pushing and shoving, losing their belongings or just abandoning them in the stampede that followed. The Germans yelled to pick them up. For a while, I was dragging an enormous bundle that did not belong to me and abandoned it as soon as I could. Local youngsters were quick to snatch those bundles away. We got a preview of what arriving at a German concentration camp might look like. Now, Jews were again segregated and men and women were separated. While the men were forced to form a square in the yard adjacent to the German guards' building and wait to be cleared by the German "border customs," women were pushed into a sliver of space, a triangle formed by two walls left over from a wall that used to run around the whole yard. Into that tiny space, they pushed at least a hundred women. The force of the stampede almost slammed me into the wall, but I could still see some of what was going on in front of us. The men in the square sang Jewish folksongs and the whole yard took on a surrealistic, unreal character. Why did they sing? Ordered by the Germans? To the Germans' amusement or to drown out the screams that would soon be coming from that "customs" building?

A German in civilian clothes, the whiteness of his shirt stood out on the black, bleak background of the whole scene, approached the group of women, and picked out two or three girls. For what purpose, I could only guess. He picked the most presentable girls, young, tall, and well-dressed, and led them away. Soon, while the men were still standing in that square, singing the melody of *My Shtetele Belz,* the popular, sentimental Jewish pop song that also reached us in our corner, we were ordered to go, one by one, through the "customs." I don't remember much of it. Bewildered and scared by the whole thing, I handed the officer whatever money I had in my hand, it was not much, which he took as if it rightly belonged to him and waved me away. I found myself outside the building, in no-man's-land, out of the reach of the Germans. All in all, it took only a few moments, and it has left almost a blank in my memory.

After they finished with the women, they took the men through the same "customs" check, but the men were given much rougher treatment. I was waiting at the roadside, already in the no-man's territory, for the men to come out. I don't know where I got a bottle of iodine from, but I can still see myself standing there on the side of the unpaved village road with the iodine bottle in hand, using that iodine on the wounds of the men coming out bruised and often bloodied. Finally, Gabriel's father appeared. He had blood on his face. The bruises and wounds were not only of the Germans' making. Polish youngsters waiting around and trying to take away what the Germans had left, had their share in it, too.

On No-Man's-Land

At last, we were all in no-man's-land, the neutral zone, a large field fenced off by barbed wire that divided the Germans from the Russians. It was late November and the field, swarming with people, was sprinkled with snow. People had been sitting there for many days in the cold, outside, without any shelter, and some, as we were told, had already been sitting there for at least two weeks.

Someone informed us that two children had already been born there in the field, and some people had already died there, too. Food was very scarce, brought in by smugglers, and very costly, and nobody could predict how long we would have to stay there, waiting for the Russians to let us in. The Russians might open the gate and let us in, or they might not, and nobody knew when it might happen. In all that commotion, Gabriel met his half-brother Jakub who had left Łódź a day or two before us. Jakub's wife with their tiny baby remained in Łódź while he went to the Soviet side with the same hope that many others had, that he would eventually be able to bring his family over to safety having prepared a proper place and secured "papers."

I moved ahead as far as it was possible to the barbed wire and the makeshift gate marking the border. A Soviet soldier with a pointed cap on his head and a long rifle with a bayonet stacked on top of it was guarding the gate. Moving along the fence, back and forth, his long trench coat tangling between his heavy boots, he directed his rifle toward the people on our side of the fence and kept repeating two words, like a chant, "*davay nazad, davay nazad!*" It sounded more like a plea than an order. He was addressing it to the people on our side while the people kept pushing closer to the gate. What does it mean? There is some similarity to the Polish words that mean "give back, return." What have these people taken away from him that he wanted them to return? I had translated his Russian order incorrectly, which actually meant "move back!" and now thought with some scorn about those who had done something like that to this good Soviet soldier who was now almost begging to regain what belonged to him.

An older, haggard-looking woman standing not far from me was mumbling another Russian word, also new to me, "*pozhalusta, pozhalusta*" (please, please). But it reminded me of the Polish word *żal*, signifying a deep feeling of despair caused by nostalgia or a plea for mercy. The woman kept repeating her *pozhalusta* plaintively, addressing it to the soldier on guard. This sounded to me not only as a plea for mercy, which of course it was, but also as a somewhat excessive and therefore perhaps undignified lamentation, taking into consideration that we had just arrived. Having foremost myself in mind, I forgot that this woman and many others might have already been there in that naked, snowy field for quite a while. Finally, tired by the day's experience, I squatted, trying to rest my head on my forearms, and the duet of the soldier's monotonous "move back" and the woman's heartbreaking "please" threw me into a kind of torpor.

The Soviets Open the Gate

Soon, however, my moment of rest would end. Something was happening on the other side of the wire fence and the resulting commotion snapped me out of my lethargy. We were, it turned out, very lucky, incredibly lucky. We hardly had time to come to our senses after what we had been through at the border crossing, and before we could even begin worrying about the situation in that cold, wintry field, it all began to change.

What people were waiting for, hoping for, was turning into reality: the Soviets were opening the border and letting us in. Someone had arrived there, at the other side of the gate, by car, or was it by horse? Some were swearing it was a car, others a horse. It was most probably a horse as the Soviets were not rich enough for cars. A moment later, the field was illuminated by a reflector, someone was giving a speech, and we were told that the Soviet government was welcoming the refugees. We may go ahead to the nearest train station on the Russian side, some 15 kilometers further to a place called Zaremby Kostzel'ne (Zaręby Kościelne). There would be a train there, we may board it, and it will take us to Białystok.

Elated despite the tiredness, we marched all night. And while we were going east, large crowds as big as ours were moving in the opposite direction, to the Germans, and I wondered who they were and why they were going to the German side. They did not look like refugees from the territories taken over by the Russians. Only later I understood that cross-border smuggling was already underway on a considerable scale.

I marched on my sore feet, as others did. Nobody knew what was ahead of us, but this was a rather happy march and some people were even trying to sing. The Germans could not claim us now, and the yellow armbands, if kept, would only be a sad souvenir.

CHAPTER FOUR

TO THE URAL MOUNTAINS

Bialystok was full of refugees, and homeless people. It was the Białystok of Gabriel's imagination, crowded, with lines everywhere. The Russian authorities did what they could, providing lodging in the Białystok suburbs, in the summer cottages that were now empty. We were lodged, some twenty people in a room and straw mattresses were provided. There was also a soup kitchen and a portion of daily bread for everyone.

I did not perceive the living conditions as a particular hardship; at least I do not remember it as a time of hunger or especially terrible deprivation. This was a temporary situation anyway, and everything around was so very interesting. Gabriel and I walked a lot, happy that we could spend so much time together. We discovered the city and learned to read Russian from the signs over the stores. *Parikmakherskaya* means barbershop, and *khleb* had the same meaning as in Polish: bread. It would not be too difficult to learn a language with so many similarities! And the Cyrillic lettering seemed like fun! Soon, we found a way to the reading rooms, to the so-called "Red

Corners"[55] that the Soviets had opened. I remember especially fondly a reading room in the center of the city, a showcase of reading rooms, grateful for the warmth in there and the culture, the civilized indoor plumbing, warm water coming from the faucet, and the many journals and newspapers available for free.

Gabriel also met other members of his family in Białystok: his half-sister Pola, a sweet young woman; and her husband, whose name was Mojzesz (Moniek) Hostik. I had never met Pola before, but now I felt that we would become good friends. She was my sister Sala's age, and like her, she was also expecting her first child. Right away she told me that Gabriel and I "should get married, you know." What did she want to tell me, I wondered? Did she want to tell me that she would like to have me as a sister-in-law? I certainly would have been glad to have her. Or was she just afraid that we would "live in sin," without the blessing of a rabbi? I did not ask her, and she did not elaborate; I guess she had more nagging problems on her mind. But I was glad that Pola said what she had said.

Unfortunately, after a while, Pola and her husband decided to return to Łódź and took their [Gabriel's and Pola's] father with them. Pola's husband had planned to reach Vilna and from there, via China, eventually get to America, but those plans turned out to be unrealistic after the Soviets occupied Lithuania. Not willing to risk a voyage deep into the Soviet Union, they decided to return home to Łódź. Thus, the family was again and even further divided. Tragically, their father never managed to reach home. I found out about the Hostiks only recently from the records of the Łódź ghetto, that they returned to Łódź and even had a child born there in 1942. Was this their second child? I found no trace in those records about Pola's first child, due in the spring of 1940. The conclusion seemed obvious; Pola, her husband, and their child had perished in the Holocaust.

55 These were communist cultural centers or clubhouses of sorts, often housed within other buildings or institutions, and offering classical Communist texts, newspapers and magazines published by the regime, and inspirational posters.

Will We Be Coal Miners?

Soon, our stay in Białystok would also come to an end. To prolong it was neither possible nor did it make any sense. As soon as Soviet companies started recruiting people for work in the faraway places of the Soviet Union, in the Urals and beyond, we registered to go. Jakub, Gabriel, and I decided to register with the first company that came our way, and it turned out to be recruiting workers for coal mines in the Ural Mountains. They were taking anybody, promising that there would be work for all, and not necessarily only in the mines but all kinds of work. My brother and his wife decided to wait a little longer in Białystok, but finally, they too registered to go to the Urals, though to a different place.

Our mining company paid each recruited future worker 100 rubles, ten *chervnovtsy*, which were large red bank notes. How much was it? The minimum wage at that time was eighty rubles per month, the wage of a cleaning lady, and people lived on it, though it would be very difficult to say that it was a good life. And what would I be doing there, and what could I do? With the typical carelessness of youth, I did not bother myself too much with such questions. Besides, we were told that miners make five or six times that much, and Gabriel had decided that he was going to be a miner, no less, so the unspoken assumption was that I would have nothing to worry about.

The First Trip to the Ural Mountains

We traveled to the Urals in freight cars, about twenty people in a car. Soviet freight cars have been described perhaps a thousand times. They served to transport large masses of people: soldiers, prisoners, deportees, cattle, and all kinds of goods. Prisoner transports were tightly guarded by armed guards, and the prisoners were crammed into overloaded cars.

Ours was a luxury train by comparison, not overcrowded; there was a place for everybody to stretch out on a straw mattress, a blanket to cover us with during the cold winter nights, and the cars were heated by round iron ovens that stood in the middle of each car, the so-called *buriuka,* hence the car was called *teplushka* (a heated car). Though the fire in that oven burned constantly, sending a steady flow of warm air into the corners of the car, this was, nevertheless, not enough to melt the white frost covering the walls.

I liked to watch the flame jumping around in the oven's little window as if it could give me answers to questions not even asked, about the life awaiting us so far from home, in unknown places, among strange people, and about my parents and sisters I had left so far behind. But most of all, I liked to look outside, sitting, weather permitting, in the partly open door of the car, leaning on the door's frame, my legs dangling outside.

The sheer vastness of the country was overwhelming. The snow-covered enormous empty spaces, the black massifs of dense forests, the tall pines and firs against the white background, gilded by the cold, northern sun of an early afternoon. What views! What beauty! To me, a city child, who had never previously had the occasion to admire nature in such splendor, this was spellbinding. But such moments could not last; it was getting cold in the car, and people were complaining, the door had to be closed.

The trip to the Urals lasted two weeks. The train stopped at large stations a few times and we received meals at the stations' restaurant; for the rest of the time, we had to make do with the so-called "dry rations" of bread and other basic foods, provided by the personnel accompanying our train. Hot water for tea was readily available along the whole way; each passing station had those small structures announcing in big letters *Kipiatok*, which means boiling water. Initially, everybody mistook that for the station's name, wondering why all those stations had the same name.

Altogether, it was a rather monotonous way of traveling, especially after the initial excitement had dissipated. Once, when the train stopped at a large station so we could have a hot meal, some of us, Gabriel and I among them, had overstretched the mealtime a bit, and our train moved away, leaving us behind. As it turned out, there was nothing to worry about, because the laggards were sent to catch up with the freight train by a passenger train, going in the same direction but at a much faster speed. Since it paid to be tardy, on the next occasion we would deliberately overstay, and thanks to this trick, brought some welcome variety into our journey.

"I Am Not Concerned about the Boys, for You I Worry"

This presented us also with the opportunity to get acquainted with the natives for the first time. As foreigners, we were arousing a considerable amount of interest and as people running from a war, we were treated with genuine compassion. Russian women were shedding real tears over me, a girl so young, without parents, going into the vastness of their country which as they knew could be cruelly tough. At one station, while we were sitting at a table in the restaurant, a woman in a white smock approached me, took me by the hand, and led me into the kitchen where she put in front of me an enormous plate full of cold cuts. "Eat," she said, "eat as much as you want." "The boys would have a ball," was the first thought that came to my mind and I ran to call Gabriel, Jakub, and some others. And they had a ball, indeed, but the woman that invited me was not happy. My Russian was still just elementary, but I understood what she said and remembered it. "*Rebiat ne zhalko, tebia zhalko*" (I am not concerned about the boys, for you I worry).

At another instance, while Gabriel and I were resting in the warmth of a passenger train compartment, a woman, poor and haggard looking, offered me a little herring. I can still see her, standing there with her offering. She was holding the little fish by its tail in her outstretched hand while tears ran down her cheeks. She tried to tell me something. It was about a girl, obviously a daughter of hers, that was "just like me" and whom she had lost. I did not understand all of what she tried so painfully to convey to me, but the gist was clear. The scene confused me and I did not know what to do; I felt sorry for that woman and was at a loss for what to say, how to react, but urged by the people around, I finally took the little herring and said politely "*spasibo*" (thank you), which made all of them in the compartment smile happily. Someone even offered me his place on a bunk, on a sheepskin, and covered me with a warm blanket, telling me to sleep tightly till we catch up with the freight train; they would wake me up in time.

Kizel, Permskaya Oblast

Finally, our trip came to an end in Kizel, in the Perm Oblast (region) that was renamed Molotov in the years 1940–1957. Kizel, Kizil, or Kyzyl was a small city and the capital of the Tuva Autonomous Oblast of the Southwest Asiatic Russian Federal Socialist Republic (SFSR) on the Yenisey River, in the foothills of the Urals, founded in 1914, and originally called Belotsarsk until 1917. I remember it as a small sleepy town with wooden sidewalks and it was cold, icy cold. The temperature on our arrival, we were told, was over 50 degrees below zero on the Celsius scale, and we were warned to cover our faces before sticking our noses out from the warmth of our pretty cold *teplushka*.

So, I had arrived at the Ural Mountains, a place at the end of the world, the name of which I only vaguely remembered from geography classes and had never even dreamed of seeing. This was the Ural Mountain range in the northwest-central Soviet Union, extending about 21,000 kilometers from north to south, from the Kara Sea to the steppes of the Caspian Sea, and traditionally dividing Europe from Asia.

The densely forested Urals, the forests that I had admired from the partially open door of our *teplushka* on the way here, were rich, we were informed, very rich in mineral resources, precious stones, and metals, such as iron, manganese, nickel, chrome, copper, bauxite, asbestos, coal, and oil. Huge industrial centers were created in the 1930s at Sverdlovsk, Magnitogorsk, Nizhni Tagil, Perm, and Chelyabinsk. Now, we, the *bezhentsy,*[56] were brought here to work on developing and multiplying these riches. I must right away add, however, that we were not perhaps the company's best investment deal.

56 Russian for refugees and used to refer to the Polish citizens, mostly Jews, who fled from the territory occupied by the Germans into that taken by the Soviets.

We spent the first few days in Kizel in makeshift accommodation set up in a school. This was mainly for resting after the long trip and for small chores like washing, laundering, and adjusting to the new and strange surroundings, as well as for meetings with some local "important people." This was a disparate group of officials from the city authorities, from the trust—our employer—and with them some representatives of the local intelligentsia who were interested to see the newcomers, people from abroad, refugees from the recent but distant war in the West. Some were Jews. Of those, I remember best a coalmining engineer with whom we would later become friends, and a Jewish actor/theater director, a very Semitic-looking handsome man, who gave a speech in Yiddish. They all came to greet us, and everybody tried to be reassuring and spoke warmly.

Gabriel ventured into town a few times, but I stayed inside on his urging, afraid of frostbite. My coat and my shoes were not adequate to face the winter temperatures of Kizel. True, he was not dressed for the winter either, but the "rugged man" prided himself to be frost-proof, one of his "manly" ambitions that he paid for dearly. After a while, however, when either the cold had eased up a bit, or we had all learned to adjust, we transferred to the places where we were supposed to settle. Gabriel, Jakub, and I got assigned to the coal mine, *shakhta* number five, a few kilometers from Kizel.

Mine Number Five

It was an almost brand-new mine, only recently opened for exploitation. With all fairness to the company that brought us there, I must say that they tried to keep the promise that all kinds of work would be available, and people would be employed according to their abilities. But there was no demand for all the tailors, cobblers, salesmen, and such, and the choice of jobs offered, besides that of down in the mine, made for a rather short list.

Gabriel wanted to be a miner and nothing could have persuaded him to look for something else. Whether he insisted on it for the cause, the glory of the profession, or for the money it is difficult to say now—

perhaps it was for a bit of all the above. I remember what he told me, "A miner working with a pneumatic drill earns a lot of money. It's easy; the drill does all the work, anybody can be a Stakhanovite,"[57] and he seemed childishly yet earnestly to believe so.

As for myself, there was a great demand for cleaning ladies, washerwomen, and this was what women were mostly offered, but when the director of the mine asked me what I could do, and I rather sheepishly said that I could use a typewriter, he assigned me to the mine's main office, saying "Let her get acquainted." Perhaps he had a daughter of my age at home, and so the next day I started my new job that paid eighty rubles per month, the wages of a washerwoman, the minimum Soviet wage at that time, but which certainly beat scrubbing floors and cleaning toilets.

Internship in the Coal Mine's Main Office

My job, or rather internship, was not very demanding. The executive secretary, the boss of the place, a tall blonde middle-aged woman, tolerated me and others were nice to me. I managed to pick up some Russian since I left home, but my knowledge of the language was still limited, and I was happy to have the opportunity to concentrate on learning it faster. There was no school I could have attended after work, so I learned on the go, so to speak. Having started to recognize the Cyrillic lettering by deciphering the signs over the stores in Białystok, I since read whatever came into my hands and asked questions to everybody who would listen. I remember the trouble I had with learning the conjugation of the verb *govorit* (to speak). Listening to people, I was able to discern the difference between the ending of that verb for the second and third persons, but what was it for the first one? How do you say, "I speak"? I kept asking anyone who would listen to my questions, often helping to express myself with my hands, "You speak, *ty govorish*; he, she speaks, *on, ona govorit*; and I speak, *ya govorit*? Right? No, not right?"

57 Workers in the USSR who exceeded their daily norms received praise and rewards.

People did not understand me, and I could see from their faces that they did not know what to make of this strange girl. Finally, someone, a Tatar, said after listening to me with great attention, "You know, I don't know the language very well myself, '*sam po ruski plokho govoriu,'* [I do not speak Russian well] and I am also a *natsmen.*" Now I got it! *Govoriu*, of course, is the word, I had heard it plenty of times. And by the way, I learned from that man something else, not only a word and not only a new word, but a new, important notion. *Natsmen* (*natsionalnoye menshinstvo*), a member of a national minority, a word that defined me, too. I was a member of a minority, and perhaps would remain in this status for the rest of my life!

The main office of the big enterprise was an interesting place to work at. It also made for a good observation point of life in that strange, new country. I was not overloaded with work, perhaps because nobody believed that I could do much, and indeed, I could hardly do much. So, I was practicing, pounding the old Underwood typewriter and copying for my practice something or other from an occasional newspaper, and nobody bothered me.

Typing away diligently for hours, I watched the miners waiting to be received by one of the director's deputies. Some were coming after their shift and they had the dirt of the pit still on them; others arrived before work, washed but still with traces of coal on their hands and faces, all patiently squatting along the whitewashed walls of the long hallway. Apparently, they had some grievances, personal problems to discuss with the bosses. Sometimes they would exchange a few words with their neighbors in hushed voices, but more often than not they just sat there quietly, smoking their *makhorka*.[58] I wondered who these people were, and where they were from. Big men, strong-looking, as one had to be strong to work in the pit. I had never seen workers like these miners; in Łódź the only big industry workers I knew were weavers, textile workers, the mainstay of the Łódź industry. These here were different, and they sure looked different, too. Were they the real

58 Most workers in the USSR at this time could not afford readymade cigarettes and rolled their own from an inexpensive and inferior local type of tobacco known as *makhorka*.

proletariat of the "dictatorship of the proletariat" that the Soviet Union so proudly proclaimed to be? Do they really rule this country?

One day, the editor of the local two-page newspaper came into the office. He urgently needed to get an article retyped, but the blonde, tall boss of the office, sent him away with a contemptuous gesture implying that it was too late, and don't you see, it's almost four o'clock, come tomorrow, maybe... But he could not wait till tomorrow, and I can still see the imploring expression on his face when he turned to me, as the last resort, "Would you do it, can you do it?" he asked hesitantly. I sat in the office long after everybody had left, finishing the two or three pages. "*Spasibo*, *spasibo,*" he repeated more than twice, happy with the result of my work. I was happy too, as for me it was a breakthrough, of sorts and now I knew that I was acquiring useful skills, and this gave me some assurance that I needed very much.

Pneumatic Drills Are in Short Supply

In the meantime, Gabriel was not doing so great in the mine. He did not get, of course, to operate the desired, powerful drilling hammer. Pneumatic drills were in short supply, as were many other goods, and while there was no shortage of qualified miners, unqualified workers, needed to load the extracted coal into the cars, were always in demand. So, Gabriel got a shovel instead of the drill and was assigned to load coal onto train cars. The cars were over 2 meters high and to throw a heavy shovel full of coal into a car, he had to raise the shovel high in the air, and this was an almost impossible task. It was very hard labor and to fulfill the production norm was impossible for him—as a youth and not physically fit for such work it was far beyond his strength. His hands were covered with blisters that would not heal, the new ones coming on top of the previous ones, constantly bleeding, and it took an effort for me not to cry when I helped him to dress those blisters and clean off the smudges of coal.

The situation was rather bleak, so he decided one day to swallow his pride and see one of the *nachalniks* (bosses) to ask for a transfer to a different kind of work. The boss, an engineer, turned out to be a kind man, and he promised to transfer him to a team of electricians, where he would learn their skills. Happy with the outcome of the talk, he wanted to make sure that the engineer would remember this promise, and here a language misunderstanding almost dashed his hopes. Before taking his leave, he asked the engineer once more, convinced that what he was saying was in Russian, "You will not forget?" But instead of using the proper (under the circumstances) Russian expression "*ne zabudete,*" he used the Polish "*nie zapomnicie*," to which the engineer nodded affirmatively and repeated a few times "*Zapomniu, Zapomniu,*" which Gabriel translated for himself as "I forget, forget," because *zapomniec* in Polish means exactly this, to forget, while in Russian it means the opposite, to remember. Was the engineer making fun of him, or what? He did not know what to think and was left confused and uncertain of what would follow. And this only added to the bleakness and depression we could not help but feel about our situation in general.

To mention the living conditions. We shared a room with Jakub and two or even three other men. Even the very notion of privacy did not exist. We longed to be alone but could not have a moment to ourselves, and it did not seem that there would ever be any improvement, because this was how all the others lived and we were no exception. True, the living conditions of the locals—and we did not get to know many of them—were better, but they were not so great either.

A Funeral for a Refugee

We had very little contact with the rest of the refugees that came to mine together with us, but one day we were informed that one of the women had died and that there would be a special bus to take us to the funeral. I remembered the woman, though I could not have said that I knew her; a very pale face and thick, short cut, very black hair, still young, perhaps in her early thirties, married. She came with her husband who also went to work in the mine. Why did she die? I hadn't heard anything about her being sick. Judging from the other women's glances and the murmurs they were exchanging, whispering among themselves, I suspected a botched abortion, and the thought made me shiver. Nobody, however, told me anything about it, and I did not ask.

The company's truck took us to the cemetery, and if our mine was at the end of the world, this place seemed to truly already be in the "other world." The snow cover that was a few meters high made the hole, into which the poor woman's body was lowered, look incredibly deep, like a real pit. Someone recited the Jewish mourner's prayer, Kaddish, and this was the end of the ceremony. We stood there for a few more moments, in silence, each one perhaps thinking his sad thoughts, about life, as it was before and of which we were all deprived by the war, and about the prospects of the new life here, under these strange and tough conditions. Then the company's truck took us back to the mine.

I remember the event, perhaps because it was my first close-up encounter with death and the first funeral that I had ever attended, even though I had already witnessed war. Strangely, however, that funeral picture has become intertwined in my memory with another memory and it was somehow pushed away by another one, that of children running around that cemetery, playing with snowballs. They were mine workers' children, perhaps there were some dwellings nearby, and they were throwing snowballs at each other, as kids everywhere do, and they were doing it with zest and joy. What struck me, however, was that they were all wearing very high, large rubber boots that belonged to their fathers, the miners. The kids were almost sinking into those boots, but they seemed not to mind it at all, happy to take advantage of the boots, perhaps the only pair in the household that was available to them while their fathers were home, sleeping after their shift in the mine.

Our New Friends, the Blumins

Among all that sadness, frustration, and nostalgia, Gabriel and I found some consolation in a new friendship with the Blumins. Mr. Blumin was the engineer who came, among others, to greet our refugee group upon our arrival in Kizel. Shortly after that, we also met his wife, and after being invited often to visit them in their home, we developed a cordial relationship. The hours spent with the Blumins in their comfortable, clean apartment—two rooms and a small kitchen, sparsely furnished—were a source of mental and physical rest, as well as a time to learn about other aspects of life in the Soviet Union, its people, and society.

David and Fanya Blumin were a childless, Jewish couple in their late twenties, and they were typical representatives of the new generation of Soviet intelligentsia; educated professionals, trained in the universities in the western part of the Soviet Union, and directed to work in the developing East. David, a mining engineer, worked in the Ural-Coal Trust while Fanya, a pharmacologist, ran Kizel's only pharmacy. They both took a liking to us, especially to Gabriel, for his sense of humor and the questions he was always asking about Socialism, the "system," economics, and politics, not knowing yet that those were questions one should not ask, while they, knowing it, would not dare to bring them up with their local friends. With us, however, total strangers, newcomers from another world, it was different, safer perhaps, and they derived much pleasure from it.

On the Abridged History of the Party

One such question Gabriel could not get out of his mind after he had already dropped the unanswerable questions about the fate of Marshal Blueher, concerned a short note he found in *Pravda* (The Truth), the official Soviet newspaper. It said, "Director, M.P. XYZ, of the N* enterprise of heavy industry is already studying the fourth chapter of the *Abridged History of the Party*."

Very nice of him, Gabriel would say, but why advertise it in the central press? Is this such an exceptional achievement? So important? And why? He kept asking these questions, truly baffled. Nobody could answer his question, but we laughed about it together with our hosts. They had never paid any attention to it, they would say, and indeed, to answer the question one would need an expert Kremlinologist, able to dissect the Soviet system.

As I would later learn, Stalin was supposed to be the author of that fourth chapter, the "philosophical" one, and the *Abridged History* was promoted as the new bible for the people to learn and repeat what it said like a mantra. The piece of news in *Pravda* was an important reminder and directive to others, regarding what they should study and think.

On the Price of a Pair of Boots

Sometimes, the Blumins would invite some other people. Once we met another engineer there, also Jewish. A short man, he was very proud of his tall, shiny boots, made of fine, soft leather. Four hundred rubles, he announced, patting the smooth top with obvious relish. This was a tremendous sum, at least for both of us, and not only for us. This was perhaps all this engineer was earning in a month, if not in two, and Gabriel could not help but remark that to work a whole month for a pair of boots, even such excellent boots, was certainly excessive, to which the boots' owner said, "The problem is not in the price; what matters is to be able to procure them, to get them…"

Now, this was food for thought as it went totally against what Gabriel had learned from his books about the laws of supply and demand, turning everything on its head. All this was certainly teaching us a lot about Soviet life, but of course, this was not knowledge of the encouraging type. It did not imbue us with optimism, either.

A Fire in the Coal Mine

We would have, however, reconciled ourselves to life in the Urals. After all, I could learn the language on the job and acquire useful skills at the same time, and if Gabriel were to get the promised transfer, perhaps things would start looking brighter. The Russians kept saying "*privyknesh, privyknesh*" (you get used to it), which somehow seemed similar to me to the American advice for newcomers, "take it easy, take it easy," and we would tell ourselves that it takes patience, remembering quite well why we came here in the first place.

But, as often happens, an unexpected event pushed us in a

different direction. One night in our fourth month at mine number five, something terrible happened—a fire broke out in the mine. Fortunately, Gabriel was not on that night shift, and as we learned the next day, there were no casualties; all the miners were taken out safely. But this was a new mine, only recently opened, and the fire was a catastrophe that upended the whole life of the mine for quite some time.

In the main office, and this I could observe firsthand, pandemonium reigned. Very important people from as far as Moscow were coming and going. The local bosses, suddenly looking so unimportant and—I hesitated to think—frightened, were taking them down to the mine, for checking and rechecking. The newcomers spoke loudly and the locals in hushed voices.

The Bigwig from Moscow

There was a lot of yelling and shouting around, suspicion was in the air, and the word "sabotage" seemed to be on everybody's lips. One such bigwig from Moscow stood out especially, a large and very noisy man, arrogantly pushing everybody around and barking orders at his comrades. I had not yet seen a Russian or Soviet man behave like this in general, and it certainly went against my naive beliefs of what socialist human relations are or should be, especially among comrades, and weren't they all comrades? I thought the scene between that VIP and the friendly editor of the local newspaper to be especially appalling: the big guy preparing to go down to the mine and the much smaller man, the editor, trying to help him put on a pair of high rubber boots. He was kneeling in front of the big guy who looked as if he was going to kick in his teeth; a slave and a master—a scared, lowly slave, and a very angry master.

Our Next Visit with the Blumins

Work in the mine had virtually stopped for a few days, and we went to visit the Blumins again. The quirkiness of fate! The twists and turns!

During that very visit, we came up with a decision that had some important bearing on the course of our lives. While talking with David and Fanya about what had happened in the mine, David, rather casually, raised the subject again of our leaving for the western part of the Soviet Union. We would find the conditions there more conducive to starting a normal life, closer to what we were used to in our native Poland. A much milder climate, for one thing, as well as the possibility to find work in the various light industries, and a large Jewish population. "You should have gone to Gomel instead of coming to the Urals," he said.

Gomel? Yes, he and his wife came from Gomel. They still had relatives there and perhaps they would even be able to help us settle there. What did we know about Gomel? At first, the very mention of the name Gomel made me laugh. Gomel to me was the place of Lazik Roitschwantz, the main character of a book by Ilya Ehrenburg.[59] We both loved that book. It was a source of much enjoyment. Ehrenburg was a popular Soviet writer, yet the Blumins had never heard of this particular book. As I only realized later, it was forbidden in the Soviet Union, even though Ehrenburg, who was in self-imposed exile in France, wrote it in around 1927 or 1928 to make up with the Soviet authorities and gain permission to return to his native country. The book, meant as an apologia of Soviet Socialism, was never quite that, no matter how much the author wanted it to be. Ehrenburg returned to the Soviet Union, but his book did not.

The main character of the book, Lazik, a poor Jewish tailor, a tragic and at once a very funny comical figure, was born in Gomel but left the Soviet Union. After numerous adventures all over the world, disappointed with life "under the capitalist system," he longed to return home, to the country building a new society, to Socialism, because "there, they at least try to build a different, new, and better world."

59 Ilya Ehrenburg, *Burnaia zhizn' Lazika Roitshvanetsa* (Paris, 1928). A Polish translation by Maria Popowska came out soon afterward, *Burzliwe życie Lejzorka Rojtszwańca* (Warsaw, 1929). It was translated into English only decades later as *The Stormy Life of Lasik Roitschwantz* (New York: Polyglot, 1960).

I also understood, at least, that poor Ehrenburg's hero, who was not a hero at all but rather an antihero, was a "poor rabbit caught up and entangled in the web of historical events," which he was unable to fathom. "And what could a poor rabbit do when history is marching through the streets?" This phrase came up in the book many times, like a refrain, and it was as if written about me, about both of us, and about so many others like us, entangled in those "historic" times. What could we do, caught up in a horrible war, in an incredibly cold and strange country, in coal mines, so far from home, from our parents, from loved ones? Yes, we could still go to Gomel, and on the spur of the moment, we decided to go. Why not?

We Are Going to Gomel

With the lightheadedness of youth, we kept to the decision that suddenly seemed to solve all our problems. After sharing our plans with Gabriel's half-brother, Jakub, who helped out a bit with the money for the train tickets, we were ready. We stopped at the Blumins to say goodbye. They gave us the promised address of their Gomel relatives and Fanya offered me a red beret. She put it on my head. "Wear it," she said, "just to avoid any problems with buying the tickets. It makes you look less foreign, more like a local girl." I had no idea, or only a very vague one, that what we intended to do was not quite legal, having conveniently forgotten that after all, we were under contract to work here for a year, and the thought made me uneasy. But there seemed to be no return.

May Stalin Drop Dead!

I went to the train station and got in line for the cashier's wicket. My heart was pounding but nobody paid any attention to me. I was glad, thinking with gratitude about Fanya and the red beret on my head, when a man, tall and big, bent over to me and said, evidently for only me to hear, "*Khtob Stalin sdokh*!" (May Stalin drop dead!). This was some statement! For the first time, I was met with such an open, hostile anti-

Soviet proclamation, and it was directed at me! I froze, not daring to look up at the man's face.

I do not know where I got the good sense not to react to him at all, as if I did not hear anything, did not see anything. The line moved ahead, I approached the wicket, bought two tickets, and that was all. But I remembered the incident and thought about it many times. What was it? A provocation? Who was that man? Perhaps just someone who had recognized me as a foreigner, the red beret notwithstanding, and just let his pent-up frustrations and hostility out? I will never know.

That same evening, we left Kizel and the Ural Mountains. And little did I know then that I would be back only a little over a year later, this time alone, again running from a raging new war, or rather the second act of the same war that began in 1939, the German invasion of the Soviet Union.

CHAPTER FIVE

FROM THE URALS TO GOMEL

The trip to Gomel was a long one. It took three days with a stop in Moscow where we had to stamp our tickets to secure seats for the rest of the journey. It was a normal, comfortable passenger train. On the first night, during a long stretch from Kizel to Sverdlovsk, we shared the compartment with only one other passenger, a Tatar woman, who could hardly speak any Russian. We were scared so we avoided talking with fellow passengers anyway. We kept to ourselves, careful not to talk even to each other, and tired of the emotions of the day, tried to sleep.

In the middle of the night, strange sounds suddenly woke me up: our neighbor, the Tatar woman, was crying, sobbing, and repeating through tears, "*oy bida, bida, bida*!" Her lamentation filled with despair sounded tragic. As it turned out, while we were sound asleep, someone entered the compartment and snatched her shawl off her head, a large woolen, flowery shawl, escaped with it, ran to another car, or even jumped off the train altogether. The woman would not stop lamenting the loss of her precious possession. And we began to worry, too, as now the militia might come and they would ask questions—where are we coming from and where are we going to, and others like this. I felt like a fugitive, and this was an awful feeling.

Red Square in Moscow

Moscow greeted us with a song and an enthusiastic announcement from the train's loudspeaker, "The capital of our motherland welcomes you!" With our belongings in hand, we went sightseeing. We wanted, of course, to see the city, but all the more so because we had to wait for our train to Gomel until the next day. And where do you go in Moscow? First of all, to Red Square of course! We looked with respect at the walls of the Kremlin and the red stars of the Kremlin towers. Then, we spent a few hours in the Museum of the Revolution on Red Square—no entrance fee—scrutinizing the memorabilia of events and people we had read so much about, and who were so important and dear to us. I was quite taken by the view of Lenin's black overcoat, embellished à la mode by a black velour collar. Lenin was pictured wearing it in many books, and this coat was here centrally on display in one of the museum's rooms.

It was already getting dark when we returned to the square. The red stars of the Kremlin towers now shone against the darkening sky and I looked at them with admiration. Swayed by the meaning attached to them as a symbol of the victorious struggle for freedom, equality, and brotherhood, I could not take my eyes off them. To me, they still signified hope for oppressed people everywhere.

Are There Rich and Poor in the Soviet Union?

We walked around Red Square some more. There were not many passersby; it was pretty cold and getting late. It was time to return to the train station. We hoped to be able to sit there through the night, waiting for the train that would take us on the last leg of our trip to Gomel.

While walking down the bridge—Kuznyechnyi Most—that was by now almost empty, in the direction of the Moscow Metro, a young Russian girl passed us by. She was tall, good-looking, very well dressed, and boasted a long, light brown thick braid coming with ease and elegance down her back from under a pretty fur hat and reaching almost to her waist. "A rich girl," remarked Gabriel. "What do you mean rich? Certainly, a beautiful girl, but rich? There are no rich and poor here, don't you know this? It's Socialism," I retorted. "Oh, yeah," he said only. This made me angry and, from one word to the next, we were deep into an argument, of all things, on the nature of Soviet society and getting angrier and angrier at each other.

This was our first such heated, angry confrontation, and it became a useful outlet for our fears and frustrations. We both have strong opinions and tend to defend them rather vigorously, and we have argued a lot ever since. We both, especially Gabriel, tend to forget such arguments rather quickly, but I still remember that first one. We were tired and hungry, and quite forlorn in that big, foreign city. And we certainly did not know what we were doing and where we were heading, or what for, for that matter. So, what else was there to do but get into an argument? Fortunately, what could have become a bad quarrel with mutual blame and recrimination, turned into an argument about an abstract subject, which we were unable to resolve, but which did indeed calm our anxiety a bit.

CHAPTER SIX

GOMEL

There Are Good People in Gomel, Too

A middle-aged woman opened the door and looked at us, a question mark written on her tired, wrinkled face. When it dawned on her who we were and where we had come from, she clasped her hands, and murmured under her breath, "David, always the goody." It sent a chill into my heart. We were ready to turn around and leave, but a man, Blumin's brother, the mathematics teacher about whom he had told us back in Kizel, entered the room, and we were invited in. He was not exactly overjoyed with the unexpected and uninvited visitors either, yet he asked how he could help. And what we needed was no small potatoes—we needed a temporary place to stay, we needed to find jobs, and get permission to register for residency in the city from the Gomel authorities. Fortunately, Gomel was not a restricted city, as were many larger cities in the Soviet Union that were simply off-limits to newcomers, unless one was directed to live there by the higher authorities for some exceptional reason.

A neighbor of the Blumins took us in. Sima was a young vivacious woman, married to a Red Army officer who was absent, busy fighting the Soviet–Finnish war. Sima shared the one room that was her home with her two-year-old little girl, and she would share it with us too until we could find something better, or until her husband returned. She could save some space for us, and she could also use the additional income for renting it, she told us, and I appreciated her trust and directness. And she would, of course, wait for the payment until we could start working.

There were many refugees like us in Gomel at that time. They came from all places—from the Urals, from Siberia, from the Northern Territories, would-be miners, heavy-industry workers, or kolkhozniks,[60] people like us who were not able to adjust to the harsh conditions of work, climate, and life in those distant places, and were wandering around the country in search of a more suitable, more livable place. It was enough to take a walk in the streets of Gomel to find someone, or to be approached by someone as a fellow Jewish refugee from Poland. Once, a young man stopped Gabriel in the street. "Where from?" he asked. "Oh! From Łódź, I am a Łódźer, too." He was Yosek Sharfharz and later, we became good friends. He was a Gomel "old-timer," having already spent over three months there and working as a weaver at a Gomel cooperative, Gomtextil. "You don't have a job yet? No problem, you can start tomorrow at the same Gomtextil. "But I am no weaver, I have no idea about the work," Gabriel objected. But his newfound pal would just say, "Don't you worry, I'll teach you, and you'll be a weaver in no time." The next day Gabriel was hired by Gomtextil; they needed weavers badly, and after three days of instruction, he started working there full-time, servicing first one and then two huge mechanical weaving machines.

60 The kolkhoz, or collective farm, was a regular feature across the USSR. Those who lived and worked on these large agricultural installations were known as *kolkhozniki* in Russian, here rendered with a more familiar English-language plural.

A Dashing NKVD Officer

Having solved our two main problems—a place to stay and a job—obtaining a residency permit seemed easy. But this was not so. Why did you come here, where from, what for, and go back to where you came from, or we will just send you back, and so on, with seemingly no end to it. It was frustrating, humiliating, and simply scary, but after the initial uncertainty, we finally got the word, "Yes, you may stay in Gomel." A young, dashing officer in an NKVD uniform, embellished with blue stripes, came out to the antechamber of the office where we were waiting to confirm the good news, or perhaps just to have a professional peek at us.

The infamous institution that was taking care of the country's unruly citizens, or those considered as such by the state and ruled over the innumerable concentration camps and prisons, was also taking care of welfare as well as the cultural needs of the citizens of the Soviet Union. "We will take you to an orphanage," the handsome officer said to me with a friendly smile, evidently taking me for a minor. "An orphanage? Why? Thanks, but no, I am with him," I answered sheepishly, indicating to Gabriel who was standing nearby as if I were in his custody. The NKVD man did not need to take him to his orphanage, so he let us both be.

My First Job in Gomel

Soon, I too got a job. On somebody's advice, I went to the local newspaper's offices asking for information and was directed from there to the headquarters of the Gomel Telephone Company. They needed a typist urgently. "Just go there," I was told, and I did, and indeed, I was accepted right away. It was a super elegant place, with large rooms, and red carpets in the long hallways, all very quiet and dignified. But I was not yet a competent typist. No matter how hard I tried, there was no way to cover up my still limited knowledge of the language. After a week on trial, I was refused the job. It was not unexpected, but painful, nevertheless.

My Second Job

However, very soon after, I got another job. What a joy that the plague of unemployment was unknown there! My next job, by strange coincidence, was with the office of Gomtextil, the same place that Gabriel had started to work at less than two weeks before. Here, on the job, I learned my skills and the language. I recall that Gomtextil *kantora* (office), with a special sentiment, not only because there I learned to stand on my own feet in that new country, but also, if not first of all, because of the people I met there.

Having overcome the first hurdles, it turned out that settling in Gomel was not so very difficult. As soon as we were registered as residents, we started receiving our bread rations. There was no official bread rationing in the Soviet Union at that time, but there was a war going on, the Soviet–Finnish War.[61] The mighty Soviet Union got into some trouble fighting the tiny nation of Finland, and the war that was supposed to be won in no time became a prolonged and painful one. The perennial shortages became acute, and bread was limited; to receive it, we as residents of Sadovaya Street, were registered at a neighborhood bread store. Each morning, I would stop at the store to pick up our daily bread ration. The saleswoman would mark my name on her list and hand me the portion of bread with a smile. The smile was a bonus because I was new and had come from far away, from a different world, from abroad.

Eighty Rubles a Month Rents You a Room

Luck was on our side. Soon, we also found a room, a whole room for only ourselves. An elderly Jewish couple, owners of a small house on that same Sadovaya Street, offered it to us to rent for eighty rubles per month. This was a lot, but again, we had already learned that it was not so important how much it cost, the important thing was to "get it." It

61 The Soviet–Finnish War, also known as the Winter War, lasted from November 1939 to March 1940.

was a very tiny room, 5 square meters at the most, sparsely furnished with a narrow iron bed, a tiny table, and two stools, but did we need more? Our landlords, the Maneviches, trusted us and agreed to wait for the rent until we received our first wages, and since we had already started working, it would not be very long.

My Jacket Fetched Eighty Rubles on the Black Market

For now, however, we ran out of money, not a kopeck was left. We would sell something to tide us over to the first payday, but what? After giving it some thought, the decision was made to sell my jacket. It was a nice one from Belgium, a prewar gift from my sister Rachel, made of soft woolen fabric, a warm brown color with a delicate golden thread running through it here and there. Gabriel was upset and somehow ashamed by all this, but there was nothing we could do; this was the only thing we could spare.

Reluctantly, he went to the *tolkuchka,*[62] the Soviet marketplace, the last vestige of a free market. It was a crowded place, with a lot of pushing and shoving and haggling going on there, hence the name (*tolkat* means to push). People would bring whatever they wished to sell, ask the price they wished to get, and the customer would buy or not—it was all supply and demand. And since the demand was usually much higher than the supply, it was easy to sell anything. My jacket fetched eighty rubles. Now, we would survive till payday, dining on bread with Sitro, a soft drink popular in the Soviet Union at the time, a sweet and bubbly kind of lemonade—what a luxury!

62 Also called the *tolchok*, these semi-tolerated black markets existed in most Soviet cities, allowing people to sell, buy, and trade goods. They were especially important for refugees, who could exchange their valuable Western products for necessities.

How the Steel Was Tempered

Once we had settled with jobs that were not too demanding on us and a room for ourselves, life started to look much better. And then, I got sick. After a few days of high fever, I felt utterly exhausted, the malnutrition and all I went through during those months since I had left home, had gotten to me. Laid up in bed, unable to raise my head from the pillow, I had seemingly only one need—to cry, and cry I did, drifting in and out of sleep, crying.

After a while, still shaky on my feet, but with the fever gone, I found consolation in a book, the first book I read from beginning to end, in Russian. It was the only one my landlady had in her home, and it was called *Kak zakalialas stal* (*How the Steel Was Tempered*) by Ostrovsky, then a popular Soviet writer.[63] What a heroic tale this was! The young *komsomoltsy*[64] and their leader, the ruthless Pavel Korchagin, who was as tough on himself as he was on others, worked under incredible, inhumane conditions, fighting the elements that seemed to have all been set against them, building a railroad through a wasteland, to bring industrialization and Socialism to some faraway territories. Sacrificing their health and sometimes their lives for the cause, they worked with enthusiasm that was perhaps supposed to make a weakling like me feel ashamed.

But it did not, perhaps because, strangely enough, reading that book, or rather fighting through the foreign language of the text, I was overcome by the exhilarating feeling of having achieved something very important on my own, conquering, I might say, the Russian language, and I was overjoyed by it. While digging through that cruel yet engrossing tale, I got the feel for the language. Henceforth, I was able to read this language like my own. The book opened the door for me to read and enjoy better things later, to become acquainted and fall in love with the great, rich Russian nineteenth-century literature.

63 Nikolai Ostrovsky's *How the Steel Was Tempered* (1934) was a bestseller in the Soviet Union.

64 The Komsomol was the youth movement of the Communist Party. Membership was coveted and members (*komsomoltsy*) received respect.

Learning a Foreign Language

There was also another immediate outcome. Seemingly overnight I became fluent in Russian; I could not only speak it, but also write it, and I started feeling evermore confident in my job. When I returned to work after about two weeks, people noticed that I had almost lost my Polish accent. It was as if it came to me suddenly, but in reality, it was a result of steady hard work and constant mental effort. I was well aware that I was not sufficiently prepared for the job to which I so stubbornly tried to hold on. And I paid for this with exhaustion which brought me down with the illness.

I was happy to return to my job in the Gomtextil office after two weeks of absence. Now, I got to know the people and my coworkers better. My boss, Evsey Borisovitch, was the chief accountant, a kind man, who always had time to answer my questions and who never reproached me for making a mistake. He also made sure that the help the government officially provided new refugees with was available to us, and unexpectedly, we received much-needed, warm, cotton-stuffed blankets and warm felt boots, Russian *valenki.* We did not know how to use these, and they were just wasted on us. Later, when I came back to the Urals where such felt boots were very much needed, I remembered them with nostalgia. But the cotton blankets were a real lifesaving gift.

The Gomtextil Office

The rest of the personnel of the office were women, all Jewish. There was Ms. Stolberg, a friendly, cheerful, still young, good-looking, and well-built former pilot and parachute jumper turned accountant, in charge of the cooperative's payroll. We got our money from her, I was told. She would just laugh it off when others were trying to impress me with stories of her heroic past. And was I impressed!

Her desk was to the left of that of the chief accountant's desk, and on his right was the desk of Mrs. Kazhdan, a middle-aged, evidently well-educated, serious woman, a mother of two teenage sons. There was a certain air of mystery around her, and the whispers and allusions about her past, which would occasionally slip from her office colleagues' lips in small bits and pieces, added to that air. Little by little, I got to know that she and her husband were once high Soviet officials holding responsible positions in the Soviet Far East, but that they had lost their positions during the purges of 1936–1937, and that Mrs. Kazhdan's husband was arrested and most probably shot. After that tragic turn of events, she and her children moved away from there in a kind of self-imposed exile as far as she could get, took an inconspicuous job at the least important place as "our" Gomtextil was, and that this possibly saved her from sharing her husband's fate, and allowed her to keep her two young sons. Mrs. Kazhdan was the first person with a biography that, as I realized only later, became rather common in the Soviet Union from the 1930s onward: a single woman, with a child or two, her husband arrested or executed as an "enemy of the people," a class of people, the political, cultural elite that made up postrevolutionary Russia, beaten and decimated by Stalin's "Great Terror."

In the far corner of the office was the table of another woman, Sima, skinny, swarthy, a lonely, single woman, a proverbial spinster, one might say. Yet, she too had a smile for me, and when I mentioned that I intended to enroll in high school night classes in the coming school year, she started coaching me in algebra. She would bring me some algebraic formulas, with explanations and exercises to work on almost daily.

The fourth woman, also the accountant's helper, I remember less. She was older, a very neat woman, her hair always properly coiffed, her blouses always embellished with some handmade lace collar. She clearly remembered better times, the times before the revolution, and she tended to keep to herself.

They were all interested in my Polish background, in life abroad, even if Poland did not seem to be a truly foreign country to them; it was not Western Europe, after all. There was even a Russian saying, "*kuritsa ne ptitsa, Polsha ne zagranitsa*" (A chicken is not a bird, Poland is not abroad), which whenever it was mentioned in my presence, always came with the disclaimer "no offense meant." Yet, they wanted to know about the war, the Germans, and particularly their treatment of the Jews. This, however, was rather a taboo subject, for now, Germany was an ally, and whatever anybody was thinking of that unexpected, strange, and frightful alliance, this was not something to talk about in public. Neither were other subjects, even if they were only remotely connected to politics.

One Does Not Talk Politics in Public

It took me some time to get used to that Soviet code of behavior. One day, I came across a small note in *Pravda* about Trotsky's death. To me, it was a very interesting piece of news, and on arriving at work, I shared it with my coworkers right away. "Trotsky died, killed in Mexico," I announced, wondering how and by whom, and why, clearly showing that the news had stirred up some emotions in me. The answer to my announcement was dead silence. No head turned or rose. Only after quite a few moments, and I can still see myself standing there, surprised by that lack of response, Mrs. Kazdan said, just so into thin air, not addressing it to anybody in particular, "To a dog, a dog's death."[65] Why such a harsh statement? I wondered, not daring, however, to say anything more aloud. Could it be that her husband was accused of Trotskyism, the most horrible "sin of the day," and was shot for it? Was this why she felt compelled to react to my piece of news broached in public?

Sometime later, perhaps even a few weeks later, I was walking with her after work on the way home, and while we were talking about unimportant things, she suddenly said, without any preamble, "You know, Hannushka,[66] I once knew a girl, a lovely young girl, very idealistic, she came to us from France and was working for the Comintern. She was arrested, for spying or something. I hope she was innocent though, and she'll be able someday to return to her France again," but from the tone of her voice, it was clear that she didn't believe this would ever happen. What was it? A warning? Was she telling me that politics is a dangerous business and that even a mere interest in

65 In Russian, "*Sobake—sobach'ya smert.*" This is a common Russian proverb.

66 Gannushka in the original. Russian does not have a letter H and it is often replaced by a G. The "shka" at the end is a form of endearment.

politics might not be good for you? I had not been thinking in those terms then, but her tragic little story, though I later heard and read about innumerable equally tragic and horrible ones, stuck in my mind and has remained with me ever since.

The City of Gomel

The first summer in the Soviet Union, in Gomel of 1940, was for us mostly a time of hard work. Especially for Gabriel who would put in many overtime hours to make up for the lack of experience in his new job, as well as for the additional money. Nevertheless, we also found some time to look around, to get to know the place where fate had so unexpectedly brought us. Gomel was a medium-sized Belarusian city, second only to Minsk, the capital. In a way, we could have also laid some claims to Gomel as our ancestral city, because Gabriel's father had some Gomel connection: either he had lived there for some time before World War I, or his father before him had, though there is no way of knowing this exactly. Poland, as a country, also had some claims on Gomel, as it had once occupied the city, as well as a big chunk of what became Belarus.

As I remember it, and I spent over a year there, Gomel was a clean, sleepy town. The main streets Sovyetskaya and Komsomolskaya, which ran perpendicularly to each other, were long thoroughfares with very little traffic and just a few stores which for the most part, stood empty, with no wares, no customers. With the situation slowly improving after the successful end of the war with Finland, the distribution of goods also improved, and at the big food store on Sovyetskaya, I would sometimes buy meat patties that were advertised as beef, but judging by their excessively red color, were probably horse meat. They tasted good, though, and were affordable. There was some industry in the city, mostly textile, and one larger textile mill was named in honor of March 8, International Women's Day. Salek Epstein, Gabriel's schoolmate from Łódź, whom we met in Gomel, worked there, and Dora's brother Berl had also found a job there. But most of the businesses were small cooperatives, like Gomtextil, various food processing places, and such.

The Sozh River Flowed through Gomel

The Sozh River that flowed through the city added flavor to it, and the beautiful park on the high bank of the river was a place for rest, play, and meditation. Here, on the shore of the Sozh, Lazik Roitschwantz contemplated life, and twiddling the scarce growth on his chin, decided to leave his native town and country and find a way abroad. By the strength of Ehrenberg's imagination, Gomel was for me, first of all, Lazik's city, and sometimes I would catch myself looking around as if expecting to find his characters: the high-bosomed Fenusya Gershanovich, whom Lazik was in love with; the old *moil* who in his days performed circumcision on so many male Jewish children, and what a waste this was! They grew up to become high Communist officials and turned away from Jewishness! And, of course, citizen Puke, the zealous, vigilant woman, Lazik's fanatical nemesis, who brought upon him countless troubles just because he had the bad fortune to sigh at a moment when sighing was not, according to her, appropriate, and she interpreted the inadvertent sound as being politically incorrect. Sometimes, it would seem to me that I was seeing them all around, perhaps because Gomel was over 40 percent Jewish. Only in the fall of 1940, when I enrolled in the Evening High School for Young Workers, leaving Gomtextil for the *Oblono* (*Oblastnoye Otdelenye Narodnogo Prosveshchenya*), the Regional Office of Education, in a way a parallel to boards of education in the U.S., did I get in touch daily, with more of the non-Jewish population of Gomel.

A Letter from the Łódź Ghetto

When I look back at those first months of my life in Gomel, the enormous mass of impressions, the emotions of setting up "a household," of working a full-time job, of getting used to new surroundings, and new people, it makes for a rather blurred picture. In addition, I see all this as if on a small screen on the background of a larger one, something like the picture-in-picture feature some TV sets now have built in. On the larger picture is the war, the German invasion, and events of the recent past—our leaving Łódź, saying goodbye to my parents and sisters. How are they now? What do they do, and what do they live on? How do they live there now? Under that terrible fear? The German occupiers? And what does it mean to live in a ghetto? It was all hard to imagine and painful to think about.

There were no letters while we were on the move, but now, having a permanent address, we began to receive letters from home. My parents were startled and frightened by my move from the faraway Urals to a part of the Soviet Union so much closer to home. The news that some of those who had found refuge in the Soviet Union intended to return or were even actually seeking ways to return to the occupied country was much talked about in the ghetto, as I understood later on from reading memoirs of survivors. My father must have heard such talk, and my change of address alarmed him. He was afraid that I too might think about returning home and he warned, almost begged me not to do so. "Stay where you are, do not come home now, this is not the time for it," he wrote.

I still have this postcard in my memory. I remember the way he embellished the capital letters. Somehow, this made the warmth of my father's love almost tangible. The warning had also conveyed, without dwelling much on it, how horrible the situation was over there. Despite all we had gone through during the last few months since leaving home, neither Gabriel nor I were thinking about looking for a way to return to Łódź. We did not harbor any such thoughts, knowing quite well that there would be no return. Nevertheless, my father's warning meant a lot to me; it was encouraging endurance and patience.

Dark, and Still Darker Clouds on the Horizon

The papers in the Soviet Union seemed to almost totally disregard what was going on beyond the borders, in the "near abroad," in the Polish territories occupied by the Germans, and one would not learn much about the setting up of the ghettos in what was contemptuously called "former Poland," or "*Panskaia Polsza*" (Polish Lords' Poland). We had to rely on letters from our families. This was the source from which I learned that at the beginning of January 1940, barely two months after I had left, the Jewish population of Łódź was concentrated within a small and poverty-stricken part of the city, and walled in. And, as in any disaster, one can find something positive perforce to be consoled with, so here, too, some consolation could have been derived from the fact that since our family had always lived, almost as if by birthright, in that poor part of the city, my parents did not have to move out of their place to somewhere still considerably worse, and go through the trauma of forced deportation. For the better-off population of Łódź, to move into the squalid slums of Bałuty, where the ghetto was mostly concentrated, added considerable hardship to the catastrophic situation.

Of all my close relatives, only my sister Sala was forced to move out of her place, because through her street, Oblegorska, also a place of very poor dwellings, the Germans had decided to run the ghetto's border, dividing it from the "Aryan" side, and thus Oblegorska had to be rendered "free of Jews," too. Yet the letters from home were restrained, no details were given about their life and no answers to my specific questions. Were they wary of the censorship established in the ghetto?

Gabriel's mother's letters were also very brief, yet full of love for her eldest son. In very few words, she told him the wrenching story of her lonely fight to survive with her two boys, without her husband. Gabriel's father did not manage to return to Łódź, and remained somewhere around Komarów, far from Łódź, but in places he was somehow familiar with. He had grown up in Komarów, and at that time, his mother was still living there. He was, as Gabriel's mother wrote, in a German forced labor camp for some time, but when he was let go, he was still not able to reach her and the children in the Łódź ghetto. The letters did not say why. One could only surmise that this was because traveling for a Jew was out of the question, or because the ghetto was walled in and tightly guarded, and there was no way of getting in or out.

By the autumn of 1940, although our personal situation in Gomel was improving and life for us was becoming easier, we felt hopeless about the general situation. This was the year of the greatest German military successes. By then, they had conquered almost all of Europe, France had fallen, Belgium, where my sister Rachel with her family and my aunt with her husband and child lived, was also overrun.

It seemed that the Germans were invincible. Who would stop them? Is there such a force in the whole world? I believed that the Soviet Union, the "natural enemy" of the Nazis would do it someday, but as it turned out, they were not enemies anymore: Stalin had a pact with Hitler, and there was nothing but dark clouds on the horizon.

Evening School for Working Youth

In September, Gabriel and I started attending the Evening School for Working Youth. Looking back to those faraway years of our youth, I am still wondering where we got the energy for all this. The school's schedule was a tough one with four or even five times a week of regular classes, from seven P.M. until ten P.M., not to count homework. And a full-time job plus household chores, and everything else! Gabriel was working three shifts, but when he started attending school, he was relieved from the second, the afternoon shift, and after the night classes he would go directly to his night shift. Yet, attending school was for us both, something of the utmost importance, as if the world would depend on it. I would like to understand the nature of our motivation, what was it?

A month or two later, I changed jobs. I left the office and started working as a typist at the regional school board. As Gomel did not have a developed public transportation system, to get to work at the office, I had to walk there and back every day on foot, and this would take a big chunk of time from my busy—and now much-busier—daily schedule. As I remember, there were only two buses there, one running along the main street, Sovyetskaya, and the other, along Komsomolskaya, and neither could take me to work. I did not consider the daily walk a hardship, I rather liked it, but it was time-consuming. The new job was located closer to our place on Sadovaya Street and a short distance from the school, and this added some two hours to my day. As much as I liked to work at the office, with the friendly people who were always so helpful to me, I had to say goodbye to them.

I left the office grateful for the start it had given me, and for what I was able to learn there. I felt more confident now and passing the examination, based on which I was hired at the new workplace, was no problem.

My New Job

The regional school board differed greatly from Gomtextil. It was, one might say, a cultural institution and an important office, the importance of which was underlined by its location in the center of the city. Another indication of its importance was the large office space for the director and his deputy and separate rooms for the many school inspectors, as well as the large administration office where an older gray-haired and very strict Russian lady bossed over me and another middle-aged typist. There was more typing here than at my previous job, and the material, pertaining to education, school programs, and so on, was interesting. Also, I got a pay rise which I felt was well deserved, and was proud of. I remained with the school board until the time came for evacuation in July 1941. The Germans were by then already pretty close to Gomel and the city's authorities appealed to the population to move east, deeper into the vast territories of the Soviet Union.

Hanna working as a typist at the *Oblono* in Gomel, 1940.

By a strange whim of memory, I can recall the last name of the school board's director, whom I saw perhaps only once. He was Mr., or rather Comrade Dayneka, a slightly built, middle-aged, and rather soft-spoken man. As for the inspectors, I recall some of them, but I have forgotten their names. Most were men, and only two inspectors were women: Tosya (unfortunately I don't remember her last name), and the other, a very Semitic-looking, large woman, a party activist, whose name has also escaped me. There was, of course, an understandable distance between a young typist and the high-positioned inspectors. Yet I was a young girl, and not a bad-looking one, and they all treated me in a very friendly way.

Once, one of the inspectors gave me some lyrical poetry to read, wanting to know how I liked it. I did not know if he had penned the poems himself, but it was wasted on me, anyway. At that time, I would still rather admire poetry about "The Cause," poetry with "meaning," and would consider anything else as "too sentimental." I was callous enough, and perhaps conceited enough, to voice my opinion. The inspector was disappointed and there were no more poems for me. One day, another of the inspectors took my picture while I was sitting at my old Underwood, typing. The photo came out quite well and I was very happy to have it. He was kind to give me two prints of it and I sent one home, to my parents, to Łódź. They acknowledged receiving it and were elated for me.

Tosya

One of the women inspectors, young, lovely Tosya, became my friend. She had graduated quite recently from a pedagogical institute, and this was her first job. Tosya worked on the methods of teaching reading to first-graders, and I often typed her material. Sometimes she would dictate it to me, and then she would lean over me closely, as if telling me secrets, and sometimes she would indeed, in the middle of dictating, switch to share with me her latest secret thoughts, mostly about love and passion. She had married right after graduating from college, and her husband, a young army lieutenant stationed near Gomel, would visit her at weekends. On Mondays Tosya's red lips would be more swollen than usual, and she would be sure to share with me some of her feelings, with a shy smile, one married woman to another.

I was not used to being intimate in such a way with anybody, and sometimes felt embarrassed, which I tried hard to hide, but as she seemed not to notice the embarrassment, she didn't pay any attention to my certainly awkward attempts to hide it either. Before I left Gomel, Tosya gave me the address of her parents who lived in Nizhny Novgorod. Gabriel and I used the address as a mailbox through which we would be able to reestablish contact, after we became separated because he was drafted into the army, and I evacuated from Gomel. I liked Tosya very much and she could have become a dear, close friend. I hope she and her lieutenant survived the war and lived a happy life together ever after, but I never heard from her again

As Spring Should Always Be

The year Gabriel and I spent in Gomel was our best war year. We adapted to life in the new country, we were working, our earnings were sufficient for our needs, and we started attending evening high school classes. It seemed that there was even some future ahead of us. The park on the Sohz River was beautiful, and the spring of 1941 was almost as spring should always be. On a Sunday afternoon, even we who were always so busy were able to find some time to go for a walk and sit on the bank of the Sohz River and enjoy its beauty. Lazik Roitschwantz was sitting there once! The thought made us laugh, and recalling his adventures, we would now tend to dwell rather on the funny than the tragic side of his exploits.

The Year of Soviet–German "Friendship"

Around the middle of 1940, many new refugees arrived in Gomel. They were people, who, after having ended their first year in the far-off places of the Soviet Union, the Urals, Siberia, and others, were wandering around the vast country looking for a place where they hoped to find less harsh living conditions, a more livable climate. Others, having given up hope of bringing over their families left behind forever, as it seemed by then, wanted to return to what used to be their homes, and many of them had registered with the Soviet authorities to go back to German-occupied Poland.

The German–Soviet "friendship" of the day was allowing for population exchanges. Rumors—we had heard them too—had spread that the Soviets were delivering even some German Communists who lived in the Soviet Union into German hands, arrested during the last purges (1937–1938), and that the exchange took place over the border at the Bug River. To our then-disbelieving ears, this sounded like horrible lies, but later, it all proved to be true.

Among those registered to return was also Gabriel's half-brother, Jakub. Having lost hope of ever being able to bring his wife and baby girl from Łódź over to the Soviet Union, he had left the mine after having finished a year of work there and went to Białystok, where he registered with the Soviet authorities to return to Łódź. Poor Jakub, he was in such a hurry to get home as fast as possible that he did not even stop in Gomel to meet with us. He waited in Białystok for a few months to be sent off to the other side, but this was all in vain. One day, the would-be returnees were rounded up by the Soviet authorities and sent off to a different destination. Instead of going to Poland, they were transported to Siberia.[67] As fate willed it, Jakub survived the war there, while his wife and child perished in the ghetto or one of the numerous German death camps.

Approximately at the same time, my brother, Mayer, with his wife, Dora, also came from the Urals and settled in Gomel. They had a tiny baby girl, born quite recently, and I was happy to see them all. They could not settle in Gomel, and had settled in a small town, Rechitsa, along the Sozh River, not very far from Gomel. The only drawback was that Rechitsa could only be reached from Gomel by an antique steamship and that the ride took at least two hours each way. Dora's two

67 Most of the Polish–Jewish refugees who had signed up for repatriation were deported in June 1940.

brothers, Abram and Berl, had followed them, and they came a bit later, too. They settled in Gomel.

Twisted Lives

Our tiny room was constantly invaded now by people returning from the faraway places in the Urals and even farther, and seeking, as we did before, a place to stay. We tried to help, and fortunately, we were able to do so, at least to a certain degree. Acquaintances or total strangers passing by and in need of an overnight stay, refugees in need of some help, advice, or some food, knocked on the door of our tiny room. Kindly, our landlords, the Maneviches, did not protest about the traffic on their doorstep.

I must mention some of these people with whom we came into contact then: a young man, I don't remember his name, a funny guy with a sad face, making up one-liners just in passing, "What kind of a country is this," he would say, critical of life around him, where *kak* ("shit" in Polish means "how" in Russian) is a word, and a pair of shoelaces is an outfit?" (This is because shoelaces were sold at men's clothing stores and were often the only article available there). He did not survive the war.

There was a young girl, pretty, cheerful Rywcia, whom I knew from the last peacetime vacation, which I had spent with my sister-in-law in the village. It was only one year earlier, though it seemed as if a lifetime had passed since then. Rywcia stayed with us while waiting for a pass to go to a town in the former Polish territory, now under Soviet occupation, to join her fiancé there. She got her pass three days before the German invasion began, and left happy, her dream was going to come true. Instead, she got caught up in the war and perished.

There was also Mr. Kunitz, a man in his forties, educated, and cultured, who came to Gomel to look for a position as a teacher of German. Later, in the Urals, I met his family. I was told that in his letters to them he had described us, his Gomel hosts, as a "very young couple who often quarreled about their school copybooks." It was true, we did quarrel about the notebooks, Gabriel always complaining that I had again taken his, and right he was! Mr. Kunitz got his teaching position in a small town not very far from Gomel but was swept away by the war, killed by the Germans, if not shot still before the war had begun by the vigilant NKVD on suspicion of being a German "spy," just because he knew German.

A Food Parcel to the Łódź Ghetto

During that year of the German–Soviet "friendship," it became possible to send food parcels to the Łódź ghetto. We received mail from our families more regularly now and were allowed to send one parcel per month, its weight limited to 8 kilograms. Our pitiful gift of barley, sugar, and soap was, however, extremely important to them. Those parcels, as I read after the war in the already mentioned *Chronicle of the Łódź Ghetto*, had a positive "impact on the economic life in the ghetto."

One day, my sister Sala wrote to me, asking for a parcel for herself, similar to the one that I had sent to my parents. I had received only one letter from her, an open postcard, and I can still see it in my mind. Her baby son had died shortly after he was born, a healthy baby, beautiful "like a cherry," she wrote, and my heart ached for her and her child. That she asked me for help, the sister that was always helping me, caring for me, the sister I looked up to, threw me into despair. I could not forgive myself that I did not think about it myself. "Don't cry," Gabriel consoled me, "put together a parcel, we'll send it in a few days, somehow." A few days later Germany invaded the Soviet Union, and the new war, or the new phase of the war that began in 1939, was upon us.

War Again

War had been in the air for some time now, especially since the beginning of spring. People were talking about the war all the time, and military units were passing through the city day and night; tanks and heavy military equipment rolled through the city's streets going west in the direction of the German–Soviet border, yet war, nevertheless, came suddenly and unexpectedly.

June 22, 1941. Sunday morning. Gabriel, back from his night shift, was getting ready to go to sleep, while I was off to the kolkhoz market for some sour cream and cottage cheese, as usual on a Sunday morning. Yet, this time something was different in the market, there was something in the air, some nervousness, absentmindedness; people seemed to pay little attention to the normally celebrated acts of selling and buying.

War? I was stunned and ran home as soon as I could. Gabriel was already on his feet and busy tearing his passport to pieces. It was a so-called Nansen passport, issued under the auspices of the League of Nations, which he had received in Poland on his eighteenth birthday, like all stateless persons who resided in Poland. This was, for reasons difficult to understand, the status his father had had in Poland; he did not have citizenship, despite being born in Polish territory and living there all his life. Gabriel inherited that status.

A Polish passport, Gabriel decided, was bad enough under the changed circumstances, and this strange document may become a real threat in case it needed to be explained to the Soviet authorities. And since there had been some arrests shortly before the outbreak of the German–Soviet hostilities, especially among the refugees, a "preventive measure" by the NKVD, more such measures could be expected and it was better to be on the safe side. With this in his mind, Gabriel destroyed that unfortunate document.

There was no need for explanation, I understood without words what he was doing and why. There was war, and we were strangers in this strange land and, as such, subject to suspicion, even more so than its "regular" inhabitants, the native population, all watched by the always vigilant state security forces.

We listened to Molotov's speech;[68] there was no doubt it was true that Germany had attacked the Soviet Union, all pacts notwithstanding,

68 On the day of the German invasion of the USSR, June 22, 1941, Foreign Minister Vyacheslav Molotov (1889–1986) delivered a speech on Soviet radio. For those not near the western border, this was the first news of the war.

but still, it was unbelievable. What will it bring, how will it go, and what will now happen to our people in the ghetto in Łódź? What will the Germans do to them now? Will I ever see my parents, and my sisters again? Suddenly, a feeling of panic seized me, a fear so strong, so overwhelming that it almost brought me down. Despite all the lessons life had already taught me, or perhaps because of them, I knew that any bad situation could always still get worse, and I was expecting it.

Yet on the surface, at least for a while, life went on as if nothing had happened. I would go to work as usual, people talked about the war, of course, and listened intently to the loudspeakers, but nobody had been drafted yet, and the war still seemed to be rather far away. A national guard was organized, and workers at the factories were issued rifles. Gabriel brought one home and I looked at it almost with hatred. What would we do with that outdated, 100-year-old specimen of military equipment that belonged in a museum? Would we fight the Germans with it? I still had the German tanks in my mind, as they rolled into Poland, conquering the country in such a short time.

No matter how veiled the news coming from the loudspeakers was, it soon became clear that the Germans were advancing very fast, that they had already crossed the old Soviet border; that Minsk, the capital of Belarus, some 100 kilometers from Gomel, had also already been taken. Everybody, it seemed, started talking about evacuation. Some larger factories with their machinery, personnel, and families, had already evacuated. Some offices were also leaving town. Some of the inspectors at the school board left, the Jewish female inspector vanished one day, and little by little so did others. Our bosses who were still there told us that everybody was free to evacuate, and that there was no need to show up to work as usual.

"Death to Jews and Communists"

One morning, while still at work and sitting at my typewriter, I heard some strange noises coming from the street and ran to the window to see what was going on, as did others in the room. A man was running in the street, waving a jacket—or was it another piece of his garment?—

as if it were a flag, and yelling with all his might, "*Smert' Zhidam*[69] *i komunistam!*" (Death to Jews and Communists!). He was clearly drunk. After having bumped into a newspaper stand serviced by an elderly Jew, accidentally or on purpose, he overturned it, but got caught up in the smashed kiosk, and fell to the ground. People, yelling and cursing, who had been chasing after him for a while, had now got to him. Two militiamen showed up, apprehended the "demonstrator" and put an end to the commotion. But what an ominous scene this was!

The war was only in its third week, but the Germans were already closing in on our area. Yet between them and Gomel were the Pripet Marshes, Gomel being situated on the Marshes' edge. The Germans were not interested in pushing through the treacherous terrain. They could afford to wait. They were already far beyond Gomel to the north as well as to the south and could certainly just close the ring at their convenience. The city authorities were appealing to the civilian population to leave, to go east, deeper into the Soviet Union. Freight trains were provided for the evacuation of women, children, and older men. People were free to board the trains. All that remained then to do, was to wait until the train was ready to move. Nobody knew when the train would start moving—it could take a day or a few days, or just a few hours. There was no schedule, but there was also no need to buy tickets. The trip was free.

Gabriel Is Drafted into the Soviet Army

Gabriel urged me to evacuate. He had to stay in Gomel, waiting for the draft summons: men eighteen to fifty years of age were not allowed to leave without permission of the Voyenkomat, the Military Authority. Leaving without it would make him a deserter. But he was afraid that I might somehow not manage to get out in time and find myself alone, trapped under German occupation. He made me promise that I would not waste time needlessly and go as soon as he left.

69 In Russian, this name for Jews is derogatory.

I would evacuate, of course, and I would not stay in the city a moment longer waiting for the Germans to take it over, but I also would not leave before he got his draft summons. It was July 10 when it came. It said to report to a military training camp in Orel, well over 320 kilometers from Gomel. There was no exact date set; all it said was to show up there at a "reasonable" time. Transportation was not available; the draftees were supposed to use their feet or whatever luck would provide them with along their way. What was a "reasonable time" under these circumstances? Better to leave right away, without delay.

On July 12, on a sunny afternoon, I went with Gabriel to see him off as he joined the army. The highway leading from Gomel to the East was crowded with people, but almost no vehicles were on the road; young and middle-aged men walking in small groups or alone, all going in the same direction, draftees on their way to their respective military training camps.

We walked in silence. There was nothing more to say. We were both aware that he was going to a war that was going to be long and horrible. Would we ever see each other again? Would we survive? At some point on that highway, we had to say goodbye to each other. Gabriel urged me to hurry back, it was getting late, and he wanted me to return safely, before dark, to what used to be our home. He would later catch a few hours of sleep, somewhere under a tree along the road, and then go on further.

It was time to part. There were no tears. We kissed. "You come back," I told him. He held me for a short time, nodded, as if in agreement, and went straight ahead, not turning around even once. I stood there, motionless, desolate at the roadside for a few more moments, watching him disappear, blending in with the others on the road moving in the same direction, and then I turned slowly back and continued my lonely return to the city.

CHAPTER SEVEN

EVACUATION

The state of panic that came over me with the beginning of the German–Soviet hostilities had somehow already subsided. The war was here, and whatever I would do next must proceed from that fact. Now, everything seemed to have become rather anticlimactic. There were things to do, and decisions to make, and I was the one to make them by myself—I was alone now. Do not dwell on what you cannot help, do not give in to self-pity, just do what you have to do, I told myself, though certainly not in so many words. The evacuation was now first on the day's agenda.

The next day, in the afternoon, my sister-in-law, Dora, came to Gomel with her baby girl, not yet three months old. We were going to evacuate together, and she needed my help. Berl, Dora's brother, brought them to my place from the small town, Rechitsa, up the River Sozh where they had lived since their return from the Urals. My brother, Dora's husband, had to stay behind. He, too, could not leave his home without the permission of the town's military authorities.

A young woman, Mania, also a Jewish refugee from Poland and an acquaintance of mine, joined Dora and me. She, too, had a baby, an infant boy, no more than ten days old. Mania was alone; her husband, whom I saw only fleetingly once or twice, was arrested a few days after the outbreak of the war. The Security Police had then swept the city, perhaps to prove vigilance in the face of the war that had just begun, and many of the refugees fell victim to it, and among them was Mania's husband. She had no idea where they were keeping him. A week later, when she went to the hospital to give birth, she still did not know anything about his whereabouts or fate. Now, with her tiny child in her arms and barely able to keep herself on her feet, she joined us for the evacuation.

Another woman joined us as well, a tall blonde woman called Estera. She too had a child, a toddler, and a boy just over a year old, but no husband. I did not know Estera before we started preparing for evacuation, nor did I know where her husband was, or if there was one at all. A quiet woman in her late twenties, preoccupied with her son, she, like the rest of us, was from Poland and wanted to join us, and this was good enough. I perhaps remember her well—it's strange how our memories work—because she had a little stroller for her boy and this stroller turned out to be of great help to all of us later on, when we finally arrived at our destination, northern Kazakhstan. We stuck together because after all, we were indeed strangers in a strange land—we had all come to the Soviet Union only a little over a year ago—after the German invasion of Poland in 1939 had brought us here, and now we had to flee from the Germans again. Though the natives were friendly and kind, we felt better among ourselves, speaking the same language, and we were glad to stay with "our own."

At the Train Station

We gathered at the train station. Berl, Dora's brother, helped us load our belongings on the train, and said goodbye to us. As much as he was worried about his sister and the baby, little Mirele, he could not join us since he had been ordered to stay in Gomel. Berl did not survive the war and we never found out where and when, and under what circumstances, he perished.

Since nobody knew when the train would start moving, we lingered outside our car in the warm July sun, chatting idly away our anxieties about the war and the trip into the unknown. Suddenly, Mania broke out sobbing and wailing, "My child, my child, oh, my God, my child!" She looked scared and confused, and what was coming through her sobbing was more of a whimper, a long, soft whine, than a shrill cry. Then, looking at us straight, her eyes bewildered but dry, she said in a strangely quiet voice, "He is dead. The child is dead." And suddenly, the unbelievable, unexpected fact became clear to all of us, her child had died! "How come? What happened?" Everybody wanted to know, astonished, numbed by the shocking, disturbing event, to say the least. Only a few days before, she and the child had been released from the hospital, and was not the child well then?

We looked helplessly at Mania and the tiny, still unnamed baby, with sorrow and compassion. There was no doctor at the station, and the now again sobbing Mania kept repeating, "He is dead, he is dead." What was there to do? A dead baby should be buried. But who would take care of it? Mania was unable to stand on her feet, the two other women had little children to care for—was I the one to whom that burden had to fall? We looked at each other, and somehow it seemed natural even to myself, or perhaps to myself more than to the others, that I had to take on the task, and I did, somehow automatically, half-raise my arms, because of course, the dead child had to be buried.

To Give a Dead Child a Proper Burial

Someone put the little body, wrapped in a diaper, on my half-outstretched forearms. A few drops of saliva, dribbling out of the dead baby's mouth, touched my bare skin. It made me shudder with disgust, mixed with fear. Was the baby dead? Definitely? Yes, the little body was stone still, the little face gray-bluish, and its features blurred as if seen through a thick layer of water. I did not know much about babies, there were none in the family when I was growing up. Once, I picked up a little child of a distant cousin for a few moments, and my dress got damp. The grimace on my face made the onlookers laugh, and this was the end of my knowledge on the subject.

I glanced once at the tiny face, enough perhaps to remember it forever. Someone mercifully covered it with the end of the diaper, and off I went. To give the dead baby a proper burial. Shocked into some mental numbness, I seemed to have but one thought in my head, an imperative, working like a drone, "Give the dead baby a proper burial." But where to go? For some reason, I decided to go to the nearest hospital, located about a half-an-hour walk from the station. However, there they refused to take the dead child from me. Hospitals, I was lectured by a very busy and impatient nurse, are not for dead children. We are here to help sick children, this one cannot be helped anymore, it is dead, she reprimanded me sternly. May I leave it in the morgue then, I tried timidly, and the nurse threw me an icy, quizzical look for an answer, and scowled, "What child? Whose child is it anyway?" And she angrily interrupted me when I started mumbling my explanation about "the woman at the train station who was going to evacuate…" "Go, bury it," she repeated. "This is not a cemetery, it's a hospital!"

My next stop was the police station, maybe the "friendly" militiaman would help, but they were busy evacuating their offices, too busy to pay any attention to me or my problem. Yet one of the men gave me, while running past me, the same advice, "Go to the cemetery." I had lived in Gomel for over a year but had no idea where the cemetery was. Perhaps it was on the other side of the city, and even if I had known where it was, how was I to get there, anyway? I had been wandering for a long time with my little "burden," this parcel on my still-outstretched forearms. I was getting tired myself, my arms were growing stiff, and numb. I felt at a loss, having no idea where to turn to for help next. How could I have been so irresponsible, taking on this strange mission, having no idea what I was getting into? I was now reproaching myself. Yet, all that time, the thought that this "burden" I had in my hands was not just a parcel that was getting somehow heavier and heavier, but that it was a dead child in need of being buried, would not leave me for a moment.

Frustrated, I sat down on a bench for a moment of rest. I was almost at the end of my wits. Should I return to the station, and bring the dead child back to Mania? What else could I do?

And in that instant, I suddenly decided to go to the tenement where Mania used to live, to her neighbors, maybe some of them were still there, and maybe someone would help. I knew the place; it was not too far from where I was and I knew it was inhabited mostly by Jews.

The unusually quiet, half-empty street, in an already half-dead city, with very few passersby on the normally busy streets, and the dead child in my arms—all this seemed so unreal, eerie, and scary. I hastened my steps. It was already growing dusky when I reached the place and the room of Mania's neighbor. I will never forget that middle-aged, poor Jewish woman in her small, dreary room, watching me with her sad, understanding eyes. "Mania's child...dead...put it down there, I will bury him tomorrow," she said, pointing to the end of a cot along the wall.

Only now, relieved of my burden, a thought that made me tremble, sprang to my mind: What have I been doing, running around with that dead child in my hands, having only one thought in mind, that it had to be buried? What about my train? Is it going to wait for me? What if it has already gone? What if it was the last train leaving this already half-besieged city?

And I started running as fast as I could. I ran back to the train station, praying that the train would still be there. While running, the sad eyes of the woman who had delivered me of my burden seemed to follow me, and another thought kept turning like a drill in my mind: Why was this woman staying here in this lost city? Why wasn't she also evacuating? Wasn't she afraid of the "death masters" that would take the city soon? Did she not know they would bring destruction, pain, and death? Only a year-and-a-half ago I ran from them for the first time, and now I was even more frightened of them than I was before. My previous experience had made me acutely aware of the danger that comes with them, and it had instilled in me some kind of instinct, a sixth sense, telling me, ordering me, "Run for your life!"

Fortunately, my train was still there. Mania was sleeping. I told my friends about the "qualified success" of my mission and soon fell asleep, too. It was a restless sleep. The unfamiliar look of the city, the angry nurse at the hospital, the sad eyes of the woman that promised to bury the dead child, and the thought, "where was Gabriel now, where was he sleeping?" made me toss on the train's hard bunk. In the middle of the night, the train suddenly jerked and started moving. Our evacuation had begun.

A Digression: Why Did This Baby Die?

I will have to move far ahead in time now to continue with the story of Mania's dead child. The episode at the Gomel train station kept coming back to me, and with time gone by, different aspects of the story have imposed themselves on my memory, demanding answers. Sometimes, I would have that disquieting, repetitive dream, which filled me with dread; kaleidoscopic bits and pieces of little children, dead or alive, broken-up fragments that would never form a whole, clear picture, a mishmash, a pair of attentive eyes, belonging to who knows who, a train rolling by. That past incident had made a much deeper impression on me than I was aware of in the beginning.

I recalled the story for the first time many years after the event while recounting my wartime experiences for the Shoah Foundation. The interviewer, a young, sympathetic woman, visibly taken by the drama of the story, asked me the question, "But why did the child die?" It took me rather by surprise. I never asked that question then; there was no doctor at the station, as I have mentioned, who would have certified the cause of death. The mother had said so, and "everybody" could see that the child was dead, and in my mind, there was not even a shadow of suspicion of "foul play" on the part of Mania, to use an expression from detective stories.

Well, this was then, half a century ago, but now, with all the experience of the Holocaust behind us, after having heard so many hair-raising Holocaust tales, I should perhaps be more critical, and analytical. Yet, I could still not bring myself to think about Mania in any way implicated in the death of her tiny child.

By now, it is part of history. The Germans were demanding "quotas" of children for deportation, which meant death, as a pay-off, a ransom for allowing the ghetto to exist a little bit longer. Warsaw's

Czerniaków committed suicide protesting that demand,[70] Rumkowski of the Łódź ghetto made such bargains with the Germans many times. Similarly, the ghetto mothers had "a choice" when deported with the children: a mother could abandon her child and this way prolong her own life for a while or share the child's fate. And it is a well-known, documented fact, that mothers were choosing death with their children rather than abandoning them, rather than sending them to a lonely, horrible death. These are heroic cases of sacrifice, telling the story of the modern-day Niobe, the Jewish mother in the Holocaust. On the other hand, tragic cases when children were sacrificed, killed, either for the "good" of a group of grown-ups, escaping and trying to hide from the Germans or, in an extreme, most tragic situation, by their parents, when this seemed to become the only "solution," are also known and documented.

All this was very unsettling, to say the least. The question "Why did this child die?" seemed rather innocent. How could it then suddenly become colored with such dark suspicions? This was unseemly, and now, I felt the need to share my story with others, the need to talk about it, and I would sometimes tell it to willing listeners, some of my friends. Their reactions varied.

One of them, reacting very emotionally to my wandering around the almost empty city, asked if I was aware of the danger to myself and added that she wished she would have been able to guide me and make me leave "my parcel" on the bench on which I had sat down for a moment, tired and despairing about my unfortunate mission. I knew what she wanted to say, but no, the thought had not crossed my mind, then.

Another one said that it was "really silly" of me to take "something like that" upon myself, that I could have been arrested, accused that the child was mine and that I had killed it. "Mania," she added, "was a bad woman, she knew that she was putting you in danger, yet let you go ahead with it." Well, I knew my friend was talking from the heart wanting the best for me, and that she had said what she said, only because she was scared for me.

70 Adam Czerniaków (1880–1942), chairman of the Warsaw ghetto Judenrat, committed suicide rather than oversee mass deportations from the ghetto.

Still another of my friends, a physician by profession, asked me another question, quite a creepy one, taking into consideration that such questioning could lead to an indictment. "Do you know," my friend asked, "that such a tiny baby, less than two weeks old, if not fed for a day, would of course cry, but not for long!" "And did Mania," she went on, "have enough food for the baby? Or for herself, for that matter?"

I have told and retold the story of this dead child many times. And the question "Why did this child die, was he sick?" has come back again and again. I used to answer that these were times when death was "having a ball," ghastly times and that the first victims were the very young and the very old. Children could not survive the deprivations, the lack of nourishment, lack of medical care. Little children were also dying because their parents were losing their battles, worn out by hard labor, hunger, and general circumstances that were rendering them helpless. So harsh was the lot that had befallen their parents, and first of all, their mothers! As I learned after the war, little Mirele, my niece, did not survive, did not live to be a year. Though she seemed to be a healthy child, some disease claimed her. And this is perhaps, in general, a sensible explanation, the only one I believe I can give, though my listeners did not always seem to be satisfied.

Sometimes, I would notice glances that told me that my story betrayed some naivete on my part. And I began wondering. I was and still am far from casting any suspicions, but while the story of the Holocaust is indeed rife with cases of ultimate sacrifice on the part of many mothers who deliberately and consciously chose death rather than abandoning their children, as the "death masters" demanded, also not uncommon were the horrible stories of sacrificing a little child when, for example, the safety of a larger group of people trapped in a hideout, could be jeopardized, betrayed by a baby's uncontrollable crying...

Now imagine a young mother, left alone, with no means of survival, her husband just arrested and put away, who knew where and for how long? The woman, escaping the war zone, leaving the city bound to fall to the Germans any day now, and going into the unknown? Here one does not need to even mention postpartum depression, the circumstances were sufficiently depressing, as they were. And indeed, was she able to breastfeed her baby? I do not know this; I do not remember her feeding it, anyway. And did she eat enough? And was she able, in her expected state of mind, to remember to breastfeed her baby? And what was this child to her, the unhappy, tragic mother? A gift of life? Or a terrible burden? Withholding food, what an "easy" way of getting rid of the "burden"!

I have no answer to any of these questions. I never even asked any of these questions then, they simply were not within the realm of my thinking. I would have had to be an entirely different person to have had these kinds of thoughts and I am not out to blame anybody or to cast suspicions now, either. But then, maybe, just maybe, if to scratch away at the story just a little further, one could uncover yet another layer under my little story, and a much more tragic, complicated story would emerge. Yet, as it is, the "case" is closed, and it will perhaps never be solved.

One More Digression

I tried to become friends with Mania. But despite the long journey from Gomel through Kazakhstan to the Urals that we made together, and the tragic story of her dead baby, there always remained some distance between us. We never talked about her dead baby, she never asked me any questions. Soon, she left the Urals. In the early autumn of 1941, the Soviet government had established contact with the Polish government-in-exile in London and had issued an "amnesty" for Poles held in Soviet camps and jails. Many thousands of such prisoners were set free, and Mania's husband was among them. He somehow managed to find her and she left to join him.

I never met Mania again, though our paths did cross again once, in a rather interesting way, if indirectly. But to tell this I must again jump to a different time and place, to a completely different world. The twists and turns of fate! Many years after the war, in a different time and it would seem a different life, I went with Gabriel to visit Israel and met Mania's husband there, who by then was not her husband anymore but the husband of Marysia, another friend of ours. They lived with their daughter in Jerusalem and we went to see them.

Marysia left Poland for Israel in 1956 and worked at the Israeli Ministry of Commerce. She got married in Israel, which I knew, but I had no idea who her husband was. Yet, as it turned out, we were not quite strangers. He recognized me at once. He said that he remembered me from Gomel. I could not recall having ever met him, especially in Gomel. I thought about this, but I couldn't recall it.

After dinner, while we were still sitting around the table reminiscing about the war times, as it is common when survivors of those times get together, Marysia's husband wanted to know what I did in Gomel, where I had lived, and so on, and all this was becoming a bit annoying. However, when he asked me how I got out of Gomel before the Germans took over the city, I realized, to my surprise, how clear the images of the evacuation from Gomel were still in my memory: my sister-in-law with her baby, Mirele, Mania, her dead child, the half-dead city, the train station, and the train ready to leave the city any moment leaving me behind, and I started talking about all this.

He listened attentively. "And who were the people you were evacuating with?" he prompted me on one occasion. "There was a woman with us whose child died at the train station, but this is a sad story I had better not tell it now," I replied. But he insisted, and I told him the story of the dead baby boy and how I had tried to find a way to give that child a proper burial. "And this woman, Mania, what happened to her later on?" he asked again. Surprised, I responded, "Mania, did I mention her name?" "No," he said, "there was no need; she was Mania, my former wife."

How dreadful! So, he was Mania's husband and I had unwittingly told the man the painful story of his own child! I was very sorry and apologized, but he said that there was no need for it. "This was so long ago," he said. Of course, he knew that the child had died, it was almost due when he was arrested, and he thought it had died right after birth in the hospital. He did not know the details, but they did not matter so much anymore as all this was so long ago. And after a moment, he added that the history of his marriage with Mania was a complicated one. She joined him during the war, but they parted later. She returned once again, only to leave him finally for good after they arrived in Israel.

Of course, how could I have forgotten? I had met this man, Mania's husband, in Łódź, after the war, he came to see me; he had a problem and came to ask for my help, he told me then. Mania, he told me, had left him after they had returned from the Soviet Union to Poland and he was adamant to get her back, would I talk with her, please, he knew I could influence her "for the good." Strange, I thought, another mission for Mania, but this time I flatly refused. I cannot meddle in such a thing, I said. What could I say to Mania? Now, I tried to remind him of the episode—how silly of me!—but he, in turn, refused to remember any of this. No, he said, we did not meet in Łódź, only in Gomel. Besides, he added, this is not important anymore, he had forgotten all this business with Mania long ago. Of course, I was not going to try to refresh his memory. He went into denial mode, perhaps for Marysia's sake, yet it was so obvious from all that strange talk at that dinner table that though he had been married to Marysia for about twenty-five years and had a daughter with her, a handsome soldier girl now home for a holiday vacation from the Israeli army, the memory of Mania was somehow still alive for him, that Mania did still matter to him.

The whole situation became awkward, and it was high time to change the subject. Yet I still would have liked to have known where Mania was and how she was doing but I could not bring myself to ask. And while I was still hesitating, ask or not to ask, our friend, Marysia, as if having guessed my state of mind, said, "Mania, if you want to know, married a *frume* here, an Orthodox Jew, a *Lubavitcher*[71] or something like that, and has had many children with him." "How many," I asked, not able to curb my curiosity, and she said, "At least four, from what I have heard." And this is all I have to add to my story about the "incident" at the train station in Gomel.

71 Lubavitcher refers to a follower of the Rebbe of the prominent Chabad-Lubavitch Hasidic dynasty. During the war this was Rabbi Yosef Yitzchak Schneerson, the sixth Rebbe of Lubavitch. He was succeeded in 1950 by Rabbi Menachem Mendel Schneerson, the seventh and last Rebbe of the dynasty, who grew Chabad into a worldwide movement.

From Gomel to Kazakhstan

Let me return to the story of the evacuation from Gomel. The entire trip lasted about two weeks and was rather uneventful. Only once was our train bombed, and not the train directly but the train station where we had stopped. Since the evacuation transports were not accorded priority moving rights, the train often languished for hours on the back rails, and the bombardment that the station came under did not do any harm to our train that was on hold for the moment, far enough from the target of the German planes. From that rather safe distance, we were even able to observe the havoc the German planes were playing on the station. I remember the image of a Russian woman that stood outside our car. With her arm outstretched accusingly towards the sky, her fist clenched, and with a loud cry, "Twenty-five years of pain and suffering, so much blood, so many victims, and now this, to boot!" she struck a very dramatic pose, fit for a poster or a sculpture, perhaps. She seemed to blame the sky that was so exceptionally blue during that nice summer day, or the force beyond it, for all that terrible suffering the Russian people had endured during the first three decades of our century: the war, the Revolution, the Civil War, and now "this," the German invasion, and war again.

Otherwise, the trip was, as I have already mentioned, rather uneventful. Certainly, it was not a tourist trip set on sightseeing, but overall, the conditions were not too harsh. I do not remember suffering from a lack of food, which means that it must have been rather sufficient. The sanitary conditions were much more difficult to endure. It was summer and a hot one. At longer stops, we would use the station's facilities to refresh ourselves, but since from one such stop to another, the train had to cover long stretches of open spaces and be in motion sometimes for a whole day, if not longer, we did not enjoy this luxury too often.

Longer stops were also used to socialize, meet fellow travelers from other cars, and share our thoughts about the trip, about life awaiting us in the unknown places to which the train was taking us, about the war, the invaders—how far they had already gone and how far they would go before the Soviet forces would push them back, and that they would eventually be pushed back, there seemed to be no doubt in my, or anybody else's, mind.

Where Do You Think They Are Taking Us?

The train was taking us farther and farther into the vast country, leaving behind the war, the enemy planes, and bombs falling from the skies. The train stations and the isolated settlements we were passing by were illuminated at night, the best sign to show how far away from the war and its darkened dwellings we were. Yet nobody had any idea where we were or where we were heading, or what our final destination was. Wherever the train would bring us, this would be it. Yet not everybody was so fatalistic. The younger evacuees were especially keen to take their fate into their own hands.

At one of the stops, I got into a chat with two Polish–Jewish refugee women traveling in the car next to ours. These young women, one of them in advanced pregnancy, were both firmly set to leave the train before it would arrive at its final, unknown destination. "They are taking us to some kolkhozes in the wilderness, what do you think, where are we going? And what will you do there? What will you do in a kolkhoz?" they asked me. They both eventually said goodbye to us when the train stopped in Kuibyshev, a large city on the right side of the Volga River. One of them had some friends or relatives there.

We, my "group," did not know anybody there or in any other place along the way, so we decided to go as far as the train would take us, and beyond the Volga River anyway. For some reason that was not clear to me then, and for which I have no explanation for now either, I was rather adamant not to get off the train before the Volga. Did I believe that the Germans would be able to push as far as the Volga, but not any farther?

One early afternoon, after about two weeks of almost constant motion, the train suddenly stopped, and we were told that we had arrived. We were in northern Kazakhstan at a small train station, the name of which has escaped me.

The first night was spent on makeshift bunks in a school turned into a temporary shelter for refugees. Early the next day, when I went outside the school, I saw the steppe in front of me, a sea-like, flat, open space, not interrupted as far as the horizon by even a single tree or house. The tiny Kazakh village was on the other side, behind the school. It was a new vista, a panorama like nothing I had ever seen before, strange and frightening but also at the same time wonderfully beautiful, unexpectedly and indefinably beautiful. Yes, I told myself, this must truly be the end of the world.

The Village in Kazakhstan

With my sister-in-law, Dora, we went to the village, just to look around and perhaps to get some warm water; she was dreaming of bathing the baby. The child had endured the deprivations of the trip wonderfully well, her mother miraculously had enough milk to feed her, and little Mirele, now in her third month, was able to keep her head up and sometimes smile at us when she was not sleeping. A pretty child she was going to be, I thought, looking at her clear features and touching her tiny, warm face. Sometimes I liked to carry her, to feel the warmth of her little body. Perhaps, it helped me push down the memory of that poor dead boy deeper into the subconscious. A bath was what this child needed very much.

The Kazakh woman in the first hut we entered asking for warm water, wondered, "Warm water?" Water in general was not a readily available commodity here, and warm water? A bath? For the child? "What strange things these newcomers are talking about!" the wide, thick-featured face of the Kazakh *khoziaika*[72] seemed to be saying.

72 Mistress of the house.

We Are Not Staying Here

It did not take us long to decide that we would not be staying there. Dora and I wanted to get to the place in the Ural Mountains where she and her husband had spent the first year of emigration. They had left only half a year earlier, looking for a less harsh place to live. Kamensk-Uralsky, an industrial city, seemed now like the pinnacle of civilization in comparison with the Kazakh village, and a most desirable place to live. And maybe her husband, my brother, would later find her there, if and when he managed to get out alive from the territory that was presumably already under the Germans. Also, I would have a better chance of finding a suitable job there, while here all I could count on was working on the farm, labor beyond my physical strength, in the Kazakh kolkhoz. Those girls, who left us at Kuibyshev, knew what they were talking about, after all. Mania wanted to join us, while Estera would go with us as far as Chelyabinsk, a big city in the Urals, which was on our way, and where she had relatives. They settled there after arriving in the Soviet Union at the beginning of 1940 and were smart enough, or patient enough, not to seek any "greener pastures" in the western provinces of that vast country.

Having made up our minds, I went to the train station to buy tickets. Luckily, passenger trains were running in all directions but the west, and we had enough money to pay the fare. Since these were our first hours in the village and no authorities had yet been busy "settling" us in or registering us, it seemed to us that we did not havc to ask anybody's permission to leave. Had we asked, we may have been denied, just in case, but as things stood, we were not escaping, just leaving. After all, we were not brought here by force! We managed to hire two kolkhoz youngsters who said they had a horse and wagon to get our belongings and us to the station. The horse turned out to be a miserable little pony and the wagon was a sort of strange basket-like vehicle on one wheel. But don't look a gift horse in the mouth! The basket was big enough to carry our rather sparse belongings, and off we went. The pony with the basket at the head of the procession and we on foot, following. The station was about an hour's walk away and the train was scheduled to leave late in the afternoon. We had plenty of time. Happy that our adventure was going so well and that soon we would come to more familiar places, leaving the Kazakh village with its dark, small, sad huts behind, made us breathe easier.

All had been going too well, however, and something was bound to happen. And indeed, midway to the station, out of the blue, something snapped in the harness connecting the horse with the cart. The horse took fright, swerved, and dashed forward, kicking the cart with his hind leg on the way. The cart turned over and our belongings were scattered on the road. The boys ran after the horse, and in a few moments, they and their horse were out of sight. Still, we did not lose our heads or our determination to get out of there. Fortunately, we had Estera's little stroller. It saved not only the day but also, perhaps, our whole venture. We put part of our belongings into the stroller and two of us went with it to the station. While one stayed there keeping an eye on the load, the other returned to those waiting at the roadside for another part of the belongings. And so, thanks to the "providential" stroller, we made it to the station, and saved our belongings, too. In installments, turning around three times, we were all at the station, still in time to board the train for Chelyabinsk.

We arrived in Chelyabinsk the next day. Estera's friends had lived there, in the safety of the remoteness of that place through the outbreak of the German–Soviet war, until the victorious end of it; they returned home when the war ended. They worked hard but were relatively comfortable there, yet tragedy had found its way to them, too. A daughter of theirs, a young girl, of my age, was struck by lightning and killed instantly. Just an accident! She was walking home from work in the fields, holding a tool of her work—a shovel—up on her shoulder, when it happened. The story stuck in my mind and came back to me many times. Perhaps, because the death of that girl, unknown to me, was so unusual, perhaps because she was my age, I do not know, but it made me think more often than anything else, how fragile human life was, the life of each one of us, my own life too. How easy it is to lose it, even far away from the war.

Still another day by train, and we reached our destination, Kamensk Uralsky, or rather one of its suburbs, a settlement, or *posiolok* as the Russians called it, Uralski Alumineviy Zavod, the Ural Aluminum

Mill. It was a huge complex, producing aluminum for the aircraft industry. Started here just a few years earlier, it was still growing and developing. Suffice to say that while at the time of my arrival, there were only two very tall smokestacks sending smoke up into the air, when I left the place three years later, seven or even nine were doing just that.

CHAPTER EIGHT

RETURNING TO THE URAL MOUNTAINS

The Ural Aluminum Mill's settlement was spread out on a large chunk of bare land in the middle of nowhere and was covered with neat rows of barracks, elongated squat, whitewashed structures of equal size. In front of the settlement ran a railroad, leading from a nearby, similar place, some 8 kilometers away, to the center of town and beyond, up to the aluminum mill. Where the settlement ends, behind the barracks, there were some half-dried tangled bushes most of the year. From afar, they looked like a dark line of barbed wire. During the long winters, those bushes, buried deep under snow, were not visible at all, and then it seemed that the barracks stretched into the horizon, with just no end to them. To the right of the barracks, there were some other structures—outhouses, and they too were under snow during the winter, their "content" deeply frozen, yet grown into a sizable hill. There was not a tree between or around the barracks and there were no streets or sidewalks.

It was summer, dry continental summer when we arrived there and the ground was firm, but summer here is ominously short, and right after it comes the muddy season. Then, stepping out of the barracks, one would almost right away tread in mud heavy enough to lose your shoes in it. Thus, the railroad tracks also became the only safe walkways for pedestrians and communication lines uniting the separate settlements, dwellings, or production sites with each other. Walking often meant jumping from one wooden railroad tie to another. I sometimes tried to count those ties to measure the distance to the center, to my place of work, to any place I would need to reach. Sometimes, I would get confused, when I counted. The count would not tally, and I would then start again, which would not matter anyway, since the only purpose of the count was to make the tedious walk seem shorter.

There were about fifteen whitewashed barracks in the settlement. They looked sturdy, in good shape, and almost new. They had been built quite recently and were quite livable, especially compared to the huts of the Kazakh village. Inside, each barrack was divided by a long hallway, on each side of which were rooms, thirty altogether, and one room to a family. The rooms were assigned "turnkey" furnished, with two single iron beds, a small table, two stools, and in the corner, close to the entrance, an oven, a solid brick oven for cooking and heating. The railroad, which provided the inhabitants of the barracks with a "walkway," also provided them with coal to keep their rooms warm during the severe winters. The open cars of the passing trains carried loads of coal for the aluminum mill, and when they stopped right across from the barracks, which happened quite often, the inhabitants helped themselves to the coal. The rooms in the barracks were kept rather decently heated.

At least two of the barracks were inhabited almost exclusively by refugees from Poland. They were now already old-timers there, and they took us in. An older woman with a baby in her arms greeted Dora, "You are back, I see. You should not have left here in the first place," she admonished her. This was Ida Heker. Actually, despite her worn look, the woman was only in her early forties then, and was not the grandmother, as I had assumed, but the mother of the baby she was carrying in her arms. She also had a seventeen-year-old daughter, Gina, who came out to take a look at the arrivals, too. Later, I became close with the Heker family and Gina became my lifelong friend.

Dora was put up by Sima, a refugee woman living in the same barracks. She had been living by herself at that time as her husband had left for the western part of the Soviet Union half a year earlier and had not been heard from since. Mania and I found a temporary place with a couple, also refugees from Łódź, Ewa and Dawid.

Job Hunting

I began job hunting right away, and it did not take long to find one. People were needed and my Gomel experience and proper papers from my last job at the regional school board were helpful. I walked into the first personnel director's office and told my story, careful enough to omit the stop at the Kazakh village on the way from Gomel. At first, the director looked at me sternly and even with some suspicion as evacuees were not supposed to come here on their own but rather be directed by the authorities whose business it was to settle them "where they were needed." But after giving my "case" some thought, he decided that it would do no harm to employ me, and since people were badly needed, he directed me to a less important manager who offered me a clerical job at one of the less important offices of the aluminum mill. Thus, I landed a job in one of the numerous offices connected with the Uralski Alumineviy Zavod at a desk, across from a middle-aged man whose name was Lobanov. He had the title of "statistician" and one of his main tasks was to prepare statistical accounts of productivity.

On the Uses of Statistics

I can't remember much about that stage of my "career," but one story stands out. My duty, among others, was to collect daily data on the production of gravel in preparation for the monthly accounts of that product. I had no idea what the product looked like or where it was produced, but one day I learned. I got the data needed for my forms by phone from the stone quarries and summarized it every week. One day, however, the phone of one of the quarries went dead.

My boss needed the summary urgently for his monthly account to be sent to his higher-ups. "Go there and get me that data," he told me. Well, there was no point in arguing or pleading; it would be in vain, and I knew it. Yet, I also knew that it must have been at least a 15-kilometer walk and that there was no transportation, and I was scared. All the more so when I noticed the expression of concern on the face of the office manager, an older woman, an evacuee from Moscow, with which she reacted to the news about my assignment. "Some assignment Comrade Lobanov gave me," I thought, but off I went.

I walked, alone on the empty road, not a dwelling along it, just a high stone wall on one side and flat fields covered with some skimpy growth on the other. From time to time, I would run to make my trip shorter. Not a car or truck, not another human being walking in the same or the opposite direction, but finally I reached my destination safely. The manager at the quarry looked at me with surprise, "You came just for that data? Lobanov needs it that badly?" he wondered, not showing too much admiration for the man or his statistical zeal. "You wait here for a moment," he told me. Soon he would be dispatching a truck in the direction of the aluminum mill, and "you will get a ride." I was lucky, the truck that was delivering gravel from the pit, got me back home in no time. I felt glad that I had not tried to plead with Lobanov, even though I was tempted to, but most of all, I was angry because of the futility of that silly assignment. Truly "Sisyphean" work, I repeated to myself. I was told at the stone quarry that yesterday's production was the same as the day before, which was only to be expected, since those numbers were almost a constant, anyway, I knew that much already and had wondered about it before. I learned that the numbers that went into our statistics were just "approximate" numbers, and the data that were so scrupulously entered into my forms were more often than not pulled out of a hat, "*s potolka,*" as the Russian saying goes, literally meaning off-the-ceiling. My "accounting," it turned out, were a sham, an exercise in futility. Corrupted statistics? I saw many more and much graver signs of corruption later, but this was the first that I had come face to face with, and I wondered why? What for?

Zoya Trofimovna

I stayed at this particular job for some time and got to know some of the people there. The office manager, the Moscow evacuee who was dismayed with Lobanov ordering me to walk to the stone quarry to make that useless trip, as she knew it would be, was Zoya Trofimovna. A tall, lanky woman, her dark, graying hair smoothly combed back, she had something in her eyes that made her rather plain face very attractive. It was a strong face with slight traces of small pocks, and dark attentive eyes that evoked trust. This was a woman that would care for stray cats, dogs, or lonely young girls who came from afar and had no evident family ties, for sick alcoholics, those unable to beat the disease, and such. We had in the office one such alcoholic, an accountant, a middle-aged man, also an evacuee. I had never seen anybody with signs of acute alcoholism before. His hungry (for a drink?) eyes were asking for pity. He would work without a hitch for a while, till he would get hold of a drink again, and then, forget work, forget everything, he would vanish for days. But it was wartime. The newly introduced wartime laws, aiming at strengthening workers' discipline, were harsh, and in full swing. For not showing up at work without a good reason, a sickness certified by a doctor, one could easily be sent to a labor camp. And his kind of disease was not considered a sufficient reason.

Russian Patriotic Pride

Here, in that office, people liked to talk politics, or joke about it, as in none of the other offices I had worked in before. The excitement of the first weeks of the war had heightened people's interest in political events and had also loosened their tongues a bit. One of the political jokes of that time, as told by someone at the office, has stuck somehow in my mind, perhaps because it was a joke saying a lot about Russian patriotic pride. It was in connection with the then, much written and talked-about visit of the British minister of foreign affairs, Eden,[73] in

73 Anthony Eden (1897–1977) visited the USSR in December 1941.

the company of the U.S. envoy, Hull,[74] to the Soviet Union, and it went something like this: Two interlocutors were talking about the event. "*Eden i Hull priyekhali v Moskvu*" (Eden came to Moscow and Hull, the American envoy with him) said one and the second answers, "*Nu, i hull z nim*!"[75] The play of words, the likeness of the name "Hull" to the Russian popular expletive, made for the joke. It was the beginning of the war, things were going badly for the Soviet Union, the Westerners came to offer help and cooperation, and the Russians were making jokes about it. The whole office roared with laughter!

My Other Jobs

After a while, I left the office and Lobanov, and with no regrets. Being at the disposal of the Personnel Office of the aluminum mill, I was often assigned to fill other jobs, always on the same low clerical level. For a short time, I was a so-called *tabelshchitsa,* a factory timekeeper, and my duty, among others, was to check the workers' presence at work at a few construction sites. To do this, I would have to get up high in the buildings under construction, where the workers worked. The cold wind of the Urals almost blew me away, but I did not mind this. I disliked this job for another reason. It became most unpleasant, especially when large groups of students from junior technical schools were brought in to work there. The students, very young boys, fourteen and fifteen years old, left jobs in droves, while absenteeism became under the harsh war laws, a criminal offense. When caught, they would be imprisoned. Sometimes they would come back to the same jobs, the same place, but as prisoners, under guard. The sign on my list "absent" took on a sinister meaning. Luckily, I was soon relieved from that job, and what helped me was the introduction of the food rationing system. It also became my duty to distribute the ration cards while checking on the workers' presence, but since so many were leaving their job, on

74 Cordell Hull (1871–1955), the U.S. secretary of state, did not visit the USSR until 1943, but the joke seems to rely on his presence.

75 Blasphemy upon him.

the very first day of the system's introduction, I was left with quite a lot of undistributed cards, which I dutifully returned to the Personnel Office that very day. And, soon enough, I was transferred to a different job. Distributing ration cards in a place where the fluctuation of the workforce was so high could become a lucrative source of free goods, and it was not to be left in my care.

For a certain time, I did some secretarial work at a small office at the aluminum mill's inner railroad. There was not much to do there, just take telephone messages for my boss, who was very busy elsewhere, and would come in from time to time for a few minutes to check those messages. I had plenty of spare time—almost all my time was spare—and I used it, grateful for the chance to read, undisturbed. The office was equipped with a typewriter, but there was almost nothing to type, so I used it just for practice, so as not to lose my typing speed, as well as to work on my language skills. For this, I tried translating and typing whatever I could get my hands on from Polish into Russian.

Transferred yet again, my job for a while was to check the numbers of freight cars coming in and out of the aluminum mill. This job involved night shifts, which was not easy. To walk, alone, during the cold and pitch-dark Ural nights, along the freight trains, finding my way in the maze of rails by the dim light of a lamp I carried in one hand, while writing down the numbers of the cars with the frostbitten fingers of the other, and checking those numbers against my list. Yes, this was work.

Studying Chemistry at the Local Chemical Technicum

I got a break and became a student of the local Chemical Technicum. This was the only school there that would give me the equivalent of a high school diploma, as night classes at the local high school were not available. My goal was to get the diploma that would pave the way into a university to study what I wanted to—philosophy. I was quite determined to reach that goal.

Even though I did not intend to become a chemist, I liked what I was taught at the technicum and liked being a full-time student. The teachers were great, mostly evacuees from Moscow, the subjects were interesting, the mathematics teacher could not have been clearer, and even I was getting somewhere with my studies. However, this became clear after a while, I had to take into consideration that the student food ration was much skimpier than a worker's ration, even that of a low-rank clerical worker. The students, exclusively girls and mostly local ones, had their families' support, while I, being alone, had to rely only on my ration. Four hundred grams of bread daily, soup in the canteen, and almost nothing else soon brought me to a state of exhaustion. To think that I had over two years of this before me seemed too much. I had to find a shortcut to reach my goal, and not perish on the way. With this in mind, when an opportunity to get a job at one of the canteens came along, I quit at the end of the second semester.

Yet Another Job

This opened a new era in my life in the Urals. I got a job in one of the huge wartime canteens that were feeding many hundreds of people daily. Soon I was promoted to a cashier, and then again promoted, this time to the ranks of an office clerk, whose task it was to keep the canteen's books. This was a "clean" office job, quite a promotion, indeed. And it was much more than that; working at a canteen during wartime turned out to be truly lifesaving for me. One would not starve working in such proximity to food, even such very poor and severely limited, rationed food as served by the canteen. One of the waitresses, a woman from Kyiv, a wife of an army officer serving somewhere on the fronts, once said to me when we got to know each other better, "When you first came to work here, I wondered how old you were, fifteen or thirty? Now, I can see, you are nineteen." And this speaks for itself. I had a lot of jobs and got a lot of experience from the three years I spent in the Ural Mountains.

Reestablishing Contact with Gabriel

It did not take long to reestablish contact with Gabriel. Our plan worked. I wrote two letters, one to Nizhny Novgorod, to Tosia's parents, and the other to Kizel, in the Urals, to the Blumins, and almost immediately received two letters from Gabriel that were already waiting for me at those places, in care of those good people. I wrote back at once, and soon we had direct contact. His first few letters—and I could not complain because he wrote often—were positive, even optimistic. He had arrived at the military camp and had started training to become a radio operator. This would take some time, he wrote, and that I shouldn't worry about him, the army would take care of him, he got a new uniform, and everything was going to be fine, just "don't forget me!" Just in case, I sent him eighty rubles, half of what I still had when I evacuated. I had a job now, and my earnings would see me through. The money never reached him, however, because he had left the training camp in the meantime and was on the move. A sudden, unexpected twist dramatically changed his situation, and he wrote to me about it with some embarrassment.

One morning, not long after he arrived at the camp, he was told that he was being transferred to one of the special "work battalions" for others "like him," sons of kulaks, ethnic Germans, former citizens of Poland, inhabitants of the "liberated" western Soviet territories, and other such "untrustworthy individuals." I could feel how shocked he was by the sudden change. He was drafted and went without hesitation. Nazi Germany was the mortal enemy and he considered it his obligation and duty to contribute to its defeat as best he could. Convinced that the cause was just, he would fight for it. Now, the rejection left him with a bitter taste. I was shocked too, and felt somehow ashamed, while at the same time, in a certain way, also relieved. So, he would not go to the front, so much the better. Of course, neither of us could know or anticipate the year-and-a-half-long stretch of terrible suffering that was about to begin for him, or how close and how often he would come to the abyss during that horrible time, though not being directly in combat, and yet more than once, so close to a most dreadful death.

The Work Battalions

With this still ahead of him, for now, he was writing and telling me about his life under the new conditions, in the work battalion. He often kept changing places, assigned with his group to dig anti-tank ditches, and with the front lines moving deeper and deeper into the country, he was always close to the front lines. There were not many details in those letters, perhaps because of the military censorship, or because he did not want to burden me unnecessarily with describing the deprivations and the hardships of his life. Sometimes he tried to make light of his predicament, sometimes he would even make fun of his contribution to ditch-digging, and I knew that such hard labor was just beyond him.

Soon, I would see the work battalions here, at the Urals, and this brought the horror of Gabriel's situation much closer to me. I could not only perceive it mentally, but I could almost palpably feel it. In the fall of 1941, the Ural Aluminum Mill got a shipment of men, young men badly needed by the expanding enterprise, which was very important for the war effort. Regiments and battalions of soldiers conscripted in the western Soviet territories into the regular army before the outbreak of the war, and now not trusted with arms and participation in combat, were transferred into *stroybat* (labor battalions) and dispatched to the Urals and other industrial places in the eastern territories to strengthen the workforce there, or to replace indigenous workers drafted into the army. Suddenly the place was swarming with young men, with familiar-looking faces. The first to come were deportees from the Baltics: Lithuania, Latvia, and Estonia. They stood out by their looks, as well as their European-style dress, and they did not last long. After a few weeks, they were not there anymore. Either, they were transferred to other places, or after a while, they blended in with the locals, changed by the harsh living conditions and hard labor to which these young people were so evidently not used. Then, Poles, mostly Jewish, from Białystok, Lwów, and so on appeared, and among them, some former refugees from western Poland, who had settled in those parts of the Soviet Union and were called for military service there. These newcomers, still militarized, living in military barracks, wearing their military garb, but very poorly fed, were worked to the bone here, as if the unwritten policy was to make these "untrustworthies" pay a price for being saved from death at the fronts. This was what I had heard, but I could see the results of this treatment with my own eyes. Very soon, many of them became completely destitute. Exhausting work and far too little food wore many down very quickly. Soon, one could see some of the members of the labor battalions begging in the canteen at lunchtime, waiting to gulp down the few spoons of someone's leftover soup, or grabbing a plate with even the tiniest amount of gruel left on it right from under your nose, to lick it greedily, obsessively. Turned into paupers, their uniforms in tatters, and dirty, they soon seemed to have lost even the look of human beings, not to mention the young men that they were. I watched them, and my heart ached with compassion and fear. Is this what life is like for a member of those battalions? Is Gabriel also living under such unbearable conditions, digging trenches, almost under fire, so close to the front lines, hungry, in a state of utter exhaustion, and destitution? Would he also succumb to this? I had not cried since that day when on hearing the news of the German invasion of the Soviet Union, I was seized by panic and thought in horror and fear, what next? Now, I cried and I could not stop crying.

A Most Economical Way to Survive

Yet life goes on. I tried to adapt to the new environment as best I could, learning to disregard difficulties when I could not have done anything to avoid or solve them. This was not an attitude stemming from a deliberate philosophical principle; it was rather a matter of character. My inherent, somewhat fatalistic streak, and at the same time my inborn optimism, made me believe that things would somehow "come together" and that the difficulties would be overcome. My experience of the last two tumultuous years had taught me that this was the most economical way to survive. Do what must be done, do your part, but also remember this: It is not the end of the world yet.

I was getting to know the people around me, those living in the same barracks, and first of all my hosts, the nice couple from Łódź, who had taken me and Mania in. Ewa, a woman of thirty-something, plain but friendly, was very proud of her family name, Harnam. Her brother, a young Communist, was killed by the Polish police while urging workers in his native Łódź to join a strike, and the event was commemorated by a song that used to be quite popular before the war in the Łódź left-wing milieu, "In front of the Biderman factory, he stood, comrade Harnam, on guard (of our cause) he died," etc. Ewa worked at a vegetable warehouse, which was a good job for wartime, because a carrot, a potato, or a leaf of cabbage would enhance one's diet greatly. Her husband, a burly man, worked as a truck driver, and later, when huge American trucks showed up at the aluminum mill, he was entrusted with driving one of those. They were happy to be together, far from the ravages of war. I enjoyed talking with them, they were optimistic about the war's outcome, and this was what I needed to hear.

I Love to Travel but I Will Not Go to Tashkent

As the summer of 1941 was coming to an end, my brother, together with Dora's younger brother Abram, unexpectedly and miraculously showed up at the settlement. They left their little town near Gomel after the local Soviet authorities had already gone. There was no more *Voyenkomat* to draft or release them. In the meantime, the Germans were already far ahead of them. Moving on foot, mostly during the night, they were able to get out of the war zone. How did he manage, I wondered, to cross the front lines, to get out from behind enemy lines, from the other side? He told me that he had given away his "European" clothes, the good, tailored coat made in Łódź by the best Bałut tailor, a Mr. Lenga, and that he had thrown away that gorgeous felt hat that I had taken such care of while we were escaping from Łódź right after the outbreak of the war. Instead, they both got themselves some local *fufaikas*, old, quilted cotton jackets, to blend in with the locals, to make themselves as inconspicuous as possible, and avoiding highways, they had traveled to Kamensk-Uralsky, expecting us to be there already. It was a guess, and fortunately, the right one. Dora and I were, of course, overjoyed to see them and overjoyed that we had managed to get out of Kazakhstan. It was scary to think what if we had stayed there? And what now? I was convinced that they would try to settle here for good. After all, the place was familiar to them! I wished they would, they were now my only family. It would certainly be easier for all of us to stay together. However, my brother ran into some difficulties with settling here with his family. Either he had a problem with obtaining a room, or perhaps the year they had previously spent here was tough, having prompted them to leave for Gomel in the first place. Or, perhaps, they were influenced, in addition, by Abram who wanted to try his luck in some other place and had convinced them to do so as well? I don't know, but one day they decided to move to the south of the Soviet Union, toward Central Asia. Tashkent was there, the breadbasket, "the city of bread," as the title of a popular book about the times of the October Revolution suggested,[76] and it was tempting to try its warmer climate, too.

I would not see my brother till 1946 when, after the war, he returned with his wife to Łódź. I would miss them but decided against joining them. I had a job and was already in touch with Gabriel. He knew my address and we could write to each other. I decided against moving and remained in the Urals, alone. Though I "liked to travel," I stayed where I was.

New Friends: Gina

I was getting used to the new surroundings and new people. Little by little, I made new friends. My closest friend at that time was Gina, the girl next door. She was still attending high school, and she was in the tenth grade. She studied for two years at a gymnasium in Łódź before the start of the war, and she was very well-read. She was lucky, I thought, she would soon get the high school diploma I coveted, and I told her so. But she was not very excited about that prospect. She had a problem that made her feel unlucky, that made her suffer—she was greatly

76 Alexander Neverov's popular Soviet children's book, *Tashkent, City of Bread*, was first published in Russian in 1923 and subsequently translated into multiple languages.

overweight! And come to think of it, it was a real problem, indeed. A good-looking, petite girl, at seventeen, weighing about 80 kilograms, was serious. This is unjust, she was telling me. We lived on a very poor diet, barely subsistence level, and here she was, plagued by such an abundance of flesh! It seemed like a curse to her. She needed more food than I did, was hungrier than I was, and she was only seventeen and wanted to be liked and loved, wanted to find a boyfriend, and it did not seem likely to her, at least not any time soon.

She came with her parents, Dawid and Ida, from Łódź, where Dawid had been a carpenter and Ida had worked in a textile mill. Here he got a job in his trade, or close to it, not as a cabinet maker as he was in Łódź, as such a job did not exist here in the Urals, but he worked with lumber anyway, busy with whatever they were producing at the carpenters' division of the aluminum mill. Ida Heker now had her family and a baby to care for, little Vova, born "unexpectedly" in her "old age" as she would never forget to add. In the evenings, back from work, I would often stop at their place, to talk, sometimes to help out a bit with the chores that Ida was buckling under, or to go for a walk with Gina. They were a family and this was perhaps what most attracted me to them, with my own family now so far away on the other side of war-torn Europe, and Gabriel with me only thanks to the thin thread of our letters, little messages written on sheets of paper torn out from a copybook and folded into triangles, military-style letters, an envelope being a prewar luxury.

Oskar

From time to time, others also stopped by at their place, newcomers to the aluminum mill would visit the barracks, looking for people coming from the same places they had come from, from Łódź or Poland in general, and the circle of friends, or just acquaintances, would grow. Some remained there for a long time, and others came and went. One became a friend for life—Oskar. He came to the aluminum mill as a member of a labor battalion. Escaping the Germans, as we did, he too moved to Białystok and managed to somehow find work and stay there.

Conscripted to serve the obligatory three-year term, and then promoted through the ranks, he one day became a labor battalion member, too, and was transported to the Urals with a whole military unit. He wanted to fight the Germans and felt deeply offended by the refusal. A dedicated Communist, he had served a prison term in Poland for distributing illegal Communist literature, and he wanted to fight the Fascists for the cause, for his parents and younger brothers left in the Łódź ghetto, and his wife in Białystok, now also under the Germans. "Don't they need dedicated people, willing to give their lives to fight that horrible enemy?" he wondered. Oskar told me that the Russian officer who had escorted his unit to the Urals was almost crying that after fulfilling his mission, he had to return west, to the front, while he, Oskar, was almost crying about being refused that honor. He would later try to enlist with General Anders' Polish Army, but as a Jew and a Communist, he would not stand a chance.[77]

Giza

At the aluminum mill, I also met other Polish refugees who became my friends and whom I met again later after the war. I met Giza Lvov, an interesting, even a bit eccentric woman. She lived alone, her husband was lost somewhere on the other side of the front lines. She did not believe she would ever find him again. She most probably knew something about his fate or, more likely, there was something about their relationship, which she preferred to keep to herself, and indeed he did not come back to her, if he survived the war at all. Giza was not a resident of the barracks, and she lived in the center of the town in one of the tall, seven-or-more-story-high buildings designated for the *inzhenerno-tekhnicheskie rabochie* (ITR), the engineers, professionals,

77 During the period of cooperation between the Polish government-in-exile and the USSR (July 1941–April 1943), the Poles were allowed to form a military force to fight under Allied command. The Polish Armed Forces in the East is usually referred to as Anders' Army, after its commander, General Władysław Anders (1892–1970).

administrators, and generally, the bosses. These were good buildings with large apartments, now inhabited by more than one family in each; one family to a room was the rule, widespread in the Soviet Union, with the amenities, bathroom, and kitchen, shared by all the inhabitants of such "communal" dwellings. I was once in such an apartment, visiting a family of Leningraders whose daughter, Aviva, was a co-student of mine while I was with the Chemical Technicum and I admired it. The head of that family was an important physician, and that's why he was assigned that living space.

Giza's share in these luxury dwellings was a tiny room, adjacent to the kitchen, the so-called room for the *dom rabotnitsa* (domestic worker). She was, of course, happy to have the privacy of this space, and I liked to visit her there; we weren't bothered there by others and could talk freely. Sometimes I would read some of Gabriel's letters to her, she liked them very much, and was the only person to whom I would read them. Sometimes we would just talk—about what life would be like after the war, where we would live, here, in Poland, or somewhere else? She wanted to paint, she confided in me. She would go to an art school, and she did indeed attend the Warsaw Academy of Arts after the war and became a painter, a well-respected portraitist. To this day I cherish her portrait of our son Henryk as a boy of about eleven. We saw each other from time to time after the war, and she always gratefully recalled that I encouraged her to hold on to her artistic ambitions. She maintained that I was the only one of her old friends who did not consider her ambition of becoming a student at the age of well over thirty a "crazy" idea. She was happy in her bright studio on the Plac Konstytucji in Warsaw, but, alas, her happiness was short-lived; Giza died of cancer in her early forties.

Rutka

I met yet another woman at the aluminum mill, with whom I was friends after the war for many years. She was also a lucky inhabitant of one of those small servants' quarters, in one of the big buildings in the town's center. She shared that room with her then-husband. Rutka was a redhead, a teacher by profession, born and educated in Warsaw. In 1942 or 1943, she gave birth to a son. Somehow a picture of her, bent over the baby in the process of changing the child's diaper, has stuck in my mind—a young woman, a picture of health, her red hair blazing and throwing a reddish shade on her face that expressed the most loving dedication that she was giving to her task! What was it in that scene that made such an impression on me, imprinting it in my memory forever? My nostalgia for what I could have eventually had and what might be taken away by the war? For Gabriel, for the family we hoped to build someday for ourselves, and which might never happen, now?

Poor Rutka, her husband left her pretty soon for another woman, and I tried hard to understand why. Rutka seemed so much nicer to me, better than the other woman! I tried to understand till I finally understood that these things are beyond understanding, and this made me, understandably, very sad. Will something like that happen to us, to me and Gabriel, too?

Nina Chekrygina

I made friends with yet another girl, Nina Chekrygina, a Moscovite, a Russian girl. A beautiful girl, slim and graceful, her features like the most delicate carving in marble. She lived with her mother in one of the other barracks. The mother, also very thin, was much taller than her daughter, she was always dressed in black, and with her face darkened by troubles and deprivations, she sometimes looked like an apparition. Nina's father was an artist, a known futurist painter, whose name I looked up in one of the Soviet encyclopedias, and he had died years ago. Nina was a student at Moscow Lomonosov University, where she studied Western and Russian literature, and she introduced me to a host of books, especially books from nineteenth-century England: Thackeray, the Austins, in Russian translations. I could not get enough of it. She once showed me her college transcript, and I remember going through it almost in awe, reading the titles of the courses she had taken, the marks she had gotten on the exams, and taking it all in. One day, I would have one like that too, I was sure of it!

As a student at Moscow University, Nina knew many of the younger crowd of Moscow artists, musicians, and performers. Now, touring the country, some of them were visiting such remote places as ours in the Urals, as well. The performances took place usually in the local *Dom Kultury* (House of Culture, if to translate it awkwardly, yet literally). It was a popular Soviet Union institution, a kind of public club, and a community center. They screened movies and staged concerts, poetry recitals, and the like there. In addition, the large hall was used for important local meetings, or it doubled as a dance hall. The center also housed a library and a reading room. Needless to say, I liked the place and used to spend whatever free time I had there. Nina, in whose company I would sometimes attend a performance of the Moscow artists, would invite me to meet them, her friends, behind the scenes, which was not only fun but also something of a window into another, wider, brighter world that was virtually unknown to me till then, a fascinating world! I felt indebted to Nina for her friendship and those initiations and kept her in my grateful memory, but we lost touch with each other when I left for Leningrad later to become a student there, and she returned to Moscow when the war had taken a turn for the better.

However, I heard about her once more, though many years later. In the early sixties, I was with my family on vacation at a Baltic Sea resort and met a Russian woman, Zina, there. She was a translator from Polish to Russian, and vice versa. Zina, a vivacious woman in her late forties, had come on vacation from Moscow with her four-year-old son. She had come at the invitation of the Polish Association of Writers. She had learned Polish, she told me, with the specific purpose to become a translator of Polish literature into Russian. Fascinated by the new trends in Polish literature at the time of the "Polish October,"[78] she wanted to bring it to Russian readers. The intellectual movement in Poland, as a proponent of change towards liberalization and freedom, was then

78 A period of relative political and intellectual openness in Poland in the latter half of 1956, following the death of Stalin and the so-called Thaw in the USSR.

at its highest, and Polish literature and ideas being ahead of what the Russians were allowed in their country at that time, became very popular in the Soviet Union. Zina was a graduate of the Moscow University Department of Russian and Western Literature, and while chatting with her, I asked if she did not by any chance know Nina Chekrygina. Oh yes, she said, she knew her very well; Nina taught literature in one of Moscow's colleges, she had been married, but not anymore, had a grown son, and was very, very fat. I was disappointed, not knowing why. It seems as if I hoped to hear something more exciting about the beautiful, graceful, intelligent girl who had been so full of promise and had made such an impression on me. I felt disappointed. Zina disagreed. "Look, she is alive, has a nice job, a son, she will perhaps have a grandchild or even two, that, according to our standards, is very good." And, she added with bitterness, even though she tried to laugh it off, "Look at me, I am almost fifty, my older son is about thirty, and my young one here is four. I could not afford a husband but could afford a child, and I got one. That's our life!" Her chilling answer could make one shiver even in the middle of that warm, sunny August day, but it was only reflecting, unfortunately correctly, on life as it was there. I knew something about it myself, and there was no need to convince me.

Adapting to Life in the Urals

This digression has taken me too far away from the Urals, however, and it's time to go back there. My life there was stabilizing, and I moved to Sima's place after Dora and my brother had left, and with the money I was earning and a roof over my head, which was free, I did not have to worry about the necessities. Sima was a quiet woman; I spent almost three years sharing a room with her yet knew almost nothing about her. She worked hard, as everybody else did, and we did not see each other much. Later, I sometimes wondered how it was possible to live so close and be so remote, and I faulted myself. I am certainly not the gregarious type.

My time was divided between work, waiting for letters from Gabriel and writing letters to him, and getting acquainted with the new place and conditions. I found my way, as I have already mentioned, to the *Dom Kultury* and mainly to its library and reading room. The hours spent there among the books, in that cozy, well-heated place that seemed to be cut off from the outside world, from its bustle, the days growing shorter and colder and muddier, were a gift. I wanted to read them all, to digest them, for them to become mine. They had the *History of Philosophy* by Aleksandrov,[79] which I went, sometimes with Gina, to read there, but also, almost unbelievably out of place, Plato's Dialogues, in an old Russian edition. This was new, I had never tried this kind of literature before, and I liked it. Plato's parable of the cave made me muse almost romantically about "true life," which passes by us while all we are seeing, sitting in the cave, are merely shadows of life. And what is that "true life"? Interestingly, the romantic streak or ethos of the Marxist philosophy, with which I was already acquainted at that time, seemed to me not only to coincide with Plato's concept of the two worlds, and the demand of striving toward achieving the knowledge of the highest "Good," but to reinforce it!

Sometimes, performances were staged at the *Dom Kultury*, and with the war raging in the western provinces of the Soviet Union, artists, often of the highest class, would come to these remote places in the Urals, not able to perform in more prestigious places. Here, at that *Dom Kultury*, I attended a piano concert of one of the best, Emil Gilels, a young musician who later became world famous. I have never forgotten the shine of the black piano, the white teeth of the keyboard, and the young man with his reddish mane of hair, bent over this piano and playing, playing, playing. I did not have much musical education, and I was hardly familiar with classical music, yet the beauty of those sounds overwhelmed me. This was unforgettable, an initiation of sorts, a first for me, which turned me into a zealous music listener for life. Of the other artists who came to our place, I also remember Yakov Flier very well and a prominent Soviet pianist, but the impression from that first concert remained unsurpassed. Many years later, in the late

79 Georgy Aleksandrov (1908–1961), a prominent Marxist philosopher and Soviet politician, published his *History of Western European Philosophy* only in 1946. She may be referring to one of his earlier works on Aristotle.

seventies, an epoch later, I went to Gilels's concert in Toronto, but the musician was not young anymore, and neither was I. The concert was great, but of course, it wasn't possible to evoke the beauty of those old feelings.

During the autumn of 1941, notwithstanding the war raging in the west and still going rather badly, the steady losses of the Soviet army, and the fast advancement of the enemy, life in the Urals seemed bearable, even normal. The lights in the evenings were on, there were no blackouts, and the war was far away. The radio announcements were casting a heavy, black shadow, but the Soviet counteroffensive near Moscow in December 1941 that threw the Germans back after they had come so frighteningly close to the capital and were already boasting about capturing it, brought the first glimmer of hope. It strengthened people's belief that the Germans would be defeated, though by then it was already rather clear that the cost would be enormous, and that it would take a long time.

The lights were still on, but the rhythm of work was getting faster, even feverish with the introduction of longer work hours and the almost total cancellation of holidays and days off. Food became scarcer, ration cards were introduced, but there was no problem with obtaining your ration of the daily bread, or whatever else was allotted—the ration of sugar, half a kilogram per month, per person, or some of the other food staples. Also, the soup in the *stolovka* (the canteen) was not yet as watery as it would later become and salt was still available. Later, the *miaso-ryba, zhiry, muka* (meat or fish, fats, and flour) on the ration cards seemed promising, but they remained mostly a name on the coupons, a legend. I, for one, never saw any of those in any of the open stores. There were, of course, stores, but they were mostly empty. There were, of course, also "secret" stores, for the higher-ups, but I never saw any of those from the inside and only had a very vague idea of their existence, as this was far beyond my "level." And the toughest times were still to come.

1942: The Most Horrible Year of the War

The most horrible of all the war years was 1942. After the momentary success of the Soviet forces near Moscow, the Germans, after the winter recess, were pushing ahead again, capturing kilometer after kilometer of Soviet territory, taking city after city. However, detailed knowledge of what was going on at the front was not available here. If there were any newspapers at all, they were not accessible, practically nonexistent, or again not available at my "level," and one had to rely on what the loudspeaker would tell you. And the loudspeaker told stories of heroic deeds of this or that tank operator or a foot soldier single-handedly destroying an enemy tank, or a unit heroically holding on under enemy fire and causing them heavy losses in some battle, and of the army's "orderly retreating to preliminary positions."

The repetitiveness of that sorry chant made me shiver. Kyiv, Kharkiv, Zaporizhzhia on the Dnieper, and other places beyond the Dnieper were lost, and the fronts were coming closer to the Volga River. This was chilling news. The Germans captured city after city, but there was no news of what they were doing to the population. And I knew what they were able to do to innocent, unarmed civilians. There was also no mention of the Germans' treatment of the Jews in those Ukrainian and Russian cities in the western Soviet territories that were heavily populated by Jews. So, it was no wonder that there was nothing about what was going on even further to the west, in occupied Poland.

It had been more than a year since the last letters from the Łódź ghetto, scarce, short letters that nevertheless spoke volumes. Over a year had passed since I received that tragic postcard from Sala in which she had asked for a food parcel. How are my parents, my sisters, Sala and Helcia? I would close my eyes, trying to imagine them, but there was nothing, a blank, not because the memory of them had already faded but simply because of the total lack of any new information. I did not have anything, any new input to feed my imagination, I just had what was in my memory, and this was no longer enough, I was unable to envision what their life was like.

Summer Brought No Relief

The summer of 1942 was hot, dry, and very sunny, but it did not bring any relief after the first harsh Ural winter. On the contrary, the dreadful news about the war and the growing scarcity of food made things considerably worse. I got to know hunger pangs, having to start the day without anything to eat because I was careless enough or not rational enough to divide my ration of bread properly, or was too hungry in the evening and ate it all instead of leaving something for the next day. It was demeaning to have to think about food almost all the time. Malnutrition became a common occurrence, and there were rumors about starvation. A little later, I too was so weakened by malnutrition that I got sick. The glands on my neck swelled up and I was afraid of a recurrence of my illness from a few years before. I went to see a doctor and he gave me a prescription: a coupon for an additional portion of soup daily in the canteen for a month. It turned out to be the most effective medicine.

Allied Help

In the middle of the year, the general food situation eased up a bit, perhaps due to Allied help. First, heavy American trucks had arrived at the aluminum mill to replace the old, worn-to-the-hilt local ones. Until then, trucks running on wood were quite common here. The truck driver would feed a few pieces of wood into the burner and the truck would move ahead slowly, coughing and puffing up black smoke from the exhaust pipe mounted to its side, towering over it. The new trucks looked as if they came from a different century, even a different planet. Dawid, my neighbor, entrusted with driving one of those huge machines, could not stop telling us wonders about them. Then, some American foodstuffs also showed up. I knew them by name, but don't remember ever having seen any of those, at least not in 1942: canned meat, white canned lard, powdered milk, and egg powder. Some of these delicacies went into our rations, distributed through the canteen, which meant into the daily soup. And by that time, our daily soup was not even made of cabbage any longer but mostly of *krapiva* (nettle), a weed that's supposed to be very healthy and "good for you," with lots of vitamin C! The help was a proverbial drop in the bucket. Yet perhaps it helped to organize a much-needed children's kitchen, which supplied little children with lifesaving bottled food. I think that little Vova's chance to survive increased greatly, thanks to those bottles his mother was bringing for him from that new kitchen.

Why Did Gabriel Stop Writing?

Letters from Gabriel arrived regularly, and this sustained me. He still wrote often, but the tone of his letters was changing, becoming less and less optimistic. One of those letters, I can still see it in my mind, was especially ominous. His coded address was the same, but he was moved around a lot, all the time in the proximity of the front lines, insofar as there were still such lines. He wrote this letter sitting with his unit in a boxcar that was again being moved somewhere. He said in the letter that he was writing on a sheet of lined copybook paper, which he had placed on the flat bottom of a pot hanging on his buddy's back. The train was moving, and only in this way, he could keep the paper steady and in place. People were leaving the labor battalions, going home, escaping, he wrote, and the battalion he belonged to had shrunk considerably; those who did not have too far to go to reach their families had already left. What was he to do? Everything seemed to be crumbling. Should he also leave? Try to get to the Urals? No, he would not do it, not yet anyway, he had no stomach for desertion, and this was the exact phrase he used, "He does not have it in his heart to just take off and leave like that. This is not the end yet!" I repeated that sentence a few times, very scared for him, and myself, too.

By the end of that summer letters from Gabriel stopped coming, and this became something almost impossible to deal with. At first, I thought he was on the way to the Urals, that he would show up any day, that with his labor battalion in disarray, he had left it, as many others had, "going home" as he again told me in one of his last letters. But wouldn't he write on the way if this were the case? Summer was coming to an end, the muddy, rainy season was again upon us, the first snow whitened the normally dark industrial panorama of the aluminum mill, and nothing, no letters, just nothing. I did not believe that he was dead, I just could not see him that way. The newsreels showed pictures of enemy soldiers scattered on the snow-covered fields, laying there in strange poses, dead enemy soldiers. I watched those pictures, but no, Gabriel was not lying somewhere like that, this could not be, this was just impossible to imagine. Or, perhaps, he was captured by the enemy? He was so close to the front lines, and the lines were often breaking down, in many places quite recently. This much even I knew from the skimpy information received from the loudspeaker. For some time, there were no more stable front lines, so might he have fallen into the Germans' hands? But this was a horrible thought, and I tried hard to push it out of my mind. I did not know what to think, I did not know where to turn to for information, and I would not have gotten any, anyway. I tried to go on, waiting and hoping, sometimes hope against hope.

With German Victories Comes the Upsurge of Antisemitism

The year was coming to a close, but there was no respite in sight. With German victories, antisemitism was on the upsurge and it became almost palpable. Till then, I had never experienced open antisemitism in the Soviet Union, directed toward me. I would come to experience it later, see it raising its ugly head of hatred at the end of the war, or right after the victorious war, but not earlier. If I stated that I was Jewish, I would be met sometimes with an unbelieving glance and a remark, "but you don't look it," or in some cases, I would half-jokingly be asked to say *kukuruza* (corn in Russian) as a folksy test of sorts: some Russians believed Jews were supposed to roll the letter "r." But now, with the tides of war turned against the Soviet Union, with the Germans pushing victoriously ahead on all fronts, the Russian antisemites' powers of recognition suddenly became greatly improved, and I could see and feel antisemitism rising. The glances, and the epithets hurled after you when you walked deadly tired along the railroad tracks on your way home from work, became an everyday occurrence. The few Polish Jews still living in the settlement started thinking with some apprehension and suspicion about our native neighbors, and in the quiet of our rooms, we spoke more than once about what we could do next, where to go and how, and would we have any time to go anywhere? Wouldn't our neighbors do the job before the Germans arrived?

Rumors and Tales

During those times, I also often heard recurring rumors that the kolkhozes would be dissolved and that the aluminum mill would be turned into an American concession. I heard it many times and from many people and wondered about these rumors. Were they just an expression of what the Soviet people were dreaming about? The kolkhozes, a constant thorn in the body of Soviet society, introduced by mass terror, brought suffering to millions and ruined agriculture. I did not have too much experience with the collectivized Russian villages but knew that those who grew wheat had no bread for their own needs. I remembered the farm worker in Gomel, who walked for a long time with me from the market to my place, to exchange some milk she had brought from her kolkhoz for the bread I was able to spare from my ration. Now in the Urals, I tried to repeat my experience in barter. I gave a farm worker from a nearby village some fabric I had brought with me from Gomel in exchange for some milk. I got two cups of milk and a promise of more next week. When the worker did not show up anymore, I decided after a few weeks to visit her. I took advantage of a ride to the village, but what I saw there was so appalling that I forgot what I had come for. Though I was then not in envious shape, taking anything from that utterly impoverished woman would have been a crime. How happy and rich in comparison was that prewar Polish village of Dora's parents that was still fresh in my memory! Sad and hungry, I returned to my accommodation on the settlement. Of course, I could not stop wondering "why?" Why so much suffering, and poverty, why such horrible helplessness? This was too big, too difficult for me to fathom.

While the resentment toward the kolkhozes was not difficult to understand, the rumor about the Ural Aluminum Mill puzzled me more. The aluminum mill was on a scale of those grandiose projects of Socialism, like the Zaporizhzhia Dam, the power station, the "biggest in the world," the pride of the Soviet Union, and this too was to be resented? This was to become an American concession? That rumor was harder for me to understand, Gorbachev and *perestroika*[80] were still over half a century away.

Gina's Father: Dawid

I was certainly not the only one with doubts and questions. One day, late in the afternoon, it must have been on a Sunday, a day off, I was sitting outside the barracks taking advantage of the still-warm August sun. A neighbor, Dawid, Gina's father, came outside, too, and approached me. We started to chat, but what I had expected to be some usual neighborly small talk, turned into something else. Right away, he began confessing how disappointed he was with what was going on around us and "generally in the Soviet Union." This was certainly not the Socialism he had fought for all his life, he complained bitterly, asked "what can you call this?" and on and on he went. He decided, he concluded, to write his thoughts down, he wanted to inform... "Inform? Who?" I asked, looking at him with surprise. There is a saying in the Soviet Union, a cynical one, perhaps, but born by experience, "*Ne nravitsia sovetsksia vlast', pishi zaiavlenie v NKVD*" (You don't like the Soviet order, complain to the NKVD [the secret police]). But he seemed not even to hear what I was trying to tell him and he kept repeating with an almost maniacal insistence that he had to write, he had to make it known, and would I please translate it for him into Russian, he could only write in Yiddish.

80 Perestroika (restructuring) was the term used to describe the failed attempt to modernize the political and economic infrastructure of the Soviet Union in the 1980s.

I tried to talk him out of it, repeating that it was futile and dangerous, and finally, I refused to do any translating. I never got to know what he did with his "idea" in the end—did he curb his wish "to inform" those poor leaders who knew nothing of what was going on in the country? Or was his family able to talk him out of it? But a few months later, Dawid and a few other people from the same shop where he worked, were arrested. There was a rumor, again only a rumor, that an "anti-Soviet" leaflet was found in the shop. It could have been true, but it also could have been a provocation, or just a rumor prompted by the arrests. Gina's father never returned home. In 1945 Gina was officially informed that her father had died in prison of "natural causes." She was then a student at Leningrad University.

The NKVD Is Vigilant

Shortly after Dawid's arrest came many others. As if the suffering caused by the war, hunger, and excessive hard labor were not enough, massive arrests had to top it all. The security police worked hard, and many people were dragged away, many never to return. The "cleanup" was thorough and fell hard on the refugees of the settlements, and especially on former members of labor battalions. The arrests touched many lives deeply and tragically. The Russian saying "*Od sumy i od tiurmy ne otkazyvaysya,*" which can be roughly translated as "nobody is insured against becoming a beggar or a jailbird," seemed to be coming true. To console her after her father's arrest, Gina's coworkers once asked her during a smoke break to just look around and see something for herself; almost everybody had some family member in prison, or a camp, almost everyone was in prison or would be, so don't despair, it's just a fact of life!

Victory at Stalingrad

And yet, as the year 1942 was nearing a close, news about the German defeat at Stalingrad reached us.[81] This was the first bright ray of light in the darkness, a promise of better times to come. I watched the historic moment in awe, the meeting of the two Soviet armies, one coming from the south and the other from the north, as it was shown on the newsreels. The divisions from Siberia, soldiers newly introduced into battle, many in white camouflage, well armed, looking strong and enthusiastic, projected the image of victory, and what a sight this was! Now the Germans were encircled by Soviet forces. This put a ring around them, a ring that would squeeze them into submission. And soon, pictures of thousands upon thousands of German prisoners-of-war would arrive on the newsreels! How different they looked now, those conquerors, those demi-gods, monsters who had unleashed on us such horrible suffering!

With the Stalingrad victory came a visible change in the public mood. Of course, the end of the war was not yet in sight, it was still well over two years away. But with that victory, the war had reached a turning point, everybody seemed to believe so. The prevailing feeling was that the fortunes of war had tilted toward the Soviet Union. Now, it became easier to believe that the day would come when Hitler would finally be beaten.

But all that easing of tension notwithstanding, life was still bleak, hungry, tough, and not getting easier. And I had to deal with my grief; there was still not a word from Gabriel. What had happened? It had been over half a year without a sign of life from him. Who should I ask? Where should I look for an answer?

81 German troops only surrendered on February 2, 1943, but when Operation Winter Storm, the attempt to break the encirclement of the Sixth Army, was abandoned on December 23, 1942, it was clear that their defeat was inevitable.

Crime and Punishment

Day after drab day passed by and time seemed to stand still—it's no wonder that I haven't retained much of that time in my memory. On that bleak and black background, one memory stands out. I walked as briskly as I could, on my way home from work. It was a bitterly cold winter day, and I kept my head down to lessen the impact of the wind blowing into my face a little when I noticed and then picked something up from the snow-covered ground. It was a bread ration card with coupons for two days of bread for a family of four. No name on it, no address, and no possibility of returning it to the rightful owner, though I am not sure at all that if I had known it, I would have returned it. The temptation to keep the find was very strong. Yet, a whole family left without bread for two days, a true misfortune, and it was a heavy thought to bear, so maybe, I would keep it, but just maybe! I bought the bread—two whole loaves of dark, fresh, good-smelling bread. A fortune! I went to the market, sold some of it, and bought a bit of that coveted white American white lard instead. Now, I'll have a feast. I shared part of that feast with little Vova who, just then, was left in my care for a few hours. We ate the bread, piece after piece, greased with lard, and it was good! Little Vova was happy and stayed healthy after the feast, but I was punished. I got sick, very sick, my stomach not used to fats, revolted against the lard. I can still see myself moving helplessly along the seemingly endless barracks hallway, holding on to the walls, and then going back slowly to my room, only to repeat the same trip almost immediately, over and over. I was punished, and it was a pretty heavy punishment.

A Letter from Gabriel

Some more time passed by. One day in late March, on a still cold and cloudy morning, while I was leaving the barracks on my way to work, the postman handed me a letter, a little triangle, a military-style letter. Gabriel! I knew it was from him immediately. I burst into tears before I could even open it. A single sheet of lined paper and a few sentences on it. "I am in a hospital, sick with typhus, I am better now, I was in captivity, I'll write again. Are you well?" The miracle I had almost stopped hoping for! I stood there, in that dreary, wintry hallway, looking at that piece of paper. The handwriting was his, but it showed how sick he had been still while writing. His hand was unsteady, the letters big, and uneven, as if coming from a child's first writing endeavor. I cried and could not stop crying. Gina showed up in the hallway, "He is alive, alive," I answered her puzzled look. "So, what are you crying about?" she wondered.

Soon, more letters came, and once even a snapshot. This one became my favorite. Later Gabriel would send many from different places, from Ukraine, from Romania, and especially from Budapest, Hungary, but this first one was my favorite—the same young boy who had left Gomel looked at me with that good shy smile that I loved. Soon, we started writing to each other again regularly. He had gone through unbelievable hardships. Captured by the Germans on their push toward Stalingrad, he escaped from the POW camp, was tortured, escaped again, and wandered under an assumed name in the occupied territories, working as a farmhand in the kolkhozes, and expecting nothing but death if his Jewish identity were to be revealed. He was still under the draft obligation and would perhaps be enlisted again into the army, this time as a regular soldier. It was enough to fill a book, which he eventually did, though many years later. Fifty years later, to be exact, he published his wartime memoir, *My Just War*,[82] and thus there is no need to recapitulate it here.

Gabriel's almost miraculous survival changed my life and now, there was a new purpose to it, a new hope. And at that time, other things began changing for me for the better, as well. In the middle of 1943, I changed my job again, and I started working in a huge canteen, and I worked there till the end of my stay in the Urals, in September 1944. I left then to become a student at Leningrad University. Working at that canteen became an important factor in my survival during the harsh war years. It also brought me a whole lot of new experiences. There, I got to learn more about life "as it is" than books can teach. I got to know a lot

82 Gabriel Temkin, *My Just War: The Memoir of a Jewish Red Army Soldier in World War II* (Novato: Presidio, 1998).

of new people, made friends with some, and maintained some of those friendships for years to come.

The Workers' Canteen No. 8

Twice a day, the canteen fed a few thousand workers and after the workers were done, prisoners guarded by prison guards were fed the same food. Yet the feeding time for the prisoners must have been shorter because there was always much nervousness, rushing, and tension at that time. Or was it the presence of the guards and just the knowledge that these people were prisoners that was enough to cause the tension? I looked at those people with mixed feelings, with pity and compassion, and somewhat also with fright. I was often scared by the very sight of them. They were brought to such a state of deprivation that they seemed to be robbed of humanity, those faces, especially those of the female prisoners: there was something wild and vile about them at the same time, their rough features and hungry eyes frightened me. I knew how easy it was to become one of them.

Uzbeks in the Urals

The canteen had a separate hall for the so-called ITR, engineering, and technical staff. Soon, I was transferred to wait in the ITR hall. The notion of self-service was unknown there. I carried huge trays, with twelve soup plates at once to the tables. How I did it, not spilling the soup, was a mystery to me, and one could hardly see me from behind that huge tray. Shortly, however, I was promoted to the position of cashier. Now, I was collecting money and ration coupons. This was an easier job, but I was transferred back to the general hall, to the workers' hall. The atmosphere in the ITR's hall was calmer, one might even say, pleasant, but in the workers' hall, it was more interesting. All nationalities of the Soviet Union were here, but the most visible was the Uzbeks. They were drafted to work in the heavy industry of the Urals under the special wartime laws that would make leaving an assigned job a punishable crime. Transported from the warmth and sunshine of their native land to this faraway cold place, they suffered immensely. I cannot forget the still rather young Uzbek who froze to death, having fallen asleep on his outdoor job during a subzero cold evening. He was dead, frozen, and still standing upright, leaning on the wall, when the ambulance came to take away the body.

Uzbeks received food parcels from home, among others with raisins which they would sometimes sell. They also loved to talk about the good life they had at home and about how tasty the Uzbek dishes were. Pilaf is the best dish in the world, I was told, and I was informed in detail about how to make it. All you need is rice, sheep's meat, carrots, sweet prunes, and, of course, some of those famous raisins, all goodies I could hardly remember existing.

Most of the Uzbek workers were middle-aged, the young men having been drafted into the army. Muslims, true to their religion, they would not touch pork or the piece of lard that was sometimes served with the kasha as a substitute for meat. They worked very hard and they were hungry, and they needed this food to sustain their energy during those long, cold winters. Yet, they would rather suffer than break the rules of their religious beliefs. Thus, they would leave the pork on their plates or give it away, and there were always enough takers. Observing them, I often thought about my father who suffered from starvation in the Łódź ghetto, remaining, I knew, equally devoted to what he had believed in, observing the rules of his religion that were holy to him.

Preparing Sauerkraut for the Winter

The job at the eatery was an easy one and my health and strength were improving. One day, however, I was told that I was assigned, temporarily mind you, to another job. Cabbage was being prepared for the coming winter, and workers were urgently needed for the job. A group of women—dishwashers, floor sweepers, and waitresses, transferred from their usual occupations in various canteens—was assembled, and formed into a "brigade" for cabbage slicing and sauerkraut preparation. A workplace was set up, a few long tables in the open air, at which the women armed with long knives were destroying the heavy heads of already half-frozen cabbage. The sliced cabbage was then poured into large wooden barrels, and after salt was added to it, pounded with a heavy wooden pestle till the juices would come up to the surface. My task was to deliver the cabbage heads to the tables for the cutters.

A One-legged Man

The work group was all women, and only the supervisor was a man. A big, one-legged man, he had lost his leg, now substituted by a wooden one, either in the war or in some other circumstances, I do not know. He was walking back and forth along the tables encouraging the women to work faster, better, and cheerfully. "*Vesela* [happiness], *baby, vesela*!" he kept repeating like a battle cry, and the women reacted with laughter. They seemed content to have that job, even though working inside the eatery was easier, but a few leaves of cabbage brought home would enhance the family's soup.

The image of that one-legged man, walking proudly among the throng of women in tarpaulin overcoats, their heads bundled up to their eyes in heavy kerchiefs to fend off the cold, and exclaiming his untranslatable encouragement—keep working, womenfolk, keep on—remains with me to this day. Over time, it has acquired an almost symbolic meaning for me: men were indeed in short supply.

I had no tarpaulin overcoat. I was still wearing the winter coat which I had come with from Poland over three years ago. It was much too light for the Ural weather, and now, in early October, I was cold. It had already started to snow occasionally, and because the snow would change to drizzle, my coat was constantly wet.

Anna Moysyeyevna

On my first day off from the cabbage brigade, I went to my canteen for my rationed lunch, and it was my good fortune that Anna Moysyeyevna, the canteen's director, spotted me. She had hired me a few months earlier to work in the canteen, but I had not expected that she would remember me or that she would recognize me in the crowd of her employees. Yet she did, and right away asked where I had been, and why was I not showing up at work? Who had sent me there, she wanted to know, and seemed puzzled, and even angry, when I said that it was her deputy's order. "Come back to work here tomorrow morning," she said, and I was certainly happy to do so.

A Little Stabilization

For a short while, I was back at my work as a cashier, again at the ITR hall. Here, I sat at a table at the entrance to the hall, selling the meals, receiving money, and cutting out the coupons from the ration cards. In the intervals, between lunchtime and the evening meal, I had enough time to glue all those coupons onto special sheets and add up the money for the accountant. The workday lasted late into the evening, but to complain under the circumstances was unthinkable. I still had some time in between to sit down somewhere with a book, or to write a letter to Gabriel, and on my days off for some socializing, or a movie, and especially for the newsreels. I always watched them with great interest, and now even more so that Gabriel was with the army again. He was on active duty, in combat. Sometimes, I almost expected to spot him somewhere out there. The newsreels were exuding optimism now, and this made the horrors of war a bit easier and less painful to watch.

After the victory at Stalingrad, the Soviet offensive continued, and the radio communiqués announced almost daily, names of cities taken back from the Germans. Those names were now mentioned so often that it seemed more cities had now been taken back than had been lost to the Germans a year ago. The deep, always solemn voice of Levitan,[83] the announcer, was now filled with confidence, not gloom.

83 Yuri Levitan (1914–1983) was the primary radio announcer for Radio Moscow during the war.

Gabriel reenlisted into the army after he had recovered from typhus, becoming at first a regular infantry soldier, and with time, a regimental translator and scout. He was at the front, under fire and danger, the war there was raging on, but somehow it became easier for me to believe in a happy outcome now. With the position of the regimental translator went an officer's rank and a monthly salary, which he transferred to me through the proper military channels, and I soon began to receive it.

He wrote often now. I remember his first letters from the front lines, he was on a bridgehead, he wrote, at a place where before the war an orchard had grown. Now the apple trees were half broken, injured, but still had some apples. They were, however, unreachable; to reach out for one might cost you your life, and the enemy snipers were vigilant. But the bushes bearing berries were sometimes just overhanging the trenches and the berries could be reached safely. From what he wrote, I understood that they were fighting something of a trench war, and Remarque's book, *All Quiet on the Western Front*, and the tragic story of the soldier killed by the last bullet at the last moment of war came to my mind. This image would haunt me to the very end of the war, till I got the letter dated already a few days after the war had ended, no matter how much I would try to not let myself think those thoughts for long, almost hypnotizing myself into believing that nothing of that kind would happen to him, that he would survive and return when it's all over, that after what he went through, and survived, nothing bad could happen to him again. All I had to do was to wait, and he would return, as the popular wartime song was promising, "Wait for me, and I'll return," the soldier writes to the girl he loves.[84] There were many such songs, people were humming them, this one and another one I remember, *Sinii Platochek* (Blue Kerchief),[85] the girl waving goodbye with it to her beloved, who is going off to fight the motherland's enemy, songs dripping with sentimentality, and playing to the nostalgic feelings for the "good old times" when life was peaceful and all was beautiful. The lyrics may not have been the best, but with the melodies easy to hum,

84 Konstantin Simonov, *Zhdi menia i ia vernus* (Wait for me, and I'll return) (1941).

85 Jerzy Peterburgski and Yakov Galitsky, *Sinii Platochek* (1940).

the songs became very popular and well-liked. Of the many songs, my favorite was Soloviev-Sedoy's "Nightingales, nightingales, do not wake the boys, let them have some sleep," a song about the hardships and suffering of the common soldier.[86] I happened to see Soloviev-Sedoy in person once when he came to Leningrad University to perform. He sang this song then, accompanying himself on the piano, in the big university hall. It was an enchanting evening, but this belongs to another chapter.

Promoted at the Ural Trust Food Supply

I was again promoted, and this, too, was thanks to Anna Moysyeyevna. This time, I became the canteen's "calculator." "You'll stay for a week with Katya, she'll introduce you to what it's all about, and you will be fine," she said. Ekaterina Ivanovna, Katya, a native Ural middle-aged woman, was also promoted somewhere much higher up in the ranks of the Ural Trust Food Supply, and she was indeed willing to prepare me for the job. I was familiar with the basic notions of accounting, having learned them before the war in Łódź, and now it came in handy.

I stayed at the same canteen in my new capacity for some two months, until I got a message from the bosses of the Trust that I was to be transferred to another place, some 50 kilometers away, to a small settlement where a new production place had opened up recently, and a canteen to feed some hundred people was being set up there. This meant that I was being sent "*k chortu na kulichki*" (where the devil feasts), as the Russian saying goes, to the end of the world. There was nothing I could do about it, or so I thought, and it would not help to protest or complain. It was easy to send me away anywhere, I was alone, with no family ties or obligations, so I packed my few belongings and went.

86 Vasiliy Soloviev-Sedoy and Aleksei Fa'ianov, *Solov'i ne trebozh'te soldat* (Nightingales, Give the Soldiers a Rest) (1944). The line she recalls is not quite the same as the official lyrics.

Do You Like to Swear?

I do not remember much of that place and I would not be able to locate it or name it. I was brought there late in the afternoon by one of the trucks of the aluminum mill, and the next thing I recall, I was sitting in a rather large room opposite a middle-aged woman in a reddish dress, her frizzy blonde hair well cared for, her broad face smiling at me kindly, while her vigilant eyes kept checking me out attentively. I was to share the room with her, she told me. We tried to talk, chatting about nothing when suddenly, the woman asked me, "Do you like to swear, Annushka?" Confused enough as I already was by the whole new situation, her strange question disconcerted me even more. Like to swear? I would use a swear word now and then when angry with something, I might say "*psia krew*" (dog's blood) or "*cholera jasna*" (damn it), for example, which was often used in Poland. No, this was not what she had in mind, the woman answered, still smiling politely. "What about real swear words?" "Oh, Russian swear words?" Certainly, during all these years in Russia, I had heard some, but I could not say that I was familiar with the core Russian lexicon, and if at all, it was only vague. But to use it? No, I do not use it, and as for liking it? No, I do not, and I asked rather meekly, "Why? What for?" Noticing my puzzled look, the woman explained, "Just so, to balm, gladden your heart." Swear just for the pleasure of it? Spit out strings of swear words, as if it were some game? Strangely, I started feeling somewhat defensive. Of course, the Russian predilection for swearing, using obscenities, and all kinds of four-letter words, was widespread, but since my knowledge of the Russian language came mostly from reading, from literature, and literature in those times had not yet adopted it as its own, having renamed it "adult language," and since in my everyday relations I had heard Russian swearing, of course, but not as often as it might have seemed. Still, "just to balm, gladden your heart"? This was a first for me. This was truly something new. I was baffled and scared, too. For a moment something froze inside me, like a foreboding of some unknown and much worse things to come. She would teach me, the woman offered enthusiastically, perhaps envisioning the pleasure of teaching a novice. But there was no lecture right away, I was tired and declined it till tomorrow.

Early the next morning, I went to see my new workplace, and what a view it was! I was desolate. What will I do here in this truly godforsaken place, in that canteen that had one pot, one woman cook for cooking and everything else, and a local peasant-type guy as the would-be director of an as yet nonexistent eatery, who seemed to be quite content about the whole business, and me, to take care of it, but of what? I was not a pioneer, I did not feel that I was capable to build an eatery from scratch in the middle of nowhere, and I doubted that anybody expected me to do so. The whole thing seemed to have been a misunderstanding, but how would I clear up the whole mess? Fortunately, I did not have to. While I was looking around in desperation, the telephone rang and conveyed a message from the Trust's office to me to come back. What a relief! Anna Moysyeyevna, she must have been behind this, again, I thought with gratitude. Bless her!

Three Sisters, Not by Chekhov

I did not return, however, to her place, but was assigned to a different canteen and worked there, in the same capacity, till the end of my stay in the Urals. It was a smaller place, with a much smaller crew, only two cashiers, and both happened to be Jewish refugee women from Poland who had come to the Soviet Union at the same time and in the same way as I had. Ewa and Pola were two sisters from Central Poland. Their third sister, the oldest, Mina, who had also arrived with them, lived in another place, but also in the Ural Mountains. Pola and Mina had come to the Soviet Union with their husbands before the end of 1939 and Ewa had come with her fiancé. They had planned to get married soon after, but the war struck and there was no time for ceremonies. Now, all three men were sitting in Soviet concentration camps, arrested over a year ago on some trumped-up political charges and sentenced to ten years each. This was a very popular sentence and as the Soviet saying goes, "ten years you get for nothing."

Ewa and I became friends. She was happy that I had joined the crew of that canteen. She felt relieved working with me, she was telling me. She was not very good with the Russian language and taking care of the food coupons and the money seemed too much for her as well. Afraid that she would make some mistake and bring upon herself unpleasant consequences, or that someone would frame her, now she could breathe easier, being accountable to me.

Sometimes when the cold was too bitter to return after work to my barracks which was at least a few kilometers away, I would stay overnight with the two sisters. Once, while I went to sleep, Ewa stayed up till late, mending my skirt that had begun to come apart. She treated me like a younger sister, and her care and tenderness warmed my heart. It had been a long time since I had experienced it from anybody, and it brought back Mother, my siblings, and it brought back Gabriel.

I met all three sisters after the war in Warsaw. One day, Ewa came to visit us. She found out where I lived and simply knocked on the door. They all returned to Poland when the war ended, she told me, but none of their men did. Pola's husband did not survive the camp, he died shortly before the war ended and she was duly notified about it. Mina's husband survived the camp but found another woman and remained with her in the Soviet Union. Ewa's boyfriend served his ten-year sentence to the end, and after that, returned to Poland. He had hoped to find her, but Ewa by that time was already married to a different man, a dentist, with whom she lived happily for many years and had a child, a girl, named Tzipora. Ewa was desperate to have a child but was not able to conceive for a long time. And when it finally happened, her former boyfriend showed up. Now, she would not return to him, even though some of the old feelings toward him were still alive, because her child had a father and they were a family.

Shortly after that, Ewa with her husband and child left for Israel, and so did her two sisters who remained single. I would often think about them; three sisters, like in Chekhov's play, yet from another story, another time, different angst and suffering; but their lives could also fill a novel, they also deserved a story, a play, in any case, they deserved not to be forgotten.

The Chief Cook and the Canteen's Director

Of the other people I met at the new canteen, the most memorable characters were the chief cook and the director. The cook was a tall and very skinny young Ukrainian, almost bare bones, quite unusual for a cook. His name has escaped me, but one of his often-repeated sayings still rings in my memory like a refrain of a sad song, "*Shchi i kasha—pishcha nasha*" (cabbage soup and kasha is our daily food—in Russian it rhymes). This was what he cooked day after day and what the canteen fed some 600 workers twice daily. The popular saying, reflecting life's monotony, conveyed feelings of melancholy and frustration, but in his rendition, it was just oozing with these feelings, deepened in his case, perhaps, by his frustrated professional ambitions being forced by the circumstances to limit his art of cooking so severely.

The director of the canteen, Yarmoshchuk, was a stocky half-Ukrainian, half-Russian but a total Leningrader. He did not care too much, however, about the city's name, Leningrad. For him the city's name was Peter, not Leningrad or Petrograd or Petersburg; the name of the city had changed many times before it was named Leningrad, and the proud old inhabitants of former Saint Petersburg often liked to use its abridged name, Peter. Called up into the army at the beginning of the war, he was wounded defending the city, and thus the war came to an end for him. Nurtured back to health and discharged, with a medal for bravery, he came to the Urals where he went to work within the food supply organizations. His wound had left his right arm and hand stiff and without feeling, but he "got out of hell," as he would sometimes say rather lightly.

By that time, I had already met all kinds of people in the Soviet Union and had become smart enough not to expect to find the "new Soviet man" as the official ideology envisioned him/her, but Yarmoshchuk was a very special character. He certainly was a good organizer and he worked hard to keep his canteen running smoothly. Hungry for recognition, he once invited a journalist of the local newspaper, fed him a good dinner, and received in return a glorious write-up, praising him highly as a "*vzortzovii director*" (a model director), tending to the needs of the workers. What he needed this for, I could not fathom: would his bosses higher up in the organization look at him more favorably? Didn't they know how such publicity was won?

Once, being perhaps a bit drunk, he showed off his stiff right hand, tightly covered by a leather glove, commenting, "They all steal, I am not against it; too bad I have only one hand, had I had both, I would steal with both." Did he steal and how, I had no idea. He was given to cynical, cruel jokes, remarking once on a case of a director of one of the canteens caught watering down the soup, which had been served there, "Big deal, they say, a ton of water contains 5 grams of fat, so what's the problem?" Yet, if he did steal, he was probably not a large-scale crook. About what big-scale stealing meant, I got a hint from our pantry keeper, Semion Porfirievich, an older local man. He worked in food supply for years and in many capacities. Once, he served for a certain time as an actor, he told me in confidence. Where there is food, there is also waste; food gets spoiled and it has to be written off, he explained. It's all, of course, done in full legality: the waste is estimated, weighed, and so on, and the protocols are duly signed, but when a ton was spoiled, 2 tons would be written off. So, you see where the crooks are? People blame the salesgirls, selling you your portion of daily rationed bread, sure, she would get her few additional crumbs, but the thieves were higher, much higher, and they didn't steal crumbs.

Motya Abramovich

My education was certainly getting more detailed and deeper, and one day it was summed up, of sorts, by Motya Abramovich, an evacuee from Babruysk. He was an older man, his two sons were serving in the Red Army, both officers, one a major in the artillery, the other a captain, both somewhere on the front lines. Motya Abramovich worked at the transport division of the aluminum mill and moonlighted producing for his private customers something resembling galoshes, shallow rubber boots worn over regular shoes or on *valenki* if one was lucky enough to own a pair of those felt boots. Warm and light, they were excellent for the snow and cold of the Russian Ural winters. Motya Abramovich made the "galoshes" out of pieces and scraps of old tires, using the aluminum mill's facilities and vulcanization tools. The tires belonged, of course, to the mill. He would gladly, he told me, buy the scraps and pieces he needed for his "production," but they were not for sale, and the only way to get them was to steal them. His whole "enterprise" was, of course, illegal, and Motya Abramovich was a lawbreaker, even though he hated to be one very much.

That winter, my last in the Urals, I bought a pair of high boots that were supposed to be leather. Being now better off, supported with Gabriel's pension every month, I could afford it, but my "leather" boots turned out to be fake and soaked up water like a sponge. What I needed was a pair of galoshes, and Motya Abramovich made them for me from those stolen pieces of rubber. We often talked about the war and life in general, about our loved ones left under the Germans, he with his wife had gotten out in time, but still had many relatives left there. We also talked about the hard times, how poor people lived and how crooks had it very well. He would often end the conversation with a confidential sigh and a declaration, "I will tell you a secret, dear girl, '*Eto ne sotsialism, eto venerism*'" (this is not Socialism, this is a venereal disease). In Russian, the word for venereal disease rhymes with Socialism.

There Will Be a Future for Us

The summer of 1944 was approaching fast. Almost three years had gone by since I had come as an evacuee to the Urals. And what next? I had survived the worst, the war would come to an end, and perhaps soon, and it would certainly be a victorious end. It was time to think again about the future and go back to my old dream. I still needed a year of high school to get the coveted diploma. Universities began reopening, and advertising admissions. I saw an advert in the local library that Leningrad University, which was still in evacuation in Saratov, would receive applications from prospective students and it took my breath away. For the first time since the outbreak of the war, they were opening their doors to new students!

I decided to see the director of the Moscow high school that was functioning here in evacuation and ask permission to pass the final exams as an extern, together with the high school students, during the examination session coming shortly. This was a daring idea, which I got from a book I once read. The hero of that novel did just that, he passed his exams for a medical school as an extern, and later on became a respected, if not even famous doctor—I am not sure about the details, but never mind! Yet, I was skeptical until the last moment that such permission would be granted. I was, however, sure that if granted I would be able to prepare myself properly. I was overjoyed when the high school director, an older man, having heard me out, after a moment of hesitation, said yes. Why not? And he kindly gave me the schedule of the session that was already in preparation.

Taking Exams As an Extern

I did not have much time, and there was so much to do, and so many gaps to fill. I did not doubt that I would manage literature, history, or science, like physics and chemistry, but mathematics was still my bête noire. Written algebra, would I pass this? I tried to convince a girl I knew from my Chemical Technicum, to do the same, to take the same "shortcut," trying to strike a deal with her. She was very good at math, so she could help me prepare, while I would help her with the other subjects. But she took one look at the two volumes, the textbooks for Russian literature and Russian history, and just said no, this was not for her, she would never manage. Too bad, I liked her. I still remember her name; Boyarskaya, half-Russian, half-Bashkir, and so good at math! It's very easy, she would just say, when I struggled with it.

Well, I would do it alone, then. I had two months to prepare before me. And I was prepared. The Russian essay that frightened Boyarskaya was "easy" for me, and the oral exam turned out to be something of a triumph. My examination question required me to talk about the Russian poets of the second decade of the century. I started with Alexandr Block, my favorite, reciting his lines by heart, and then Bryusov, in which lines one could hear the rattle of arms, and the clatter of hoofs, the sounds of the revolution. My textbook said so, and I repeated it faithfully but also added as if an afterthought that there is another poet whose lines are also so expressive that one could hear sounds there, although of a different kind; one could hear laughter, and I read the few lines I had memorized from Khlebnikov, lines which made me fall in love with his poetry. "*Razsmeytes smekhachi! zasmyeytes smekhachi, chto smeyutsya smekhami, chto smeyanstvuyut smeyalno, o, zasmeytes usmeyalno.*"[87] I did not know any other line of Khlebnikov, besides these were quoted by my textbook as an example of an empty play of words. But I was intrigued and greatly impressed by those few lines, and I got a round of applause from my classmates for reciting them! I got an A. Such a good start made it easier for me to successfully pass the rest of the exams. I passed them all, and I did very well in physics, chemistry, geometry, even trigonometry, and the scary algebra too, though with less success. I got my diploma and immediately mailed it to Saratov. I think I remember all this so vividly and with such detail because I felt that I had indeed achieved something important. I was proud of it, as a matter of fact, prouder, perhaps, than I was later in life after achieving my subsequent academic degrees, even my doctorate, or later my publications, books, and articles that always tended to leave me with an aftertaste of a job not quite done to my liking. Getting a high school diploma was equal to breaking a barrier. Also, I was the first in my family who was going to get a university degree. And I had done this against all odds.

In the meantime, Gina also decided to apply for admission to the university. She hesitated at first, to my dismay, and she even dropped out of high school having only a few months left to finish the tenth

87 Viktor "Velimir" Khlebnikov (1885–1922) was a Futurist Russian poet. His 1908–1909 poem *Zakliatie smekhom* (Invocation of Laughter) opens with the four lines she quotes. His plays on words and unaccustomed uses are truly a challenge to translate. One translation reads: O laugh it out, you laughsters! O laugh it up, you laughsters! So they laugh with laughsters, so they laugherize delaughly. O laugh it up belaughably! See Marjorie Perloff and Craig Dworkin, eds., *The Sound of Poetry / The Poetry of Sound* (Chicago and London: The University of Chicago Press, 2009), pp. 100–101.

grade. She decided then that she would rather go to work, earn some money, and get a better ration card, which under the circumstances, was understandable. For some time, she was a cashier in the same canteen where I worked later. I had followed her example and advice in seeking employment there, but after a while she quit the canteen and went to work at the aluminum mill, learning to become a cutter there. Now, having changed her mind, she decided to apply to the university, after all. The teachers at her high school where she spent over two years after arriving with her family in the Urals knew her as an excellent student and there was no difficulty with obtaining the diploma. I was glad that we would be going to Saratov together.

Gina got the response from the university quickly. Her diploma showed straight A's from the top down, and she was admitted without any entrance examinations. Now, for me, I had begun a waiting period. I was working, as usual, but my thoughts were with the postman: would there be a letter from Saratov for me or not yet? Some time went by and I began doubting that such a letter would ever come. The high school was short of diploma certificates, which was nothing unusual as there was a shortage of everything. As an external student, I got a *spravka* instead of a formal diploma, a statement listing all the subjects I had passed, and the grades I had received. This was just on a regular sheet of paper, but it had all the necessary stamps, round and rectangular ones, which made it as formal as formal could be! But maybe this was not enough to be admitted to such a prestigious institution as Leningrad University?

But finally, my day came. One morning Gina showed up at my workplace with a letter in her hand, it was for me from Saratov. Come for the entrance exams, it said. I was overjoyed!

Why Quit Such a Nice Job?

All I needed now was to pack my few belongings and make some rounds to arrange to leave my job. Enlisting in a university was recognized by the law as a sufficient reason for obtaining release from one's job, and I received it promptly. People were asking me, though, with some surprise, where I was going and why? Are you not happy here? You have such a nice job! "*Teplo i mukhi ne kusaiutsia*" (You have it warm, and flies are not disturbing you) so where are you going? You'll starve there, don't you know? Leningrad? People are still pretty hungry there! And what are you going to study? Philosophy? What's that and what for? I felt uneasy about explaining that philosophy was a "legitimate" subject of study, and often in answer to that last question, I would say that I would be studying history, which was usually received with a little less derision.

I was glad to leave the Ural Trust of Food Supply. I was, of course, aware that the job at the canteen had helped me to survive the tough times. During the year and a half of working for the Trust, my health improved, and I was now able to look ahead with a greater degree of confidence.

Shortly before leaving, I saw Anna Moysyeyevna, the canteen's director. She had always been kind and helpful and I owed her quite a lot. When I told her where I was going and why, she was glad for me. She smiled at me and wished me well, actually "Bless you" she said, which was rather unusual for that time and place and made me remember it as a cherished gift.

CHAPTER NINE

STUDENT TIME

The cavernous hall of the Sverdlovsk train station, the first stop on the way to our destination, Saratov, was crowded, chock-full of men in military garb, soldiers, and officers. Some were just milling around, some took up the station's floor sleeping or just resting, and some were running, hurrying to their trains. Their gray-greenish trench coats seemed to be everywhere, and the heavy odor of makhorka and cigarette smoke permeated the stale air; the whole station seemed to be enveloped in a nondescript gray-greenish shadow of dirt. To secure seats for the next stretch of our trip, from Sverdlovsk to Saratov, we had to stamp our tickets here, but considering the competition, our chances looked rather slim: the military moving to the West, to their units, must, of course, come first. We spent a long sleepless night perched on some steps inside the station, amidst a mass of soldiers, sleeping, snoring, and pushing to find a place to stretch their legs. It looked like we were in for a long wait, and perhaps we would have been, if not for Gina's resourcefulness. She saved the day! Early in the morning, while I remained at the station with our belongings, she went to the city to find the headquarters of her last employer, the Ural Aluminum Trust. To her surprise, she was met there with more than just understanding; girls enrolling in university, graduate schools opening up again and admitting students, and life returning to normal, this sounded all so optimistic that she made them almost happy there, she told me on returning to the station with our tickets properly stamped for the next available train, and even some additional food coupons for the next few days, to boot.

From Sverdlovsk to Saratov, from the southern tip of the Ural Mountains to the Volga River, there are some 2,000 kilometers. I do not remember how much time it took us to reach Saratov. The trip in a car packed with soldiers, as was the whole train, was uneventful. I slept one night through, lucky to have found some space on an upper bunk, but nothing about the rest of that trip. I do remember though that bright morning when bent almost in half under the weight of my backpack, I disembarked on the platform of the Saratov train station. Someone representing the university was waiting there and directed us to our temporary new home, the university's dormitory. We were not the only ones coming to enroll; people were coming from everywhere, the most convincing evidence that the university was serious about starting a new academic year. There would be a new beginning!

Saratov

Saratov, situated on the right bank of the Volga, was a medium-sized city. Some 640 kilometers to the northwest from here was Moscow, and only about 320 kilometers to the south was Volgograd, then known under the name of Stalingrad.

Founded by the end of the sixteenth century as a fortress guarding Russia against the hostile nomads of the steppe from the east, Saratov became an industrial and agricultural center in the nineteenth century that would develop and grow in size and importance during and after the war, reaching about half a million inhabitants during the war years. At this time, the city's population growth was mainly because it hosted many evacuees who came to Saratov with their institutions, like Leningrad University, or with their factories and heavy industry plants, which continued operating there. The native population was mostly Russian, with a mixture of national minorities—Chuvashs, Mordovians, and Tatars.

Saratov boasted a rich historical past. The Soviet encyclopedias and dictionaries stressed the fact the Ulyanov/Lenin family lived there, even though it was a rather short stay. The same sources also pointed out with pride that Saratov was the birthplace of many heroes of Russian history, of famous revolutionaries of the nineteenth century, and foremost among them, Nikolay Chernyshevsky. Going back even further into history, to the seventeenth century, the Stenka Razin peasant and Cossack rebellion against the tsars was played out here and many of the Saratov inhabitants had supposedly participated. This last event was not, however, very much in vogue at the time I came to Saratov. During the war, such events were rather played down and for understandable reasons: it was not "politically correct" to laud rebellions against the state, even those of the distant past, even against the tsarist state, now that the state was engaged in a war against the nation's mortal enemy. The presentation of Saratov's historical high points, to which we were treated upon arrival at the university, omitted them discreetly, as did the history books then and later during the first postwar years.

Of course, moving from the Ural settlement to a big city, with many cultural amenities was a boon, and it felt that way to me. I liked to walk along the streets, real city streets with buildings on both sides, streets that led to a square, and from there to more streets, revealing new vistas as you walked along. I was a city girl, and I preferred those tunnel-like city vistas to the open spaces around the Ural settlements which seemed to lead to nowhere. I often felt lost there, at the end of the world. Not so here, I felt much more at home.

It Is a Small World

Little by little, I got to know the city better and appreciated its cultural institutions. In Saratov, there was a theater and a symphony hall, and many art and history museums. There was also an opera and ballet theater with which I was rather well acquainted during my stay in Saratov. A funny thing happened the very first time I went to buy tickets for a performance there. In the foyer of that theater, I met Salek, an acquaintance from Łódź, from the Youth Section, from the time when we were still teenagers. We had not seen each other since we had left Łódź, or perhaps even a year before that, and now six years later, here we were! We were both surprised. It's a small world, indeed! So, Gabriel is with the army, he commented, and you are a university student! He seemed overwhelmed. He got married, he told me, lives in Saratov, and "do you need money?" he wanted to know, he wanted to help out. "Thanks, but no," I declined. I did not need any help and reciprocated with advice to join a night school, to take advantage of the opportunity to get an education. Well, I or maybe the Yentl in me was always advising, urging anybody who asked for it or not, to learn, to study. We met again after the war in Łódź, and later in Israel, where he eventually moved with his family, and where Gabriel and I visited. Whenever we met, he always recalled that I advised him to study and that he sincerely regretted not having listened to my advice. Yes, I always proselytized for education, and though not always successful, I hope I did manage to convert some.

Saratov University

Among the many places of higher learning located in Saratov, the most important was Saratov University. It was one of the oldest in the country, founded in 1909, and in 1921 named in honor of Chernyshevsky, a radical revolutionary, writer, critic, thinker, and most of all, a prisoner of conscience, who had spent twenty-seven years in the tsar's prisons. One of his books, *What Is to Be Done?* influenced generations of revolutionary youth in Russia, and gave inspiration for many books by those seeking an answer to the question he posed, and most prominently to Lenin's own, *What Is to Be Done?* with consequences that became rather well known. Saratov University also boasted many world-renowned professors and scholars in the past and of having prepared many thousands of specialists from the Soviet Union in almost all fields of knowledge and industry. There were departments in almost all fields of science. Humanities, history, linguistics, and languages were also well represented, but there was no Department of Philosophy.

Leningrad University in Saratov

The arrival of Leningrad University, evacuated from Leningrad for the duration of the war, had enormously enhanced the level of learning as well as the status of Saratov University and knowing that, the arrivals treated their host a bit patronizingly. The host university was "provincial" while the guests were from the great city with "European" aspirations. The newly arrived students were let into that "secret" right away with numerous stories and anecdotes to make that point. I can recall one such anecdote. The university owned a subsidiary farm, which provided, in part at least, vegetables for the students' and employees' canteen, and students, as well as professors, were obliged to work there for the good of all. Professor Aleksandrov was a Leningrad University world-famous mathematician, and he too would share in that work, but unfortunately, his contribution was not up to standard. Professor Usov, then deputy rector of Saratov University, reprimanded him and published in the university press an announcement, "Professor Aleksandrov is to be strongly reprimanded for weeding the carrots carelessly." Of course, Professor Usov immediately became the laughingstock of the newly arrived, and proved their point; this is a "provincial, parochial" place!

Whether the story was true or not, there certainly was something to the Leningraders' claim. Leningrad University brought people who would not have come to Saratov otherwise and greatly enhanced the host school's intellectual status. I heard such opinions, and anecdotes, from trusted, reliable sources. Włodek [Włodzimierz] Brus, the foremost Polish reformer-economist of the 1960s, knew about it from his own experience and shared his knowledge with me. Escaping from Lwów before the German onslaught, he managed to get to Saratov already in 1941 and stayed there to work on his doctorate in economics. The Leningraders were a true intellectual tour de force, influencing the host university's life, he maintained, citing as an example the Gukovsky brothers or philosopher Vladimir Resnik, who made Włodek read Hegel's *Phenomenology of the Spirit*—in German!—and discuss it with him in detail!

I too remember the intellectual excitement that Professor [Grigory Aleksandrovich] Gukovsky, a historian of Russian literature—the other Gukovsky [Matvei Alexsandrovich] was a highly respected specialist in European Medieval history—was able to stir up. I will never forget the public university lecture on Pushkin read by Professor Gukovsky. The enormous auditorium was bursting, and many more people were crammed into the outside hall, corridors, and steps. The enthusiasm of the listeners was indescribable and for me rather perplexing. Gukovsky spoke about Pushkin, stressing the poet's "Russianness," which made the crowd go almost wild. The professor was a marvelous speaker, but this alone would not have explained the temperature of the event. It was a lecture given at the right moment; it was the fall of 1944, the war was going well and visibly coming closer to a triumphant end, and the wave of Russian confidence and patriotic pride was reaching a peak. Soon, just a few years after the war, this pride would be easily manipulated into Russian chauvinism, directed against "cosmopolitanism," which would also include official antisemitism. But this would come later. For now, the professor's quotations from Pushkin lauding the delights of the Russian countryside, buckwheat blooming in the fields, moved the public almost to tears. To me it all sounded overdone, I was rather attuned to Soviet "patriotism," if any, rather than to a purely Russian one, and quite possibly such overzealous outbursts of nationalistic emotions scared me just a little, even there and then.

And, of course, I could not have agreed more with the laudatory words about Professor Vladimir Resnik. He became my first teacher of philosophy and I remember him fondly and with gratitude to this day. He was a philosopher, an intellectual, and an educator who influenced his students in many ways, but unfortunately, his role at the university was cut short for political reasons. At the end of my first year at Leningrad,[88] Vladimir Resnik was removed from the Faculty of Philosophy. It was a

88 The author refers to her first year in Leningrad, not with the University of Leningrad in Saratov.

sad story and a truly ominous sign that dark political changes were on the way. I will return to it later.

Rossiya and Evropa, Russia and Europe

The University of Saratov had two dormitories for the arriving students. These were former city hotels, named Rossiya (Russia) and Evropa (Europe), respectively both located on the same street, and facing each other. The buildings, each four stories high, had similar good-sized rooms accommodating four people each. As it turned out, there were also differences. Evropa was in much better shape than Rossiya. First, the plumbing in Rossiya was almost constantly in disrepair, defective, and often breaking down. When necessary, we would run across the street to use Evropa's facilities. On top of this, Rossiya quite often suffered blackouts, either because of shortages in the city's general electrical system, which when cuts were unavoidable, preferred to cut Rossiya's side of the street rather than the other one, or because of Rossiya's faulty fuses. While Evropa boasted a rather steady flow of electrical current that permitted proper illumination of the rooms in the evenings and even the use of small electrical appliances, such as a hot plate allowing for tea preparation, Rossiya was often engulfed by darkness. "Of course, everything is as it should be," a newly arrived student, a tall blonde girl with a Muscovite accent, summed up the situation once, repeating and paraphrasing the traditional verdict of Russian westerners, "*V Rossiyi t'ma, v Evrope svet*" (darkness rules in Russia, enlightened is Europe). Critical of Russia's backwardness, the westerners traditionally juxtaposed Russia with European progress, sometimes doing so with considerable bitterness and anger. The girl from Moscow pronounced her judgment with an ironic chuckle, and we all laughed.

My Dormitory: Rossiya

Gina and I were assigned a room in the Rossiya. Soon two other girls, one from Tbilisi and the other from faraway Siberia, joined us. The girl from Tbilisi was Margarita (Rita) Idelson, also an aspiring philosophy student, and before long Rita and I struck up a friendship that would last far beyond our student years. Rita was already over thirty, and an engineer by profession when she came to Saratov; a latecomer, one might say, yet still below the age Plato recommended for commencing studying philosophy, she said with a laugh. Intelligent, perceptive, and hardworking, Rita was endowed with an uncanny ability to convey her knowledge to others with admirable lucidity. She would become the best student in our class and seemed well on her way to a good academic career. Yet this was not to be, through no fault of her own.

New students were coming daily, and they were mostly, if not exclusively, girls, a sign that the war was still going on. The girls came, dragging their belongings in wooden suitcases or just bundled up in a blanket. Many brought bags with dried bread, heavy black Russian bread, turned into crackers. Parents were sending their daughters off to study at one of the most prestigious universities in the country and they did their best to provide for them, for the trip, and for the first, perhaps, hungry days in the new place. They gave them the best they could. As the girls unpacked the bags and took out the bread collected at home sometimes for weeks, often they found to their dismay that the crackers were covered with mildew, spoiled, and had to be disposed of. I still remember the expression on the face of the girl who had to throw away her bag of bread, the expression of embarrassment and regret, to waste bread was a shame, and the loss pained her as she knew what it took to prepare it for her. This image has come back to me often. It somehow epitomizes for me the level of poverty and deprivation that had become so common in the Soviet Union during the war.

Preparing for the Entrance Examinations

After the first few days of getting acquainted with each other, with the future professors, and with Saratov University where we would be studying until the time came to leave for Leningrad, we got the schedule of the entrance examinations and sat down to work. The exam that worried many the most was Russian history, a very broad subject. I remember the instructor sharing a few tips with us. "Don't tell me, when asked about the Crimean War, that we lost it because our officers were good-for-nothing while the soldiers were true heroes. I will fail you for that right away," he warned us. "It was the other way around," he continued. "The officers were great, we had great leaders, heroes, Admiral Nakhimov, and the like, while the soldiers, subjugated feudal peasants, did not want to fight, they did not see any purpose in fighting." The instructor warned us not to repeat the easy and popular—and popular because it was so easy—cliché: the "bad" officers versus the heroic "masses." This interpretation, he admonished us, was a travesty of Marxist teaching, forgetting somehow to add that on this basic formula, it was also once considered proper and essential from the same Marxist point of view that these schools of history were once built.

"Tough Is the Rock of Knowledge"

We formed a study group to prepare for the exam and started meeting every morning for sessions lasting a few hours. At one of the first such sessions, a woman approached us, she would like to join our group. She was a ballerina, a chorus girl to be exact, with the Saratov Opera, but, you see, she was forty now, her dancing years were over, she had to learn something to be able to move on with her life and she asked would we take her in so she could prepare for that horrendous history exam with us? We did, and she became a fixture in the room. She came regularly, never late, and sat there quietly, reading her piece, moving her lips while reading. Then, trying to memorize what she had just read, she would raise her head, cover her ears with her hands, and move her lips even faster to repeat what she had just read. From time to time, she would stop for a moment, shaking her head as if in despair, and let out a deep sigh, pronouncing more to herself than to us, "*gryzem granit nauki, devushki!*" (Tough is the rock of knowledge, girls!) I adopted the expression, and I have used it ever since, sometimes half-jokingly, sometimes quite seriously, as an encouragement when my task gets too demanding, and I come close to quitting. Then, it becomes a call to resist the urge to quit. The image of that slim, petite woman of forty poring over her history book is still with me; it makes me smile as I recall the efforts and aspirations of my youth when biting into the "tough rock of knowledge" seemed to be the most important thing in the world for me.

You Must Have Been Born Somewhere along the Volga?

The history exam went without a hitch. I answered the questions, and my professor was satisfied with my answers, but he wanted to know where I came from, and from which part of the Soviet Union. "You have a slight accent," he told me, and he tried to guess which part of the country he could ascribe it to and where I had been born. "Don't tell me," he said, "just talk to me some more." He listened attentively when I talked "some more," but then he shook his head, and admitted that he could not be sure, but perhaps I had been brought up somewhere along the Volga because I do accent the letter "o" a bit too strongly. He was quite surprised that I came from a place much closer to the Vistula than the Volga and had not spoken Russian until I arrived in the Soviet Union, a few years earlier.

My First Academic Year Begins

With the exams over, it was time to begin working in earnest. There was no set program of study, but we were offered what was available at

Saratov University. Since there was no Department of Philosophy, we were directed to study languages and history. I took Latin, which was taught by an older man obviously with a lot of experience and even more patience. I sincerely regret that all this lasted only one semester, enough to get the taste of it, but nothing more. Unfortunately, Latin was not offered at Leningrad University. Teachers of Latin, as well as teachers of logic, interestingly, I am afraid, were then a dying species in the Soviet Union.

Of all the other subjects I took, and there must have been quite a few, I recall vaguely only the lectures in comparative linguistics, and I remember these more because of the lecturer than the subject itself. It was getting cold in Saratov, it was November or even later, the auditorium was cold, too cold to take notes, and the female professor who was lecturing was clad in a heavy fur coat. I can still see her imposing figure in that heavy, long almost to her ankles, gray fur, walking back and forth on the podium, explaining the intricacies of the Old Church Slavonic tongue. One day, she gave me an assignment for the next seminar, to prepare a talk about Marr's linguistic theory. I dutifully went to the university library and spent a whole day there reading up on Marr.

Who remembers Marr now? Stalin made him "famous" by blasting him for real and made up "sins" in his *About Linguistics* booklet in 1951, as a result of which Marr was pushed into the abyss of nonexistence and his school was dismantled. But in the forties, Nikolay Yakovlevich Marr, who died in 1934, was still revered in the Soviet Union as a scholar, and his school of comparative grammar that tried to establish a linguistic kinship between the Caucasian languages and the languages of the world dominated the field. Marr and his followers were aspiring to achieve a monopolistic position in Soviet linguistics. Marr had declared that all he wanted was to replace "Marrism" in linguistics with Marxism. Translated into plain language, this meant that Marr's linguistics should, as the only true expression of Marxism, be recognized as the only true theory in the field of linguistics.

I was then, of course, far from such thoughts, and what I read interested me, it was new to me, it made me think, and preparing a talk for a seminar, for the first time, seemed important and exciting.

But the next morning, I could not remember what I had read in the library just the night before. I knew it was on Marr, but what? Not a word, not a sign, just a blank, not even the title of the work in question. This scared me a lot. How will I be able to study? What was I to do? Doomed! Now, that I finally had the chance! Frustrated, disappointed, and almost in a panic, I was upset. Fortunately, it was only a temporary setback.

Other Polish Refugees at the University

In Saratov, there were also other Polish–Jewish refugees, and some were students of the Saratov–Leningrad University. I was happy to get acquainted with some of them. I met there Sylvia Bartel and her boyfriend (later her husband), Szulim Weisblum, as well as her two sisters, Genya and Zosia. Three sisters, again, very different from the sisters that I was acquainted with in the Urals, different from the point of view of their upbringing, education, and aspirations, but also with very interesting life stories, to say the least, and they also deserve a play or a novel. Of all three, I knew Genya the least as she joined the Department of History in Saratov and remained there when I left with the university for Leningrad, but she struck me as the most caring soul, one who treated her sisters as her charges, always doing something "for them." A small girl, my size, I remember her as I once saw her, bent almost to the ground under a heavy sack of potatoes she was hauling home, alone. As Sylvia, who had spent her childhood in an orphanage, told me, Genya was indeed a "caregiver" to her, before and even after that orphanage. Albeit the three sisters came from a very poor background, orphaned early in their life, the oldest, Zosia, still managed to become a mathematics student at Lwów University before the war. Sylvia was the one I met first. One day, she stopped me on the steps of our dormitory, Rossiya. She heard that I was from Poland, she told me. The rest was easy and soon I got to know others, among them Basia Holcman, a Warsaw girl, a biology student. New friendships were started, and some, like the last two mentioned here, have lasted to this day.

Polish Patriots in Saratov

Some of the Polish refugees congregated at the Union of Polish Patriots [Związek Patriotów Polskich, ZPP]. At first, the name had a confusing and, for me, even suspicious ring to it. What was it, I wondered? Patriotism was a notion from the rightists' vocabulary. Communists were internationalists, not patriots, and the "national question" was secondary, always "subordinated" to the "social question"; that's what my books were teaching me. So, who are these "patriots"? As I soon learned, it was an organization set up in Moscow, in April 1943, on the initiative of Polish Communists, Wanda Wasilewska, and Alfred Lampe. Communists who have gone patriotic! I smelled something fishy in it, and it certainly was, but it was also a sign of changing times. Communists going patriotic would go a long way, adopting nationalism in its pretty extreme forms, antisemitism included. This would come later, though not so much later.

As for now, however, the newly formed union took care of the many thousands of Poles, former Polish citizens who found themselves in the territory of the Soviet Union, willingly or not, of those who were deported forcibly from the places taken over by the Soviets in 1939, and then stashed away in the furthest corners of that vast country, or many of its concentration camps. In 1943, those detainees were released from the camps, and the "Patriots" were of great help in resettling them. Saratov got its share of those Poles because the city of Engels, in the vicinity of Saratov, could provide them with accommodation. Russified Germans who used to live there—Engels being the capital of the German Autonomous District on the Volga—had recently been deported to remote locations. Stalin's methods of solving or preventing eventual problems which national minorities could cause were in full swing.

The Patriots were taking care of the resettled Poles, there was some financial help coming from Moscow, Polish schools and orphanages were set up, books in Polish were published, and a Polish weekly was issued. The Patriots grew fast, and soon there were many local organizations. Saratov had one too, and the leaders of the new organization were mostly former Communists who later, upon returning to liberated Poland, would take up high positions in the government. Edward Ochab, the future member of the Politburo of the ruling party, the Polish Workers' Party (Communist) in Poland, later its first secretary, had been in Saratov for some time. So had many others who would become well known in New Poland—Naszkowski, Nasilowski, Brus, Haber, Pol, and the like. The union was a lively place, and it was interesting to visit there from time to time, to participate in some debates about political events concerning future Poland, or just to listen to interesting speakers, and to get to know some new people.

During my time, Włodek Brus about whom Sylvia, clearly in love with him, would tell me a thousand stories—how talented, brilliant, and so on he was, and what a great future awaits him in Poland when the war is over—was not in Saratov anymore, having left to join the Polish army. He would indeed achieve great influence as an economist in Poland, and first of all, as one of the foremost reformers in the 1960s. Marian Naszkowski became a cabinet minister, Ferdynand Haber would be the deputy chief of the Party's propaganda for many years, but his daughter would become a dissident, and in post-communist Poland would be the coeditor of Adam Michnik's daily *Gazeta Wyborcza*. Of course, this would be a whole epoch later, and I mention it here just because I cannot resist the temptation to wonder again and again about the mysterious ways life marches on, involving individuals as well as nations in unexpected twists and turns of what is sometimes called fate, destiny, inevitability, chance, luck, or whatever else.

Zosia

One of the people I remember best from that time was Sylvia's older sister, Zosia. A mathematics student, she was offered the post of department director in the ministry headed by Władysław Gomułka upon her return to Poland. With Gomułka's downfall in 1948, she lost her post, and in the mid-fifties became an associate professor at Warsaw University, having by that time completed her doctoral thesis in economics, under the guidance of Professor Brus. I knew her best from that time since I too had joined Warsaw University's

Department of Philosophy then, having finished my course of studies. Zosia passed away in 1990, shortly after the death of her husband, Ludwik Pol, who had held high governmental positions for many years.

Sylvia

Today, Sylvia lives in Toronto. She and Szulim also returned to Poland after the war and she eventually graduated from Warsaw Polytechnic and became an engineer. She divorced her first husband and married a colleague, a talented engineer, but became a widow while still in her early forties. Sylvia and her second husband had two children who eventually immigrated to Canada, where Sylvia joined them. She is a good friend of mine, and we see each other from time to time, reminiscing about the times and things past or present. Szulim Weisblum, a talented mathematician, upon returning to Poland from the Soviet Union, changed his name to Aleksander Kornecki, though to us he has remained forever the same Szulim, a good friend. He too remarried, his second wife was a physician, and they had a son, who eventually also became a physician, and if my information is correct, lives in Canada now. Szulim left Poland in 1957 as these were tumultuous times, but weren't all our times tumultuous? The second wave of Jewish emigration after the war was leaving Poland; Polish-sounding names didn't make one a "true" Pole, and the "second wave" or as some said, the "second crop" was even larger than the first just after the war. Szulim, by then an associate professor at Warsaw Polytechnic, came to us one day to tell us that he, too, had decided to leave for Israel. "If I won't go, my son, when he grows up, will either hate me or be ashamed of me," he said. This was a dramatic statement, and it touched Gabriel and me deeply. We were struggling with the question for the nth time in our lives: to go or not to go and we decided to stay put. Szulim had a very successful career at Haifa's Technion and often visited the United States on academic business. He died in the States, in 1988, a day after having arrived in California on sabbatical leave at the University of Berkeley.

The War Is Raging On

The year 1944 was ending. This was an incredible year, so much had happened, so many changes, personal as well as general! The Saratov period of my journey was also almost over. Soon the university would move back to Leningrad, back to its hometown, and everybody was excited about the forthcoming event. In the early fall of 1944, the blockade of Leningrad was finally totally removed, and the city was returning to life. The Soviet army was fighting on foreign soil now, in Poland and Hungary. In the early spring of 1944, Soviet forces crossed the Romanian border, and I knew about this not only from the radio and the occasional newspaper that would come my way but firstly from Gabriel's letters. He was there with his regiment, and the unit he was directly serving with participated in the crossing of the Prut River, a border river that separated the Soviet Union from Romania. After that, the Soviets marched full force and very fast through Romania, which changed sides in the war and turned from an enemy of the Soviet Union into an ally and reached Hungary. Gabriel's letters told me, of course, no details of the regiment's movements or the battles they were fighting along the way. He sometimes tried to make it all look easy, sometimes even funny, but I knew that he was in the middle of where the war was raging, where one day they would advance, and the other, they would have to retreat, that there was still the danger of being killed, wounded, or encircled and falling into enemy hands as a prisoner of war. Now, with the almost constant push of Soviet forces ahead, he would fear the last eventuality less, though it still could happen, as it indeed almost had.

One of the greatest battles on the way to conquering or freeing Romania played out at Iasi. There was a lot of talk about that battle on the radio, and I knew that Gabriel was there, somewhere nearby. Yet, by a lucky whim of fate, he got sick with jaundice at that time and, unable to move by himself, was carried to a hospital by a buddy of his. Ivan Titov was the name of the soldier, who, during a local setback in the general offensive, carried him on his back for kilometers under artillery fire to safety. As I found out later, the regiment was directly involved in the Iasi battle and was decimated there.

Gabriel in Budapest

By the end of the year, Gabriel would already be in Budapest. He was sending me snapshots from there. Cameras were more available in Hungary, and the long siege was allowing some time for a moment of respite. I collected these snapshots of him with his unit, with others, officers and soldiers, and I knew their names. The snapshots told me about his life, letting me into it somehow. Yet the snapshots with all those smiling men in them, happy warriors, were, of course, not showing the reality of war, of life under constant tension of danger, of being killed, maimed, lost. And though I realized this, these superficial images that the pictures conveyed, fleeting glimpses of the reality he was living, were very important to me. It had been so long, over three years, how much longer would it take? My belief that everything would end well, that fate would be kind to us, was still with me, but it was tough just to wait. Waiting is somehow like living in limbo, and it was becoming harder as time went by.

Gabriel as a soldier in Budapest.

Should Women Serve in the Army?

Gabriel knew my new address, knew that I had applied to the university and had become a student, and was happy for me. His letters were encouraging even though he was not certain if my choice of field of study was the best. Philosophy? Perhaps, I would do better with something less demanding, something more concrete? But all in all, he was truly glad, and as he told me later, he was most of all glad because this meant that I would not do anything "foolish" like trying to join the army. He was afraid I might come up with the idea as the Polish army was recruiting, and I must have mentioned something in one of my letters that made him think that such a turn of events was possible. No, I had not seriously considered it. I knew my limitations, I knew that I did not have the physical strength to do what such service would require. Later, already after the war, I got to know some friends who had served and I sincerely admired their stamina, their courage, and the sacrifices they had made. Bella Ogrodowicz, a close friend, became a frontline nurse, and saved more than one life carrying the wounded to safety, often under fire. But I also knew another girl, who, her goodwill notwithstanding, served in one of the army's accounting offices, adding long dull columns of figures. I shared more than one laugh with her when she recalled her service. Not knowing what the meaning of the word *itogo* (Russian for total sum) was, she told me that she added the numbers indicating the total, doubling whatever items she happened to be counting.

Yet, I did come pretty close to enlisting once in the Polish army in the summer of 1944. A recruitment center was set up in our House of Culture in the Urals, and Gina and I went to see what was going on there. The place was crowded. Lots of people had come, and they were signing up eagerly, if not even enthusiastically. This is the only way to get out of here, one of the recruits told me, to get closer to home, to Poland, said another, to finally have enough food to eat, said some others. The recruitment officer greeted us with a pleasant, bright smile, "How nice, girls want to enlist, too," and he was ready to put our names down on his list. But we wanted to go to university, we had already sent our applications, and should receive an answer any day now, so no and we took a step back from that overeager recruiter and returned home.

Do Not Romanticize War

Gabriel was against women in the army in general, and women at the front and in combat, especially. He strongly believed that this was not a place for women, and would tell me in his letters, again and again, that war should not be romanticized, that it was a bloody, stinking business, blood and sweat, and a lot of very hard labor. He wanted me to be safe, and to wait for him, and how could I have held it against him, even if for my "liberated" self this seemed to be a rather old-fashioned view? He needed to know what he had to survive for, he once wrote. So, the change in my situation, my moving to Saratov and becoming a student, was welcome news to him. It meant that I had given up or would give up any idea of making myself into a "*bohater-dziewica*" (heroic maiden) of Polish folklore. As it turned out, I could not have done better even if I had planned the whole thing deliberately, because my going to university opened a window into the future not only for myself but also for Gabriel.

Western Allied Forces Liberated Belgium!

In November 1944, the Western Allies liberated Belgium. The Ardennes German winter offensive of 1945 reoccupied areas in the south of Belgium, but Brussels was free, and I could write to my sister Rachel. Her address in Brussels was engraved in my memory; I wrote to her and waited impatiently—would there be an answer, has she and her family survived? I hoped, not daring to expect anything. After all, there was still a wall of fire, front lines dividing Europe, would my letter even reach her?

No News about the Fate of Polish Jews

I had not heard anything from Łódź for over three years now. I knew about the Warsaw Ghetto Uprising of the spring of 1943, but the news was very sketchy, with far too little to get a picture of what went on there. Even when the Red Army liberated places in eastern Poland where the German death camps were located, Treblinka, Majdanek, and later, in January 1945, Auschwitz, it was not said that these were killing grounds almost exclusively "reserved" for Jews. Earlier yet, when Kyiv, the capital of Ukraine was liberated, there was no mention of Babi Yar, the place where over 70,000 victims, civilians, women, and children, almost the entire Jewish population of Kyiv, were killed and buried. Babi Yar remained an almost forbidden subject till 1961 when Yevtushenko was finally allowed to publish his heart-wrenching poem. While German atrocities against the Soviet population, in general, were described in detail, the fact that Jews were singled out by the Germans for annihilation only because they were Jews, was hidden in the general picture. Antisemites were utterly reluctant to grant Jews even that kind of "exclusivity" as if it were some badge of honor.

A Letter from Rachel!

It took some time, it must have been already February or even March 1945, but finally, I received a letter, a letter from Brussels! From my sister Rachel! She was alive, her husband and son were alive, and more good news, their family had grown in the meantime, a beautiful little girl had been born about a year ago while they were still under occupation! The family had survived in hiding for over a year. With the help of good people, they had found a place outside Brussels, and Rachel had given birth to her baby daughter in a convent, with the help of the good sisters and nurses in a hospital run by the convent. Half a year later, they returned to Brussels, to their apartment, and found their property intact, preserved by a man who was their bookkeeper before the outbreak of the war, and who had even kept in touch on

Rachel's behalf with our parents in the Łódź ghetto, sending them a parcel from time to time, as long as it was possible to contact them. However, this stopped in mid-1942, she wrote. And since then, nothing. Not a sign of life from our parents or our sisters, Sala and Helcia, or Sala's husband, Monek, or Rachel's husband, Heniek's brother.

By the time she wrote her letter to me, Rachel knew much more about what had happened in Poland and about the fate of the Polish Jews and Western Europe's Jews in Hitler's clutches, than I did. She knew that our aunt, the Markel family, had been deported from France, and at this time she had very little hope for their return. By then, she had met survivors of German concentration camps liberated by the Western Allied forces, who had managed to make their way to liberated Belgium and she had heard their ghastly stories about life and death in the Łódź ghetto and the camps, and she knew how slim the chances were that any of our close family there had survived.

She was happy to hear from me, to know that I was fine and that our brother was alive and well after all the misery he had gone through. It was only the three of us of the whole family that had survived and compared with thousands upon thousands of families that were wiped out altogether, this was not even a bad ratio of survival. We had what to grieve about but we also had what to be thankful for, she wrote to me. And we'll see each other, perhaps even soon, she added. I did not envision a meeting in the near future, but who knows, maybe, I certainly hoped so. We met, indeed, after the war, for the first time in 1948, after Gabriel and I returned to Poland. Rachel came to Łódź to see me and to put a stone on our parents' grave. We would meet many more times later and she would tell me much more about what they went through after the Germans took Brussels in the late spring of 1940. I remembered those events well, the frightening march of their evil forces through Europe, and the overwhelming feeling of horror at witnessing it, even from my then faraway and safe place. The Germans conquering France, Holland, and Belgium in one swipe, seemed then to take all our hope away.

Rachel's Story

At first, as Rachel's story went, the Germans did not pay very much attention to them as Jews. Some of their officers would frequent their shop, ordering a sheepskin coat or two, which had become their shop's specialty just before the war, and they paid for what they ordered; all seemed to be pretty normal. If there were expropriations, she did not know about it directly as it was evidently at a higher level. People were talking about it, and everyone was scared and uncertain of what was going to be next, but nothing especially drastic had happened, yet. Rumors were circulating in the city, rumors about deportations, about setting up ghettos. Hadn't they, after all, pushed the Jews in Poland into ghettos? Another day, another rumor. Even though the Germans were deporting people, especially Jews, and more specifically Jews not born in Belgium, Polish Jews, out to nowhere, or as some would say, back to Poland, they are not so inhumane as to deport pregnant women, they thought. Rachel got pregnant. She had a beautiful, seven-year-old, bright boy, Joseph, and the time was not conducive to plan for another child, but it happened, and maybe this was a godsend, she thought. It did not take long, however, and it became clear that living under the illusion of German humaneness would not do. Soon, their shop was taken over and the spring of 1942 saw the systematic expropriation of Jewish businesses, and the only solution to avoid deportation was to go into hiding.

Of the approximately 66,000 Jews that inhabited Belgium, only half had Belgian citizenship, by birth or by naturalization. Citizenship was not granted easily. Some of the immigrants, mostly from Poland, would live in Belgium for decades without obtaining the rights of citizenship, as was the case of my relatives there. To be a Jew was deadly enough, but to be an *Ostjude* (Eastern-European Jew), was twice as dangerous. Even having lived in the country for over ten years, your tongue would betray you as a foreigner, a Jew. It would not be easy to hide, to pretend that you were what you were not. But the locals, the Belgian population in general, were sympathetic and helpful. Rarely was there a case of a Belgian denouncing a Jew to the Germans. She would be more afraid of being denounced by a Jew, cooperating with the

Gestapo to save his/her skin for a little longer than by a local Belgian, Flemish, or Waloon, Rachel maintained. Besides, she said, the Belgian people did not have that sixth sense, the instinct that would let a Pole, for example, tell almost unmistakably a Jew from a non-Jew, as she remembered from her own life in Poland a long time ago, and of which those who had tried to hide on the so-called Aryan side in Poland during the war, were also so painfully aware.

She and her family were lucky. They found good people ready and able to help, and they survived. When I visited Brussels for the first time in 1955, I met one of these people, a middle-aged man, André, a retired postman. One day, on his daily round of mail delivery, he noticed among others a letter to the local Gestapo. It seemed suspicious to him, so he opened it, and it was indeed a letter informing on Rachel's family, denouncing them as Jews. The letter never reached the Gestapo and Rachel and her family were transferred immediately to a different place. That man saved their life. He showed me a letter he had received from the perennial Polish Prime Minister Jozef Cyrankiewicz's office, thanking him for helping Polish citizens abroad in danger during the war. The letter was dated 1948 or 1949, I do not remember, and there was a somehow surreal ring to it. Later, Rachel and her family planted a tree in memory of André at the Avenue of the Righteous Among the Nations at Yad Vashem in Israel.[89]

Thanks mostly to the attitude of the Belgian population, about 25,000 Jews survived in hiding, and half of the Jews of that country survived the German occupation, achieving the highest survival rate

89 According to the author's family, the postman—who remains unidentified—also helped to arrange the hiding place for the Sztrubels, and he might have been related to Charles and Mariette Grysouille, who provided them with shelter. The Grysouilles started to hide Jews in their home in October 1942. They not only helped the Sztrubels but also a second couple, Zelman and Chaja Winokur. When their home became unsafe in July 1943, Charles Grysouille supplied both couples with false identification cards and food coupons, which helped them to evade capture and survive until liberation. After the war, both the Sztrubels and the Winokurs attested to the deeds of their saviors, and on November 19, 1979, Yad Vashem recognized Charles and Mariette Grysouille as Righteous Among the Nations.

among the countries which had fallen to the Germans. Yet so strong and overwhelming were the evil forces that over 30,000 Belgian Jews perished.

Charles Grysouille during the award ceremony, Brussels, 1980. Yad Vashem, Righteous Among the Nations Collection, Jerusalem.

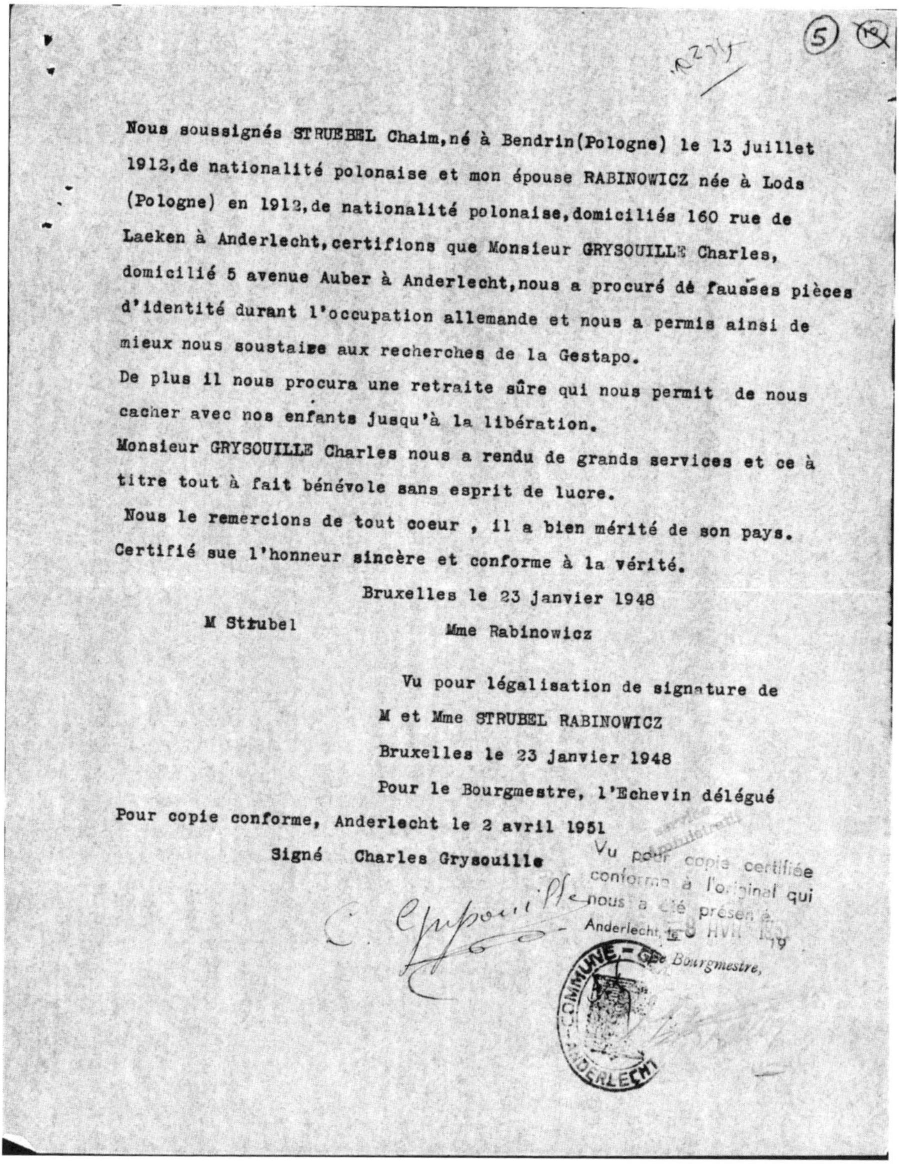

Nous soussignés STRUEBEL Chaim,né à Bendrin(Pologne) le 13 juillet 1912,de nationalité polonaise et mon épouse RABINOWICZ née à Lods (Pologne) en 1912,de nationalité polonaise,domiciliés 160 rue de Laeken à Anderlecht,certifions que Monsieur GRYSOUILLE Charles, domicilié 5 avenue Auber à Anderlecht,nous a procuré dé fausses pièces d'identité durant l'occupation allemande et nous a permis ainsi de mieux nous soustaire aux recherches de la Gestapo.

De plus il nous procura une retraite sûre qui nous permit de nous cacher avec nos enfants jusqu'à la libération.

Monsieur GRYSOUILLE Charles nous a rendu de grands services et ce à titre tout à fait bénévole sans esprit de lucre.

Nous le remercions de tout coeur , il a bien mérité de son pays.

Certifié sue l'honneur sincère et conforme à la vérité.

Bruxelles le 23 janvier 1948

M Sttubel Mme Rabinowicz

Vu pour légalisation de signature de
M et Mme STRUBEL RABINOWICZ
Bruxelles le 23 janvier 1948
Pour le Bourgmestre, l'Echevin délégué

Pour copie conforme, Anderlecht le 2 avril 1951

Signé Charles Grysouille

Vu pour copie certifiée conforme à l'original qui nous a été présenté.
Anderlecht, le 8 AVR 1951
Le Bourgmestre,

COMMUNE ANDERLECHT

Affidavit by Chaim Sztrubel and Rachel Sztrubel, née Rabinowicz, confirming the life-saving assistance provided to them by Charles and Mariette Grysouille. Yad Vashem, Righteous Among the Nations Collection, Jerusalem.

Leningrad University Returns to Leningrad

It was January and mid-winter of 1945. Our stay in Saratov came to an end. We were going to Leningrad. Full of anticipation, and excitement, we packed and got ready for the trip. A warm, comfortable passenger train would take us there. It was a sleeper train, with a separate bunk in the train's compartments for each one of us. A whole bunch of girls—the new student body was still made up mostly of girls, only in Leningrad some young men would join the ranks of freshmen—filled "my" compartment. A heated debate started right away and no wonder, this was the "philosophers" compartment and it seemed that there would be no end to the excited, noisy chatter, laughing and joking, as well as "serious" philosophical discussions. Tired from all the commotion that was going on long into the night, I finally fell asleep, when someone lightly touched my arm, waking me up, "Get up, Anya, your home city was liberated today, it was just announced on the radio." It was another Anya, my namesake, a girl from a little town, the name of which has escaped me, close to Ryazan. I liked her, and we often talked. We embraced. "Do you still have any family there?" she asked. I just closed my eyes, what could I say? The next day we arrived at Leningrad. It was January 19, 1945, and my hometown, Łódź, had been freed the previous day, and that's why I remember that date so well.

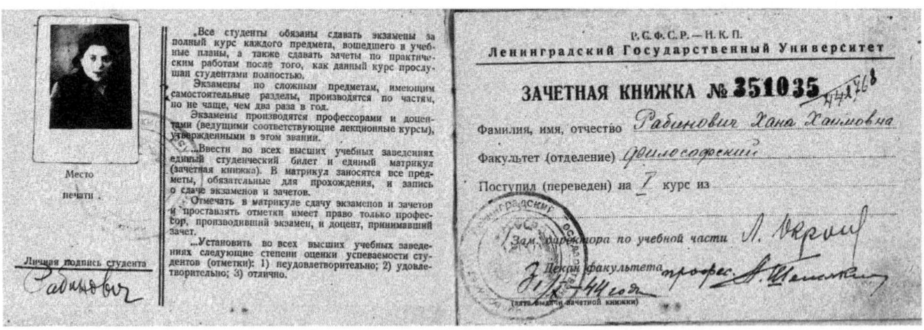

Место печати.

Личная подпись студента

„Все студенты обязаны сдавать экзамены за полный курс каждого предмета, вошедшего в учебные планы, а также сдавать зачеты по практическим работам после того, как данный курс прослушан студентами полностью.

Экзамены по сложным предметам, имеющим самостоятельные разделы, производятся по частям, но не чаще, чем два раза в год.

Экзамены производятся профессорами и доцентами (ведущими соответствующие лекционные курсы), утвержденными в этом звании.

...Ввести во всех высших учебных заведениях единый студенческий билет и единый матрикул (зачетная книжка). В матрикул заносятся все предметы, обязательные для прохождения, и запись о сдаче экзаменов и зачетов.

Отмечать в матрикуле сдачу экзаменов и зачетов и проставлять отметки имеет право только профессор, производивший экзамен, и доцент, принимавший зачет.

...Установить во всех высших учебных заведениях следующие степени оценки успеваемости студентов (отметки): 1) неудовлетворительно; 2) удовлетворительно; 3) отлично.

Р. С. Ф. С. Р. — Н. К. П.

Ленинградский Государственный Университет

ЗАЧЕТНАЯ КНИЖКА № 351035

Фамилия, имя, отчество Рабинович Хана Хаимовна

Факультет (отделение) философский

Поступил (переведен) на 1 курс из

Зам. директора по учебной части

Декан факультета

(дата выдачи зачетной книжки)

Hanna's test booklet from Leningrad University.

CHAPTER TEN

LENINGRAD

Leningrad was beautiful, cold, and rat-infested. The spectacular city, having sustained the almost three-year siege, had retained its historical center relatively undamaged. The Admiralty Spire and the dome of the Issakiev Cathedral, camouflaged during the war years, were again sparkling in the pale January sun. In the background of the snow-covered Neva, the black lacy iron railings that frame the many Leningrad bridges were showing off their full splendor. It was not easy to imagine that the horrible blockade had finally and completely been lifted only a year ago, in January 1944. And still more difficult to imagine that not so long ago, people were dying here, killed by bombs from the air and by artillery shells, yet mostly by starvation, exposure, and disease. One-fourth of the population, and "possibly more than a million," died here, as historical sources say, at least a third among them children, and only the opening of a narrow escape route to the mainland through the frozen Ladoga Lake in the winter of 1942 saved the city from total collapse. Trucks on ice not set firmly enough and still under enemy fire took the first evacuees out to safety. Frida Shulmeister, a mathematics student and a native Leningrader who became a very close friend of mine, was with one such early transport of evacuees. She lost her parents during the first few months of the siege but she and her brother were saved, having been evacuated while there was still a breath of life left in her, and her brother was drafted into the army just before the outbreak of the war. Three years later, Frida returned to Leningrad as a student. We talked often, liked each other, and there was certainly a feeling of affinity between us, and no wonder. Frida would tell me of life and death under siege in the starving city, and though, at that time, I did not yet know any details of the fate of my family in the Łódź ghetto, a place that was also under siege by the same ruthless enemy, her stories resonated with my private horror which I would only rarely allow myself to talk about with strangers.

My Dormitory on Mendeleyev Street

The siege was over, Leningrad was alive again, and getting back to normal. The university began functioning right away. We were assigned places in the dormitories; Gina and I would again share a room with two other girls, this time, psychology students, because the Philosophy Department was for some reason merged with the Department of Psychology into one—*Filosofsko-Psykhologicheskii Fakultet*. Our two roommates were Raya Makaronowa, a tall, pale girl from Russia's Far East, and Ekaterina Pronina from Ukraine. Both came to Leningrad University directly, not via Saratov. I liked Raya better, she was a "homely" girl, easy to talk and laugh with. Yet, I do not know if she graduated and what happened to her in later life. Katya, or rather Ekaterina, we all usually addressed her by her full, formal name, was aloof, and did not fraternize much. Absorbed in herself, she sometimes seemed to be studying us. She liked to write, she confessed to us once, giving this perhaps as a justification for her sometimes-indiscreet peeping. "Oh, an aspiring writer," someone said, and we knew from then to be careful in her presence. She even once read to us a piece she intended to publish, which left us rather unimpressed. But she did not become a writer. She graduated and graduated well enough to be admitted later on to the *aspirantura* (postgraduate), and became eventually not just a *kandidat nauk* (candidate of sciences), a title more or less equivalent to a Ph.D., but subsequently, a Doctor of Psychology, a kind of a second Ph.D., a high academic title very sparingly bestowed in the Soviet Union, and she specialized in child psychology. Faina, my dear classmate, and friend, when we met in Leningrad after many years and were reminiscing about the old days going through her old album with snapshots of our classmates, and talking about "the way we were and what has become of us," shared with me that piece of information, still evidently not able to overcome her wonderment. "Come to think of it, you knew Ekaterina, one wouldn't get out of her a whole lot because there simply wasn't anything there," she said, "and look, a doctor, and a child psychologist to boot, that Ekaterina, as sensitive as a log! Poor kids!" She was, according to Faina, the only one of our classmates who had achieved that much, and there were some pretty bright people in that class. Perhaps, some other qualities were needed for a successful career!

Our room was on the lower floor of the building that housed two departments—philosophy and history—on its two upper floors, at 3 Mendeleyev Street. It was a small street, not long but wide enough to form a plaza for official gatherings on special occasions. Just across from our building was the main entrance to the university, elegant and wide. The street was enclosed by the building housing the library of the Academy of Sciences. The books, hidden for safety at the beginning of the war, were now being unpacked and stacked on the shelves, a task in which my classmates and I participated. Many years later, it must have been in the eighties, a fire badly damaged that library and many of its invaluable old volumes. This was one of the many disasters that hit Russia on the brink of the collapse of the Soviet Union, and the news about that fire was mentioned by the world press. I read about it in Canada, where I was living then, and it filled me with sadness. It brought back memories of Mendeleyev Street and that heavy, gray building, and my youth. At the other end of Mendeleyev Street, which opened onto the great Naberezhnaya along the Neva River, was a post office, a place I frequented very often. Gabriel's letters from the army would come there to the postbox.

A Day in the Life of a University Student

Classes began soon after, lectures and seminars for six hours daily, from 8 A.M. to 2 P.M. At 2 P.M., there was lunch at the university canteen, a large and well-appointed hall, and after that, it was time for the university library. A gorgeous, long, and wide corridor led to the reading room. Its grand, high-arched windows looked out onto the Neva, and it was a pleasure to sit down on one of these wide, polished windowsills to take a break from reading, watch the river, or chat with a friend. The library became my favorite place, not only because of the "depth of learning" to be derived from its many books but also because it was the warmest spot in the university. It was cold in Leningrad; the northern winter was severe and there was no warm place to be found. The rector of the university, Professor Voznesienskii, in one of his speeches, lamented the deplorable situation but did not make any promises to improve the heating situation. The only hope seemed to be that spring would come early.

Saturday Nights at the University

While the university administration couldn't do much to heat the lecture halls and the dormitories, it did something to organize a cultural life worthy of a great university. Every Saturday evening, students and professors gathered in the Great Auditorium of the university for concerts, performances, or meetings with prominent people of the arts, sciences, and literature. It was not as cold as in the Great Hall. On the contrary, sometimes it would even get hot. Students would fill the hall to capacity. I remember some of those evenings well.

Once, it was a lecture with questions and answers with Eisenstein, the famous filmmaker, and creator of *Battleship Potemkin* and *Ivan the Terrible*. He wore a general's uniform with all the regalia, and talked, I am sure, of moviemaking, but I do not remember any of it. What I do recall was Eisenstein telling us that with the war coming to a victorious end, the country did not need to supply our armed forces fighting abroad anymore, now our army would supply the country. This was a striking statement, and he concluded his speech with it. After the lecture, we discussed the meaning of that statement among ourselves for a long time. Spoils of war? The Soviet Union was utterly impoverished by the horrible war, robbed and ruined by the ruthless invader, and it appealed to everybody's sense of justice that the enemy should pay heavy retribution.

Yakhontov's Poetry Recital

I have already mentioned an evening with the composer Soloviev-Sedoy who sang his popular, lovely songs and accompanied himself on the piano. It was an enchanting evening, indeed. But the most interesting and enjoyable for me were the poetry recitals. The audience participated, asking the artist on the stage for a particular poem, a particular title, and listened with utmost attention, almost bated breath. One such evening remains clear in my mind as fresh as if it was yesterday. Vladimir Yakhontov was reading Sergei Yesenin, the beautiful lyrics but also the dark verses, filled with sadness, and the short farewell poem, "*Goodbye, My Friend, Goodbye*," which Yesenin wrote just before committing suicide, in a way predicting it. The audience wanted more and started yelling, "*Chornii Chelovek, Chornii Chelovek.*" "Why do you want this?" Yakhontov seemed perplexed. "It's so gloomy, I will read you something more cheerful," he pleaded with the audience. But the audience wanted that "gloomy" piece and nothing else, and after some hesitation he obliged. Then, as if to chase away the dark mood, he went over to other lines, this time from Vladimir Mayakovsky's answer to Yesenin's "*V etoi zhizni umirat' ne novo, no i zhit', konechno, ne novei*" (To die is nothing new in this life, but to go on living is, of course, not a novelty, either).[90] Yakhontov read, "*Dlia veselia planeta nasha malo oborudovana, Nado vyrvat' radost' u griadushchikh dnei. V etoi zhizni upomeret' ne trudno. Sdelat' zhizn' znachitel'no trudnei.*" In my awkward translation, "Our planet is not

90 This line comes from Yesenin's *"Goodbye, My Friend, Goodbye"* (1925), which he left behind when he killed himself.

made for joy, let us grab it from the days to come, in this life to die is nothing new, to make life livable is a much harder task."[91] This, too, was greeted with great applause, even though at this time Mayakovsky's suicidal death was a well-known fact. Mayakovsky's optimistic answer to Yesenin did not prevent him from taking his own life a few years later, in 1930.

I was no longer a total stranger to this country and its culture, and I was receptive to the beauty of the poetry Yakhontov was reading and was fascinated by his masterful performance. I saw Yakhontov for the first time and had never heard about him before and could now better appreciate the special excitement which had preceded the evening with this artist. I loved Yesenin and appreciated Mayakovsky, but not knowing much more about them other than what the textbooks said, I did not know anything about their tragic fate. Both Mayakovsky and Yesenin took their own lives, and they were no exceptions among the great Russian poets. Violent death, either by suicide or at the hands of the government was the fate of many others of the greatest among them. Nikolay Gumilyov was shot already in 1921, accused of counterrevolutionary conspiracy. His wife, Anna Akhmatova, considered the greatest of them all, lived her life in persecution, her second husband and son imprisoned. Osip Mandelstam ended his life in the gulag. Marina Tsvetaeva hanged herself in a forlorn Kazakh hut, perhaps one like those I saw in Kazakhstan during my short stop there. I did not know all this then, but the people in the hall obviously knew, and the recital of those half-forbidden dark lines, which were in such obvious ways contradicting the always optimistic attitude promoted by the official propaganda and authorities, seemed akin, perhaps, to participating in a half-forbidden rite, and the cause of much of the excitement that one could feel in the hall.

91 From Mayakovsky's *To Sergei Yesenin* (1926).

More about Yakhontov

Yakhontov, himself, of course, knew. He was a prominent Soviet actor, associated with the Moscow Art Theater, also known for his reading of poetry and literary work, and a close friend of the Mandelstams. The audience at that reading was well-informed. I got to know about Yakhontov and his own tragic life and fate only much later. For years, he too was under constant danger of being arrested, but miraculously passed through the time of the Great Purges relatively unharmed. Relatively, because it turned him into a nervous wreck, and when he saw the signs of the times of terror returning right after the war, overwhelmed by fear that he was about to be arrested, he jumped from a window on the highest floor of his building. It was 1945, and a year later there were already clear signs that his guess or intuition might prove correct.

In Leningrad of 1946, I observed the first signs of the "times of fear" making a comeback. When, many years later, I read Nadezhda Mandelstam's heartfelt memoirs[92] from which I had learned about the fate of Yakhontov, the scene of that poetry reading from so long ago came back to me with exceptional clarity. I could hear again the voices yelling for "*Chornii Chelovek*" and saw the artist on the podium, hesitating. Now I understood what was making the atmosphere of that university hall at an evening of poetry reading so emotionally charged that it seemed to raise the temperature in the otherwise cold, unheated hall.

Celebrated Professors of the University

Another intellectual attraction of studying at Leningrad University was the public lectures by famous professors. I must recall one of them, the historian Professor Tarle, author of many books and among them

92 Nadezhda Mandelstam (1899–1980), wife of the poet Osip Mandelstam (1891–1938), wrote two memoirs, *Hope against Hope* (1970) and *Hope Abandoned* (1974), both published first in the West.

the very popular history of Napoleon. Unfortunately, I did not attend the regular course of his lectures, though I had to attend many courses on history and take exams, as my performance record booklet with its yellowed pages shows—Greece, Rome, the Middle Ages, and for the second year of study contemporary European history, and on top of all this, history of prehistoric society.

Professor Tarle taught history only for students of the Department of History, but I knew him from an occasional public lecture, and I saw the revered historian quite often in the used bookstore on the Nevsky, browsing through some old volumes. An older, white-haired man, slightly built, he was a true legend around the university, and there were rumors and jokes about him, as befits a legend. According to one of the rumors, Tarle was in exile (this turned out to be true) when a French delegation of scholars came to visit the Soviet Union and one of their historians asked where was his friend, Professor Tarle? Tarle was then speedily brought back from exile somewhere deep down in the East, south of that enormous country, and returned to his job in Leningrad.

There were also jokes: A girl (for some reason the silly student of those jokes was always a girl) was asked by the professor what could she tell him about Convent, and the girl began quickly: Convent was born in such and such year, did this and that, and the professor listened patiently but still wanted to know something about Convent's wife, was he married at all, and the girl got confused, did not know how to answer, and was sent away to read up a little more on the subject. The girl left the professor's office in tears and complained to her friends, "I told him all about that Convent and he failed me because I did not remember who his wife was, such cruelty!" Another of these "examination" jokes went like this: Tell me, said the professor, what do you know about the Renaissance, and the girl came about with a very short and quick answer—she was the mare of Don Quixote!

Yes, Leningrad, and especially Leningrad University was a different world, far removed from the world I had lived in before, and I did my best to take advantage of the rich culture it offered. I considered myself very lucky, and I was lucky, indeed. Of course, the Saturday evenings, world-renowned scholars, writers, and composers, this was the icing on the cake, for it was hard work every day and the living conditions were very modest, to say the least.

Professor Yevgenya Zelnikova

Our everyday professors, lecturers, and teachers were also, in most cases, men and women of high professional standing. To many, I am thankful for this to this day. I recall with special warmth Professor Eugenia Zelnik, my teacher of the history of philosophy. She taught a mammoth course that would go on for two years of study, the second and third, covering three centuries of Western European philosophy, from the sixteenth century till the mid-nineteenth. I only completed half of that course with her since after the end of the second year of study I left and returned to Poland.

Professor Zelnik invited me once to come to her place to pick up some additional reading material for my seminar talk. It was a small, two-room apartment with bookshelves from floor to ceiling. I stayed for a little while and as we talked about my seminar paper, she suddenly said something that struck me as very personal, albeit not out of context, since we were discussing Hobbes, the subject of the seminar I was preparing for, "We too had to voluntarily give up some of our freedoms, and now that the war has ended, we will regain them, and some more." This was food for thought, indeed, a puzzling statement for me at that moment and even, later on, I tried to understand what she wanted to tell me. Then, I saw in it only an expression of hope.

People would quite often express hope for a better life when the war would finally come to an end. I had heard this many times, repeated in various forms. Better times were expected, and people seemed to say that they deserved it. My friend Rita, remembering that I was from "abroad," also assured me with deep conviction that now, with the war over, we would have a true renaissance of art, culture, and creativity in the country, but what Professor Zelnik had said was not the same, she had expectations about regaining what they had "voluntarily given up." This was truly interesting because it seemed to be a reappraisal of the past, not only a hope for the future. Unfortunately, as it turned out, she harbored an illusion about the past as well as of the future. This phrase came back to me many times later, while thinking about the life of the "intellectual class" in the Soviet Union through the purges and the political campaigns after the war, and my own life as a member of that same "class" during the troubled times in Communist Poland.

Professor Vladimir Resnik

Professor Vladimir Davidovitch Resnik was my favorite teacher. A dark-haired, slightly built man, perhaps in his mid-forties, he had been with us since Saratov, and treated his students like friends, influencing them by his attitude toward learning, thinking, and encouraging us to read "everything," because a "philosopher" should know more than just his "small piece." In our freshman year in Leningrad, he taught a course in logic. He was not a specialist, and he almost apologized to us, but there were no teachers of this subject so he simply "had to," adding that it also did him lots of good to pore over it, as he had done once before in his youth.

Logic, as a subject, was not taught in Soviet schools or colleges during the first two decades after the revolution and was reintroduced into graduate schools only during the last year of the war, supposedly on Stalin's direct order when it became obvious that elementary knowledge of "formal" logic was indispensable for waging war, even though it was disliked by "dialecticians" and that it was not necessary for peacetime.

With the old specialists gone, our first teacher was an old man, a very old man, who used to be a great and famous logician before the revolution. For some time, I thought that he was Chelpanov himself, the author of the books on logic and a textbook that had survived the bad times. But no, Chelpanov had died in 1936, so this old man was someone else. He moved very slowly, visibly with great difficulty, and he also spoke very slowly, which students usually appreciate because it allows them enough time to take notes, but he also spoke very softly, so softly that we could hardly hear him. Once I met the old man after his class walking along the corridor, he seemed confused and was looking for a certain place. An intelligent girl, I surmised that he was looking for the washroom, which he was. I took him by the hand and led him there, but since the washrooms were the place where rats, the many Leningrad rats, liked to congregate, I stomped my feet to make as much noise as possible to chase the rats away; this was what we usually did before entering that place, and it did not always help. However, the noise startled the old man and confused him even more, so I finally kicked the entrance door as hard as I could and left him there. Gabriel used to tease me for a long time about the story, saying that a good Samaritan would have also unbuttoned the old professor's fly.

I benefited from Professor Resnik's course on formal logic. It was of great help when a little over a year later, upon returning to Poland, I tackled Professor Kotarbinski's logic, preparing for an exam on the subject at the University of Łódź. The very fact that I had taken Resnik's course and attended the extracurricular events he had led, eased the sometimes-bewildering transition from a Soviet university to a Polish one in that first period after the war. Unfortunately, Professor Resnik's time at the Department of Philosophy of Leningrad University would soon come to an end. At the beginning of 1946, he became the subject of harassment by the university authorities, which soon ended with his forced removal from his job at the university. It was a sign of the ongoing change in the political climate of the country, one of the first that I would witness myself. The momentary relaxation of the atmosphere that came with the end of the war was waning and attitudes were again getting harsher, with old and colder attitudes returning.

A Show of Solidarity and Punishment

We, his students, tried to help our favorite teacher in trouble. Fired, he was left without money and a ration card, and this was a very harsh sentence. Rita organized a collection, of whatever any of us could give to help the professor in need. We did not realize that this could get us in some serious trouble, though Rita did perhaps know that some risk was involved. She lived through the purges of 1937–1938 and lost her father to them. And she, being a member of the Party, a true believer and defender of the cause, understood perhaps that this might be considered a breach of party discipline at least. I do not remember if what we had collected was of any material help to the banished professor, but the show of solidarity certainly was a consolation. Professor Resnik moved out of the university and out of Leningrad. I recall that Rita and I, and a few other girls were present at his place when a woman, a friend of his, was packing his suitcase. We went to say goodbye, feeling strangely guilty about the whole thing. What was it that he did, what was he accused of? There were some rumors repeated in whispers that he had some bad connections, some of the people he knew had been arrested before the war as "Trotskyites," and this was enough.

With Resnik gone, Rita was reprimanded for extending a helping hand to the professor. How could she, a responsible person, a party member, transgress so far, they wanted to know. It was Augusta—I noticed her then for the first time—the department lecturer in Marxism–Leninism, and the Party's watchdog, who took Rita to task. For a while, I was scared for Rita, and it seemed that she would be expelled from the university. Fortunately, the time was not yet ripe for such punishment to be applied, and she got away with just a reprimand. But, as it turned out, her show of compassion toward a persecuted teacher was not forgotten, and she would have to answer for it later. As for the rest of us, nobody was called or asked anything, but from then on, I tried to avoid Augusta, stepping out of her way when I saw her. The tall, dried-up woman, always in the same loose black coat, with an unpleasant half-smile on her dry face and thin, tightly locked lips, looked scary. A very model of a tough disciplinarian, a juvenile delinquents' reformatory warden, a harbinger of party morality and discipline. Later, I would meet her type more than once in Warsaw.

Professor Serebryakov, the Dean

The lenient treatment that Rita and the rest of us received was owed mostly to the intervention of the then-dean of our department, Professor Serebryakov. He was the one who had hired Resnik in the first place but was now evidently helpless to prevent his firing. This must have been decided from a much higher level, above him. Still, he had some success defending his students. Professor Serebryakov was something of a legend around the university, and rumor had it that he used to be a personal friend of Plekhanov,[93] and ironically this was still an asset then. To me, he was walking history. A thin, older man, with a mustache and a neatly cut grayish beard that reminded me of my father, he had a truly fatherly attitude toward the students. Sometimes he would join us between classes to take a walk along the long corridor, asking about life and how it was going, and one could feel that he was concerned, not just asking these questions to fulfill his duty. Many years later, in the late fifties, remembering Professor Serebryakov, the gentle man and scholar, and moved by sheer sentiment, I translated a book of his, *The Young Engels,* into Polish, with Gina's collaboration, and arranged for its publication by the Warsaw publishing house, Książka i Wiedza.

White Nights in Leningrad

Slowly but surely, winter was giving way to early spring. The air was getting warmer and the days longer, and Leningrad's white nights would soon be upon us. The war was still raging, but far from Leningrad, far from the Soviet Union; the fronts were abroad, on the Oder–Neisse Line, on German territory, and in Hungary. And with the smell of spring, the days getting longer, and chasing the night away came new feelings, desires, and longings that you used to be able to keep in check, pushing them somewhere. Where to? The subconsciousness? Now, they were starting to creep into your heart and mind, almost drowning you in a kind of anxiety that is painful and sweet at once, and so difficult to deal with!

93 Georgi Plekhanov (1856–1918) was an important revolutionary thinker and activist.

Gabriel, in a photo dedicated to Hanna, taken in Austria, 1945.

"What an Injustice!"

Gabriel was in Budapest for a while staying with his unit in the Hungarian Parliament. His letters were optimistic, but I could feel how tired he was. It had been almost two years, almost constantly under fire, in battles, from the Donetz to the Danube. In the snapshots of himself or with his comrades, he looked well—miraculously he had not even been wounded once—and he was smiling and so were those men with him. I showed the snapshots to my friends, and my roommates, as they were always interested in seeing them. "Look at them," Raya once remarked, "All these men, they are all there, and not even one here, what an injustice!" We were still, indeed, a class of almost exclusively girls, though quite recently, some young men had started to join the student body. They were former servicemen, discharged from the army after having suffered heavy wounds.

Male Students Join Our Class

Our group of "philosophers" would eventually also be joined by a few others. A tall, skinny Tolya Galaktionov, whose name I remember so well because I met him many years later during my visit to Leningrad. As it turned out, he became a historian of social ideas, working in the same field as I did. Igor—I have forgotten his last name but remember him well—was a *Russkiy dvoryanin* (Russian nobleman) and that's how he would introduce himself at a time when this was not considered a title to be proud of, and not minding that people usually reacted with ironic chuckles. He was an intelligent and well-mannered young man. Igor and I once got an extracurricular assignment to check on the living conditions of families of servicemen in our neighborhood. Students were obliged from time to time to do some "useful" social work, and this was better than a day of work at the university's farm, and more interesting, too. I remember, we went to the given addresses. The conditions were appalling, which we dutifully wrote down, but if this did any good for those in need, I do not know. I also don't know how Igor fared in his career, and I have never heard about him since. Another of the newly joined students was Dima, a former tank operator, who returned from the front blind, with visible scars on his face. He was a Leningrader and lived with his mother, a very skinny, sad woman, with disaster written all over her, not only on her face but in her movements, her voice, and her dress. Dima was her only child. Everybody tried to help him. I too went two or three times to read to Dima, but the poor fellow was sitting listlessly, perhaps not even able to hear what was being read to him, and soon he deferred his studies. Of the others, I also recall Sasha, a pimply youth, who must have been no more than nineteen, yet he had already served and lost an arm in the war. He was a good student, a cheerful character, and a thinking fellow. Once I had a funny chat with him. He told me that he had read a booklet that the Party had issued for propaganda purposes. It described the poverty of the peasants in what used to be prewar Poland. As an illustration of the thesis, it stated that for a Polish peasant to buy a needle, he had to sell a goat, because the industrial goods in underdeveloped Poland were so outrageously expensive, and unaffordable for the poor peasants. But Sasha concluded from all this that these goats must have been very cheap in Poland, an incredible bargain, which wouldn't be so bad at all! To get a goat for a needle! This was bewildering. Imagine the abundance of milk and cheese, and so on, and he asked me, as an expert on all things Polish, how to solve the dilemma. Sasha was a smart guy and how stupid were the hypocritical, lying propagandists! We got a laugh out of it! I looked at these invalids, young men. For them, the war was over, but the price they had paid! And I thought of Gabriel and felt very, very tired. I had been alone for almost four years now, and how much longer would it be? And what else was coming?

Tea at Faina's

Life went on. Classes started at eight and went on till two in the afternoon. Then at the canteen, we tried to guess what would be for lunch; noodles, or mushed green peas. Most often it was gruel with a dime-sized spot of oil in the middle of the portion's surface, but sometimes it was mushed green peas, everybody's favorite. But in the canteen, we seemed to care less about the food than about meeting friends. Here I would meet Rita, Faina, and others, and there was always something to talk about and laugh about. Here, we would also sometimes spontaneously decide to meet in the afternoon for tea, most often at Faina's place. Only rarely of course would it be real tea, and mostly it would just be hot water, with a biscuit or a candy from our sugar rations, but there were always songs. And the songs were something. Faina had a beautiful, strong voice and knew them all. *Reve ta stohne Dnipr shyrokyi, Sibir, Sibir,* and of course, *Volga, Volga,* but also the less-known *starinnie* (oldies), and most of the other girls would sing along.[94] Soon, Faina and I became close friends, and our friendship lasted a lifetime.

Faina

Faina Aleksandrovna Vasilyeva, average height, flaxen hair, one blue eye, one, because the second she had lost on the front, serving in the army as a telephone operator, fighting the Germans. Discharged, after a lengthy hospital stay, she decided to study philosophy, and came to Leningrad. She came from the very heartland of Russia, the Tambov Oblast, from a family with strong connections to the village, and to the life of the peasants. A lively girl, always interested in the world around her and beyond, she was very keen on learning, and there was not even a trace of xenophobia in her. Faina, a veteran, always wore her trench coat, not for the love of it, but because it was the only warm garment she possessed, and it seemed only natural that she would gravitate toward the other girls, other veterans, and at the time there were already a few of them at the university. But no. Faina became my friend and Gina's too, the girls from abroad, strangers, foreigners.

Once, she came to me visibly agitated. "You know Marina, the other girl in a trench coat? You know what she said to me today? She attacked me for, guess what? For keeping company with you and Gina! I should be ashamed, she told me, to be friends with Jews!" "And are

94 The songs represent a diversity of styles and eras. The first is actually a Ukrainian folk song while the last one comes from a popular 1941 film.

you, Faina?" I asked. Now, she blew up at me. She could not understand how I could react to this despicable talk in such a dispassionate way, this is Fascist talk, and this Marina was fighting the Fascists, how could she, how could I, it seemed there was no way to stop her. Faina, dear Faina, was this the first time in your life that you had heard such remarks about Jews? No, she had heard it many times, people blaming Jews for all unimaginable things, and she wanted to know why? Why? Of course, I wanted to know, but I knew that there was no answer, other than perhaps that some people need to hate others, and Jews were a convenient object, Jews or bicyclists.

The whole thing did, of course, dishearten and confuse me, too. I did not know Marina, but I had noticed her, remembered her skinny, angry face, and also respected her as a soldier who had served in the Red Army in the war. I had seen some expressions of antisemitism in the Soviet Union in prewar times, though it used to be a punishable offense there. I saw it in the Urals, especially when the war was going badly for the Soviets, and I remembered that drunken hoodlum in Gomel yelling in the street "Death to Jews and Communists" the very day after the outbreak of the German–Soviet hostilities. Still, I did not expect it here, with the war coming so close to a victorious end, and certainly not from these quarters. It was painful, and a sign of change not for the better, but for the worse. And more, similar signs would soon come.

Oh, to Marry, to Marry a General!

Of my many other classmates, I have a clear recollection of only a few. For example, Dorka Bronstein, (no relation to Trotsky, and if there was any, it would have certainly been denied). She was from Minsk and had survived with her family after evacuation somewhere in the Urals and came to the university right after graduating from high school. A happy girl, cheerful despite her wartime experiences and deprivations, a bit on the plump side, blonde with gray, laughing eyes. She was an excellent student, interested in her subject of study, but, as she confessed to me once, a career was not the most important thing she wanted out of life. What she wanted was to get married, and not just married but "Ah, Anya," she told me dreamily, "to get married, married to a general!" True, the confession took place under rather unusual circumstances. Dorka got sick suddenly and had to be taken to a hospital. I called for help, and the university administration sent a car to take her there. I went with her in that car. Only very high officials had cars for their personal use, and as the ride transported us to the hospital, I too was overwhelmed, momentarily into a kind of dreamland.

I lost contact with her when I left Leningrad a year later, but I heard about her fate when I visited Leningrad again, after many years. Dorka graduated and got married, but not to a general, though. She married a colleague, a student of economics, but in 1949 the Department of Economics at Leningrad University suffered a kind of pogrom, and many of the department's professors and students were arrested. There were also some death sentences and the department's dean, Professor Reichard, was killed in the process. Dorka's husband was arrested too and was freed only many years later, during the late fifties, thanks to the changes that Khrushchev's anti-Stalin crusade brought to the Soviet Union.

Poor Dorka and her shattered dream, and there were so many shattered dreams and shattered lives during that time. Listening to Faina while she relayed this story to me, I could not stop thinking that had we stayed in Leningrad, Gabriel could have been a prime candidate for such a fate, as a foreigner, and even though he had served in the army with honor, this could have been easily turned against him. Later, when I spoke with Gabriel about the fate of Leningrad University's Economics Department, he repeated that to die for the Soviet Union, well, if this were to be his lot, he would not have had much reason to complain, there were so many ways to die in those times, but to live in the Soviet Union, thanks but no, thanks.

Anya of the Ryazan Region

Here I must mention at least one more girl, a classmate of mine, Anya, from the Ryazansk Oblast, the one who woke me up in the middle of the night to tell me that my city, Łódź, had just been liberated by the Red Army. Anya was petite, skinny, had straight short hair the color of straw, and had a few freckles, similar to my own, on the bridge of her slightly upturned nose. She was a student in the Department of Russian Literature and was extremely well-read. We could spend many hours sharing opinions on the characters of books that we both loved. Sometimes, there was also some discussion about real-life characters. Anya liked to talk about the people of her town to whom she wanted to return after graduating, about the good people and also the bad ones. There were too many of those bad ones, she maintained, recalling the corruption and drunkenness she had seen, and what it had done to their and others' lives. She would return there and fight to get things in order. She believed that education and a diploma from such a prestigious university would arm her with a proper weapon to fight this abomination. I don't know if she realized that what she had aspired to do was a Herculean task, and if she had any inkling about the dangers involved, but she was full of enthusiasm and believed firmly that she would succeed. She certainly had a noble cause as did the many heroines of nineteenth-century Russian literature which we both liked to discuss so much.

More about Rats in Leningrad

Leningrad was not cold anymore. Spring had come back it seemed for good, and the city was basking in its beauty. But the rats were still there. Going to the washrooms, we still had to stomp and make a lot of noise to chase them away, unfortunately not always with success. The rats seemed to be getting domesticated. In our room they scratched and gnawed night and day, trying to get inside through the pipe that perhaps served as a water outlet in case of flooding. The end opening of the pipe was covered with thick steel mesh that had holes wide enough to see the animals sniffing, pushing, and gnawing, yet not big enough for them to get through. We fought them, and it was a fight to the death. Raya, evidently more experienced in such matters than the rest of us, smashed a bottle into small shards, which she pushed down the pipe. It seemed to help, so we smashed more bottles with great enthusiasm, and pushed more of that breakage into the pipe. This brought considerable improvement.

Sometimes, unable to stand the scratching anymore, I would go to stay with Frida for a night or two. She had a nice room on Herzen Street in the center of the city. This was all she had inherited from her parents' large, seven-room apartment, taken away piece by piece by the Office of Accommodations, till they finally left her with this one small room. Still, it was a cozy room, well furnished, much warmer than our dormitory, and there was no rat scratching. And it was good to spend some time together, reading, preparing our respective homework, and talking, sometimes late into the night.

To put an end to the subject of the rats that have given me the creeps for years, whenever the memory would come back to me, I cannot help but recall the scene I saw in the other university dormitory, on Dobroliubov Street. This was an old dormitory that had withstood the war's ravages relatively unscathed. When I moved out of Mendeleyev Street and settled on Vasilyevsky Ostrov with Gabriel upon his return from the army, Gina had to move there. I once went to see her there. The rooms in Dobroliubov were large, eleven girls in a room, and what I saw then I have never in my life, before or after, seen again. Rats ran around the room full of people as if they were pets and as if they rightly belonged there.

The girls kept their modest stock of food, bread, and the like, in double bags hung up high under the ceiling, out of the way of the rats. But those aggressive animals were competing for the food, and competing hard, jumping up high right to the bags, real athletic jumps. I would never have believed it, had I not seen it myself. And Gina's mattress! It was scary just to look at. Shreds of cotton that the mattress was filled with were hanging from it, pulled out by the rats. It was appalling, horrible, and what was worse, the girls seemed to be resigned to all this. It had been over half a year since the end of the war, and almost two years since the Leningrad blockade had ended. All this seemed a nightmarish dream, but it was going on in broad daylight. Our previous accommodation on Mendeleyev Street looked like the epitome of luxury compared to this.

This scene has truly haunted me for a long time, and there were times when I thought that I had imagined all this somehow, so unbelievable it started looking to me as time passed by. Unfortunately, it was real. Of all the Soviet novels describing life in the Soviet Union right after the war, and I read almost all of them, only once did I come across a writer who mentioned the plague of rats in a university dormitory, not in Leningrad though, but in Moscow. It was in Solzhenitsyn's *Cancer Ward.*

May Festivities, 1945

The war was almost over, even if not quite yet. However, the month of May was here, and the May Day festivities were celebrated this year with a special sentiment. Vodka was sold freely in state stores for the first time in years, and this was almost all the stores had to offer. Everybody wanted to have a party. Our "philosophical" group decided to have one, too. Our small room on Mendeleyev Street was crowded; some of the male students came, and one of the Professors, Prezent, had invited himself as well as a colleague, another young professor. As a result of a collective effort, some vodka was bought, some food was prepared, and it was a great party. Some very pretty and talented girls attended, including Katya Sharapova, a girl with a slight limp but a terrific voice and a great repertoire of Russian romances, Glinka, Rachmaninoff, and others. She sang, and the songs, with a little help from the vodka I had downed, almost made me cry.

And then, there was Zina Akisheva, a Russian literature student, a truly beautiful girl, with slim, golden-blonde hair inherited from her Russian mother and fiery black eyes, a gift from her Gypsy father, who recited Yesenin, one of the most beautiful of his lyrics, *Sukin Syn.* And how she read this, that story of unrequited first love! The poet loved a girl in white, and wrote little notes to her but never dared to approach her. It was long ago, the girl in white was gone, and so was her dog, but when the poet returned to that place many years later, he saw another dog there that looked just the same. It was that dog's son, hence the title of the poem. And for the poet, it brought back the memory of that "girl in white," and with it the old pain. But now that memory made him feel younger, and he was thankful to the dog for having "awakened May in his heart" again. But unexpectedly, at least for me, he concluded, "*Da, mne nravilas' devushka v belom, No teper, ia liubliu v golubom*" (Yes, I loved the girl in white, but now I love the one in blue). The poem was simple and touching, and so was Zina's performance, and all this made me very sad, even among the joyous din.

And All Is Well with the Theory of Dialectics

The next thing I remember, I was babbling excitedly about a problem I had with dialectics as discussed at the last seminar on Marxist philosophy, about the nature of change in society, which I had trouble understanding, for the first but not for the last time. This time, it was about where and when, and how, as a result of the evolutionary process of change, a new quality emerges. When and where had the process been interrupted, when and where had the leap forward, *skachok*, or to put it in other words, the revolution, occurred? Is there such a point at all, can it be pinpointed, and how? Doesn't it all depend on the observer, where he is, or what tools he has at his disposal to observe the process? I truly had a problem with the whole question. I seemed to have lost the notion of revolution and this was bad, indeed, but why did I come up with this right then? My tongue in my dry mouth was twisted and I was painfully aware that I had better stop this silly babbling, but I had lost control over it. "Wait, I'll explain it to you, it's very simple," said Professor Prezent eager to help a student searching for truth. He took a chair, a high-backed one, and just jumped over it, adding, "Here it is, the *skacho*k, everything is fine with the theory of dialectics, see?" He was trim and fit, and he jumped over that chair with ease and even grace and proved the point. Anyway, it was a great party, and the next day, Berlin was taken by the Red Army.

Prezent, Lysenko, and the Science of Genetics

Prezent was teaching biology at the University of Leningrad, and we were advised to take his course, though there was no obligation. The young adepts of philosophy, encouraged to want to "know everything" had attended some of his lectures, and so did I for a short while. He was a very close collaborator of [Trofim] Lysenko and would later be accused of having brought a lot of damage to the science of biology, genetics, and agronomy, as well as to too many people who had worked in those fields and paid, in many instances, even with their lives for upholding their theories. After over thirty years, in the long, ongoing competition and struggle, Lysenko's partisans finally got the upper hand, dragging Soviet biology and genetics backward for many years.

All this was unknown to freshmen students like I was then. Lysenko was then proclaimed to be the most prominent biologist to whom the Soviet people were indebted for the achievements of Soviet agronomy and their well-being, and Professor Prezent was also considered a highly esteemed scholar. Yet his downfall was coming and was not far away. The first sign of disfavor came at the beginning of the new academic year of 1945–1946. He was late returning from a trip at the beginning of the new academic year and was reprimanded for his tardiness publicly, similar in form and methods that Professor Usov had once used in Saratov to reprimand Professor Aleksandrov. But this was Leningrad University, and I thought this should not happen here. I was sure Professor Prezent had a sufficient explanation for being late.

Of course, with the wisdom of hindsight, this was a sign of the growing antisemitic wave that a year later would come into the open, connected with the wider so-called "Leningrad Affair," and the Party's attack against "cosmopolitans," a euphemism describing mainly Jewish intellectuals. Zhores Medvedev, the known Soviet biologist of the sixties, and a geneticist, who suffered gravely as an opponent of Lysenko, described in detail and rightly criticized Prezent's role in the whole antigenetics affair. He did not, however, notice that Prezent owed his downfall more to the fact that he was a Jew than to having been a

Lysenko collaborator. Prezent was fired when Lysenko's partisans were still thriving, and still had a lot of time ahead of them. Anyway, when Professor Prezent jumped over the chair to prove to me that there was nothing wrong with the theory of dialectics, I was unaware of all this, as I was still quite "green" in many other important facts of life in the Soviet Union, present and past.

Victory! The War Was Over!

A week after our great party, the war was over. On May 8, everybody seemed to be waiting for the official announcement, but it was not coming. Only late in the evening, it was after midnight already, a commotion in the dormitory woke me up. "Let's go celebrate! The war is over, it's over!" an ebullient Dorka rushed into our room, and we joined others gathering in Mendeleyev Street, from where a rather small, perhaps a hundred strong, but enthusiastic group rushed, yelling and singing over the bridge to the Nevsky Prospekt. We expected the Nevsky to be unusually brightly lit and overflowing with people, but this was not the case. The Nevsky was not brighter than on any other evening, and it was very quiet, almost empty. Disappointed, we returned to the university.

The war was over, but not quite yet for me. I was still waiting for a letter from Gabriel posted after the hostilities had ceased. The relief when I finally received that letter! Now, I knew that he would be back, that we would be together again, and my loneliness would come to an end.

But there was no news from my family or his. Earlier, in March or April, Gabriel got an official response to the inquiry that his regiment's commander had made on his behalf to the Municipality of Łódź about the fate of Gabriel's family. The response said only that no Temkins were living in the city of Łódź. We know now much more about what happened in Poland, what the Germans did to the Jews of Poland, to our loved ones, but the detailed knowledge would come to us only when we eventually returned to Łódź, and the full scope of the horror would sink in only slowly, bit by bit. It would require time, perhaps a lifetime.

CHAPTER ELEVEN

THE WAR IS OVER

Now it was time to think about the future. One morning, I woke up with a "splendid" idea. Gabriel, after receiving his discharge from the army, would come to Leningrad and enroll here as a student. To study together was our shared dream and it had not occurred to me that he might be tired after what he had gone through during those horrible four years of war, or that he may have some other plans, or he would not feel like being a student anymore or be ready for it yet.

I went to see the deputy rector of the university and asked permission for Gabriel to be enrolled in a correspondence course, while he was still in the army. The rector, a very thin, pale, sickly looking middle-aged man, heard me out and looking at me with some curiosity, said that Gabriel could be enrolled conditionally, upon passing the entrance examination. For a moment, a half-crazy thought darted through my head: would the University send him a *vyzov* (a summons), an invitation to come for the exams, like the one they had sent to me a year earlier? Should I ask for it? No, I could not! Too much chutzpah! And not pressing my luck any further, I left the rector's office very happy with the result.

On my way back to the dormitory, I stopped at the post office, and a letter from Gabriel was waiting for me there. By chance, and chance was treating me very kindly those days, the letter said that he expected to obtain a furlough, the first one in four years, and that he would come to Leningrad, but not before the beginning of August. This was better than great! And since the academic year was over, with all the exams for the first year passed successfully, as duly indicated by the grades written down in my "index," student booklet, and feeling encouraged and overjoyed by the day's events, I decided to go on vacation. The Student Association offered some of the students a two-week vacation at the university-owned "House of Rest" on the Finnish Bay, Tereoki. The cost was modest, and I decided to go.

Vacation at the Finnish Bay

It was vacation time. Everybody or almost everybody was going somewhere. Most girls went home to their families. Gina also went to see her mother and brother, who were now living in southern Ukraine, waiting there to be resettled to Poland. The Polish Embassy was preparing for the forthcoming resettlement and concentrated former Polish citizens closer to the new Polish–Soviet border. New words came into our vocabulary, "option," meaning the right to choose between the right to return to Poland or to remain in the Soviet Union, to stay permanently here, or "repatriate" and return to the country of origin. There were talks that groups would be formed soon, and that there would be a mass repatriation, and people were very excited about it. I did not know what to make of it. I tried not to think about it for now, though it was constantly on my mind. This had to wait till Gabriel returned. For now, however, I would enjoy the good weather and the beauty of the sea, which I was going to see for the first time in my life.

I went to Tereoki, glad that my friend Rita would be there, too. A fine occasion to get to know each other better! We spent a lot of time reading, and walking, but mostly talking. Rita was very intelligent, well read, and talking with her was not only interesting but also educational. She had an uncanny talent to explain the most complex questions in a lucid, precise way. She would make a great teacher of philosophy, the subject she truly loved, and she was, in my mind, the most promising student in our group. We got very friendly in Tereoki, but her future did not turn out the way I had wished for her. Rita had a tragic life and I will return to her story later.

We Met on Mendeleyev Street

The two weeks in Tereoki passed quickly. Gabriel was supposed to come to Leningrad on August 1 or 2, and not knowing the exact time of his arrival, I kept going to the train station every day, looking for the train from Kyiv, since he was supposed to come from the south. On the third day, it was as sunny and bright as the two before that, I left my room early in the afternoon in the company of my two roommates, Raya and Gina, intending again to reach the train station. We were still on Mendeleyev Street when suddenly I saw Gabriel turning from Naberezhnaia into our street. He must have noticed me too, because just as suddenly he stopped, while I left the girls and ran toward him. "The room is all yours," Raya called after me, "we are not coming home today!"

So, we met, after more than four years. Neither of us could believe that all this was happening for real. It was surreal, this street, this city, it was all dreamlike! We stood for a moment just looking at each other, then sat for a while in one of the stone niches along the Neva, just to catch our breath, and went "home" to my room in the dormitory. The room was not "all mine" and Ekaterina was there, and she would not budge the whole evening. The psychologist and writer would not give up such an occasion to eavesdrop, she needed "material" for her science and creative writing, perhaps, and would not allow us a moment of privacy. I have never forgiven her for this, and this, perhaps, has kept her in my memory forever.

After the first two or three days, filled with so much emotion that I was on the brink of tears almost all the time, the dean's secretary, an older woman, I am sorry that I do not remember her name, told me that we could have the room adjacent to the dean's office. It was vacation time, the room was not being used, and we used it till the end of Gabriel's furlough. Soon after Gabriel arrived, I rather casually informed him about my "great idea" of enrolling him in the correspondence course and about the entrance exams he would have to take. If he was shocked, he did not show it. He would later say that I had not left him any alternative, and he took diligently to the books. He had two weeks to prepare himself, and after four years of war and God knows what horrors, and not having even seen a book through all that time, this was a tall order. I, certainly, had not shown a lot of imagination imposing my "great idea" on him, but I had no doubt that he would manage, and I wanted so much for him to be able to share the dream with me that had been ours since our early youth, and the realization of which now seemed to be within reach.

A Correspondence Student

Gabriel passed his entrance exams. His Russian essay was very good, history and geography were a cinch, and of the gaps in his knowledge of the history of Russian literature, he was absolved by the female examiner. She "understood" that young men were suffering from shell shock from the war fronts (and how true it was in Gabriel's case, too!) and that this could be a sufficient explanation as to why he did not remember the name of the hero of Griboyedov's famous play, *Gore ot uma* (The Woes of Being Wise).

We were, of course, both overjoyed that he was admitted as a student to the correspondence course. It brought hope for the future to both of us and it felt as if a door to that future had truly been opened. By the end of the month, he was ready to return to his unit, hoping that now it would not take long, that demobilization would soon follow, and that his war would finally be over for good.

Beware of Military Discipline!

On the eve of his departure, we went for a stroll. Gina joined us, and the three of us were walking slowly along the Nevsky, taking in the early evening traffic on that famed boulevard. Gabriel was telling us some of his funny stories, of which he always had a pocketful, and we were laughing and sharing a fun moment. At the same time, a military police patrol passed by, set to catch some transgressor, a drunken soldier, or some other such "catch." And they did, a lowly sergeant having a good time, strolling with two girls. Gabriel did not notice the patrol, did not salute the young second lieutenant, the patrol's leader, and was stopped, properly rebuked, arrested right there, and led away. It all happened so quickly! A moment and they were out of sight!

Yet I did notice where they took him and stormed the office of whoever was in authority or on duty there. It sounds even now, perhaps, funny and unbelievable, but I did "rescue" him. The duty officer hardly listened to whatever I was excitedly trying to explain to him and just pressed an invisible button under his desk, and gave a short order to an orderly, who pushed his head into the half-open door, and almost momentarily Gabriel, with his belt and shoelaces in hand, showed up. "What did you say to him?" he was curious to know. I said that we had been at the Kirov Theater a few days before, and I had been humming the General's aria, unable to get even one note right, ever since. Then, I laughed and told him, "I didn't say anything, I sang, I sang the General's aria from Eugene Onegin, you know, 'Onegin, I love Tatiana madly, madly, madly,' and he let you go."

Now happy that the whole silly incident was over, we returned to the dormitory. The situation had the potential to turn nasty. A night in a cell with drunkards was unpleasant enough, but it could have had many more and much graver consequences. Gina was anxiously waiting for us. With the experience she had with arrests, police, and especially secret police, she had good reason to be scared and to be worried about us.

An Unexpected Result of My "Great Idea"

My "great idea" had a lucky and unexpected side effect. It brought about a happy, though unforeseen, result. When Gabriel returned to his regiment, he realized that the coveted discharge was not to come so soon, after all. The demobilization had begun, but the first to be discharged were older soldiers, at least ten years his senior. He would have to wait his turn and it would be at least a year, if not two. And in the meantime, the political and military situation had changed again. The Soviet Union's continued participation in the war, this time in the war against Japan, became a real possibility. The regiment was abuzz with rumors about an imminent dispatch, as a part of the whole Third Southern Front, to the Far East. Fortunately, chance was again kind to us. The demobilization laws stated that students who had interrupted their studies because they were called up for active duty, could now be discharged immediately to continue their course of studies. Gabriel, now a student admitted to Leningrad University, fell into this category. He got his discharge, and was finally able to say, "farewell to arms." The entrance exams, and the effort that went into them, had paid off. And in October 1945, he was back in Leningrad, for good.

It was almost unbelievable that all this happened. That it was happening so quickly seemed simply short of miraculous. Every day was bringing another event, another change, and many were happy, though there were some bad ones, too, a mixed bag, so to speak. Upon his return from the military, Gabriel obtained a transfer from the correspondence course to a full-time study program. This was now a simple matter, just a formality, even though at that time the university was already teeming with men returning from the military, discharged after lengthy wartime service. Even our philosophy class was no longer an almost exclusively female club.

Gabriel decided to study economics, and there was no difficulty with this either. What was, however, truly difficult and for a time almost hopeless, was to find accommodation. The dormitories were overcrowded, to say the least, incredibly congested and Gabriel was duly informed when transferring from the correspondence course to the full-day program that the university would not provide him with accommodation. As a student, he obtained the right to register in Leningrad as an inhabitant temporarily, to obtain something akin to a "student visa."

When we came to the municipality to get this "student visa" stamped into his document, the clerk, an elderly man to whom he presented his papers, stood up to shake hands with him, impressed with his military medal, "Glory," and with a bright smile on his face, almost solemnly declared, "Citizen, the right to live in the city of Lenin is awarded to you forever, '*na vechno.*'" As was explained, this was a special privilege for the bearer of that "Glory" military medal, whether he had come to study here or for any other purpose. To obtain a Leningrad permanent *propiska* (resident permit), the right to live in Leningrad was a coveted prize for an outsider during the Soviet times. To limit and control the growth of the largest cities, especially Leningrad and Moscow, severe rules were instated about who may and who may not be admitted to live there.

A One-eyed War Hero

His medal, "forever," was nice, but it still could not provide you with a place to live. There just was not anywhere, not even a tiny bit of space! I had my place with the girls in the dormitory, but Gabriel, the bemedaled warrior returning from the fronts of the war, was homeless. Friends of mine from my Saratov time, Sylvia and Szulim, both mathematics students, were lucky to have a tiny room for the two of them in one of the dormitories, and they put us up for some time. Also, Gabriel was stashed away with some male students in another dormitory for a while.

To rent something somewhere in the city, was out of the question. We did not have the money to pay for it, even if such a place were to be found. I was at my wit's end when my girlfriends came up with some advice. On the Fifth Line,[95] on Vasilyevsky Island, there was a dormitory, half-destroyed during the siege of Leningrad and it was just being prepared for renovation. Its manager, *Tetya* (Aunt) Sonya, lived there on the first floor, the only one that still has some livable space, and my friends told me to talk to her, to give her a gift, and that she would arrange something for us both on that floor since Gabriel was

95 In the southern half of Vasilyevsky Island, there is a series of parallel streets leading north and south. These bear an unusual naming pattern with numbers assigned to the sides of each street. The numbering starts with First/Second Line in the east and ends with Twenty-Eighth/Twenty-Ninth Line in the west of the island.

lawfully registered as a student and a Leningrad inhabitant. I heeded their advice, and we were lucky again and we got a room! Not on the first floor, nothing was available there, but on the second. A room was there, alright, the walls were whole, the ceiling over them too, and it had a fine door separating it from the wintry hallway. The room's two-paneled window had glass in one panel, while the other one was covered instead with cardboard, a one-eyed war hero! There was no heating and the Leningrad winter was already upon us and promised to be rather ferocious. But there was electricity. I could use a small hot plate and have hot tea on demand!

We cleaned up the place, *Tetya* Sonya provided some standard dormitory furnishing, two narrow iron beds with cotton-filled mattresses, a table, and two stools, and we were home! In the middle of the room, we installed a small iron stove, a well-rounded contraption, like a rich man's belly, that was popularly known as *bouryouka*. We were very familiar with it from our travels in cattle cars through the Soviet Union's long distances. A long pipe that went from the stove through an opening in the window's cardboard—good it was not all glassed in—was supposed to direct the dangerous fumes out of the room. But usually, there was more smoke and fumes than fire in our "oven." The fire was barely licking the surface of the slivers of wood. It was too wet for the fire to catch on, and the flames would fade and wane. Our efforts to keep the fire going were more often repaid with fumes that made my head spin. Yet I must admit that the room had very good ventilation and the fumes would be gone if we opened the door to the freezing hallway for a few moments.

That's how we lived through the 1945–1946 winter, the first winter after the victorious war. We spent our days in the lecture halls, or in the library, which was also never sufficiently warm but managed somehow to stay healthy. Gabriel would later say that for him, compared to what he had during the four years of war, the living conditions were luxurious. What saved us were our youth and the warm goose-down comforter, Gabriel's "spoils of war." He sent it to me in early spring 1945 from Budapest where he had participated in the fierce, protracted battle that the Soviet army had waged for that city. To say that the comforter was of great help in that half-destroyed dormitory in freezing

Leningrad, would be an understatement—it may have saved our lives. But what truly, and most importantly, perhaps, helped us to survive that first winter after the war, was our quiet joy that we had found each other again, that we were together again.

Who Can Afford a Winter Vacation?

At the end of February came the mid-semester break. We had both passed our exams with good results, and Gabriel and I were offered a two-week pass to a resort, in one of the university's "vacation homes." The place, Shirokoye, was halfway between Leningrad and Moscow, in the woods, with fresh air and clean, warm rooms, and it was free. I was sure that my friend, Ben, was instrumental in arranging this for us. Ben was a senior student, I do not remember of what, a refugee from Germany, a Jew expelled from there with his parents who were Polish citizens once upon a time, and therefore Hitler felt it right to throw them back over the border to Poland before the war, in 1938. I got to know Ben upon my arrival in Leningrad. He was an activist, always involved with the Student Union, and social committees, and was always looking for volunteers to help.

I was happy with the offered break, a warm room for two, for two whole weeks, what could be better? But unexpectedly, Gabriel refused. No, he would not go, it was not the time for breaks yet as he had only been a student for four months and he had hardly started working. How could he stop now? I tried to convince him that we would take whatever books we needed with us, that we both needed that break, but all this was in vain. Why? For a brief moment, I thought that it was because of Ben, but this seemed ridiculous, too silly even to consider. I could not understand it. It was heartless, he should have gone, even if only for me. I was really at the end of my tether, and perhaps, if I had used such an argument, he would have given in. As if anticipating it, he admitted that yes, he knew that I needed it, I should go, that he was happy that I was given the chance, but no, he could not afford a break, he would not jeopardize the academic year! He had to stay here and work, he needed it, even if only for his peace of mind. "Give my place to Gina," he said. "She needs it too, you both go, and I'll be fine."

He did finally convince me, as he had before when he had sworn to me that he hated sweets, leaving his whole ration of sugar for me, not even touching it. But I remembered that he used to like sweets, as any normal teenager does, yet I went on nevertheless to convince myself that perhaps he had changed during the war, the war had hardened him. Don't they say, after all, that it is "manly" not to like sweets? And he was not a teenager anymore, he was a man. So, I went to Shirokoye with Gina.

There were other girls from the university there, and we shared a room for six. It was truly a nice, hilly place, situated amidst thick, evergreen forests. An older man, the resort's handyman, awaited us at the train station with his sleigh. Bundled up in sheepskins, we got a ride to our destination through the wide, snow-covered fields, by the moonlight. It was a bucolic land of dreams, something out of a Russian classical fable or opera!

I found myself at the pinnacle of luxury, or so it seemed to me then. The room was clean and warm, the people friendly, and there was even a doctor or nurse at hand to help those who needed it. The food was much better than at my university canteen, and the ration of bread was more than sufficient. A glass of milk every second day was a welcome addition to our diet; a woman from a nearby kolkhoz brought the milk in exchange for a loaf of bread that we were able to spare among the six of us, the usual in the Soviet Union barter, as it was before as well as during and after the war.

One day, the milkwoman came almost in tears: she told us that they said we were going to have a war again. Is it true, she wanted to know, could it be, a war while we have not yet had even enough bread to get our fill? Her lamentation struck me. A war, again? I did not know what she was talking about, it was perhaps nothing but a silly rumor, I thought. But later, when I put together some dates, it became clear to me that the rumors were not without a cause. Since the beginning of 1946, the relations between the Soviet Union and the Western Allies were becoming more visibly strained, and the Cold War had started to replace the cooperation if not friendship that had developed during the common struggle against Hitler. Churchill's Iron Curtain speech was fiercely attacked by the Soviet press and radio. The kolkhoz loudspeaker—we had it in our room but kept it off as rest is rest—was spreading anti-Western propaganda, raising the specter of war. It had resonated with the poor kolkhoz woman and had brought her to tears.

The vacation house was rather well equipped for the vacationers' rest. There were even skis there, but there was no gear, and none of us possessed adequate boots to enjoy skiing, so we took long walks through the forest, on the thick, white snow, and that was good enough. But no, I was not happy in Shirokoye. I did not sleep well and had bad dreams. I repeatedly saw myself in my dream at the post office on Mendeleyev Street, where I used to receive Gabriel's letters, and the woman who used to hand them to me with a smile was looking at me sternly, not smiling anymore. Her face seemed to have changed, I did not recognize her. Was it her or some other person? I tried to recall where I had seen that face, whose was it, and these efforts were painful and in vain. I returned to Leningrad feeling guilty, nervous, and even more tired than I had been before the trip.

It was back to the daily routine of lectures, classes, the library, sometimes a movie, a Saturday evening at the university, but somehow those had lost their earlier luster. It took us some time to get over the Shirokoye episode, our "split." Gabriel looked askance at me as if wondering if I was still cross with him and I felt guilty for holding his need to work, his feelings of duty against him. Even if it was a bit much, was it, after all, a "vice"? There were truly big gaps in his knowledge to fill in, but one cannot "heat an ocean with a needle" as the Russian saying goes, and a week or two of rest would not have done any damage to him or his plans. And he seemed to feel a little guilty, too, for having let me down. Yet, slowly but surely, spring was coming to Leningrad again. The days were getting longer, the sun, although pale, was out more often, and the air was warming up. Also, the renovation of the dormitory had begun, and one day the window in our room was glassed-in afresh, no more half-blind war hero there. The new glass sparkled in the pale sun, and we threw out the stove; it was not needed anymore.

Spring Cleaning

One day, early in the afternoon, following a sudden urge, I left the library and went home to clean up our room. It looked like a cave. The walls were almost black, covered with soot, which our stove would usually produce in abundance whenever we tried to heat our room a bit. Suddenly, I could not stand this anymore, and I took a rag and piece by piece rubbed the soot off the walls and the ceiling, too. The walls that appeared from under the layers of dirt were not white, of course. They were grayish, a color I would not exactly call pearly-gray, but still a great improvement, and I felt satisfied with the results of my effort.

In the meantime, Gabriel alarmed by my disappearance from the library, came home and caught me in the middle of that almost Herculean task. We spoke Polish among ourselves when alone, but on seeing me at my work he suddenly said in Russian, and with scorn, "*Raba byla i budesh*" (a slave you've been, and will be), and started to help. We finished the cleanup, scrubbed the floor, which to our surprise was made of good wood, and parquet, and we had a palace! To top off my happiness, I gratified my aesthetic impulse and spread my only scarf over the cotton-filled pillow on the bed. The little flowers on the blue background brightened up the room and brought spring inside.

With spring upon us, the white nights returned, and the air carried the sweet smell of the shrubs, which had come alive again, all covered with fresh, moist little leaves. With spring, the examination session was also coming closer, yet it was now harder to work diligently. We now spent more time in our room, cherishing the privacy it provided.

Are We Returning to Poland?

Amidst all of this, a new problem came to our attention. It was not all that new, but now it was a problem that had to be faced and resolved without further delay. The treaty that was signed the previous year between the Soviet Union and the new Polish government about the repatriation of former Polish citizens to Poland was coming to the stage of realization. People were preparing to go and the problem for us was what to do. Stay or go? Most people were, of course, waiting impatiently for that moment to come, and they were ready to go as soon as possible. Most of our friends went without any delay, but some waited till the end of the academic year. There were also some who decided to stay, but there were not many. I remember only two such cases among the people at our university. One, a man, born in Lwów, and preparing his doctoral thesis on Russian literature, told us, "Here are the graves of my ancestors, and here I will stay."[96] This was a clear, though somewhat pompous, statement of his intentions, and I remember it mainly, perhaps, because of that pomposity. What he finally did, I do not know. The other was a third-year economics student, a woman, I knew her only by first name, Anya. She was born and had lived in Warsaw till the war and had started university there a year before the war. "No," she told me, "I am not going. Where to?" She had not forgotten Poland, the ghetto bench at Warsaw University, and all that, and she did not have anybody there to return to. "Isn't that enough?" she asked me somewhat accusingly.

There was no fixed date set for the option, and we were hesitating, unsure, and tried not to talk about it too much. I was mulling over the question myself, and I knew that Gabriel was doing the same. Perhaps, we did not want to influence each other. For some time, I kept trying to convince myself that the best would be to leave the decision solely to Gabriel, whatever he decides, that would be it. I understood Anya's point of view, and I shared her fears. After all, what good memories did I have of life in Poland? And whom did I still have there? Who was left? Who was waiting for my return? My parents were no more; my two sisters were no more. By now, it was clear that all my family there had been wiped out. And what would I do there? And what about the right to an education I had fought so hard for and now I had the university here? There was a lot to think about, and if only those thoughts had influenced my decision, my choice would perhaps have been obvious.

96 Lwów, although part of Poland before the war, remained in the USSR afterward.

Yes, We Are Returning to Poland

Amidst all this agitation and commotion, I got pregnant. Our son, our first child, was due to be born. I will never forget the wave of happiness that overwhelmed me when I, silly me, realized the fact. The conditions were appalling, the uncertainty of our existence mind-boggling, but the feeling of joy was indescribable. Did it influence our decision to return "home"? Perhaps, though not directly. One evening, the hour was late, but the sun was still in the sky, one of those Leningrad white evenings filled with nostalgia, we were sitting in our room. Arkasha, Gabriel's classmate and friend, was with us; they were preparing for an exam that was the day after the next, and after a few hours of intensive work, it was time for a break. I too had pushed my books aside to join them for tea. Now Arkasha was telling us about his life. He was born in Leningrad, his father had died in the war, and he and his mother had been evacuated from Leningrad when the ice on the Ladoga Lake had set and returned after the blockade was over. He was her only child, and his mother supported him while he studied. To complement her meager income from her job as a school librarian, she produced socks on a small mechanical device she owned, working evening or even night shifts at home. She would produce a pair or two of socks, and then sell them on the black market, making twice as much as she did from her salary. She had to be very careful though not to be caught doing it; if caught, she could be imprisoned for "speculation," a punishable offense. Yet that income kept them going, and despite the risk, she would not stop. As I listened to his story, I could see that small round machine in my mind, I saw the sharp metallic shine of its needles, going up and down in a steady, monotonous movement. I could see such a device, even though it was a long time ago, so long that I could not recall the person working on it, and I must have been a very young child then. It was in Łódź, the Jewish Łódź that was now obliterated, the Łódź of my parents, my childhood. And overwhelmed suddenly by a painful, acute, nostalgic feeling as if stung by those needles, I half-stated, half-asked Gabriel that very same evening, "We are going home, aren't we?" He nodded affirmatively as if he was simply waiting for me to ask the question. And so, among all this, my pregnancy, morning sickness, torn by contradictory feelings, we suddenly knew what we had to do: we are going home, we are returning to Poland.

A Small Beige Blanket for the Baby

One June morning, we went to the Passport Office, the OVIR, presented our papers verifying our place of birth and former Polish citizenship and were told that permission would be granted soon. On the way back from the office, we went for a walk on the beautiful Nevsky Prospekt, taking it in as something valuable and beautiful that we had already lost. I remember it was rather sad. We were again facing the unknown. What would be with our university studies, where would we live, on what would we live? There was a lot to think about, perhaps too much. We stopped at a few stores that had recently opened on the Nevsky but were still mostly empty. In one store, we bought a small beige woolen blanket, with the little child to arrive in eight months in mind, but also, perhaps, because there was not much else to buy.

ZAGS, the Marriage Registration Office

With the summer session at the university over, the examination results properly recorded and stating that I had finished my second year in philosophy, and Gabriel, his first in economics, we were ready to leave. There were still some errands to run, and all this kept us both very busy. One day, Gabriel returned from his errands, saying that he had stopped at the ZAGS office in the Vasilyevski Ostrov municipality. He had gone there to ask if we needed any witnesses to register our marriage. He thought to ask Arkasha but was told that no, there was no such need, we could go there tomorrow, and he made an appointment. The next morning, as I was getting dressed, not quite awake yet, he reminded me, "We are going to ZAGS first," and I wondered absentmindedly: ZAGS? What's that and what for? And while uttering this, I understood that I had said something wrong, and heard him say *idiotka*, female for idiot in Polish. This brought me back to my senses. I uttered "Aah," a sound of recall, and looked at him. He had an expression of hurt on his face. *Idiotka*, indeed. No, it was not a Freudian slip on my part, and it did not thwart our marriage from surviving for well over fifty years now, with some more, I hope, still ahead of us. We went to ZAGS. The ceremony was utter simplicity. Later, in the late fifties, Palaces of Marriage were built in the Soviet Union to "strengthen the institution of marriage" that was once doomed to be abolished as one of the last vestiges of the "bourgeois hypocritical morality." Young couples were married there with all the pomp, white dresses, wedding bands, flowers, music, and tears of their elders. But then, right after the war, it was very simple. No witnesses, the clerk, a young girl, put our names into her large books and asked me which name I wanted to use, his or my maiden name, I said his, then she said, "You pay fifteen rubles"—very affordable!—gave us a formal certificate that stated that according to the laws of the Soviet Union we were duly married, and wished us good luck. There were no flowers, no wedding bands, I don't know if it would have been possible to find these in Leningrad at that time, even if we could spare the money to buy them. My sister Rachel, when she came from Brussels to Łódź to visit us a few years later, was upset that I was not wearing a wedding band, and promised to send me one, which she did upon her return home. She sent me a small parcel containing chocolate, tea, and coffee, and hidden in the package of tea was a wedding band. Now I had that smuggled ring, and I could show the world that I was a properly married woman. Did I ever regret or miss the commotion connected with the ceremony of getting married? I was very happy arranging our daughter, Helenka's, wedding, and I did my best to see that her dress was beautiful, that the reception was as nice as it could be, and I even planted special flowers in our backyard to have them ready for the occasion. But as for me, yes, perhaps, to have a nice white dress to wear for my wedding would have been great—I did look good in white when I was young. And is there a woman who wouldn't like to have a memory like that? Even my friend, Roma Granas, a true revolutionary, an emancipated woman, a woman who once got into a public political argument, face-to-face, in person with Khrushchev, once confessed to me that one of the things she regretted most for not having had in her life was a white wedding! But such thoughts were not on my mind then, on the Vasilyevsky Ostrov, in that rather shabby office. With our parents and most of our loved ones gone, with almost nobody to share the good news with, and again facing a trip into the unknown, a very uncertain future, my thoughts were not the happiest.

I shared the news, though, with *Tetya* Sonya, and also informed her that we would be moving out soon, having decided to return to our homeland, Poland. She told me that she knew about it already, and I wondered how? "The man from the secret police, you remember the one with whom I came to your room the other day?" she said. He wanted to have a look at Gabriel and me and he had told her why. "But don't worry, it's nothing," she assured me. And then she added somehow dreamily, "At least over there, in Poland, people have enough potatoes to eat…" Enough bread, enough potatoes, that was the level of the Soviet people's dream! I felt goosebumps all over.

"It's Good to Be a Citizen of Great Britain"

There were still some minor formalities to take care of, and one day I went to the university library to get the librarian's statement that I had cleared my library account having returned all the books I had borrowed from there. On my way back, walking slowly along the sun-drenched Naberezhnaya, along the Neva, I was stopped by a colleague. He had heard that I was leaving, going abroad to Poland, and was it true, he wanted to know. He mulled over my affirmative answer for a few moments and then said something that made me remember him, and his name, to this day, "So, it is true! Sure, it's good to be a citizen of Great Britain!" It was so strange, a surreal joke, one might say. I laughed, and so did he. I was going to Poland, and here he was saying Great Britain! Little did I know then, or could even imagine that eventually, further down the line, Petya Veprentzev's joke would almost come true. I could not help thinking about it when many years later, I was asked by the Canadian judge of peace upon receiving my Canadian citizenship if I would mind swearing my allegiance to the queen of Great Britain? Would I mind? Why? No, I was very happy to do so. I had finally arrived, I hoped. And it had been a long trip.

CHAPTER TWELVE

BACK TO POLAND

Before leaving Leningrad, we decided to try once more to find out if it were possible to remain in the Soviet Union as Polish citizens temporarily until graduation, as Polish students abroad. We were very worried about our studies. To come this far, despite all the obstacles, and put it all at risk now? This was difficult to even think about. We thought our whole future was at stake.

A representative of the Polish embassy, Mr. Volpe, came to Leningrad on official business. We somehow found out about it and went to see him. We met him in his hotel room, on Herzen Street. I can still see us sitting there, in that fancy room, talking with the representative of the new Polish government in Warsaw.

There Was a Pogrom in Kielce!

Mr. Volpe was very cordial and well-wishing. He looked with special interest at Gabriel's war medal ribbons, which he was wearing on his jacket, Soviet style. There were generally no Poles serving in combat in the Soviet army during the war, and knowing about it, he was curious about his service, and why we wanted to stay here longer, and before we had time to say a word, answered it himself, "It's because of Kielce, I understand," he said. We had no idea what he was talking about as there was generally not much information in the Soviet press about what was going on in Poland, and we did not know anything about Kielce. Trying not to get into much detail, he told us it was quite horrible, a pogrom that took place quite recently, at the beginning of July 1946, a bloody pogrom that took over forty Jewish lives, returnees from Nazi concentration camps. This was what he told us, and it could have scared one from ever wanting to return to Poland again. Right after the war, after the great catastrophe, which annihilated almost all the Jews of Poland, a pogrom, and on such a massive scale! Terrified and numbed by the news as we were, we tried to explain to Mr. Volpe why we had come to see him and that we would like to postpone our return to Poland to continue our university studies here, being uncertain if it would be possible to continue studying there.

There Are No University Fees in Poland

On this matter, he assured us, there was less to worry about. University studies were free in Poland now, so there were no tuition fees, some very good professors from Lwów and Vilna universities, both renowned, prestigious institutions, had moved to Łódź, and a university was already operating in our native city. There should be no difficulty transferring. He wished us the best of luck, but as for staying here longer, he could not help us. He told us that there was a plan to eventually send students from Poland to the Soviet Union to study, but this would still take time, as it did indeed. Three years later, we would see off many of our new friends who were going to the Soviet Union's universities for their education.

So, we were on the way to Poland, our native country which we knew almost nothing about, even the language had become rusty, as it was not being used much. And how will we be received there? By now, we knew that there would be no enthusiastic welcome, to say the least. Would it be possible to live there at all, to bring up our child?

We stopped in Moscow and stayed there for a few days, thanks to the help of the Union of Patriots. I met Giza there and I was happy to see her. She too was returning home and was also worried. What will you do there, she asked me, how will you live there, on what? The same questions were weighing heavily on my mind, but I answered her rather lightheartedly that I may try to become a teacher and earn enough to be able to continue my studies because this was my greatest worry. "Maybe, maybe," she said somehow skeptically. "But universities are now free in Poland," I repeated what I had recently learned, and what seemed most important to me. Yes, but nevertheless...what prospects did we have here, if we decided to remain? The Soviet Union was familiar ground, but who do we have here? And did we really want to live here? And would we be able to survive on our meager stipends for three or four more years, and with a little child in our care?

"Should Have Bought a Leica"

I told myself to chase away these thoughts, to forget them, it would all settle somehow, and for the better! And as if it were a sign that things were indeed going to improve, I regained my normal appetite in Moscow. I could not believe how suddenly it had returned. The awful morning sickness was gone, I was hungrier than ever, and I started to eat for the proverbial two. On the account of the Patriots, Mr. Volpe had provided us with a bundle of canned mackerels and Spam, which had seemed almost a fortune to me. "Should have bought a Leica,"[97] he reproached us, "you'll need some money to start."

Good advice, but we did not have a Leica, and neither did we have the money to buy one on the black market from one of the Soviet veterans returning from defeated Germany. All we had brought with us was a wooden suitcase filled with books, and another one with our personal belongings. We also had a typewriter, and two new aluminum

97 Leica is a premium German manufacturer of optical equipment. Leica cameras were small yet expensive and price-stable, which is why Russian soldiers liked to bring them along when they returned home.

pots, which I was proud to have bought in a Leningrad store; a family needs something to cook in, and the fact that the pots were available in the store, was a positive sign of the times changing for the better, that the industry could spare some aluminum to produce something useful for the public, and not everything had to go into making planes, tanks, and such, anymore. I also had a new winter coat, a heavy coat made by the half-illegal Leningrad private manufacturers. It was very warm, indeed, and it had a fur cap made from real moleskin fur, the seller assured me, and to him, it was the coat's greatest asset. We spent a rather big chunk of Gabriel's army discharge money on it.

We only stayed in Moscow for three days—there was no reason to prolong it, and this was no time for tourism. In the late afternoon our friend Gina, Gabriel, and I boarded the Moscow–Berlin train. Gina's mother was already in Łódź.

Goodbye to the Soviet Union

I was overcome by mixed feelings saying goodbye to the Soviet Union, goodbye to Russia. I had spent over six years there, I was just eighteen on arrival, a stranger in a strange land. I left my family behind in Łódź and would never see them again. I survived because I had escaped in time, before the arrival of the barbarians who were set on wiping us, the Jews, off the face of the earth only because we had been born; I survived thanks to this country that hosted me, let me live and work there, and achieve goals I could not have even dreamed of before. I lived with the people of that country, some good, some not so good, and participated in their everyday struggles, their hardships, and by now knew how tough this country was and could be. I had come into contact with the common Russian folk, as well as with the educated ones, and I had the chance to become acquainted with some representing the intellectual circles. I studied the culture, literature, history, and traditions of that country.

Yet, I could not stay there; I could not have made this country the country of my choice. I would simply be afraid to opt for staying there permanently. But why? I made good friends there! Was it the system then, Socialism, was this what I was afraid of? But the socialist idea was still dear to my heart, wasn't it? And there would be a socialist system in Poland, too, it seemed certain now, but it need not repeat the same pattern, with all its drawbacks. Perhaps it will be a better one, a kinder one? Has Gabriel not fought for Russia, no, it was for the Soviet Union, which was Nazism's greatest foe? Nazism was also our deadly enemy, and there was a distinct difference there for us. Hadn't he also said that to fight for the Soviet Union was alright, but to live there, was another matter? And the antisemitism that was raising its ugly head there, we had seen ample signs of it, but what about Poland, don't we remember? And now, Kielce, they had a pogrom there, did they not?

Bread, Give Us Bread!

At Smolensk, our train was virtually surrounded by children, hungry, emaciated, half-starved, begging children, their arms outstretched toward the people on the train, *"Dyadya, Tetya, dai khleba"* (Bread, give us bread!). I will never forget this. The children of the victorious power that smashed Hitler's might! With tears in my eyes and that image in my memory, I left Russia, leaving the Soviet Union behind. In confusion, I repeated to myself tangled lines from Nekrasov and Tutchev, "Thou art so pitiful, Poor, and so sorrowful, Yet of great treasure full, Mighty, all-powerful, Russia, my Mother!"[98] and "Russia cannot be understood with the mind alone."[99] Indeed, it is beyond understanding.

98 Nikolai Nekrasov (1821–1878), from his unfinished epic poem, "Who Can Be Happy in Russia?" See Nikolai Alekseevich Nekrasov, *Who Can Be Happy and Free in Russia?*, https://gutenberg.org/ebooks/9619 (accessed November 1, 2022).

99 This is a frequently quoted line from a short 1866 poem by Fyodor Tyutchev (1803–1873). The full text reads "Russia cannot be understood with the mind alone, no ordinary yardstick can span her greatness: she stands alone, unique—in Russia, one can only believe."

Here, They Throw Jews Off the Trains!

When our Moscow–Warsaw train passed the new Polish–Russian border, I bought a Polish daily, the first I had seen in many years. I looked through it excitedly, and one of the first news items which sprang to my attention, though tucked away somewhere inside the paper, was a note saying, "Yesterday, again two Jews were thrown off a train," going from some place to another, somewhere in Poland. The casual mention of this seemed to suggest that this had been, if not a common occurrence, not an isolated one, either.

And a Soviet Reassuring Joke

I must have gone pale reading this piece of news, since one of the Soviet officers sitting in our compartment and who had engaged in friendly conversation with us, suddenly said to me, "Do not worry, Miss, I will tell you a good joke. Do you know what's an urna (a ballot box)? An *urna* is a box into which goes Mikołajczyk and out comes Gomułka."[100] He wanted to cheer me up and unwittingly delivered a concise and apt description of the real political situation in Poland. Whatever was going on in the country, we—the Soviet Union—are in charge and watching, and Polish independence should not be taken too seriously. The joke's message was unmistakably clear.

100 Stanisław Mikołajczyk (1901–1966), served as the prime minister of the Polish government-in-exile from 1943. After the war, he returned to Poland to run in the elections that Stalin had promised the Allies would be free and fair. However, as the joke makes light of, despite his popularity, his communist rivals, including Władysław Gomułka (1905–1982), allegedly won the majority of the vote.

CHAPTER THIRTEEN

ŁÓDŹ

The Łódź Fabryczna train station, from where we had left over six years ago to escape the Nazis, looked the same, and yet it was a totally strange place as if an eternity had passed in the meantime. Over there, I remembered, my mother and Helcia standing, waving goodbye to me. The station was much busier then, now it looked rather sleepy.

While Gina and I sat on our belongings, Gabriel ventured downtown to find the place where Gina's mother lived. It did not take very long, and he returned in the company of Oskar, whom we had last seen in Leningrad. He had stopped then at our place before leaving for Poland. Gabriel returned from his short first glance of the city, visibly confused, "You have no idea how narrow and small Piotrkowska Street is, imagine, just a small town street!" It used to be the proverbial grand avenue for us! And after a moment of hesitation, he added, visibly very upset, "A daily newspaper is two zlotys." It used to be fifteen groszy, and even this was not very affordable; the new price seemed sky high, and it struck and worried him. "Well, Oskar can afford one,"—it was sticking out from his jacket pocket—"we'll manage somehow, too." I wanted, perhaps, to calm his fears, and mine too, but the terseness of my remark only brought those fears out in the open, instead of dissipating them.

Łódź As a Stopover to the West

Jews, returnees from the Soviet Union, and there were about 5,000 in Łódź at that time, were taken care of by the Jewish Committee. Most of them did not intend to make Łódź, or Poland in general, their home. Łódź was rather a short stopover before Czechoslovakia, from where the way led to the West, to Germany. There, after some time in the camps for displaced persons, the refugees would embark on another trip, to some other Western European countries, and those lucky ones, who had relatives in Canada or the USA, would wait for admission, which would come after a long procedure of securing visas. Others would go by way of Italy to Cyprus, which would eventually lead them to Mandatory Palestine. State borders were still amorphous, and the migration of the mass of people looking for a place to live after having gone through the hell of war, ghettos, and camps, was still going on. At the same time, there was also a movement, though a much lesser one, from the West to Poland: people were coming back after liberation from the camps, some had decided to return to their country of birth for good, others just in search of their families, or for what was left of them, if any. A year later this almost-free border crossing would be stopped; to leave or to enter Poland, passports, exit visas, and so on were again required.

We Came to Stay Here

We came intending to stay. The next day, we registered with the Jewish Committee, and, it was a very pleasant and unexpected surprise that we were offered a place to live in the "Bursa." It was a Jewish dormitory for students and would-be students, a youth hostel of sorts, which the Jewish Committee, supported by the Joint,[101] UNRRA, and perhaps other such international relief organizations had recently opened in Łódź. We spent a year and a half in the "Bursa," almost till the time

101 The American Jewish Joint Distribution Committee (AJDC, JDC, Joint) was an important philanthropic organization operating in Poland before and after the war.

when Gabriel got his first job upon graduation. It was truly a life-saving place for us and it virtually saw us through college, providing room and board. And it also provided the company of about a hundred other young people, most of whom were determined to stay put in Poland, the country of their birth, language, and the opportunity to study in a chosen field, and to build a future for themselves, and this was very important too. Most of those young people were survivors of the ghettos and the camps, some, like Gabriel and I, had returned from Russia, and most were sole survivors of their families, their lives being spared through a string of miracles. And they all wanted to do something with those miraculously saved lives, as they indeed did. Doctors and engineers, journalists and scholars, working for many years in Poland, Israel, the USA, and Canada, as well as in many countries of Western Europe, and even in Australia, came out of that group of young residents of that dormitory in the years 1945 to 1948. Later, the political convulsions that Poland experienced almost regularly, turned this group of people into emigrants, dispersed all over the world, which was, after all, perhaps inevitable: dispersion being a seemingly eternal, inherent fact of Jewish life.

Tracing Life and Death in the Łódź Ghetto

Here, for the first time, we also found traces of our families that had perished in the Holocaust. One morning, I was "discovered," or better to say, recognized by a girl who had known me and remembered me from the time we both attended elementary school. She had also been a close friend of my younger sister, Helcia, having lived almost next door to my family in the ghetto. Suddenly, the people around me were not strangers anymore. My parents, and my sisters, were no longer totally lost for me. I had found a thread to hold on to, by which I was able to contact them in a way and bring their suffering during that last horrible stage of their lives, when I was away from them, somehow closer to me. I was overwhelmed by deep emotions. Just having found even these mere shadows of the life and death of my loved ones, seemed to have been reason enough for coming here, for returning home.

Many of those young girls and boys knew each other from the Communist youth organization that functioned in the ghetto, and my Helcia was with them during that time. They all knew me through her, as she had told them with pride about the "sister who went to Russia." Suddenly, there were now many people around ready to share their memories of Helcia and my father with me. Dorka Zorek (later Francuz) lived at Helcia's place during the last few months of the ghetto, before being deported to Stutthof. Dorka Flug worked with Helcia in one of the ghetto workshops producing cotton-filled comforters. She kept praising Helcia. She was such a good friend, always ready to help. Dorka told me this more than once. Helcia was so adroit with her hands, and without her help, she would have hardly been able to manage with her work on those dreadful comforters. Marysia Finkelstain (Ostrowska) also remembered Helcia fondly, and so did Yuzek Smietanski, who also remembered my father; Lucek Dobroszycki told me about the radio that was hidden in our place, and how much it mattered to them all to have it and to be able to listen to the world. Marysia Frydrych (Wiener) was a next-door neighbor of Gabriel's mother and her two younger sons, Ignas and Monek, and this was another source from where we derived glimpses of their life and suffering.

Soon after arriving in Łódź, Gabriel and I went to the Jewish Committee's archive. I received my parents' death certificates there, and my father's *Kennkarte*, the German identification card with his snapshot on it. My father's naked, shaven, skeletal face looked at me, his eyes so very sad and tired, that it put me to shame. What did they do to him? They starved him, and forced him to shave his beard, too! He was strong enough to last until March of 1944; he endured hunger for so long! In mid-1942, the food ration in the ghetto fluctuated around 600 calories, which meant that at that time people were already constantly hungry and wasting away. Already in 1942, famine tremors and death from starvation accounted for over 15 percent of all deaths in the ghetto. Those most wasted away were deported to the annihilation camps, and people from Łódź were being deported to such a camp, Chełmno, already in 1942.

Touching the mere shadows of the ghetto reality took a tremendous emotional toll. Even though I painfully felt the need to know more, I seemed scared to ask for more, and the people around us were also not very eager to dwell on the subject. I did, however, try hard to find a trace of my sister Sala's fate. But no matter how hard I tried it was all in vain. No trace and nobody came forward with any kind of information. Her name vanished rather early from the register of the ghetto inhabitants; I found it mentioned there for the last time during the first half of the year 1942, in connection with an address change. This much I found out from the Yad Vashem records of the Łódź ghetto when these records became available, and I obtained a copy. As is also well known, deportations from the Łódź ghetto to one of the most notorious camps, Chełmno, started very early, already in the first months of 1942, and the only conclusion I could draw was that Sala too must have been among those early deportees and that it was there that she met her death.

I wrapped the documents received from the archive and hid them so well that I could never find them again. How I searched for that envelope later on! But to no avail. It was gone. I hid it so well and buried it so deep, but the painful image of my father's shaved face remained with me forever.

Hanna and Gabriel after their return to Łódź, Poland, in 1946.

"Kikes Are Coming Back"

One day, I ventured out with Gabriel to Dworska Street, where my grandparents had lived for as long as I could remember. This was also where I had lived with my parents and Helcia for at least a year before the start of the war. The frame house on the left side of the yard was gone, its wood used perhaps as fuel during the cold wartime winters. As for that brick house on the right, all that remained from it was a half-ruined front wall yawning with empty holes where windows used to be. But the lilac tree was still there. It had grown taller during those war years. It was not in bloom now, but it still had a rich green leafy crown.

On the way back, we passed a small alley street, Kielma; my grandfather Mendel used to live there, and my Uncle Benjamin, Mother's brother with his large family, also lived on the opposite side of that street. It used to teem with children and grown-ups, always in haste, going back and forth about their business. Now, the street was quiet, almost empty, with most of the houses along it half-ruined. Only at the end of it, at a corner house that was already part of Brzezinska Street, two young men were working on a scaffolding, busy painting. The young workers' eyes followed us. We had interrupted the monotony of their work and provided them perhaps with an entertaining moment, "Kikes are coming back," we heard loud and clear, and their easy laugh would sound in our ears for more than only a moment.

Łódź University

Yes, there was a university in Łódź, and this elevated my native city, from the city of textile factories, and tall chimneys spewing dark smoke into the sky, to a higher level of civilization. Enrolling was simple. Our Leningrad credentials, student books—indexes—were viewed with some suspicion, but they were legitimate documents, and I was accepted as a third-year student in the Department of Philosophy, then headed by Professor Janina Kotarbinska, the wife of the distinguished Polish philosopher, Tadeusz Kotarbinski. Professor Kotarbinska, herself a Holocaust survivor, wondered why I had taken so many history courses as a student of philosophy. I could not explain to her then that those were all mandatory courses. There were no elective courses at Leningrad University, and I think that this was a universal rule there. But later, if asked the same question again, I would have ventured a different answer: the programmers of my student curriculum made me take so much history to better prepare me to perceive the world's development as leading to history's "natural," "crowning," and "inevitable" end—the socialist system. Professor Kotarbinska, a logician and analytical philosopher would perhaps consider such an idea at least strange, and rightly so, but I think this was it. Still, whatever the case, studying history was interesting in itself, and did me no harm; on the contrary, I learned to appreciate it even more as a useful background for my favorite subject, the history of philosophy.

To become a full-fledged student in Professor Kotarbinska's department, I would have to pass some additional exams which were mandatory here for students of philosophy during their first two years of study. I don't remember what they were, but I did fulfill the conditions because, in October, I began attending classes, lectures, and seminars regularly. Professor Benedykt Borenstein, previously from Vilna University, a tall and distinguished-looking gentleman, who held his head a bit stiffly to one side but his back very straight, taught Kant. He read with his class the *Prolegomena to Any Future Metaphysics* of that great German philosopher, whom he treated as if they were good old friends. He commented on the text, Kant's life, and his times with familiarity and an abundance of details, which made the difficult reading fascinating. Gina and I were the only two students in his class in permanent attendance. For a short period, another girl joined us, but she did not stay long and anyway kept to herself, no matter how much we tried to befriend her. From time to time, one of us would ask a question concerning the text, and sometimes the professor would address a question to us, and any answer, even the most insignificant answer, always seemed to be appreciated.

I also attended a course on the history of philosophy taught by Professor Wasik formerly from Vilna University. His assistant was Dr. Czajkowski, a pleasant man, who was much easier to talk with than the professor himself. Professor Wasik conducted a regular, but not a very popular seminar, and I, as a regular attendant, had to prepare a paper to be presented at the seminar. Since I had spent the war in that exotic country which, as it was well known, had brutal soldiers wearing heavy, awkward-looking tarpaulin boots, but no culture or science or any of those things, not to mention philosophy, I was asked to tell them what all that Marxist philosophy is about. I tried my best, presenting my paper about dialectical materialism, my heart pounding, and I managed to conceal the trouble I had with the subject, even at that rather elementary level at which I knew it at that time. Docent Czajkowski was impressed, and he said that he did not expect this philosophy to tackle such difficult problems, and he seemed sincere. But Professor Wasik was not impressed at all. He gave me a new assignment though, after which if done to his satisfaction, I would have fulfilled the requirement for another semester in my beloved subject. The assignment was to write eight or ten reviews of books or articles in philosophy that I could choose from a long list he gave me. Professor Wasik liked my reviews much better than he did my paper on Marxist philosophy. On that occasion, he also wanted to have a little chat with me about the Soviet Union. Well, he said for a start, they don't even have a decent library over there, to which I quickly tried to assure him that they do, the Lenin Library in Moscow, for example, with 2 million volumes, to which he remarked sarcastically, sure they have, they took the books away from everybody like they tried to take away timepieces from everybody, and on this note, our discussion came to an end. But I got my passing mark, and thus received the required credits.

Leszek Kolakowski

As I mentioned already, Docent Czajkowski was impressed with my Marxism paper, but one of the students was not. He had some reservations about one of my formulations and would not let it go. When the class was over, he still wanted to argue about it and we did, though I have no recollection what it was about and, as an argument of last resort, he told me, "Kolakowski would not agree with you either, what Kolakowski says is different and Kolakowski is right." "Who is Kolakowski?" I asked. "Let's go ask him," he answered, surprised by my ignorance. Let's go, I agreed. We went to Professor Kotarbinska's office, and there he was. Leszek, a tall, fair-haired, skinny youth in outgrown, baggy slacks. Whether we had resolved the question that brought me to make my acquaintance with him, I do not remember, but we became friends. We studied at the University of Łódź at the same time and attended the same seminars there and at Warsaw University. Later, we became colleagues at the Department of Philosophy at Warsaw University, and when he was eventually promoted to the post of chairman of the department, he also became my boss. We also left Poland at the same time, in 1968, with my family and me trying to immigrate to the United States, while he went to Canada for a two-year stay, invited to teach there at McGill University, which would eventually turn into a voluntary exile.

Kolakowski went through a long and interesting ideological and philosophical evolution. He began as a political Marxist activist, taking the pronouncements of what was officially and rather vaguely and crudely formulated as the body of Marxism as well as its political correlations, to the extreme, sometimes also to the dismay of the older, more experienced, and tempered Marxist politicians. He was then one of the most influential members of the group of young, enthusiastic, aspiring writers, poets, and intellectuals, all unrelenting fighters for Socialism. Some of those young men, no older than twelve at the war's outbreak, styled themselves as veterans as if to make up for the missed occasion to participate in the "great event" and become heroes during "those heroic times." One comes to mind immediately, a talented mathematics student always in a worn-out Russian trench coat, topped with a dirty military cap bought from some Soviet soldier at the Łódź black market. He was a popular figure in our student organization in postwar Łódź and grew to become a respected mathematics professor at Warsaw University in later years. Those young "revolutionaries" formed an informal group or should I say movement which became known in the history of the first postwar years in Poland as the "pimpled" ones.

We must remember, those times were the times of the great postwar overhaul in Poland, the time of rising Stalinism, and the role of the uncompromising, extreme, young, intellectual revolutionaries could have become an ominous one. When the old professors, who had gained influence and fame during the prewar years, under the "old regime," not ready to collaborate fully with the new one, were pushed out of the universities, the very presence of pushy, uncompromising "heirs" waiting to become their replacement, intentionally or not, it does not really matter, was of consequence. Adam Schaff, who directed the whole operation of "reforming" the university system on a "philosophical and ideological" basis for the Party, had many willing and eager helpers. Sometimes, the extremism of those helpers was even too much for him, as he recalled in one of his later books. It is not easy to imagine, but it is true. Kolakowski stood up once, the year was 1950, in Professor Tatarkiewicz's class and read a letter criticizing the professor for neglecting Marxism in his history of philosophy. And Kolakowski, Baczko, Sladkowska, and Holland, all dear friends of mine, came to Schaff with a formal complaint about Professor Kronski. He did not know anything, they claimed, about Marxism, and demanded that he be fired from the Institute, and Schaff asked them to leave his office. I have no reason to question his veracity, but I had no idea then of what was going on, I liked the Tatarkiewicz textbook, learned from it my history of philosophy, and it was way, way better than the Russian–Soviet Aleksandrov, which I had learned to dislike while still at Leningrad University. And I respected Kronski as a man of great learning, an expert in the field of German philosophy, Marxist scholar or not. Professor Resnik of Leningrad University had taught me this attitude. So how come I did not know what my friends and colleagues were after? Where was I? Perhaps, because I was at the Institute only part-time I stayed out of it, but first of all, because I was busy at that time preoccupied with my new baby, our sweetest little daughter, Helenka, and could not care for much more. How good for me!

With time, Kolakowski, like many others of the "pimpled" ones, grew up and became fully accepted and highly valued as a party philosopher and historian of philosophy, author of many articles, as well as of biting polemics with Catholic Church theologians. Some of his writings of that period, though they always wear the stamp of his wonderful erudition, became characterized by a rigidity that was prevalent in the usual output of many other "proper" Marxist dogmatists of the Soviet mold of that time.

Well, this period did not however last long, and soon Kolakowski, true to himself and his inquisitive mind and the need to search for the truth, became one of, if not the foremost political and philosophical critic of the doctrinaire, institutionalized Marxism, the official ideology of the political system of People's Poland. Now, his main endeavor would be directed to uncovering the "true" meaning of Marx's oeuvre. Convinced that it was lost, buried under the weight of the 100-year-long history of the theory, he started a period of searching for it. The irreconcilable differences between the theory's noble promises and the doubtful political deeds and results led him to search for a new understanding of Marx's teaching, a search for the "original meaning." With the mid 1950s, and especially after Khrushchev's denouncement of Stalin, such tendencies were also becoming popular among the Left in the West. Disappointed and frustrated by the reality of the hitherto embraced socialist system, intellectuals took up a search to examine anew and revise some entrenched tenets of the theoretical Marxist heritage. So, for example, the writings of the "young" Marx were searched for important values that allegedly were not continued by the "old" Marx and were therefore lost. In a similar vein, Engels was criticized as "spoiling" the "true" Marx, and Lenin hardly deserved to be called a Marxist, not to mention Stalin. Notions like Marxism as an "open" system, Marxism without the notion of the "dictatorship of the proletariat," a notion allegedly disliked by Marx and used only a few times by him, Marxism as the philosophy of the individual, and so on were promoted. Those attempts at revision of what Marxism "should become," born by noble intentions, no doubt, coincided with the equally noble search for a kind of "Socialism with a human face," "Socialism, which we could like," and so on. In short, a search for a "better" Marxism and a "better" Socialism or Communism was going on, in the West as well as in some of the "People's Republics" at least, and first of all, in Poland, a search for a more acceptable, and "true" teaching that would restore the real humanistic meaning of Karl Marx's heritage. At approximately this time, Kolakowski, still a proclaimed Marxist, started to plan, if not also to write his book, *History of Marxism*, the three volumes of which he published while already living in exile in England. This fundamental work witnessing the author's enormous learning and being conceived in the spirit of the author's still ongoing search for the "true" meaning of Marx's heritage reflects his own ambivalence toward this heritage.

I read Kolakowski's book not just with great interest and intellectual satisfaction. Reading it was also an emotional endeavor for me. It brought back to me the many discussions on that subject within the Department of Philosophy as well as outside it, in some of which I had also participated. It moved me enough to write an essay on Kolakowski's own ideological and philosophical evolution, a fascinating subject in itself, an evolution that seemed to reflect the intellectual evolution of a whole generation of intellectuals in the postwar era, and not only in Poland. It took Leszek a great deal of effort to bend his extreme views, to grow out of his youthful extremism, and grow into what was recognized and accepted as "proper" by the official party censors and in the same way, it can be said that it took him an equal amount of trouble to grow out of Marxism altogether, to say his final farewell to Marx. Tracing the "fate of that strange doctrine, which began as a protean humanism and ended with the monstrosities of the Stalinist tyranny," Kolakowski defended Marx against his continuators who misrepresented him and allegedly overlooked the most important ingredient of his teaching, which I found somehow akin to Marx's own frowning about his followers, disavowing them rather contemptuously, "He is not a Marxist, if they are."

The *History of Marxism* belongs to the stage of Kolakowski's ideological development when he was still a committed Marxist, and was proud to proclaim himself as such, but at the same time so very far from what was the official, institutionalized, dead humdrum allowed by the Party and State that there was no place for him in Poland anymore. Kolakowski himself, as his *History of Marxism* witnessed, liberated himself in the process of writing it, which makes the book all the more interesting for showing the difficult process of his unlearning, of growing out of the dogmas he had accepted in his youth. My essay, "Reading Kolakowski: Marx and Marxisms," was published by the Journal of the Polish Academy of Sciences (Archives of Philosophy) in Warsaw in 1992. By then, we were already all living in a totally different, changed world, a new epoch, one might say, a post-socialist one.

In the fall of 2003, I watched an interview with Kolakowski on an educational TV channel on the occasion of his receipt of the "American Nobel," as it was called by the Polish press, the Library of Congress Prize for outstanding achievements in the field of humanities and social sciences. I watched with pleasure and pride.

Taking a Break from Studying

But let me return again to the faraway postwar time. For now, I was done with studying philosophy or anything else, for that matter. It was late January, and my child was due in February. Nothing was more important now. The doctor assured me that I was fine, and everything would turn out well, all I had to do was relax and take it easy, which I did or I tried to do anyway. I used the free time to read or reread a lot of Polish classics; Prus, Zeromski, and I derived a lot of pleasure from it. Especially Prus as his *Lalka* (Doll), seemed hilarious to me, making me laugh out loud, and my baby, kicking inside me, seemed to laugh, too.

On February 14, late in the evening, Gabriel took me to the hospital by a *dorozhka*, a horse-driven buggy like those still used nowadays in tourist places for the tourists' enjoyment—there were still not many taxis in Łódź at that time. The nurse on call said that it might still take a lot of time, and there was no reason for him to wait there as he would not be allowed near me, anyway. These were the hospital regulations, and to my surprise, he left at once. But Gabriel went home so obediently, because he was sick. He was running a high fever and was seriously ill the whole day before, but he did not tell me anything, and I had not noticed his symptoms. As it turned out, I went into labor, and he took to his sick bed—quite a division of labor! Just a silly pun, but it somehow amused our friends, and we remembered it for quite a while.

The hospital was very quiet, not a sound. It was a small place, once a private clinic with still noticeable traces of former elegance. The Germans had taken it away from the Jewish prewar owner, and after the war, it was taken over by the Polish government. Too anxious to be able to stay in bed, I spent the rest of that night walking, if not running, along the dimly lit hallway. I was alone with my pains, recurring at pretty long intervals that were not yet strong enough to make me yell for help or get panicky. The silence, the white clean walls, the shine of the floor's linoleum in that dim light, all this gave the place a somehow mysterious and ominous look. I was scared.

Henio, Our Son, Is Born

My son was born the next day, Friday, February 15, at 5:35 P.M., a healthy boy, weighing 3.65 kilograms. There was no doctor at the birth, only a midwife, a tall, skinny woman with a shrill voice. She seemed professional and trustworthy but went suddenly into panic right after the child was born. I was hemorrhaging and she lost her head for a moment. "Should I give you a shot, should I call the doctor?" she repeated a few times with trepidation. Her questions, though I heard them, seemed to be about someone else, not myself, and all her fears were no business of mine. I was feeling weaker and weaker and being so weak felt good. "Do not sleep, keep your eyes open," she slapped my face, and gave me the shot. The hemorrhaging stopped. When all the commotion was over, the nurse, a middle-aged, well-rounded, short woman, brought my son to me. My father's brown eyes looked at me from the child's little face. I felt the salty taste of tears in my mouth and an acute painful sting of mixed emotions. There was joy, surprise, but also sadness, and a touch of something else. Disappointment? Fear? Perhaps all mixed together? Only three years had passed since my father's death, and his memory was dear to me. Yet the child's likeness to my father momentarily brought back the much too painful fresh memories, and the perhaps crazy thought that with the inheritance of the likeness comes also the inheritance of fate. I wanted, and expected perhaps, my son to take after Gabriel, if not for any other reason than just because Gabriel was luckier than my father. I looked back at my son, Gabriel's son, smiled at him and prayed for a better lot for our son than my father's was.

My midwife was so proud of what she had done for me that the next day she told me half in secret that in the big city hospital just yesterday, a young woman had died in a situation like mine, she had bled to death. "You are lucky," she added, not giving herself any credit. Yes, I knew that luck was on my side!

In the afternoon, there were visitation hours, and my friends came to visit. Basia and Gina came, Oskar came, but no Gabriel. What was going on? They told me not to worry, it was just a cold, and he could not come to see me or the child, because a cold, it's catching, you know! They were taking good care of him, they told me. Basia and Gina joined forces to cook a tomato soup for him. The soup became something of a legend later on and we would joke about it for years. By mistake, Gina added sugar to it instead of salt. And since it still did not taste right, Basia added some more, and finally it became as sweet as...sugar! But their next effort was successful and Gabriel got his soup.

They kept me in the hospital for ten days, and Gabriel did not show up. The blonde, short, fat nurse was a good Catholic and she pitied me, the abandoned young mother. Once, to cheer me up, her round face beaming, she told me not to worry and that she would be glad to hold my son, the poor fatherless child born out of wedlock, for baptism, to do such a favor for a single, unmarried girl brings good luck!

Moving to a New Apartment

We continued living in the dormitory. Gabriel was now a third-year student at the Department of Law and Economics, while I took a leave of absence, now totally immersed in mothering. A year later, Gabriel, who was almost done with his course of studies, got his first permanent job. It was with the Łódź Party School, run by the city's committee of the Polish Workers' Party. He was offered the post of managing the school's library, and he was satisfied with the job. Later, he would repeat more than once that this was his best job ever. It allowed him to spend a lot of time browsing through books, which he did sitting mostly up high on a ladder to check out the books on the upper shelves, while at the same time preparing for his final exams and seemingly oblivious to anything else.

Gina, Hanna (with baby carriage), and Gabriel.

At that time, the first and most difficult period of mothering and nurturing was behind me. We had by now a beautiful, one-year-old boy, and I wanted to continue my studies. But first, we would say goodbye to the dormitory. With Gabriel's job came a "fringe benefit," the assignment of an apartment, or to be exact, a room with the use of common utilities and a kitchen in one of the buildings that the City Party Committee took over after the war. The Soviet model of communal living was being introduced in Poland. There was not much space available due to the destruction that the city had suffered during the war; there was still very little new construction around, and what was available was grabbed by new “owners,” institutions that were quick enough or strong enough, or important enough. The apartment, in which we were allotted our “living space,” was in a very modern, elegant building built just before the outbreak of the war, at 20 Wolczanska Street. It was not a very large apartment, just three rooms, and a small additional room, the so-called “maid’s room,” but the rooms were of high quality and the amenities were great. I was especially enchanted with the bathroom, never before had I seen such beauty; green tiles all over and shining steel, and hot water from the faucet! The building also had a nice garden, so all in all, it was a perfect place to raise a child. We got one room with the addition of the maid’s room, which Gabriel used for work, often sitting there late into the night. In that room, he also prepared for his finals, sometimes working with a friend of ours, Halina, a co-student of his, while in the adjacent kitchen I would prepare something to eat for the baby or for all of us.

I have a memory from this time. One day, it must have been the end of May, I was preparing spinach for Henio, having devised a way of preparing it that would make him like the food that was good for him. And the child liked it, as we all did, and while eating, we talked about the latest news, the emergence of the Jewish State. Halina had a very interesting, even heroic past during the war; a Jewish girl, she was smuggled out of the Warsaw ghetto in 1942, just before the start of the first great deportation. She jumped over the ghetto wall to the other side, and subsequently worked for the Polish Workers’ Party, involved in transporting arms, running a printing shop, and so on—some most dangerous assignments. She became well acquainted with the leaders of the then Communist underground, who now, in 1948, were the rulers of Poland. Zenon Kliszko, she told us, was unhappy about the UN decision to recognize the Jewish State. But the Soviet Union voted for it, too, I wondered. Yes, but Kliszko, Gomułka, they adhere to the “Polish way to Socialism…” Never mind them, we finally decided. I was happy about it all. I also thought that my father would have been happy, too.

1948–1949: A Time of Deep Political Change in Poland

Poland was changing around us. The two leftist parties, the Polish Socialist Party and the Polish Workers' Party (Communist), were uniting and establishing a new party—the Polish United Workers' Party (Polska Zjednocznona Partia Robotnicza, PZPR) that became Poland's only ruling party for the next forty years, until its demise in 1989. The new United Party pushed Poland closer toward Stalin's or the Soviet model of "Socialism," toward a fully fledged totalitarian society. The fundamentalist Communist elements were taking over, and the days of Gomułka and his comrades seemed to be coming to an end.

Naming a Child in Such Changing Times

Small, otherwise insignificant stories often add color and bring the great changes of the times around us into sharper focus. One such story seems especially telling to me. Our neighbors in the apartment, a young couple, had a child, born during that summer of change. The father of the child was an instructor in the city's committee of the PZPR, and he had a problem. One morning, when he saw me in the kitchen we were sharing, he decided to tell me his problem. He wanted to name his boy Wiesław, in honor of the leader Wiesław (Gomułka), but he could not do this now, Gomułka was in disgrace, so what was he supposed to do? Name the child Bolesław? For the new first secretary, Bierut? But what if…? I did sympathize with him; he had a problem, indeed. I wanted to advise him to name his boy after some member of his family. This was what we had done. We named our son Henryk, and this name was also in a sense the result of a compromise, but the situation demanded compromises, and there was nothing one could have done about it, or so it seemed to me then. Gabriel wanted to name our son Chaim, after both of our fathers. But how could you do this to a child who had to grow up and live in Poland, go to school there? It seemed to deliberately invite problems for the child. Yes, I understood my neighbor's problem, we had had a problem, too. Ours was solved by the list of official names that the municipality's registry presented to us, one was allowed to use any name on that list but none that was not on the list, and there was no Chaim there. So, we decided on Henryk—at least it started with an H! And remembering all this, I skipped our story and advised my neighbor, a bit tongue in cheek, "Yes, Wiesław is definitely out, Bolesław, hmm, who knows, so maybe Włodzimierz (in honor of Lenin), that would be safer, wouldn't it?" And what do you know? He heeded my "advice" and named his son Włodzimierz! And there are many Włodeks around, and not only in Poland but in the West, too. Revolutionary-minded young couples were giving their sons the name Vladimir.

An Exam with Professor Kotarbinska

In the fall of that year, I was back at the university, attending seminars, preparing papers, and fulfilling other student duties. The seminars were much more interesting now, especially those led by Professor Ossowska on ethics and Kotarbinska on analytical philosophy. These seminars were well attended and the students were intelligent, interested in the subject, and generally more advanced in philosophy than I was at that time, which made the lively seminar debates all the more interesting for me, and just as exciting. I was also attending some of the lectures by Professor Nina Assorodobraj who was teaching a course in sociology, introducing me to big names in Polish sociology such as Krzywicki and Czarnowski, the latter being her own professor in prewar Poland. Later on, she became my boss as the head of the Department of History of Philosophy and Social Thought at Warsaw University.

To earn my BA, I had to take one more exam. Only one, but this was a huge exam on logic, the basis of which was Professor Tadeusz Kotarbinski's fat, solid textbook. I would be examined by Professor Janina Kotarbinska, and I knew that I would be seriously scrutinized: Professor Kotarbinska had little trust in the girl that came from "that" country and would sometimes mix a Russicism or two into her speech. While a Gallicism was nice and evidence of a good prewar education, and an Anglicism would show some worldliness acquired during the war years, a Russicism was something else. It was just not done.

I studied Professor Kotarbinski's book back and forth, and then again. Never before or after did I work so much to prepare for a single exam. I knew the subject and I understood it. I also acquired some reservations in the process of studying it. The professor's reism, as a form of materialism, for example, seemed too simplistic to me and his extreme nominalism also begged questions, but I learned a lot. From many points of view, this textbook was an eye-opener for me. And I took the professor's warning against the overuse of what he called large "quantifiers"—never, ever, always—to heart. This was in a sense an antidote to what I had been pushing into my head reading Marxist literature since my early youth: Marxism operates with nothing but large quantifiers, general laws, a priori notions, masses, not individuals, all large scale. I passed the exam but got a mere C+. Well, I did what I could, and received my BA.

Mothering Is a Great Job

For the first year of his life, I was with our Henio almost all the time, doing some of my work while he was sleeping or leaving him with Gabriel to attend a seminar or a lecture. He started walking, running even, before he reached his first year, and talking on his first birthday. He stood up on his little feet at seven months, and holding onto something, a chair, a table, he would walk around it. By then he had grown out of his crib and we bought a bed for him but could not find one with a safety net, so Gabriel sat down to pleat one, to keep the boy safely behind it. I still have an image in my mind: Gabriel pleating that white net carefully and patiently, and the child walking on the bed, holding on to the bar to which Gabriel was attaching the net. As I was leaving the room, I looked over my shoulder to wave to the child who was calling me back, "Mamm, mamm, mamm!" and I took in the picture that I would cherish forever. We were a family. A strange and sweet feeling came over me, a feeling of security which was unknown to me. No more loneliness, or being alone. We knew what we were doing, why we were here, and where we were heading. Later on, I would have more than just one moment in my life when none of these would apply, but when recalling that one beautiful, fleeting moment, I would always derive strength and courage from it.

My First Teaching Job

Our son was over two years old now, the most beautiful, lovely, and lively boy, and it seemed time to introduce him to daycare, so that he would be with other children, and I could get some more free time. There was a daycare on the same street, just across from our building, and he liked it. I would leave him there for half a day, and when I got an offer to teach part-time at a technical high school, I took it. As befits Łódź, the textile center of Poland, the students were textile workers on leave of absence, assigned to two years of schooling, after which they would be ready for promotion in their factories. Most were young men, in their early twenties, but some were much older, experienced textile factory workers, and there were also some women, rather young girls. I was to teach an introduction to philosophy, which was not, of course, the most important subject for them, it was just meant to add a "touch of humanistic thinking" to the technical curriculum. There was no program or instruction of what that should be, and I could teach whatever I wanted. I decided to teach some basic, elementary notions, explaining terms used in philosophy, ethical theories, and I made it livelier by adding some stories about the great philosophers' lives. The class met twice a week, the students seemed to like me, and I felt comfortable with them, too. I remember, we often joked and laughed. Among others, I tried to convey to my students some basic notions of Marxism, such as that of surplus value, the notion explaining the mechanism of capitalist exploitation, and here I got a surprise. My students listened to my explanation very attentively and almost immediately started calculating how many hours of their work goes to the state, the present owner of the factories, and what is left for them, and they concluded that they were more exploited now than they had been before the war, working for the capitalists. They got me into hot water! A lively debate followed, and it was, no doubt, educational, I think first and foremost for myself.

CHAPTER FOURTEEN

WARSAW

In the fall of 1949, we moved to Warsaw. A few months before that, Professor Adam Schaff, during his weekly visit to Łódź where he lectured at the university, offered Gabriel and me jobs in the newly created Party School in Warsaw. The new school, offering a two-year course of study, was to be a serious academic enterprise. The Party needed better educated cadres, and people able to teach there were in great demand. Gabriel and I had just graduated in time. Gabriel would join the Department of Economics, and I the Department of Philosophy, led by Professor Schaff himself. I would be one of his assistants, and I was thrilled.

Professor Adam Schaff

Adam Schaff became the foremost Polish Marxist philosopher of that time. He had received a chair at the University of Łódź upon his return from the Soviet Union in 1946. The son of a rich and prominent Lwów lawyer, he joined the Communist Party a few years before the war as a young man and a student in Lwów. After graduation he continued his education for two more years at the Sorbonne in France where he earned a doctorate in philosophy. The winds of war brought him to the Soviet Union where he continued his studies, and obtained the highest Soviet academic title, doctor of philosophy, from Moscow University. A highly educated man, with what used to be called a very good *Kinderstube* (upbringing), born to a totally emancipated, Jewish-by-origin-only family with connections to the cream of the Polish intellectual elite; he was also a polyglot. And all this was certainly showing. A handsome, sophisticated man of the world, Schaff was, of course, a tremendous asset to the Party, vitally interested in converting young Poles to the cause of Socialism and Marxism, and being a stupendous organizer, his head full of imaginative ideas, he was able to find support for those ideas with the top party leaders.

Schaff engaged us to work with the new two-year school, but he was already looking beyond it, organizing a higher educational establishment, something similar to the Krasnaia Profesura (Red Professors) that the Soviets had in the thirties, the Institute of Social Sciences (INS), a three-year course of postgraduate studies awarding doctoral degrees, or as it was then called in the Soviet manner, candidate of science degrees. I would eventually be associated with the two-year school, called in short the Party School, and the INS, from where I would later receive my doctoral degree in the history of philosophy.

The Stalinization Process Had Begun

The years 1948–1949 marked the beginning of a grandiose overhaul of the Polish economy, political life, and cultural and educational institutions. The United Workers' Party was tightening its control over all areas of life in the country. Marxism, which was almost nonexistent at Polish universities, would soon become an obligatory subject for everybody, regardless of their subject of study. The existing chairs in social sciences and philosophy would be replaced by new ones, and the old venerable Professors Kotarbinski, Tatarkiewicz, Ossowski, and Ajdukiewicz were sent into semi-retirement, barred from teaching. New departments and chairs were set up at Warsaw University and in the provinces, headed by new professors, trusted members of the Party, and professed Marxists.

Gabriel's appointment for the new job came through in no time, but mine must have run into some snag, and I decided to go to Warsaw to find out what the problem was.

My First Visit to Warsaw

This would be my second visit to Warsaw after the war. The first time, a year earlier, I had gone there with my sister Rachel when she came from Brussels to visit us in Łódź. I knew that it was a difficult trip for her and she had left her children in her husband's care, undertaking that trip almost into the wilderness, or so it must have seemed to her, to the East, to the Soviet-dominated part of Europe, behind the Iron Curtain. I had not seen her for twelve years, since her last visit home, and so much had happened in the meantime—the war, the Holocaust. I was in my early teens then, and now I was a married woman, even though I did not wear a wedding ring, and I had a sweet little son. We were both overwhelmed by the meeting. We cried reminiscing about the past, our parents, and our two sisters lost in the Holocaust. Rachel came because she wanted to see me, the only survivor of the family remaining in this part of the world, but she also had a self-imposed mission; to put a stone on the grave of our loved ones. Our parents had both died in the ghetto, so there was a possibility that we would find their burial place. Yet, as it turned out, it was impossible to find our mother's grave. "There was too much traffic here at that time," the cemetery keeper explained to us. Instead, he pointed us in the direction of the place where, he swore to us, our father, who had died in March of 1944, was buried. He checked it out in his books. At that time the number of inhabitants of the Łódź ghetto had decreased considerably, people had died already, and thousands upon thousands had been deported, and the cemetery bookkeeping was easier to maintain, so here it was, the grave of our father. And on this place, we put the stone, a memorial to all our beloved, our parents, both sisters, and brother-in-law, who had no graves of their own. We stood there, Gabriel, Rachel and I, and Andrzej Pawlowski, our non-Jewish friend who would remain one for life, each one of us silently taking in the moment. I never went to that place again. I could never bring myself to go, and there was no need to. It was engraved in my heart and memory.

I took Rachel to Warsaw before her return home. We both wanted to see the monument commemorating the Warsaw Ghetto Uprising. It took us some time to reach the place, even though it could be seen from afar, and we stood there in the middle of an enormous, almost endless field of rubble, a wilderness of a new kind, one produced by the forces of the last war. A few years later, a new city had grown around the monument, right there on that thick base of rubble, made of stones and bones of the former inhabitants of Warsaw's Jewish Quarter. "A cemetery, a cemetery, here and in Łódź, just the same," Rachel kept repeating, talking more to herself than to me. I knew she was doubtful about our prospects here, and she wanted us to join her and our brother in Brussels. In the beginning, right after our return from the Soviet Union, she had even sent people to get us safely over the borders, but by now she knew that this was in vain and that we had no intention to leave.

On the way to the train station, we stopped at a café on Marszałkowska Street, the main Warsaw thoroughfare. The once grand avenue was lined with small ground-floor dwellings, remnants of the old buildings destroyed by the bombardments and fires that the city had sustained many times during the war, or hastily constructed temporary wooden shacks, open for business. A smiling young girl brought us coffee and put the change on the table after we had paid the bill. Rachel wanted to tip her, but not knowing our money, she looked at me as if asking "will this be enough?" It was not, and she gave the girl so much more that the girl herself said "Oh, that's too much," and complimented Rachel on her pearl necklace, "Your pearls are very beautiful," the girl said and I noticed those pearls then for the first time, wondering why I had not paid any attention to them before.

Soon They Will Lock You All Up Here

We were sipping our coffee in silence and Rachel was massaging her tired feet, when she then turned to me and said once more, "It's not too late yet, you know, with time they will lock you in here for good." And after a moment, not seeing any reaction from me, she added with a shrug, "But then, what do I know of universities?!" I looked at her, my dear older sister, who was always something of a mother figure for me and Helcia, the two youngest in the family. She had an expression of scorn on her face and at the same time, of hope that my obstinacy might yet result in something good for me. And it was the expression I used to sometimes see on my mother's face, when she wondered what would become of me.

What Caused the Snag?

Now, one year later, I was again in Warsaw. The city welcomed the arrivals with clouds of dust. There was a lot of reconstruction and rebuilding everywhere. The remnants of buildings bombed out or consumed by fires were coming down under sledgehammers and big machines, filling the air thick with dust, and the din, the noise they produced seemed almost unbearable. I quickly reached the Party Central Committee, then located at 2 Chopin Street, and Comrade Magda Treblinska, one of the deputies for the chief of personnel, was ready to receive me. But it was a strange, if not outright hostile, reception. I was too young to teach Party cadres, she told me. Well, that's not so bad yet! What else did she have against me, I wondered, when she suddenly burst out, "My mother did not send me to university!" with a very strong emphasis on the "me." And with a "You must wait, we will let you know," uttered in a decisive, angry way, I was sent off! This was baffling, what did she have against me, did she read my resume at all, and where did she get those silly bits of information about me? Not giving up, I went to see Tadeusz Daniszewski, the director of the Party School and therefore my future boss, who, as I knew, was eager to hire me. Daniszewski, a historian who, I knew, had spent many years in the

Soviet Union, was friendly and reassuring. If he had known anything about the "snag," he would not have told me, anyway, but he was exuding an "everything will be fine," attitude, and with this I returned to Łódź, still wondering all the way home if I would get the promised job. To move to Warsaw and obtain such highly placed jobs in such a short time was a big advancement and a promotion of which I could not have even dreamed about only three years earlier upon our return from the Soviet Union. After all, with not much to offer and virtually no connections in this old and yet new country of ours, Gabriel and I had rather modest expectations. But we were not the only ones advancing and being promoted with such speed. Most of our new friends were also moving to Warsaw, and many recent graduates were offered important jobs.

Gabriel, Henio, and Hanna, 1949/1950.

Moving to Warsaw

I got the job and we moved to Warsaw in the early fall. This time we had many more things to move, one does amass belongings indeed, but our new employer covered the transportation cost. We were also assigned an apartment with two rooms, a kitchen, and a bathroom in a renovated building on the corner of Grojecka and Slupecka, with three windows overlooking the Plac Narutowicza. This was a separate apartment, no sharing with anybody, it was all for us. It was our first real apartment, our home, and it was a joy. We spent almost twenty years in this building, changing apartments once. With the birth of our second child, Helenka, we moved to a larger apartment, one floor up, with three rooms, a kitchen, and an "impressive sanitary center," as one of our friends put it.

"You are lucky, truly blessed," the woman who was running the neighborhood newspaper kiosk in front of the building once said to me. I used to buy an occasional weekly there, returning from a walk with my children. Looking at them admiringly while they were holding on to me, she repeated, "You are lucky." She knew I was Jewish and that I was not supposed to be here at all, but I was, and had such gorgeous, sweet children, and lived in such a nice building. She touched my hand while handing me over the change, as if she wanted some of my "good luck" to rub off on her. Life was very generous to us.

The Party School

The Party School was an academic institution under the auspices of the Central Committee of the United Workers' Party. I met many interesting people there but disliked the place almost from the very beginning. It was too "high" for my taste. From the very beginning, there was something that made me think that I was rather disliked by the school's leadership, and not trusted. There was nothing tangible but I could not shift the feeling that they had some reservations about me, and this made my life difficult there. I have often wondered what that might have been. Yet, little by little, I was pulled into the new life, and my work seemed interesting enough to make me disregard other "inconveniences." There, I met many good people with whom I became friends for life.

Hanna, Helena and Henryk, October 1951.

Sławek Krajewski

My closest coworker was Sławek Krajewski, a very mild-mannered, conciliatory by-nature man, a Moscow University graduate. Sławek was a "hereditary" Communist. His grandfather was Adolf Warski, one of the founders of the SDKPiL (Social Democratic Party of Poland and Lithuania) in 1893, and of the Polish Communist Party in 1918, a member of the Polish Sejm for many years between the wars, and a victim of Stalin's Great Purges, arrested and killed in 1937. Sławek's father, Władysław Stein-Krajewski, married to Warski's daughter, was a member of the leadership of the Polish Communist Party in prewar Poland and a victim of the same purges, and also killed in 1937, as was Sławek's mother. He survived by chance. By the NKVD standards, he was almost eighteen in 1937, so old enough to also be arrested and share their fate. Luckily, he remained untouched. Sławek grew up to become a scientist and a philosopher, teaching and writing about the philosophy of science, a field in which I was a total stranger, but his general interest in Marxist philosophy brought us to work together on a popular brochure titled *What's Marxist Philosophy?* to which I contributed the part about "Historical Materialism." Sławek initiated me, so to speak, into the business of writing for publication.

Right after the war, many places in Warsaw and around the country were named after Adolf Warski, including big factories, shipyards, and mines. Sławek was a celebrity. But I wouldn't say that this had made him vain. He was always the rather unassuming and a bit absentminded scholar who avoided controversy. And he was always ready to make a show of self-criticism when accused ever so slightly of some political transgressions. I remember on more than one such occasion when Sławek would offer his self-criticism even before he was asked for it, always disarming those looking for a fight. But in 1968, when the government and the party leadership had unleashed the antirevisionist and antisemitic campaign, and Sławek was called to answer for some of his remarks, he gave the inquisitors a decisive "no." He was right in his condemnation of violence used against students who demonstrated in March of 1968, he maintained, and would not revoke it, and was thrown out of the Party for that refusal. But he was allowed to keep his job.

At that time, the authorities had had enough of scandals with other children of former party luminaries who had taken up the banner of dissent, and thus Sławek retained his job at Warsaw University but was refused promotion for twenty-five years, remaining the longest-serving "docent," associate professor. Ironically, his promotion to full professorship came only with the fall of the Communist regime.

Assistant to Professor Schaff

For a while, Sławek and I were the only two people in the department, apart from Adam Schaff whom we would see only twice a week when he came to deliver his lecture. He was very busy elsewhere, including at Warsaw University, where he headed a chair of philosophy. As his assistant, I conducted seminars with the students, going over the professor's lectures and reading the recommended texts with them. Besides this, the professor entrusted me with a special task: I was to provide him with examples, and "quotations" to illustrate the theses of his lectures. So, when he would elaborate in his lecture on the main laws of dialectical materialism, let's say, on the "third law" of dialectics which says that quantitative changes at a certain point must result in a qualitative change, I was supposed to provide "illustrations" in support of the theory to liven up the lecture. To keep the students' attention, the examples should be "relevant to their lives" and the political reality of what was going on in the country. I regret that I never told Professor Schaff how Professor Prezent had once "proved" to me the correctness of that same "third law of dialectics," jumping over a high-backed chair. Schaff had a rather fine sense of humor and would have laughed, but I doubted that he would agree to repeat Prezent's "proof" for his students at the Party School. Anyway, finding those examples was a very difficult task, an almost impossible task. I had had problems with the laws of dialectics since my student days and was not sufficiently inventive to come up with enough examples that this law indeed functions and how, but those which I had somehow managed to come up with were incorporated into the lectures. I felt queasy when the professor made those examples part of his text and read them out loud, but Schaff was an impressive lecturer, and especially then and there, he would be able to get away with anything, even my lame "examples."

It was also my duty to edit his carefully scripted lectures, and sometimes I was unable to find some of the facts he was citing, simply because there were no such facts. I once spent a whole day looking up some "laws" mentioned in the lecture, and finally, unable to locate the term anywhere, asked him for its meaning. He gave it a cursory look and said insouciantly, "Have no idea! Let's skip it!" He was an easygoing man, and in those difficult, controversial times, when high-strung devotion, often bordering on fanaticism, could cause trouble for people around, this was a rather redeeming feature.

Schaff did not remain as chairman of our department for very long and he moved on to other things; to chair a Department of Philosophy at Warsaw University and to organize the Institute of Social Sciences. I was his student at Warsaw University and received my MA degree in philosophy there, having completed my thesis, *On the Classical and Marxist Theory of Truth*, in 1951.

Other Members of the Department: Stefa

Of the other people in the department, I should mention Stefa Iwinska. A generation older than I was, she had joined the Party as a young girl in prewar Warsaw. She spent many years in the Soviet Union, and most of those years in concentration camps, arrested for her own "sins" or for the "sins" of her husband, a leading Polish Communist, who was shot in the Great Purges. Though not a "philosopher" by education, she was trusted by the school's leadership as an organizer, able to hold the department in check, and for a short time, she even chaired the department. Gabriel and I eventually became friends with her and that friendship lasted till the end of her life, in 1987, when we had already lived abroad for almost twenty years. There was something very decent in her, and one could trust her knowing she would never act against you based on what you had entrusted to her. And one could talk almost freely with her; in private she would laugh with you about the more surreal incidents so visible on the surface of our everyday life under the system of "building Socialism."

What had mostly attracted Stefa to the ideal of Socialism was the notion of equality. When Svetlana Stalin published her revelations about her father telling, among other horrors, of the many mansions the dictator kept for his exclusive use, Stefa felt especially disgusted with that "sin" against the principle of equality. And when someone sarcastically asked, "but did he not have even more concentration camps?" she would not be taken aback by the remark, not because she took terror and concentration camps lightly, as she had suffered from it horrendously herself, and not because these "sins" of terror and violence did not pain her, but because they were, she seemed to reason, "temporary," not inherently belonging to the notion of Socialism. Terror and violence were rather an aberration of Socialism, while the principle of equality was very basic, and there could not be Socialism without it, and the breach of that principle should be considered especially dangerous! She finally renounced her party membership in 1981, after General Jaruzelski gave the order to shoot at the miners who occupied the Wujek coal mine, she told me, and Jurek, her only child, was arrested for participating in a solidarity event.

It took her a long time to tell me anything about what she had been through or had seen in the Soviet Union, and when I once tried to tell her something about my own experiences, she shook her head and advised me not to tell anybody about it. Ever! "Why?" I asked then, playing stupid, but she refused to continue this talk, and this was already after Khrushchev's revelations denouncing Stalin at the Twentieth Party Congress of the Soviet Union in 1956.

Gina

At one time, in 1950, Gina, who had also graduated in the meantime, joined our department. She wanted to return to the Soviet Union to study there for a doctoral degree, and at that time the government was sending many students there to continue their education. Gina was admitted to the program, but then someone at the Party's office in charge of student exchange got vigilant, and she could not go. Her father's fate, a prisoner who had died in a Soviet prison, got in the way, but she was offered a job with the Department of Philosophy at the Party School instead.

Ola and Dr. Schleyen

A little while later, Dr. Schleyen became chairman of our department, and two other younger members joined as well, including two women, one of whom was Ola Jasinska, First Secretary Bierut's daughter. I remember her well and I knew her from my student days at Warsaw

University. Ola was a nice, friendly, and unassuming person, easy to talk to, and never took advantage of her position of "first daughter." The other woman, who later on married someone who was very quickly advancing to the highest positions in the Party's leadership, made herself known as a pushy, aggressive, and arrogant creature, whom we, the old timers, tried to avoid.

Since I have mentioned Schleyen, I want to recount an episode that characterized the atmosphere we were living in, but for that, I have to move ahead of time a bit. Schleyen was a doctor of chemistry, a well-read and well-educated man, but at the time that he became our chairman, he was hardly able to work anymore, suffering from some heart condition, and he passed away shortly after that in 1956. In his younger years, he had fought with the celebrated Dabrowski International Brigade in Spain, and though officially this was still considered a great honor, in 1949–1956 those people came under suspicion of having been influenced during their stay in Spain by Trotskyite ideology, and many of them were arrested and persecuted in other ways. All this was no help to Schleyen's ailing heart. He was one of the gentlest and most tolerant bosses I had ever known, he was a good-natured man, and if his heart had not been that sick, it could have been rightly said that he had a truly "good heart." His wife, who was in Spain with him, became a professional translator of Spanish literature, eventually introducing many of its important titles into the Polish language. Not having had any children of their own, they adopted a girl, a child orphaned by their comrades fallen in Spain, and brought her up as their own from earliest childhood till she was eighteen. By then it was 1968. The Party had embarked on a new course trying to resolve its latest political crisis by turning to antisemitism. Now, the Schleyen girl had discovered that the Schleyens were not her "real parents," and that they were of Jewish descent, to boot, and she would not have any of this. She renounced them as parents and left Mrs. Schleyen, by then a widow, alone and heartbroken in her old age. Everybody who knew them and heard about this tragic story, a telling indication of the poisonous atmosphere we had come to live in, was also heartbroken. I still remember that girl. I knew her as a small child, a chubby girl, with yellowish straight hair, blue eyes, a delicate blush on her cheeks, a happy child, so Slavic, so typically Polish, and when she was older, a healthy, robust-looking girl. She was always the Schleyens' pride and joy. At first, I could not believe the story was true, it seemed so cruel. It caused me pain, and I could not forget it.

Students at the Party School

My relationship with the students at the school was generally good. As mentioned earlier, they were mostly grown men, with only a few women. The school provided most of them with a great opportunity for advancement in life, and they were eager to learn. I tried to teach as best I could, but my efforts were often thwarted because of the students' lack of preparation. Sometimes they were almost illiterate, accepted to the school as a kind of reward for having joined the anti-Nazi resistance during the occupation, for involvement in the armed struggle against the anti-communist underground right after the war, and later, they largely came from the lower chains of the party apparatus. Some were grateful for whatever we, the teachers, did for them. I remember one of my first students, a man in his forties. He would show me his hands, saying, "You see, comrade, these hands, they are used to tilling the soil, not to holding a pen or a book." He would rather keep working with a plow, but the Party had told him to do otherwise, and he did. He became a regional secretary, and later always greeted me warmly whenever we would occasionally meet. This was not so with many others. Some preferred not to recognize their humble instructor when they saw me at some conference or other such occasion. Their careers had taken off after graduating and many became important first party secretaries of provinces, and these were positions of great power, from where they would look to the capital for further promotions. They certainly preferred not to recognize the girl who used to correct their illiterate papers.

Once, I ran into trouble trying to explain to my students some intricacies of the philosophical notion of truth, and the criteria of truth in general, classical, and Marxist philosophy. I had just recently defended my MA thesis on the subject and could not help but show off my recently acquired knowledge a bit. It was too much, and one of my students brought me back to my senses. He wanted to know why I make the whole thing so "unnecessarily complicated." Don't we possess a perfect "criterion of truth"? The best one, he instructed me, is the attitude toward the Soviet Union, and that's it. I did not know what to do, whether to cry or laugh. It would be laughable if there was not an implicit accusation of my lack of appreciation of the Soviet Union in what he said, even if he did not perhaps mean it. This could be, of course, fraught with unpleasant consequences, to say the least. It took patience, a lot of it, to explain to that student how he was not right and why, and luckily not all the class was as dumb, and I had somehow weaseled out of it.

Spineless Intelligentsia

The students were, in general, politically more trusted by the school's leadership than the teachers. The students were party workers, sometimes with leadership experience, and they certainly would be future leaders, while the teachers, especially the "girls," just received some education, that's all! The old conflict between the workers and the intelligentsia or the old anti-intellectual prejudices were still very much alive here. To be sure, we were repeatedly told by the school's leadership that we had to have something to give our students, but we also had to learn from them. We had to learn party devotion, party discipline, and first of all, the principles of *partiinost*,[102] whatever that was. These were supposed to strengthen our "party backbone" and make "true party people" out of us, the mere spineless intelligentsia! To achieve this lofty goal, we were assigned to the most trusted or experienced students to assist them during their visits to party organizations around the city's big factories and to learn what it was all about. The whole thing was nothing new; it was borrowed from the brotherly Soviet Party, which in early Soviet times widely used the slogan of "bolshevizing" a field

102 A term for a person with a non-compromising, partisan mindset that would pursue the goals of Communist Party ideology.

of science or an institution upon which the Party did not yet have a firm grip. Later, while studying the history of debates in the Soviet Union in the early thirties on "What Is Marxist Philosophy?" I found that this demand of raising the level of *partiinost* was widely used at the Krasnaya Profesura Institute (Red Professors Institute) in Moscow, of which our postgraduate Institute of Social Sciences in Warsaw was a replica. There, they called that principle "bolshevization." I was amused reading about the loud protest against that "bolshevization" by one of the professors, V. Sten. He was "already a Bolshevik and cannot see any sense in the whole new enterprise," he wrote. It was a courageous protest, and the fate of the protester was tragic. He was eventually shot, as were many other students and professors at that Institute, whether "bolshevized" or not. Now, I became the object of "bolshevization!"

Edward Gierek

I was assigned to Edward Gierek. He was a student in the group I was teaching, and though generally a rather good student, he had trouble with getting through the four laws of dialectics. I could not blame him for that too much, since I had a lot of trouble with those, too. Gierek was a large man with an interesting background, a Silesian miner who emigrated in prewar time from Poland to France and Belgium and had spent many years there working in the coal mines and doing party work. Deported from France for political activities after the war, he went full-time into party work upon returning to Poland. The Party saw great potential in him and sent him to school to get some education. And the Party was right; Gierek had a great future before him. After graduation, his career took off. He became the first secretary of the province of Silesia, "Katanga," as that province was jokingly dubbed,[103] and in

103 The province was likely nicknamed "Polish Katanga"—after the Congolese province—due to the fact that it was a rich mining area and that the purported mentality of the local Silesian population was that they differed from the rest of

1970, after Gomułka's downfall, he became the first secretary of the Party and Poland's ruler for almost a whole decade.

I remember accompanying Gierek on a visit to the electronic equipment factory in Warsaw, named then for Rosa Luxemburg if I am not mistaken. Gierek walked through the factory halls, stopping occasionally to exchange some words with the workers, and to listen to their complaints which were mostly about the low wages, high production norms, and the obligation to pay party dues; the factory boasted having the highest party enrollment among the Warsaw factories. Complaining, the workers sometimes got excited and talked angrily, calling the obligation to pay party dues an additional, unwarranted tax. Gierek kept calm, nodded seriously, and smiled occasionally. Finally, we went to see the factory's party secretary. A young man, he sat at his desk, and we both sat on the other side of it. At a certain moment, the secretary's shirt that was unbuttoned at his neck (it was a hot summer day) opened a little wider showing a medallion on a chain that he wore around his neck. Gierek reached out and pulled the medallion out from under the shirt, and the rudeness of this gesture made me freeze inside. "What's that?" he reproached the secretary. "First secretary of a Party organization wearing religious artifacts?" The poor secretary blushed. "Souvenir from my dead mother," he said only, and Gierek, the polite, well-mannered man that I knew, had obviously found himself again, and he simply said, "I am sorry." Well, I thought, somehow relieved, not all of my students would have apologized! The whole incident remained in my memory for years. Did it strengthen my "party backbone"? Did it "bolshevize" me? All it did, was show me firsthand a bit of real life inside a large Warsaw factory, which certainly gave me some food for thought.

the Polish population and were not understood by them. Fittingly, Gierek was also sometimes labeled "Tshombe," after Moïse Tshombe, the secessionist leader of the sort-lived State of Katanga.

The Doctors' Plot

Stalin died in March 1953. Shortly after that, the Doctors' Plot was called off, and Beria was denounced and shot.[104] I clearly remember the moment when I learned that the Doctors' Plot had been called off. It was Good Friday and I had to attend a meeting early in the day to discuss the grading rules to be used in the forthcoming exams, and since our housekeeper had already gone home for the holiday, Gabriel stayed with the children. The meeting was tedious, as such meetings usually were, but in the middle of it, Roma, then the school's director, left the room. She said she had to leave for a moment, but she did not come back for quite a while. When she finally showed up, she had the look on her face that said: great, historic news! A few moments later I ran home, ran on foot from Piekna Street to Grojecka, quite a distance, to let Gabriel know the incredible news: it was all a lie, the doctors were not killers. We had not believed it for a moment, anyway, and we were right not to believe. And it was not the first lie. There had been many lies before: there were the Great Purges, and all those widows I had known, their husbands, often party officials shot in the subsequent purges, lies, lies, and all the pieces of the puzzle were falling into the right places! Perhaps this would be the last one?

Is Nothing Going to Change?

Events followed each other now with tremendous speed. Beria was denounced, the camps, the arrests, and the massacres were his fault. He, himself an old British spy, was to be blamed for all that horror.

104 The rise of antisemitism in postwar Soviet Union culminated with the so-called Doctors' Plot, in which a large group of prominent doctors, most of them Jewish, were accused of engaging in a conspiracy against the state. Formal accusations and arrests in 1952 led to widespread distrust of Jewish doctors and grassroots attacks against Jews throughout the country. Following Stalin's death, the doctors were released and rehabilitated. Lavrenty Beria (1899–1953), head of the NKVD, lost the subsequent struggle for power and was executed in December 1953.

Eyebrows were raised, a British spy, like in 1919, again?[105] Is nothing going to change? And it seemed that not much would change. I had attended the party meetings at the Central Committee a few times, and one of these meetings, attended by all who worked there, from the cleaning women to the bosses of departments, stands out in my mind. One of the instructors was accused of having hidden some episode of his activity during the occupation and was strongly criticized for it. He should have come clean when he was accepted into the Party and not hide anything of his past, even if what he did hide was not in itself something horrible. The poor man, under the barrage of questions and reproaches, was mumbling, giving some unintelligible answers. Suddenly, I felt nauseated. I saw myself standing there in that huge room full of strangers, being questioned and rebuffed and reproached for whatever it might be, and simply feeling scared.

Am I a "Rotten" Liberal?

It had been almost five years since I started working at the school, but I still could not get rid of the feeling of uneasiness, and finally, the day came when I could not take it anymore. I do not know or remember what the last straw was, what had directly triggered my decision or impulse to say "enough is enough" and resign from my job. My resignation caused something of a scandal, as one does not resign from a place like that. From here you can be fired, but to leave of your own free will? Unheard of! Almost tantamount to resigning your party membership, this was just not done, not in the spring of 1954. Much more time would have to pass until giving up your party membership would not be punished by the loss of a job, not to mention some other grave consequences, like having to give up your apartment, for example, or not being able to obtain any other job, at any other place. But in 1954, just a year after Stalin's death, all this could still happen to you for having committed

105 A reference to the 1918 "Ambassadors' Plot" to assassinate Lenin and overthrow the Bolshevik government—and to its alleged main culprit, the "Ace of Spies," Sidney Reilly.

such a "mortal" sin. I was labeled a "rotten liberal" for it, which made me angry. I knew very well that the "L-word" was anathema to Communists like it is nowadays to some extreme conservatives, but I still could not refrain from protesting, especially against the "rotten" part of the label. Liberal, well that was not so bad, is not liberty the root of the word? But why "rotten"? I was young and did not feel rotten at all, I replied somehow tongue in cheek.

Quitting the Party School

Still, times were changing, and this had perhaps emboldened me to write my short letter of resignation in the first place and to leave it with the school director's secretary. My letter was very short, and it said only, "Please relieve me from my job at the school." It sounded more like a cry of "let me go, I cannot take it anymore," more than anything else, and I was fired immediately. Writing my letter of resignation, I did not intend to protest against anything, to demonstrate or take up a "cause." With a full load of teaching, and work on my thesis and the two small children at home—my little daughter, Helenka, was not much over two years old, a sweet, healthy girl with big, starry green-gray eyes—I needed some respite as I was, perhaps, tired and overworked. Now, I was free but confused and unhappy. I wanted to leave this place, but I wanted to have a job. What now? It was March, our children were at that time in the mountains with our housekeeper, Maria, as we had sent them there for the clean air for a whole month, and the first thing I did was pack a few things, buy a train ticket, and join the children. I needed to embrace them, to hold them more than anything in the world. Gabriel saw me off at the train station, advising me to stay there a few more days, to wait out the stir I had caused, to let it blow over. I had sent in my resignation without consulting with him. He was not at the school at that moment at all, and I did it in his absence, intuitively fearing, perhaps, that he would try to calm me down and talk me out of doing anything rash, but after it happened, he did not reproach me for what I had done, and he was very sweet and tremendously supportive about the whole incident.

Crime and Punishment

Times were changing; there was no doubt about it. Roma was not stupid and was not mean either. She summoned Gabriel to her office and reproached him in front of her deputies and visiting inspectors from the Central Committee. For what? For not having been able to prevent his wife from "misbehaving"? For not condemning me for what I had done? He just laughed in response. "Do you expect me to divorce her?" He posed that question, and this seemed to him such a hilarious thought that he had to laugh. And yet, it was in the Party's tradition, or code of behavior in the not-so-faraway past, that women would divorce their husbands when they got into trouble with the Party, not to say arrested or sentenced, as it was often the case in the thirties, during the Great Soviet Purges. This was a "normal" thing to do for the woman left alone with children, if she was not also taken away to the gulag as a "member of the family of an enemy of the people." In such a lucky case, the woman would often divorce her husband, mostly just for the children's sake, to cut them off from their "no good, an enemy of the people, father," and to change their blemished name so they would be able to go on with their lives. Yet, this was 1954, after Stalin's death and after Beria, and it was Poland, where such practices even during the peak Stalinist period were not common, though not unheard of either.

Having overcome the first few moments of anger, Roma changed her mind. She was not oblivious to the winds of change. I was ordered to attend a meeting of my party organization at the school where I was supposed to be condemned by the whole "collective" but at the last moment she decided not to come to that meeting, and without the prosecutor, the meeting was canceled. There was no mood to condemn me among my colleagues, either. "You won by default," someone told me with satisfaction. I won, but not quite. Professor Adam Schaff was very sympathetic and told me not to worry. At that time, I was a student at the Institute of Social Sciences, working there on my doctoral thesis. This, he told me, would remain unchanged, I would be transferred to full-time status, and receive the stipend to which full-time students of the Institute were entitled. But the higher-ups said no, I had to pay for my “crime.” I could continue working on my thesis with the Institute but without pay; there would be no stipend for me. I missed the wages I had earned at the school. It was not easy to get by on Gabriel’s earnings alone, especially since covering Maria’s wages was just impossible and we had to have her if I were to work at all. Gabriel took on some additional work and we both took whatever material we could get to translate from Russian, and this somehow saw us through till the fall, the start of the new academic year, when I was assigned a new job at Warsaw University. The transfer was meant as some kind of punishment. The salary was lower, and the “prestige,” well, of a mere (!) university department was not comparable with the Party School, but I was very happy. Later, when the social prestige of the university and especially of the Department of Philosophy had earned the respect it well deserved and the party institutions with the Party as a whole had gone down, some of my friends would say jokingly that I was clever going for that change as early as I did.

The Department of Philosophy at Warsaw University

I joined the crew of Professor Nina Assorodobraj, a sociologist who was then head of the joint Departments of History of Social Thought and History of Philosophy, with a salary reduced by one-third. But after the 1956 upheavals, university teachers got a raise that brought their salaries to an equal level with those at other academic institutions, among them also the Party School. With reforms introduced at the university, the mammoth group headed by Professor Assorodobraj was divided in two, and History of Philosophy became a separate department, led by Tadeusz Kronski till his untimely death in 1958, and after that, by Leszek Kolakowski. I remained with the department till the political turmoil of 1968 turned our life upside down and forced us to leave Poland for good.

I'll Be Teaching the History of Philosophy

My transfer to the university opened a new era in my professional life. First of all, the atmosphere at the university was visibly different from that of the Party School. I felt much freer, the vigilant eyes that I felt upon me at the Party School all the time were gone, and this was a tremendous relief. For some time, I taught a course on historical materialism. This was an improvement, too, as I could forget about dialectical materialism. The base and superstructure, their interaction, causes and effects of change in society, and the individual in society—these were interesting subjects. Though the answers and solutions stemming from what was called historical materialism were becoming more and more unsatisfactory, I wanted to work on them. I would not, however, make any of it the theme of my doctoral thesis. I knew by then that I wanted to stay in the field of the history of philosophy and social thought. I liked to analyze social ideas, describe, classify, compare, and understand them. One of my early papers, prepared for a seminar at the Institute of Social Sciences, had as its subject a nineteenth-century Polish Socialist, Stanisław Worcel. I compared his views with the Russian Narodniks[106] and the results were considered interesting. I presented Worcel as a Polish counterpart, a forerunner of the early Russian Socialists, and used my knowledge of the Narodnik ideology and its criticism by Lenin for it. Why not continue working on the subject and include the whole group of these early Polish Socialists, the group of which Worcel was one of the founders and leaders? I was encouraged in my intentions by Bronek Baczko, who was also busy working on his thesis concerning social movements in nineteenth-century Poland while simultaneously organizing the Department of History of Social Thought at the Institute. He would eventually chair that department and become my official adviser. For the time being, Anna Sladkowska, soon to be Julian Hochfeld's wife, was also there finishing her thesis on Edward Dembowski, a mid-nineteenth-century radical and philosopher of the Young Hegelian mold. Soon, there were others, a "class of titans," as

106 Narodniks were the members of a nineteenth-century Russian revolutionary movement that tried to motivate the Russian peasants to rise against the tsar.

Tadeusz Kronski dubbed the group. Seven young and talented men: Radgowski, Sikora, Beylin, Szacki, Hinz, and Mrowczynski, I am not sure if Zimand was there too. There were seven altogether, but I do not remember who the seventh was. This was truly a good class, all future professors, authors of interesting works, journalists, and also future dissidents. There was perhaps some inevitable logic in it because the deeper they dug, the more disenchanted and disappointed they became with what they were digging into.

At first, there was some mild opposition from Professor Schaff. He was not only the Institute's director at that time but also, unofficially, of course, the leader of the so-called "philosophical front," the nickname reflecting the militaristic penchant of the ruling party. Yet the title that the Institute students had accorded him was not a militaristic but a "civilian" one. "Prince Adam" became Professor Schaff's nickname. He had plans, which the Central Committee urged him to carry out, to get his students to describe contemporary Poland, to talk about the "dialectical contradictions" of the new social order, and how to overcome them to "help the leaders." At first, then, he was not so happy about my idea. He had a "made-to-order" subject for my thesis, "New social laws of the transitional period." No more, no less. Luckily, I was not that ambitious and quick enough to see that this was pure nonsense, a trap that I should avoid by all means. The leaders didn't need my help. Wasn't it said that to "discover social laws," one has to be a leader because only from the "height of the leader's perspective" can one see them, anyway? I had the good sense to say no, I was not knowledgeable enough to undertake something like that, and so, I got my project, The Polish People Communes, accepted as the subject of my research and eventually, my doctoral thesis. I knew I could do it. It was an interesting piece of history of socialist ideas in nineteenth-century Poland, and the higher-ups finally gave their approval. The history of social thought in Poland and the history of philosophy in Poland, as it was developing and becoming interconnected with the mainstream of European philosophy, was recognized as an important and worthy research subject, if not for any other reason than that the Party needed to show that it was rooted in the past, in the Polish intellectual tradition and revolutionary movements. The nineteenth-century radical

Socialists, the Communes of the Polish People, were soon recognized as favorite forerunners.

Joining that group at the Institute of Social Science, if only part time, and my main job at Warsaw University, did me a lot of good. I defended my thesis successfully at the beginning of 1956, but I only published it in 1962. Even though my thesis was recommended for publication by the Institute, I did not rush because I had my doubts about its methodological assumptions. At first, I was unable to specify what exactly I did not like about it and it took me some time to understand what the problem was. I analyzed that group of former soldier-rebels, forced into exile after the lost insurgency against Russia in 1831, as if I had intended to run for the post of their ideological leader, prescribing what they should have done and thought in their time with the wisdom of 100 years of hindsight. It made me laugh. To put it in a nutshell, my dissertation was written, as almost everything that was written at that time, from the point of view of what was considered "politically correct" at that given moment. It was a horrible thing to do to the researched period of history, and I was not yet the most extreme adherent of that "methodological" directive! It took me some time to edit my manuscript and it was finally published by the Book and Knowledge Publishing House under the title *The "Polish People," A Survey of an Ideology*, to mixed reviews, some saying that it lacked this or that, but Adam Ciolkosz, the leader of the Polish Socialists in exile, himself a professional historian and author of a two-volume *History of Socialism in Poland*, found my book to be the "first honest account of an important fragment of history of Polish socialist thought coming from Communist Poland." I liked that "honest" adjective very much; that's what I wanted my work to be. Dr. Ciolkosz was very helpful to me later on, when I, myself an immigrant, was looking for a job in the USA. We exchanged many letters then on various problems, general and private. I was deeply touched when he tried to console me in one of his earlier letters saying that he knew very well what it meant to lose one's country, but we should not give up hope, we shall return. He died in 1978, but his wife Zofia Ciolkosz, who lived to be 100, did see the new Poland. As for me, I went back to Warsaw to visit a few times but would never want to settle there permanently again.

Poland after Stalin's Death

There were many signs that times were changing and they were coming from within the Party. By the end of 1954, a meeting of central [Communist] Party activists in Warsaw took an openly critical stand toward the party leadership. Also, by the end of 1954, Gomułka was freed from prison and though it was only officially announced in the spring of 1956, we knew about it before. It meant that a major shift in policy would come sooner or later, and people started talking about things that were previously taboo. That Socialism was abused, that people were jailed for nothing, that some had died in prison. Independent clubs were forming and multiplying around the country, and people were talking and talking. The *Poem for Adults* by Adam Ważyk, published in the summer of 1955 and inspired, as rumor had it, by some from the highest party leadership, came as a shock. The shock caused was not so much by what Ważyk had said, but that it had been allowed to appear in public.

> They lived by the aurora,
> and gave darkness,
> they lived by the idea,
> and parted with the people,
> they lived by their dreams,
> and lies became their daily bread.

People were reciting it excitedly, in agreement with its message, while some were writing "counterpoems." A reform movement was being born, and the Party School's director, Roma Granas, became one of those at its head. "The thaw" was coming, welcomed by most and opposed by some.

After the Twentieth Congress

In February 1956 came the Twentieth Congress of the Soviet Communist Party in Moscow and Khrushchev's so-called "secret speech" denouncing Stalin. It was read in Polish translation at all party meetings around Warsaw, causing a considerable stir everywhere. To distribute the "speech" or not to distribute must have been subject of some haggling within the party leadership, and as a result, a huge pack of at least a few thousand copies of the "speech," landed temporarily in our apartment, hidden to prevent it from being confiscated by the side that was against its distribution. Early one morning, Roma's driver brought it up to our place for safekeeping and picked it up again two days later.

Shortly after the Congress, Bierut, who had attended it, died in Moscow and his body was brought back to Warsaw. I stood on the sidewalk on Marszałkowska Street, watching the funeral procession passing by. It was a cold, grim day, but there were plenty of onlookers, somber men and women on the sidewalks. Were the people really moved by grief? Or by suspicion and resentment against the Soviets, held responsible for Bierut's—yet another Pole's—death? The accusation seemed to be in the air. Drizzling snow sprayed the casket, the mourners, and the bare bald head of Prime Minister Cyrankiewicz leading the procession. Jadzia Possart, a university friend of mine, standing beside me, unwittingly provided a moment of comic relief, repeatedly whispering to me her concern for the poor prime minister. "He'll catch a cold, he'll catch a cold!" Jadzia had come to the Party from the former Polish Socialist Party and had obviously retained some special feelings for her former [Socialist] Party boss.

Antisemitism Roars

Who would become the first secretary now? Soon, it became evident that there were two factions in the United Party: the Natolin from the place near Warsaw where members of that group congregated, and the Puławska group from the name of the street where most of the leaders of that group resided. The Natolin group was made up of conservatives, defending the status quo; the Puławska group of progressives, pushing for reforms. Ochab became first secretary after a lot of infighting within the Party and despite the outside pressure from the Soviets. Khrushchev came to the Party's plenary meeting pushing for his candidate and the result was a compromise, but the movement for reform, for greater independence from the Soviet Union, got the upper hand, anyway. Also, the antisemitism of the conservative faction came out into the open. The candidate of the "Democrats" was Zambrowski, a Jew, and the only bright man left in the Politburo, as insiders maintained. The conservatives, with Khrushchev's blessing, wanted Zenon Novak. At that plenary session, Roma got into a public exchange of opinions with Khrushchev, which caused something of a scandal. Various stories were told about it, but she herself told us what it was all about later on. Khrushchev had warned the Polish comrades in his speech that there might be a rift in the Party if Zambrowski were elected to the post of the first secretary. Roma interjected that "there was no such threat in our party" which Khrushchev misunderstood or intentionally misinterpreted as being accused of threatening them, the Polish comrades. And he lashed out at her! For Roma, the incident marked a point of no return in her political career. No matter how the situation would hence develop, her political career started to go downhill.

The Polish October, 1956

Now, the path to what was to become known as the Polish October had been opened. The next Party Plenary Session would decide on the change of leadership, and Gomułka would become the first secretary; inside talks had been going on for some time already. What would the Soviets do about it? Would there be a Soviet invasion? There was a lot of talk about Soviet tanks moving from the border or from the Soviet military base in Lower Silesia. The situation was rife with tension and expectations, even though nobody knew what to expect. Those were, to say the least, highly emotionally charged times.

I remember the day the Party Plenum opened. I was home when Gabriel dropped by unexpectedly. He did not telephone because the message could not have been entrusted to the telephone, as everybody knew the police were eavesdropping. The military guards at the government and the party buildings, he told me, had been replaced by the special units of the KBW, the Security Corps. This sounded as if a coup d'état was on the way!

I stayed home with the children till late in the afternoon, but then could not resist it any longer, and ran to the building of the Polytechnic where the Plenary Session was holding its debates. Everybody seemed to be there. A human chain was formed around the building to guard the place against a possible "provocation." Someone explained to me that if the "evil forces," the hard-liners of the Natolin group, were to instigate some trouble, a riot might follow and with the Russian tanks positioned just outside Warsaw, you know what could happen!

Well, I linked hands with Lena Eilstein and some students of our department. I saw some other friends and colleagues nearby, and some people just milling around, seemingly idle. It was rather quiet there, and aside from the voice of Jan Kott, the well-known dissident and Shakespeare expert, booming from the loudspeaker, reciting some impromptu political satire about the Natolins, nothing much happened. The Plenum was in session and there was no way, of course, to know anything about what was going on inside. Let's hope all will be all right, I told myself, and after all, there was a change of guards early in the morning. Did it not mean that the positive results of the debates were assured?

Only afterward, it was revealed that a Soviet delegation led by Khrushchev had arrived uninvited the very morning before the session had opened, trying to influence the decisions of the Plenum with threats. They did not want Gomułka, a former prisoner, to be elevated to the post of leader. They feared his nationalistic stand and Poland's desire for "too much" independence.

Gomułka did become the first secretary. A wave of enthusiasm swept through the country. At a mass rally held in Warsaw at Parade Square by the Palace of Culture, half a million people reportedly sang *Sto lat* (May he live a hundred years) for Gomułka, and that *Sto lat* perhaps echoed all over the world. Patriotic feelings were running high, and it was said that women were offering their wedding bands for the cause of Poland's independence. Poland was rebelling, telling the Russians to mind their own business, well not exactly in these words and not quite so much, but, nevertheless. And people sang, not insomuch *for* Gomułka as *against* Soviet dominance over Poland.

The period from the workers' strike in Poznan, and its bloody pacification by the army that reverberated through the country, till the Plenum, was a time for mass meetings. Great rallies were also held at the university and at the Polytechnic. Of the many meetings, I still remember the one at Warsaw Polytechnic. The cavernous hall was overflowing with people and speakers were hardly able to speak, interrupted by the unruly public. I admired young Krzysztof Pomian, who with the mic in hand tried, and with some success, to get a hold of the excited public. My colleagues—who were or rather weren't there—Baczko, Kolakowski, and many others, were trying to put together a resolution in support of reform. The demands from the public to include this or that, coming from the hall's floor were much more far reaching. I remember the shrill voice of a woman demanding "Return the crown to the eagle!" It sounded to me widely extravagant, even funny then, but the Polish eagle eventually did indeed get its crown back, though only some thirty-five years later.

Back to Work, Citizens

For now, however, the time of spontaneous rallies and demonstrations was over. At the grand Warsaw rally, Gomułka appealed to the people to go home and return to work. With the change in the Party's leadership, the Polish October was coming to an end. It did however bring considerable changes. Censorship was relaxed. For a short period, it seemed that it had stopped existing altogether: this was when the censors themselves went on strike in favor of abolishing the institution of censorship! The universities won a significant degree of autonomy. Also, the obligatory teaching of Marxism–Leninism was replaced by a course of the history of philosophy. Soon, I would start teaching a course on the history of philosophy in Poland and Russia in conjunction with Western philosophical theories of the nineteenth-century, a subject previously not taught at all to philosophy students. For students of other departments, I would teach a general course on the history of philosophy. Seminars were also introduced with a list of required reading that contained selections of the great philosophers through the ages, from Plato to Marx and beyond, well into the twentieth century. It was an impressive list, indeed. My teaching load was a heavy one, and I myself had a lot to learn.

Time for Apologies

During one of the many meetings at the university that were taking place before and also a while after the Plenum, I was once approached by a friend of mine who I had been friends with since student times. She told me that she must apologize for the wrong she had done to me. Employed ten years ago by the student organization, of which I was also a member, she had to write an opinion/reference for me to my employer-to-be, the Party School. She wrote, as her conscience and devotion to the cause had required her to do, stating that I had a "critical attitude toward the Soviet Union." Shocked by the whole thing as I was, all the more so because I liked that girl, a thought raced through my mind. So, this was it, this was what Comrade Treblinska had against me and why I had been pressed so hard, harder than others at the Party School, to raise my *partyinost'* level? My friend continued, visibly flustered, that Witek Woroszylski had convinced her that this was wrong, and we should all rectify the wrongs done. Well, good for Witek Woroszylski, the talented poet and writer, who had turned from one of the most extreme, rigid, young, fundamentalist Communists in his early youth into a preacher of penitence, but from where could my friend have gotten her information about my "critical attitude"? I could not recall having ever had any serious talk with her about my war years in the Soviet Union; perhaps some passing remark about my not-so-easy life during the war, even so far from the war in the Ural Mountains, gave her the idea? And this was enough for her to base her opinion on? An opinion which could and did affect my life? And did she not know that this was not an accusation to be taken lightly at that time? Well, what could I say to her now? Her "recommendation," no doubt, made my life at the school more difficult, giving me also, perhaps for the same reason, a stronger incentive to leave that place. Of course, the accusation could have brought against me much graver results; yet, I had gotten the job then anyway. The older comrades then in the leadership positions, most of whom had spent many years in the Soviet Union, and many of those in concentration camps, were themselves "critical," but of course in private, not in public, and they had disregarded my overzealous friend's opinion. In the end, things turned out for the better for me. Yet I could not help but wonder what makes a person do such things.

An Era of "Mistakes and Forgiveness"

Now, apologies were on the agenda. The Party was officially reassessing the almost two decades of its rule, describing it as an era of "mistakes and transgressions" (*era błędów i wybaczeń*) resulting from the "cult of an individual," Stalin, and, asking for "forgiveness," promised reforms meant not only to rectify the past "mistakes" but to prevent a similar situation from ever occurring again. And while some reforms were indeed introduced, and some among them were significant enough to make life in the country more livable, it soon became obvious that the critics of the past would not be allowed to go any further than the framework set up by the Party. Explaining the political and economic blunders and disasters of the Stalinist era, the many death sentences, and so on, as "mistakes and transgressions," could not be obediently accepted by the thinking public. A kind of tug-of-war ensued: the Party would not spare any effort to keep the dissidents, the emboldened intelligentsia and students, in check while the thinking people were not willing to let up their push for freedom of expression and research into the deeper systemic causes of what was called the "socialist society," and therefore a push for deeper social reforms. The confusing but also lively and intellectually stimulating time following the Polish October gave birth to a linguistic pun. Paraphrasing the Party's catchphrase, the "era of mistakes and transgressions" was countered by the "era of mistakes and forgiveness."

A New Wave of Jewish Emigration

With the greater freedom of expression, came also the reintroduction of religion into schools. With the wave of patriotism, various idiosyncrasies came to the fore, and among them, the hitherto officially banned antisemitism. This was grassroots antisemitism, not the one that would come later, officially sponsored and preached by the Party and the government. A new wave of Jewish emigration began, and now, the government again was allowing Jews, as it was during the first few years after the war, to leave Poland, either for their "historic homeland," Israel, or any other country that would accept them. As a result, in Tel Aviv, a colony of new immigrants soon came into being, nicknamed in jest "Gomułkowo," settled by those for whom Gomułka had made it possible to leave Poland. Many of our friends became residents there.

Jews, survivors of the Holocaust, returnees from concentration camps or from refuge in the Soviet Union, who had settled in Poland in the formerly German little towns of Silesia, as if trying to recreate the old prewar shtetl life there, were leaving in great numbers. Many of our friends from Łódź and Warsaw were leaving too: academics, doctors, engineers, state employees, and even former party *apparatchiks* (activists). Most were going to Israel; this was perhaps the only readily available destination. People were scared not only by the wave of grassroots antisemitism now thriving around us, but by the possibilities of what this may eventually lead to. The Kielce pogrom was fresh in people's minds and the specter of Soviet antisemitism of the Stalin era, right after the war, was a telling reminder of what could happen; the Doctor's Plot, the rumors of planned deportations from central Russia to the faraway places, job and education discrimination that were rampant there in the early 1950s, and were still in force, albeit perhaps not as extreme any longer.

We were seeing our friends off, and were ourselves thinking of emigration, and talking about it with our friends, but had decided to stay put. Gabriel and I had both become academic teachers and researchers. Ten years of hard, intensive work had brought us to a point from where we could see a clear way of doing what we liked to do most and what we could do best, and to leave now, when we had only just started, was just unthinkable and scary, too. And our main tool of work was the Polish language, the only one we felt comfortable in, the one we had learned to express ourselves in.

Far from following in the steps of many of our friends who had decided to immigrate to Israel, Gabriel took advantage of the new relative freedom to travel abroad, and the good exchange rate of the Polish zloty to the dollar—the government had set the value of the zloty arbitrarily very high—meant that a return ticket to Israel could be bought rather cheaply, and he went to see his half-brother, Jakub. Gabriel wanted to take Henio, now a nine-year-old beautiful, healthy, resolute boy on the trip with him. Let him see the world, we thought, but the events in the Middle East, the recent Suez War scared me off, and the child stayed home with me. Gabriel spent three weeks in Israel, and on the way back stopped in Brussels to pay a visit to my siblings. He returned right before New Year's Eve, in time to celebrate the incoming 1957. He brought oranges from Israel; one was still on a branch with its deep green lacquered-like leaves. It emitted an unusual, sweet smell. Someday, I would go there to visit that old, new land, I thought. The trip did not change Gabriel's resolve, or mine, to stay put.

Freedom to Travel Abroad

The relaxation of the rules about traveling abroad and, in general, about maintaining contact with relatives living abroad, especially in the "capitalist West" was one of the more tangible achievements of the Polish October. In the early fifties, it was increasingly difficult to maintain such contact. Not that it was officially forbidden, it was just regarded with suspicion by the authorities in case "something" could be held against you. I was advised by some of my friends, in the most amicable way and with the best of intentions, to stop writing letters to my relatives in Belgium and in Israel. Dangerous liaisons! I knew that my closest friends were following that advice. I simply could not, and not because I was so brave or a risk-taker. It was as a result of emotions, not reason. I missed my siblings, they were all that was left after the war from my extended family, and I cherished the contact with them.

Already in the wake of October, around 1955, among the many other rumors about changes for the better to be expected in the country soon, was one that interested me personally: a certain relaxation of the rules for traveling abroad. The borders seemed to be opening. Until then, they were almost hermetically closed, and it was almost unheard of to go outside the country for private reasons. This whetted my desire to visit my siblings in Belgium. At that time, there was an additional reason why I simply had to go to see my sister Rachel. As if there was not enough tragedy in our family, tragedy had struck again; my sister Rachel's son, little Joe, whom I had seen in Łódź when he was three years old, fell victim to polio, the Heine–Medina disease, as it was then known in Europe. In the mid-fifties, the dreadful epidemic had been in full swing in Europe, as well as in the United States. Joe, by then a young man of twenty and a third-year medical student, contracted the disease while on vacation in Spain and this was still some time before Dr. Salk came up with the vaccine against the disease. Joe was brought back to Brussels in a contraption called an iron heart and lung that breathed and kept his heart beating for him. My sister was devastated. The pain seemed to be killing her, too. The tragedy also left me heartbroken, and I simply had to go and see her.

Despite all the rumors, at first this still seemed like an impossible dream. Who would give me a passport, who would allow me to travel to the "capitalist West"? But times had changed, indeed, and what would have been impossible even two years ago did not seem so outlandish anymore. To my surprise, it turned out that travel restrictions had indeed relaxed somewhat recently and that it was feasible to visit your close family living abroad. Poland had a large population with 6 million or so of its former citizens living abroad, mostly in Western Europe and the United States, and to ease the restrictions of traveling abroad was one of the first visible and less costly changes that the government made on its way out of the dark Stalinist times.

My First Trip to the West

And so began my first trip to the West. To go, one needed an invitation from the relatives you intended to visit and a return ticket paid for in foreign currency. But by only using Polish means of transportation, as in my case, the Polish airline, LOT, on a direct flight from Warsaw to Brussels, one could obtain a ticket in zlotys. We were so isolated, cut off from the outside world in those years, as if we lived on an island surrounded by deep waters, and what was worse, we had somehow gotten used to considering such a state of affairs as almost normal. It was no wonder that I didn't believe that my plan would come true. Still, a passport office had indeed recently opened and it was issuing passports. The price for a passport to Western Europe was 5,000 zlotys; 7,000 zlotys would allow one to go over the ocean. A considerable sum when the cost of the ticket is added, and not many could afford it. Nevertheless, there were many willing to pay. A close friend of mine, Tunia, happened to work at that office. She took my application, saving me the trouble of standing in long lines, and I got a new navy-blue passport for foreign travel with the Polish eagle—without the crown!—on the cover in no time.

I scrambled together the money for the passport and ticket, and some small presents, and a LOT plane took me to Brussels. This was my first ever flight. The plane was very small and could take only eighteen passengers, but it got me to Brussels in less than three hours and it certainly seemed wonderful, not only going abroad, but going to the West; the bustling, cosmopolitan, elegant Brussels airport, as I saw it then, and my sister and brother waving to me upon my arrival. But altogether, it was, of course, a sad visit. And I was not of much help to my poor sister; Joe was hospitalized and Rachel was spending all her days at his side. A mother fighting for her only son's life, she seemed oblivious to anything else. She had gotten him through the Holocaust, in hiding, would she lose him now?

I spent a lot of time walking around the city, alone. I went to the department stores, which boasted a quantity of consumer goods that made my head spin. The abundance of goods was beyond my imagination! And the shining windows of the elegant stores, flaunting their exquisite, luxurious wares, also got a lot of my attention. More than once, I caught myself examining them almost in total rapture, never thinking that I would be interested in such "mundane" things at all. This must be very expensive and who would buy all this, I wondered. The neat, well-kept houses and clean streets, all attesting to the good standard of living of their inhabitants, impressed me, and the recent Warsaw debates about Socialism versus Capitalism reverberated in my head.

I also admired the many beautiful and historic places of that fine city, although at that time it was somewhat sleepy, and especially the splendor of the Grand-Place. The gilded Town House Tower made me wonder about the fate of its architect. Frustrated by the result of his work, the city guide informed me that he had killed himself, because the magnificent building's center came out a little bit skewed, not completely centered, and so his creation turned out to be his undoing! A special delight was the visit to the Royal Gallery where, for the first time in my life, I was able to admire one of the greatest collections of paintings: Memling, Brueghel, Vermeer, and so on. My eleven-year-old niece, Ginette, was my amazingly knowledgeable guide there. And once I even went to see an American movie, which were not being shown in Poland at that time. My visit to Brussels was coming to an end. My sister and brother packed my luggage, stuffing lots of things into it like nylon stockings, blouses, children's clothes, beautifully wrapped cheeses, and Belgian chocolate, saying that we don't have any of those in that "miserable, wretched" country, where I had so obstinately decided to make my life.

Coca-Cola, Symbol of American Imperialism

Of course, "everybody" wanted to know what "abroad" looked like. My students asked me excitedly what life was like there. How is the standard of living for people there? What are the wages? Higher than here? Twice that much? But, to my surprise, what interested them most was Coca-Cola. What was it? How did it taste? Did I like it? I disappointed them, saying that I did not like it, and they looked at me with disbelief. No wonder that Coca-Cola, no matter how much it was a symbol of "American Imperialism," would soon take over, and the appearance of Coca-Cola signs first in Warsaw and then in Moscow or Peking was an omen, presaging the new times to come.

My Second Trip: EXPO 1958

I would go to Belgium twice more before leaving Poland for good. Three years later, in 1958, I went to see the World Exposition in Brussels. Since I was able to secure a passport and visa without asking my siblings for an invitation, I traveled by train, paying for the tickets with Polish zlotys. To pass through divided Germany was an experience in itself, to say the least. This was still before the Berlin Wall had gone up, yet the border between the East and West was nevertheless very closely watched. Guards with trained dogs came into the train compartments a few times when the train passed from East Berlin into West Berlin, when it entered East German territory again, and also upon entering West Germany, again.

I was glad that I didn't have to ask my siblings for an invitation in order to obtain a Belgian visa this time. I had noticed the previous time that my relatives were a little apprehensive about having a visitor from a "Communist country" not unlike my friends in Poland who felt the same about maintaining correspondence and other contacts with their relations living in the "capitalist countries." I wondered about my relatives' reasons; "ours" I understood, but "theirs" were a bit of a puzzle to me. I was evidently less in touch with "their" reality than with "ours." I simply did not take into consideration the anti-Communist hysteria, and how widespread it was in the West.

I spent some time with my siblings again. My brother, after ten years of living in Belgium, was still a recent immigrant and his workdays were hard and very long, as an immigrant's days were expected to be. Neither could my sister keep me company much, nor could I be of much solace to her. She was still preoccupied with Joe's health. He had improved in the meantime but was still in need of constant attention. After the initial stage of the disease, when he was unable to breathe without the help of that formidable machine, he remained paralyzed from the waist down. He tried to work out, went through all possible recovery programs, but was making little progress. One time, he bravely tried to continue his medical studies that had been interrupted by the disease. Unfortunately, he was not successful. He read a lot though, and I remember one time talking with him about Alfred Young, about whom he was reading with great interest. Mostly however, I remember sitting with him sometimes listening to music, especially to Rimsky Korsakov's *Impressions from the Exposition*, a record I had brought him and which he loved.

A Few Impressions from the Exposition

I went to see the Expo a few times. The Atomnium, its official symbol, the grand modernistic sculpture reminding everybody that we had entered the epoch of the "Atom," was luring in visitors. I wandered around the international pavilions, wanting to explore almost each one of them. The countries of the world seemed to have gotten together here, each one of them trying to show off their best. In the American pavilion, which was almost empty compared to the others, an enormous chunk of redwood, a few meters in diameter, centrally placed in a large hall, grabbed the visitors' attention. It still seemed to emit the smell of some fantastic prehistoric forest. As if in juxtaposition to this presentation of the riches of nature, a seemingly endless pageant of young women modeling the latest in fashion from known American fashion houses was going on almost constantly in a neighboring hall. But the locals, as I was told by many, were mostly impressed by something else in the American pavilion: the sanitary facilities installed there, the large, super-hygienic, shining, nickel-plated place. Were they joking? Were they in this way expressing their anti-American sentiments at that time running rather high in Western Europe, especially in France and French-speaking countries? To me, Belgium had pretty good sanitary arrangements then, anyway compared with Poland they seemed to be top of the line, and I could not quite understand the natives' exaggerated enthusiasm, but it made me recall an anecdote that our Warsaw friend liked to tell,

"Question: When is a country ripe to start building Socialism?" And the answer, "When the bourgeoisie has already installed the plumbing, otherwise the country may never get it."

Of what the Soviet pavilion was showing, I remember mostly a vast gallery of social-realistic paintings. Most showed the scars of the war, many the happy life of the kolkhozes, and some were decidedly ugly. Why did they not show a model of the first Sputnik? It had caused a sensation when the Soviet Union put it into orbit, followed soon by the second one, carrying the first living creature, the dog Laika, into space. I did not understand. Just incompetence of the propagandists? Or old habits of secrecy that would not allow the public to even see a model?

Both pavilions, the Soviet and the American, had a constantly running movie show, and I saw them both. Both movies presented the vastness and natural beauty of their respective countries, and they both focused on the theme, *Shiroka strana moia rodnaia* (How wide is my homeland). Very similar in subject, they were also very similar in their patriotic tone, both a result of a similar, shallow, propagandistic effort. But there was also a difference; the American movie was definitely more technically advanced and it was shown on a much wider screen that took up almost three walls of the movie hall. Watching it, one had the impression of being in the middle of those forests, rivers, and mountains.

A Side Trip to Paris

On my second visit to Brussels, I was able to take a side trip to Paris, only two hours away by train. I had some old acquaintances there who were happy to see me and were able to accommodate me for a few days. Passing the border between Belgium and France, I wondered about the absence of any border check as nobody bothered checking my passport. "Europe" was becoming a fact of life, and the borders between the countries of what would become the European Union were if not yet abolished, very much relaxed. When I talked about it later, on my return to Poland where to go for a short excursion over the border, even to brotherly Czechoslovakia, not to mention the Soviet Union, still required visas, permissions, or at least stamps, small and large ones, one of my witty friends remarked, "You see, that's because we represent the 'new type of relations between states.'"

During those few days in Paris, I spent most of the time exploring the city in awe of its beauty. But where my poor, recent-immigrant friends lived, somewhere in a veritable slum behind the Place de la Republic, to which I would return in the evenings after roaming the beautiful quarters of the city and the Louvre all day made for such a contrast that willy-nilly I recalled Bruno Jasieński's book, *I Burn Paris!*[107] I had read it in my youth, but now I was better able to understand the desire which prompted him to write that nightmarish fantasy.

After another two or three days with my family in Brussels, my two-week vacation was over and it was time to return home, to my still very young children left in Gabriel's care. To make up for my recalcitrant behavior—leaving them for no greater reason than to have an interesting vacation—I had bought presents for them.

I would travel from Warsaw to Brussels one more time, eight years later, and I would see my siblings there again. But I would never see Joseph again; he passed away at the age of twenty-five, after having spent the last five years of his young life imprisoned in his own body, paralyzed. Gradually, he had lost his strength and his will to fight back and succumbed to some complications stemming from the dreadful disease.

107 Jasieński's book tells the story of a factory worker who, after ending up in the street, poisons the Parisian water supply system, leading to a complete breakdown of society. The French authorities reacted by deporting him. He eventually settled in the Soviet Union, where his career flourished until he got caught up in the Great Purge. In September of 1938, he was arrested, sentenced to death for alleged counterrevolutionary terrorist activities, and executed.

On Sabbatical at the Sorbonne

In the spring of 1966, I went on a four-month sabbatical leave to France. I was awarded a stipend funded by the Sorbonne or the French Government—I am not sure who paid for it but I received it through the Polish Ministry of Higher Education. The purpose of the trip had been to get acquainted with the Sorbonne and to work on whatever my current project might have been, using the university's facilities. It was a generous offer and an honor and I was glad that I got it, though the thought of leaving the children and Gabriel for such a long time was difficult.

I had just published my book on Bakunin, which brought me a promotion and a higher academic degree, and this trip was also meant as a working trip, to gather material for my next project, even though this had still not been defined. I spent a lot of my time at the Bibliotheque National but also tried to take advantage of the many cultural opportunities Paris presented, knowing quite well that such an occasion would not come my way again any time soon. At the beginning of my time in Paris, I lived at the so-called Polish House for visitors from Poland on official business, run by the Polish authorities. I shared a room with a young woman who was constantly complaining about everything: the French (they are dirty), the Italians (they are thieves), the peasants in Poland (they are rude, uncouth, and why, and for what, were they let in to live in the capital, Warsaw, she would never understand!). I was waiting for when she would come up with a litany about the vices of the Jews and decided to move out as soon as possible. I took up the offer of a friend of a friend, a woman, once from Poland, who had a rather large apartment, and moved into one of her rooms, glad to leave that xenophobic person behind.

There were many colleagues and acquaintances from Warsaw University in Paris at this time. Now, contacts with the West were encouraged and promoted, and young scholars were getting all kinds of grants to study abroad to work on their research projects, and so on. The Polish Embassy in Paris would invite French scholars as well as Polish ones to speak, and the whole colony of temporary Parisians participated in such gatherings. I vividly remember at least one of those, a very lively occasion. With a law professor from Warsaw University as the speaker and so many familiar faces around, it felt almost like being home.

I lived as if I were a student again, carefree, visiting museums, and as my French improved, I attended poetry recitals at the Sorbonne, and once or twice even a theater performance, like Mrozek's *Karol*, which in translation went under the title *Bernard* not "Charles," perhaps not to offend Charles de Gaulle. It was a very hot play then in Paris, of which I did not understand much since my French was still too limited, and this limitation was, perhaps, the reason why I was not as shocked by the play as many natives were, to the point of disrupting the show. They seemed to have felt more offended by the abundance and repetition of four-letter words in the play, than by its political aspects, and these had escaped my attention because of my linguistic limitations. Anyway, the play caused a "scandal," and was soon closed.

Tracing the Route of D'Artagnan

One of my most pleasant memories of my Paris sabbatical came from visiting the Loire Valley. I joined a student group on an excursion to the Chateaux Region of the Loire Valley. It was an international group of students, French, German, American, Greek, and so on, and we talked a lot in broken French and German and laughed a lot. Among us, there was a German who had been shot at and wounded while jumping the Berlin Wall to freedom, but luckily not dangerously wounded, a Greek art student who had escaped Greece when the Communist offensive was broken, and a young Muslim, I do not remember where from, who envied me for being "not affiliated" with any religion, as I had described myself, and did not have to limit myself in what I ate or drank, unlike him who "had to refuse" wine, or the Jewish political science student from the United States, who refused to eat at all at the very pleasant country inn where we had stopped for our supper. I remember the innkeeper patiently conferring with him about the food restrictions of the students' religion, about which the innkeeper respectfully acknowledged as "knowing very well," and they finally settled on a boiled egg for the young man's supper.

This was a memorable three-day trip and I cherish the memory of it to this day. And how I regretted that I could not have made the trip together with Gabriel and our children! I wished we could have shared all that beauty; the quaint little towns, the grandeur of the palaces, the nature, the history, and the culture so perfectly mixed into one. It was still not possible then to obtain permission for husband and wife to go abroad together, one had to stay as "collateral" of sorts, a guarantee that the person allowed the luxury of going abroad would return. The almighty state was very reluctant to give up any control over its citizens, but when only two years later the state decided that we were not needed for the most perplexing reasons of her own, they pushed, and pushed hard for all of us to go, and go fast.

At the International Institute of Social History in Amsterdam

I also used the occasion of my stay in Paris to visit the International Institute of Social History in Amsterdam, and see Professor Arthur Lehning, the editor of a full academic edition of Bakunin's works. The Institute impressed me enormously; what richness of material! I could have spent the rest of my life there, going through the amassed documents and old books. Professor Lehning knew my work; he had quoted my two-volume anthology of Bakunin's writings (with my introduction and annotations published in Warsaw in 1965) in the third volume of his work and offered me an autographed copy of his own introduction to that volume.

Goodbye to the Sorbonne

I returned to Paris to say goodbye to the good people of the Sixieme Section of the Ecole Pratique des Hautes Etudes of the Sorbonne, who had hosted me. Thank you very much! I had a good and hopefully fruitful stay in Paris. But in spite of the many things I did during those four months, the people I had met, the things I had learned, the books I had read, this had been a very lonely time. I missed my family more than ever and promised myself to avoid such lonely trips again. Little did I suspect or guess that there was a new trip, a long, and unwelcome one, in store for me, for all of us, that was awaiting us just around the corner, a new twist of fate, which would turn our lives upside down, setting us on the course of a new emigration. Only two years later, my family and I would become stateless, homeless emigrants. By then, I might say, I knew the West and should not have been so frightened by that prospect, but even so, to leave one's native country, while being well over forty and almost at the peak of one's professional career, to plunge into a totally new environment, to go for good, was scary, all the more so because nobody could have known if this would be for the better and not for the worse.

Life after the Polish October

After the Polish October, all the introduced improvements notwithstanding, life started going back to normal, which meant that the freedoms people had begun to take for granted were being steadily but surely curtailed, and the press that had enjoyed freedom of expression for a while, found it steadily eroding. A year after the October events, the student weekly *Po Prostu* was closed by the authorities. I recall the demonstration protesting that closing, which took place on Narutowicz Square, in front of the huge student dormitory. The windows of our apartment looked out on to the square, and I saw the skirmishes of the students with the police. The demonstrators, attacked by the police were at first dispersed, and many evidently found refuge in the dormitory. Then the students returned to the square, and so did the police, charging again, for the second time and working their way through the crowd with truncheons. All this lasted a few hours, and it was an ugly sight. I was looking from the window joined by our friend, Lena Eilsten. She lived in our neighborhood and stopped at our place on her way home to look at what was going on in the square. Why such ferocity, we wondered. Why close the student weekly? What's behind it? What do the authorities want to prove or gain? A "friend" of ours enlightened me, "You know, with all that's going on in Hungary, a strike by the railroad workers throughout Poland is in the making. The government has to stop it somehow, to prevent the danger of having to fight a workers' strike, and the students, those instigators, those hooligans, are a very good target, they will get what they deserve and will get more still, and this lesson will most certainly result in averting the strike." This "friend of ours" was a clever man, a hard-liner and a no-nonsense devoted party member. His career had recently taken off nicely, and he was well informed. And the Party had perhaps made the right calculation. But why should I have to choose who is a "better target"? This is not my concern, I thought, but if so, why remain in a party which makes these decisions also in my name? Can I, can we just resign? No, we could not, unless we were prepared to emigrate, which was perhaps still possible. But we were not ready to do this yet.

Advancing our Professional Careers

I got my PhD in 1956; Gabriel was not ready with his until 1960. It was clear that he needed the degree. He published some well-received economic essays, advised doctoral students for the Institute of Social Sciences, but had no degree himself. The surname of one of the students he advised there, Figa, a not very promising candidate for a scholar, prompted a pun: Figa will have a degree, and Gabriel will have a "*figa*" (*figa* in Polish means a fig, or in popular parlance, nothing). He had deemed his first attempt at a thesis on industry-agriculture relations in the transitional period (from Capitalism to Socialism) good-for-nothing, and it took him some time to find out what he would actually like to work on. And that was to describe how the socialist economy functions. He thought that he had acquired sufficient knowledge and a certain distance necessary to deal with the subject. Włodek Brus, whom Gabriel had asked to be his dissertation mentor and advisor, agreed. And since the socialist economic idea originated from Marx, he would start with a chapter analyzing his economic views. Being as thorough in his scholarly work as in all other matters, there were not to be shortcuts or secondhand sources for him. He delved deeply into Marx and after three years of steady and intensive work came up with not just a chapter but with two, almost ready-to-print, large manuscripts on Marx. Eventually both manuscripts turned into books, published in 1962 and 1965, respectively. On the strength of the first one, *Marx's Vision of the Communist Economy*, he received his doctoral degree from Warsaw University; on the basis of the second one, *Marx's Idea of Labor Money*, he got the second degree some ten months later. The bureaucracy kept itself busy, changing the laws concerning the organization of the universities. And to obtain a professorial university position, a doctorate was not enough anymore, a second degree was required.

The Myth of "Hundred Flowers Blooming": Gabriel Went to China

In 1958, Gabriel went to China for six weeks. The Chinese Premier Chou En Lai came to Poland on a state visit and invited a group of journalists to visit China. Gabriel, though not a professional journalist, represented the weekly, *Polityka,* in that group. The new weekly was trying to play a middle-of-the-road, independent role in the newly developed post-Polish October political situation. Supportive of the reform movement but wary of the extremists, whoever they might be, the weekly treaded a thin line and wanted to send to China someone who would bring back a report based on general knowledge, the veracity of which one could trust. Gabriel got the offer and was glad to go.

After Khrushchev, the myth of a united international Communist movement had lost credence. There was now the Soviet orientation, the Chinese orientation, the Cuban orientation, the Euro–Communists, the Trotskyites, and whatnot. Many of our friends put their trust in Chinese Communism. They applauded Mao's ideas, and among others the idea of turning intellectuals into part-time producers of steel, which was supposed to solve China's problem of industrialization, and eliminate the difference between physical and intellectual labor at the same time.

I remember a discussion with a philosopher friend of ours on this subject. We were in Grodno, a beautiful place on the Baltic seashore, on vacation. The resort, it was said, was built for Göring and on his direct orders, and now we were vacationing there—just thinking about it could make one feel absurdly hilarious.[108] And there, on a beautiful sunny August day, we got into a serious discussion with our friend about the virtues of that glorious Mao's idea. With hindsight, this looks ludicrous, surreal, yet it is true, and says something about the times we were living in, and about our lives. The idea of involving intellectuals in steel production or any other kind of physical labor, which by necessity would be forced labor, appealed to our friend. It's healthy to put to use your abilities, physical as well as intellectual interchangeably, she insisted. Where is such naiveté from? Doesn't it stem from the fact that people do not identify themselves with those forcibly put to the task, but rather with those empowered to put others to it? Yet, many were then genuinely fascinated by the revolutionary ardor, the supposed romanticism of the "Long March," the masses of people involved in "changing the world," and with the newly announced policy of "Hundred Flowers." Disappointed with the Soviet model of Socialism that the Polish one tried at first to mimic almost blindly, many believed that the Chinese presented something new, a new pattern of social progress, a new way of doing away with social ills and social injustice.

Gabriel went to China but he was no utopian—he had already passed this stage of life a long time ago. Hundred flowers? Freedom for diverse or even disparate views within "our" one-party system? Would it work? For how long? Just another myth? What he saw did

108 Hermann Göring (1893–1946) was an early convert to Nazism and one of Adolf Hitler's most trusted advisers. He was also one of the most important perpetrators in the framework of the Holocaust. Göring created the Gestapo and gave the RSHA chief the order to organize the Final Solution. During the Holocaust, he enriched himself with stolen Jewish property. Göring was one of the few leading Nazi criminals who were arrested after the war. Sentenced to death in the Nuremberg Trials, he committed suicide on the eve of his execution.

not turn him into a fan of the "Chinese orientation." He wrote a series of articles about what he saw and learned on that trip for *Polityka*, four altogether, but the fourth article, ready and accepted for publication, he himself withdrew. The Soviet–China conflict was coming into focus, anti-China propaganda was whipped up and he "would not add water to the Soviet mill," he told me. But the Chinese Embassy did not invite him to its receptions anymore.

More Trips

A year later, I too went on a trip abroad: to the Soviet Union. I had a new research project: the Russian and international nineteenth-century anarchist, Mikhail Bakunin. It would eventually become a book, and I needed access to the literature that was not available in Warsaw. We did not usually have sabbaticals here, but from time to time it was possible to get a few months off and a stipend to travel, even abroad, in connection with a research project. Naturally, I was very excited by the prospect of going back to the Soviet Union fourteen years after I had left there. I wanted to see the old places, first of all, Leningrad, and to meet my old friends, especially my classmates, Faina and Rita, with whom I had maintained some contact through the years.

Why Do You Want to Go to Persia?

"Why do you want to go to Persia?" wondered Tadeusz Kronski, then head of the Department of History of Philosophy, when I told him about my intention to travel to the Soviet Union. He seemed to be truly puzzled by my idea. He had been to the Soviet Union once, a few years earlier, with a group of students and professors of the Institute of Social Sciences, and had had enough! His group was hosted by the fraternal institution, the Moscow Highest Party School, and the official aim of the visit was to learn from the more experienced Soviet colleagues how to teach Marxist philosophy in Poland. Kronski was a highly educated expert in philosophy, and here he was, just to fulfill some incomprehensible ritual of the "new times," sent to receive instruction in what the hosts presented as Marxist philosophy from people whose ignorance and lack of education was transparent to the point of being scary. Aware that the security police installed listening devices in hotels and any other often unexpected places (this was common practice in Warsaw, too), he checked for them wherever he stayed, at his hotel and in the classrooms he attended, because there, in Moscow, they obviously must have many more of these devices; there they must have been ubiquitous. And he almost expected "them," his hosts, to read his unflattering thoughts. This was an Orwellian world! He returned from the three-month-long sojourn appalled and scared, and since then he has but one name for the Soviet Union: Persia.

Tadeusz Kronski

Born in Warsaw, and educated in Prague, Kronski was half-Jewish and having spent his war years in Warsaw, he had to live in hiding. The tragic death of the city after the 1944 Uprising brought him to France. But there was nothing for him to do there or to live on with his wife and child, to put it in simple prosaic terms, and since his sympathies were on the "Left" anyway, he took up Professor Schaff's offer to become a professor at the newly created Institute of Social Sciences in Warsaw and returned to Poland in 1949. Later, Kronski became head of the Department of History of Philosophy at Warsaw University.

When I first met him at the Institute and was told that his nickname was "Tiger," I found this rather funny. He did not look even a bit "tigerish" to me, yet his friend, the renowned Polish poet and Nobel Laureate, Czesław Miłosz, who left a rich-in-detail portrait of Tadeusz Kronski, called him so, and the nickname stuck to him. In 1958, Miłosz, having just received the news of Kronski's death, wrote, "Tiger. What name would better reflect that agility and buoyancy and deceptive humor? I recall him not only as a very dear friend of mine but also as one of the most decisive influences in my life. I will never end my dialogue with him...my soul was in Tiger's claws, with my full consent, of course, and with my conviction that this was for my soul's good."

Naturally, I read all of what Miłosz wrote about Kronski with great interest and was struck by the inherent incongruity in the philosopher's portrait, as it was painted by the great poet. High praise was lavished on the philosopher, on the one hand, and on the other, he held the poet's soul with his "claws." In what way had the philosopher influenced the poet? And what was the meaning of those "claws"?[109]

The Poet and the Philosopher

The most "important decisions" of his life, Miłosz said, that resulted from the influence Kronski had exerted upon him, was the decision to accept the "new Communist order" in Poland that came into existence right after the war. "At the heart of my five years as a writer and a diplomat for the people's democracy...was my philosophical star, Tiger," stated Milosz. The poet came to regret that decision and rectified it by defecting to the West while on his diplomatic post in the USA, in 1949, approximately at the same time when Kronski was returning to Poland from France. From the distance of time that had gone by, the great changes of the last decades, and the fall of the Communist system, the problem of having remained in Poland or escaping to the West seemed not so important anymore, but then it was "hot" indeed. Yet, it had to be remembered, and Miłosz stated this himself, that they both, the poet and philosopher, had developed their leftist sympathies independently in their youth and they had met as "two rivers hollowing out their beds on a plain," as the poet put it. What then is the meaning of the "claws" that the philosopher was holding the poet's "soul" by?

Kronski, a few years older than the poet, influenced him philosophically: the young philosopher had a special gift, Milosz would emphasize with utmost reverence, a rare understanding of history. He

109 Czesław Miłosz (1911–2004) devoted the final two chapters of his autobiography, *Native Realm*, to "Tiger" and to both of their struggles with ideology in the postwar years. Today, he is regarded as one of the most influential Polish poets. For his work, he was awarded the Nobel Prize for Literature in 1980. Yad Vashem awarded him and his brother Andrzej the title of Righteous Among the Nations in 1989, for providing shelter and food to several Jews who had fled the Warsaw ghetto.

possessed not only an exceptional understanding of the forces working behind the scenes of the historical process that was unfolding before our eyes but also a worthy-of-a-genius "feel" for history. By the end of the war, Kronski's view of the coming events and the fate of European culture had been pessimistic. He understood, Miłosz said, that as a result of the "inevitable historical changes," the history of the twentieth century would be a tragic one, filled with great suffering, having to bow to that "inevitable force," despite all the knowledge of its roughness. Convinced that his friend, the philosopher "knew best," he, the poet, also succumbed to it, working for "five years as a diplomat and writer" for the new Polish regime. Yet he came to regret this and escaped, while Kronski, by his returning from the West to Poland, had accepted cooperation with the forces he deemed to be "vile." There was a price to pay for these decisions. Kronski was ready and willing to pay. The poet had chosen the defiant road, and had to pay a price: he had to abandon his native land.

Reality Has Claws and an Iron Jaw

Historical inevitability, the Hegelian notion that became also Marxian, these were the "claws" that Kronski, the expert Hegelian and Marxist philosopher, was holding the poet's soul with. Historical inevitability, explained Miłosz, was the monster that paralyzed his contemporaries with fear and pushed them to accept the "new order" to "cooperate with the devil."

These "claws" rang a bell! I had heard about "them" once before, studying Russian intellectual history of the nineteenth century. A strikingly similar story played itself out between Vissarion Belinsky, the then well-known and highly respected intellectual and revolutionary, influential literary critic, and the young Hegelian philosopher and later anarchist, Mihhail Bakunin. Had Miłosz fashioned the story of his relationship with Kronski after that story? Belinsky did not read German and was a novice in philosophy when the better-educated young Bakunin was proselytizing on Hegel's theory of history as an "emanation of the 'Rational Spirit'" and imbued

Belinsky with his interpretation of the historical process. The literary critic wrote then a laudatory article about the Russian tsardom as the emanation of that very "Rational Spirit of History." The hated Russian tsardom was proclaimed as the "reality" which is "just" because it is "real" and therefore deserves affirmation. To oppose "reality" is wrong and futile, Belinsky the revolutionary declared. Those who oppose it would inevitably be crushed by its "claws" and its "iron jaws." The critic's turnabout caused an understandable stir among his revolutionary friends, and he subsequently disavowed his laudatory article, blaming the philosopher's influence for what he had written. His revolutionary friends forgave him; they also blamed Bakunin, even accusing him of playing a kind of deliberate, malicious prank on the critic.

Miłosz and Kronski, Belinsky and Bakunin, the mid-nineteenth century and the mid-twenties, the same story repeated a hundred years later! The philosopher (Bakunin) did indeed know Hegel well, and he later understood that the German "teacher" can also be interpreted differently, that "not all that is 'real' is necessarily just, or true," and that "what is just or true" might eventually become "real," as an expression of the further development of that very same "Rational Spirit." He even used this later interpretation of the German philosopher's teaching as a point of departure for his radical revolutionary program of social change, as did many young Hegelians in the forties of the nineteenth century.

And what about the monster of "Historical Inevitability" as an explanation of people's motivation in choosing political sides, of choosing a way of life? Historical determinism is a neat enough theory, but it's hard to believe that what might have momentarily motivated someone "crazed" on Hegel, motivated all those many intellectuals, scientists, and writers, who enthusiastically embraced the Communist ideals in Western Europe after the war, or all those who filled the government offices, high army posts, diplomatic posts, universities, and cultural institutions, only or even mostly because they believed that the verdict of history was already pronounced and that efforts to resist that verdict of historical providence would be futile, that refusal to recognize "historical necessity" was madness. Besides being forced by the prosaic realities of life, not high philosophical concepts, some, at least, must have also believed that the new system was right and good, that it provided at least some real answers to real social ills that were begging to be resolved.

Benefit of the Doubt for a Friend

I think it is regrettable that as a good friend, the poet did not give the philosopher at least the benefit of the doubt, and that Miłosz perhaps believed so too when he decided to return to Warsaw, but stating expressly that knowing the roughness of the "new order" and yet accepting it, and returning from Paris to work within it, he presented Kronski as someone deliberately cooperating with what he knew perfectly well to be "evil" in exchange for what? Material gain? A secure life? Fame? And having so resolved, he paid with intellectual moral turpitude. True, Miłosz in his portrait of his philosopher-friend also stressed that Kronski was an intellectual, who sought not only to "explain the surrounding reality" but also to "find a way to live, and to live honestly" in the dramatically fast-changing world. Nevertheless, he did his "best friend," the philosopher, a disservice, because the opinion of the influential poet induced others to accuse Kronski of intellectual depravity.

On the Question of "Evil in History"

I got to know Kronski rather well and, naturally, read what Miłosz had written about him with great interest, even with emotion, especially because I always felt indebted to Kronski intellectually, as a thinker and an older colleague, if not as a teacher. I knew Tadeusz Kronski for many years. He was not a dissident, not a fighter against the regime, or fiercely critical of Marxism—he even tried to defend Marxism, albeit his effort was a rather pitiful one, but he also knew, or quickly came to know, the absurdities, the surrealism of the system as well as the simplifications of the theory, and made no secret of it. He wrote about the problem of evil in Hegel's understanding of history and found there is no place for the vindication of moral evil in history. Hegel discerned the "true reality" from the "false, untrue one" that does not correspond any longer with the development of the "Rational Spirit," and became therefore anachronistic and evil, and Kronski concluded in his analysis of Hegel that no good can stem from sowing evil. He came to discern and abhor the evil inherent in the system we all lived under, and he influenced people around him with his attitude. "*Pas trop de zèle*!"[110] he would often repeat. Ruthlessness, as a character trait, was his bête noire; ruthlessness, he would grimace with repulsion, how can one be so ruthless? And what do you think of that column in today's *Trybuna Ludu*[111] that publicly chastised some poor soul of a journalist for some trifle, ideological transgression with words "reeking of hell," he kept asking us, the younger members of the department. He wanted to know how sensitive we were to that tasteless kind of writing, wanted to sensitize us to that breach of taste against which he had aesthetic objections, if not any others. He seemed to have been measuring up people's sensitivity because he believed that only by cultivating the "right" character traits would we be "able to carry over the precious values of our European heritage across the dark era," even if it were destined to last a very long time. He did share the belief of the great ancient philosopher that "character is destiny." I remember his reaction to the defection of a student at the Institute of Social Sciences, a young man privy to the political inner circle of the Polish Communist Party that caused quite a stir at the Institute. Kronski was disgusted, but not by the fact of the defection itself, never mind the motherland, he kept repeating. The motherland will withstand it, but what about his children? To leave innocent, defenseless children to such a fate seemed unforgivable and unthinkably ruthless to him.

110 The epigram "*Surtout pas trop de zèle*" (Above all, not too much zeal) is attributed to Charles-Maurice de Talleyrand (1754–1838).

111 *Trybuna Ludu* (People's Tribune) was the official newspaper of the PZPR and thus one of the largest and most influential media outlets in Communist Poland.

Not Too Much Zeal!

One episode of the relationship between the poet and the philosopher that Miłosz himself recounted, characterizes Kronski's attitude well, "Tiger forbade me to publish a certain poem, the poem I wrote after a stopover in Detroit. After being taken up to the twentieth floor by the hotel porter, I sat in my plush, overheated, room, and looked down at the neons below me, the garages, the traffic—metal fish circulating in an aquarium—and was so powerfully struck by the universal blunting of human desires here that an image crossed my mind of a man being sucked out from inside as one sucks an egg through a straw. And from that image, a poem came about a man torn from himself, about alienation. No political motives prompted me. Tiger, however, believed that the specialists of anti-Americanism (in Warsaw) would be only too pleased by the work and would pervert my intentions by reading into it a zeal to bend to party directives."

Here again, Kronski was telling his friend, the poet, "Hold your anti-American zeal! Do not make the censors happy!" And Kronski was then still in Paris, mulling over returning to Warsaw! Not too much zeal! This directive of his is so much in the vein of how my favorite philosopher, Isaiah Berlin, influenced people around him. When and where tendencies to exaggeration, to extremism boarding on fanaticism, are en vogue, "Not too much zeal!" is a sobering call.

A Fool's License

Once I asked Tadeusz why he had returned from France. It was when the Polish October was being curtailed steadily and consequently, and when the hope for a change for the better, for "Socialism with a more human face" was on the wane. Because I was not witty in French, he answered. And this was not a mere witticism. He liked to pretend, to sometimes make a deliberately exaggerated show of his fears, disgusts, and resentments, either to stress a point or to render the very actions that brought out such feelings unbelievable, by turning them into a caricature. He used his appearance, and his code of dress also as a kind of shield. I learned the expression "a fool's license" from him. He wore a colorful, brocade vest with his jacket, a piece of clothing straight from prewar Paris, which was, in Warsaw, in those times of drab Stalinist fashion, totally out of place. Here a vest like that made you immediately suspicious. Or the bow tie he wore to his lectures! This set him apart; what could one expect from a man of such habits? Any ideological transgression would be disregarded if not forgiven, he was a "fool" and that vest, the bow tie, and the French manners, at this time almost forgotten in Warsaw, gave him the "license" to transgress, to somehow explain and justify those transgressions, or so he thought and hoped. Yet, I am not sure that had he lived until 1968, all that camouflage would have helped him. Most likely, he too would have been forced out, into emigrating again, as were so many others, if not for any other reason than simply because he was, after all, half-Jewish.

My Sabbatical in the Soviet Union

At the end of 1959, I went to the Soviet Union for a three-month stay. By that time, I was deep into my new research project and needed the material I knew I would find at the archives and libraries in Moscow. I was excited about the trip, to see the Soviet Union again, to see my university friends, and especially to see Leningrad again, this was very important to me. It took some time to arrange the trip, and I started working on it while Kronski was still alive, and the head of my department. Well, I knew "Persia," knew that there was nothing to fear there for me at this time, and I had a most interesting and fruitful trip. This was Khrushchev's Soviet Union. It was not the hungry country, on the brink of starvation, that I had left fourteen years ago. The stores, in Moscow and Leningrad, the only cities I visited, were well stocked, the food in the cafes and at the university restaurant where I mostly ate, was good and not very expensive, and people on the street were dressed no worse than the people in Poland. There was a lot of construction going on in Moscow and people were talking about moving into one-family, separate apartments, a dream, after the long-suffered hell of "communal living," four, five, or more families sharing one apartment and amenities. People were also talking about "rehabilitation," the return of innocent people from imprisonment and concentration camps. I met a woman of about sixty in Moscow who had returned to the city after twenty years in a concentration camp and forced residence in the Far North when Khrushchev opened the prisons and camps. She received a pension, as other such returnees had, and "living space"; a room in a communal apartment. She was very happy and seemed to have forgotten about her horrible past. I am, she told me, a "Soviet *barinyia*," a noblewoman, a lady of leisure, and she used a lot of her time to do volunteer work in the Tretiakovka, the Art Museum, feasting her eyes on the rich art collections. But another woman, also a former prisoner, to whom Stefa, my Warsaw friend directed me, told me that the camps were again full, and to my question who they keep in the camps now, she replied: students mostly. Her information was correct; it was known that Khrushchev's "liberalization" policy was coming to an end and that the screw of power was again turning tight, resulting firstly in repression against the intelligentsia.

My Dormitory on the Lenin Hills

During my stay in Moscow, I lived at Moscow University's dormitory on the Lenin Hills. It was a huge place, a town in itself with four gated entrances. I spent my days at the Lenin Library, reading the old books, prerevolutionary or early-twentieth-century editions, and poring over the old philosophical journals that had recently been returned from the library's basement to the shelves, also a result of the post-Stalin liberalization. I used the Metro to get there. The marble salons of the Moscow underground were as shiny as ever, but the bas-relief embellishing the walls had undergone some changes: Stalin's face had vanished from there and this was yet another attempt to rewrite history.

The Yakushevs: Zhenia and Alyosha

Sometimes, overcome by loneliness and nostalgia, I would visit our friends, Zhenia and Alyosha Yakushev. Zhenia was an old friend. Gabriel and I had become friends with her at the Łódź "Bursa" right after the war. Alyosha, a philosopher colleague, was her Russian husband. Zhenia was now chargé d'affaires at the Polish Embassy, the only woman in the diplomatic corps in Moscow at that time. She too had had a most "colorful" life, that of a survivor of the Holocaust. The war had caught up with her, a native of Białystok, when she was fifteen years old and on vacation at a summer camp. She never saw her parents again. Evacuated from the camp into Russia, she spent two years in a *detdom* (an orphanage), went to school there, and later on to university. She returned to Poland after the war, but in 1949 went again to the Soviet Union, this time as a graduate student of Moscow University's Slavic Studies Department. There, she met Alyosha Yakushev, a philosophy student, married him, and remained in Moscow as a Polish citizen, having secured for herself a job with the Polish Embassy. With time, she was promoted to the high position of cultural attaché. Her duties took her to important cultural events in Moscow, and she would sometimes ask me to come with her. Once, we attended a "meet the author" event, which stuck in my mind, not because of the play itself, a tear-jerking drama that was very "hot" in Moscow then, or because of the play's author, but because of the remarks of his admirers who highly praised the author and the performance of the play for giving them, in the words of a young woman from the floor, "the opportunity to cry!" Was this the only way to make someone cry in Moscow then, I wondered?

From time to time, I would visit the Yakushevs, and I liked the evenings spent there. One would meet some very interesting people there, including Moscow University young professors yearning to break out of the stifling mold of established dogmas, and Poland being very much in vogue in the Soviet Union then, brought them to the Yakushevs. Lyosha Yakushev was a Russian bear of a man, big and gentle. I nicknamed him Chernyshevsky, because he invariably ended our discussions about the state of affairs and prospects for change with a sigh, "what we need is an organization!"

Zhenia, Lyosha, and their young son eventually returned to Poland. But they came to Warsaw shortly before a new upheaval was to take place there, the events of 1968, which threw us and them out, far away from Poland. The Yakushevs ended up in California, Lyosha teaching Russian in Monterey, and Zhenia working at UC Berkeley as a lecturer. Zhenia died in 1977 after a long struggle with cancer, and Lyosha not long after her, in a car accident.

In Leningrad, with my Russian Friends

I could go on about Zhenia and Lyosha, they were interesting people and close friends, but let me get back to my Soviet sojourn. Having, more or less, completed my research in Moscow, it was time to go to Leningrad. Faina met me at the train station, and this was an emotional encounter for both of us. She wanted me to stay at her place, but I was a foreigner now, and she understood that it would not be good for her, a Soviet citizen, to host a foreigner. I went to my hotel on Herzen Street. It was a familiar place and street; Frida used to live there.

Faina

During my stay in Leningrad, I met many of my old friends but spent most of the time with Faina because she, as a university lecturer, did not have to keep office hours from 9 A.M. to 5 P.M and thus was more readily available, and also because I used to be closer with her than with the others. Faina lived in a communal apartment close to the Smolnyj but luckily the place was a small one, just three rooms, and it was shared by only three single women, one woman to a room. Faina was the only one with higher education, a member of the "working intelligentsia" and the two other women were factory workers, but their earnings and living conditions did not differ much. Here the equality that had been postulated as society's goal was achieved.

I would meet Faina at the Naberezhnaia embankment, and weather permitting, we walked along the Neva River and talked, musing on things past, telling each other where we had been and what we had done during all those years. After graduating, Faina went to work in the Far East, to Vladivostok Oblast', teaching Marxism–Leninism at some college there. She got married to a fellow philosophy student, but the marriage was short-lived. He used to visit her from time to time even after they had divorced, "for love and philosophy," as she put it, and for some time she hoped that he would return to her for good, but this never happened.

Faina became a member of the Party while still a student and was very proud of the fact. The way she talked about it gave me the impression that for her it was something akin to being in the nobility, admitted to a higher social class. She was a highly disciplined party member and was equally supportive of whatever the Party was preaching at any given time. She had some reservations about Khrushchev's anti-Stalin stance at first, but later she would support her first secretary wholeheartedly. I was, for her, a little bit of a puzzle, and trying to "decipher" me, she once asked, "Anaya, do you like (*liubish-li*) Khrushchev?" In Russian, the verb *liubit'* means to like but also to love, and I, not wanting to get into a serious talk, tried to turn it into a joke, "How can I love him, a man I don't even know personally?" and was immediately sorry that I had put it that way because I saw that she was dismayed. She was a person with very strong feelings which I certainly did not want to hurt, and also, momentarily, a thought raced through my head that she would ask me to leave, that she would not have anything to do with someone harboring "such" views about her "leader." It was late in the evening, and the compromiser in me made me turn the conversation into a joke, and she, all her Russian intransigence notwithstanding, changed the subject, leaving the minefield of politics and ideology. But she was sad that I refused to share her unreserved adoration for Khrushchev. She was a great friend and a good, sincere human being that one could count on, and we liked each other, Khrushchev or not. Despite the ideological blinders, she was not totally blind to what was going on. The antisemitic policies of the Party troubled her and she felt ashamed of them. And with time, she became more receptive to change, more tolerant of disparate views. She presented me with a volume of Khlebnikov's poetry, knowing about my admiration for the poet, even though she herself still considered him just an unworthy "decadent." I still have that Khlebnikov volume with a long critical inscription by Faina and cherish it as a dear souvenir. Yet a few years later, she and Rita were both doing volunteer work for *samizdat*, typing distribution material not allowed by the state censors to reach the state-controlled media. I saw her for the last time many years later, in 1990, when Gabriel and I visited the Soviet Union, then just on the brink of falling apart. For Faina, this was a painful thing to witness. She was still a devoted Communist and she had fought for it in the war against the Fascists, as she would remind us, and perhaps, first of all, herself. Her world was coming to an end, and she survived it by only two years.

Rita

After the three mandatory years of work in the Far North, Rita returned to Leningrad and got a job with the Leningrad Historical Museum. She was rather happy with her job, doing some research on the history of her beloved city and publishing little booklets on famous people of the city's past. She had a son, by then about thirteen, but no husband. She had never married; she just wanted to have a child, but afterward refused to have anything to do with the child's father. It was before the age of in-vitro fertilization. Had it been available then, she would have most likely used this method. She was very cool about the whole matter; a well-organized person, she managed to exchange her apartment in Tbilisi for a large room in Leningrad and brought her mother over to live with her. The large room was subsequently divided into two, and her brother with his wife and child moved in, and thus the whole family was united. The room was part of a former grand St. Petersburg seven-room apartment that was shared now by seven families, one family per room. The common kitchen looked more like a restaurant's kitchen with so many people milling busily around there. Now imagine that bathroom there early in the morning!

We were sitting around the dinner table and eating *piroshki* (filled yeast dough buns) prepared by Rita's mother, a tall, skinny lady, in a loose black dress, and a face blackened by layers of dark patina left by the many periods of suffering in her life. We talked about Poland; they were all interested in the "Polish events" of a few years back and wanted to know what the Poles actually wanted. To my remark that Poles want first of all, perhaps, political independence from their great neighbor, nobody said anything. Had I underestimated their attachment to the "empire" of which they were, as I knew, otherwise quite critical? Had I inadvertently offended them? Was expressing sympathy for these Polish aspirations too much for them? After all, there was a common, traditional feeling in Russia of some reservation, skepticism if not mistrust about their neighbor. Anyway, the subject was evidently too "hot" to venture into, and we changed it. But next, I caused something of a stir with a casual remark that some university people in Poland were receiving stipends from the Ford Foundation to study or visit Western Europe or even the United States for research purposes. Rita could not believe it and found it even funny. The Ford Foundation! And people are taking them, those stipends? The epitome of Capitalism offering stipends to scholars from a socialist country!

Yes, this was an interesting, even memorable evening for me. It was also a pleasant one, thanks to the warm feelings they unmistakably had for me personally. I saw Rita a few more times, and she asked a lot of questions about literature, what was new, what was being translated into Polish from Western literature, and so on. For her, Remarque represented the last word of Western literature, and she was very enthusiastic about his *Arch of Triumph*, recently translated into Russian. Nothing else would strike even an echo with her. They were very much insulated, cut off from the world, and not even aware of it. And not only from the outside world, but also from the underground, great literary events in the Soviet Union that were reaching the West and causing a great stir there, like Solzhenitsyn, Terc, Daniel, and others.[112]

112 Aleksandr Solzhenitsyn (1918–2008) was among the best-known Soviet dissident writers in the West but he was not the only one. Andrei Sinyavsky (1925–1997),

And, of course, we also talked about Soviet antisemitism. Rita had suffered from it personally, and she was worried about the future. But in the middle of the conversation, she suddenly said, "And what about the Poles? It is well known that the Poles are no less if not more antisemitic than ours? How is it for you there, in Poland?" Good question! Was she defending something, I wondered? Was this a riposte in defense of some leftover Soviet pride? I did not mind and replied that till now, we did not have antisemitism coming from above, from the government, at least not very much of it, but who knows, it might come, and perhaps it would come. I had no idea that these were almost prophetic words, and that they would come true in the not-so-distant future.

I never saw Rita again but we kept exchanging letters. As if there had not been enough tragedy in her life, her son was killed in an accident at the age of eighteen, having just been admitted to college. He was crossing the street in Leningrad and was hit by a bus. She survived that catastrophe, most horrible for a mother, but not for long.

Frida

I also found Frida and saw her a few times. Frida was an engineer, working night shifts in some factory. She was married and had a daughter, Liubochka, by now six or seven years old. She had changed her address and it took some effort to find her. She exchanged her small room in the center of the city that I remembered so well for a larger one, in a lesser neighborhood. She seemed happy, working, raising her daughter, and she was absolutely and deliberately disinterested in political matters. She took me to a concert at the Leningrad symphony, and when the orchestra struck the first notes of Shostakovitch's *Jewish Songs*, performed then perhaps for the first time, the whole gilded symphony hall went wild with enthusiasm. This was not only

who published in the West under the pseudonym Abraham Terts, and Yuli Daniel (1925–1988), both writers, were convicted of disseminating anti-Soviet propaganda in 1966.

a celebration of the favorite composer's achievement, but also of the subject of the songs and of the familiar melodies, which had remained taboo here for a long time. I also visited Frida at her home, one room in a communal apartment that she shared with her child and husband, also an engineer. He did not make much of me being from "abroad." Poland, what's Poland, one can hardly call this abroad, they dyed their flag, it is a bit off-color now, and that's all, there or here, it's all the same, he tried to convince me. Frida would protest, a little embarrassed, but I made him happy admitting that indeed this was not so far from the truth. I never saw Frida again but remember her fondly. She remains in my thoughts a good friend from the faraway young years. I was very saddened when Faina told me about Frida's last years of life, in and out of psychiatric clinics. So many tragedies, so much pain and suffering!

A Scholar on Sabbatical Leave Abroad

Before I set out on my trip, I bought two bedcovers that a friend of mine had asked me to take to Moscow for some relatives of hers. They dreamed about those made-in-Poland bedcovers, and they would pay me back in rubles what I had spent in zlotys. This was a great deal and I was happy to oblige. With the money I got from them plus some of what I was able to save from my rather generous stipend, I bought a TV set, and brought it home. At this time, people were bringing things like refrigerators, radios, TV sets, vacuum cleaners from the Soviet Union, while from Poland to the Soviet Union went Polish textile. The state-run trade was somehow unable to organize such exchanges, and people took it into their own hands. It was not quite legal, of course, but very common. I could not have followed the example of Arthur Koestler who before leaving the Soviet Union in the mid-thirties bought a diamond, as he tells in his memoirs, which, when he had subsequently sold it in Vienna, provided him with means to survive for at least half a year. I did not have enough to "deal in diamonds," so I did what I could. My colleagues' commercial dealings on similar leaves were sometimes even at a much lower level. While going abroad on a research stipend, it was quite normal to take canned fish or meat with you to save as much as possible of the stipend's precious foreign currency. As rumour had it, one of my colleagues, a professor at Warsaw University, even stocked up on sugar for his two-month-long stay in Paris. Well, he had, perhaps, a very sweet tooth or had been much thriftier than others. The very same thriftiness caused some to feast mostly on bananas and chocolate when abroad, luxuries in Poland but among the cheapest food available abroad. Cheap, nutritious, and fattening, the gain in weight was somehow recompensed by saving some of the precious foreign currency! Still others would return from a six-month trip not only enriched intellectually but also much better off financially. I knew at least a few people who brought back a car bought abroad. Well, to each according to his/her ability. My TV set turned out to be a lousy one, breaking down at least twice a week to our great disappointment. A few years later, we bought a new and a better one in Warsaw, an East German Rubin; it broke down only once a month, more or less, which was a great improvement, anyway.

An Anarchist from Bulgaria Came to Visit

My book on Bakunin was published in 1964 and it was well received; perhaps the juxtaposition of Marx's notion of the dictatorship of the proletariat with Bakunin's protest against any dictatorship, which "red or otherwise still is a dictatorship," as well as his statement that "power corrupts" fell on fertile ground and appealed to many. The book found a good reception and had many favorable reviews in scholarly journals. It was also noted with a review in some radical paper in Paris; a book about Bakunin in "People's Poland" gave it a bit of an aura of a sensation. Also, Professor M. Carr, a noted specialist and author of many books concerning Russian history, wrote me a nice note.

Sometime later still, around 1965, I got a telephone call. A man, speaking a mixture of Slavic languages, asked if he could see me. He was from Bulgaria and had just bought the two volumes of Bakunin's writings, which I had edited, and would like to talk with me. Would I spare him a few minutes? He was right downstairs in the neighborhood bookstore. He came up, a man in his forties, a Bulgarian, an engineer on a business trip to East Germany; he had stopped in Warsaw for the purpose of buying these two volumes, which he carried under his arm. He had gone to many bookstores to find them, he told me, and was lucky to get them finally right here. "Does he want an autograph?" "Yes, please," he said, but this was not the only reason why he wanted to see me. There were still in Varna, Bulgaria, some anarchists, he said, and on hearing that in Warsaw, "a woman teacher" had published Bakunin's writings, they decided to send someone to buy it. Polish is not Bulgarian, but it is still a Slavic language so they would manage. To read Bakunin was an exciting idea for them. He used this trip to Germany stretching it a little to make a stop in Warsaw. The anarchists used to be strong in Bulgaria, he told me. Right after the war 400 people in Varna alone were arrested, and nobody saw any of them again. "Are you an anarchist, yourself?" he asked me somewhat timidly, and when I said that no, I was just interested in social ideas and their history, he nodded as if to say that he understood my position, and he added, "We are not for violence, for bomb throwing, we believe that the just society will come by explaining our ideas to people..." A nice guy, I thought, still not totally sure that he was who he said he was, and not someone sent over from "our" Security Police, the UB. Had he seen the book I had written on Bakunin? I nevertheless asked him and offered him a copy. He thanked me and wanting evidently to reciprocate with some gift, started ferreting around for something in his briefcase and got out a chocolate bar, which he handed to me, "If you ever come to Varna, you'll be greeted as a very best friend," he added. When I came with my family to Bulgaria on vacation two years later, I did not go to meet the anarchists in Varna, yet I kept the address for many years, just in case.

My daughter Helenka, just then returning from school, came into the room shortly before the man took his leave, and I gave her the bar. She looked at it with mock suspicion, "Is it filled with dynamite?" she asked. "It's Wedel, local production, don't you see," I said, and we both laughed.

CHAPTER FIFTEEN

SECOND EMIGRATION LOOMING

With the turmoil of the recent years over, our life stabilized, and we tried to enjoy it fully. It was a good life, and a happy one. Our children were growing, healthy, bright and beautiful, and they were good students. There were, of course, the usual bouts with childhood diseases, even with TB that was so prevalent in Poland in the postwar years that to catch it was almost unavoidable. Both children went through it at the age of seven or eight, but fortunately, it was contained quickly and efficiently, without any unduly serious consequences. Time was flying by so fast and suddenly our son was a tall fifteen-year-old boy in need of a shave, and I still see myself, inconspicuously watching my two men as they stood before the mirror in the bathroom, Gabriel introducing Henio to that arcane daily ritual. Helenka suddenly worried about her transfer from elementary school to high school and the exams she had to take. The commotion, the noises common in family life with small children, were suddenly gone.

Soon, their school years over, they would be ready to leave us. "Will we stay together with you forever?" Helenka used to ask, and now Gabriel would answer, "No, Mother and I will, but you'll find a husband and go your way, and Henio, a wife, and do the same," and she did not protest against that verdict anymore, as she used to when she was much younger, and Gabriel used to tease her that he "would marry her off" if she did not stop misbehaving. And the thought of retirement crossed my mind, once or twice. Suddenly it seemed so close, only some twenty-five more years! It was a bit scary, yet a peaceful thought. Yes, it was a good life, all the drawbacks notwithstanding, and yet, despite the many good things, the successful careers, the relative prosperity, the persistent feeling that it was all built on shaky foundations was always there. Our prosperity was dubious. In fact, all our prosperity after the war was dubious, ambivalent, because there was something artificial, temporary in our very existence here. We often thought about it and sometimes talked about it with close friends. We had an expression for describing it, "sitting on suitcases." All those years we were expecting a new "earthquake," not geological but political and social that would throw us off the shaky foundations our life was built on.

There were signs that it was coming. The Party, holding on to its power and trying to narrow the margin of freedom won as a result of the Polish October started persecuting people for possession or borrowing of books considered "slanderous to the State" as early as 1959. Books sent from abroad were confiscated by the censors controlling the incoming mail. I myself had a spat with those censors. In 1966, while on the four-month sabbatical leave at the Sorbonne, I mailed home a few books, among them a two-volume *History of Russian Philosophy,* by Zenkowsky, in Russian, but I never received them. I especially missed the Zenkowsky books, which I needed for my lectures, but my interventions at the post office were to no avail. Yet as Poland still remained the "best barrack in the socialist camp" and certainly the funniest, I was getting many such confiscated books to read through my friends, who had friends or acquaintances among the security people and feeling the need to read something more interesting than the stale officially allowed literature, would get them from that source. So, I regularly read the Polish monthly, *Kultura,* published in Paris, and other Polish and Russian émigré literature, and later on, all of Solzhenitsyn, Eugenia Ginsburg, Terc, and others.

Soon, the first trials for possessing the "wrong" books were followed by crackdowns on independent cultural clubs. The Party was showing the intelligentsia that the promised freedoms should not be taken too literally. Then, at the beginning of 1964 came the so-called "Letter of Thirty-Four." Thirty-four intellectuals, writers, and scientists addressed a short letter to Poland's premier condemning the over-intrusive censorship as endangering Polish culture. The letter was not published in Poland but was leaked abroad and came back to Poland via Radio Free Europe, causing a considerable stir in Warsaw. A student meeting was called at Warsaw University in support of that letter, but it ended peacefully and without any consequences for the students. The March 1968 student protest at Warsaw University would not end so simply.

A New Upheaval in the Making

These were signs of a coming upheaval. The first tremors came with the approaching tenth anniversary of the Polish October in 1966. A meeting commemorating the anniversary was being prepared, but the organizers were unable to receive an official permit for it. At first, the City Party Committee refused permission, but then the permit was finally granted, ironically, by the chief of the Security Police himself, Mieczysław Moczar, as my colleague and friend Krzysztof Pomian, one of the meeting's organizers, told me. "And you decided to hold that meeting?" I asked with disbelief. I saw the permit coming from these quarters as a clear provocation. Moczar was by then, and this was already known, Gomułka's main rival, vying for power over the Party, and the students would be made the first scapegoat of that internal political struggle.

Leszek Kolakowski and Pomian who addressed the meeting, were subsequently expelled from the Party. The strike against the organizers of the anniversary meeting was met with an uproar, some gave up their party membership in protest, and many others in my department spoke out against the expulsion of Kolakowski. All his coworkers were called one by one before a special commission that demanded to denounce him.

I remember my meeting with that "commission." There were two people there, the secretary of the Regional Party Organization and Stanisław Wroński, then chief editor of the publishing house, Książka i Wiedza. As it happened, a new book by Kolakowski just then set and ready to print by the above publisher, was turned by him into a rod of steel. I knew about it, and considered it an outrage and made my view clear. Wroński used to be a student at the Party School, when I was a teacher there, and I knew him well.

I added that I considered the decision unwise, and in this case very unwise, to say the least. Why so, Wroński wanted to know? Because the views Kolakowski expressed in the aforementioned book, especially in gnoseology, the theory of cognizance, I told him, were remarkably similar to the views of the revered Italian Communist philosopher and theoretician, Gramsci. Wroński gasped. I had sewn some seeds of doubt in his mind. What if he had indeed acted too hastily damning Kolakowski's ready-to-print book, and if I were right, this might have been the case. Gramsci…there was no reason for a ban then, or it might have been even wrong to do so, and maybe he would be made responsible for doing what he had ordered to do? Euro-Communism, and especially the Italian kind, was then in Warsaw held in high regard, and he knew this, of course! I had confused him, and I did derive some satisfaction from it!

More disciplinary proceedings followed, and again, in protest against them, new petitions were signed. A group of activists—students, with Adam Michnik as their leader—was suspended and threatened with expulsion from the university. This caused special indignation. About a thousand students signed a petition to the rector of Warsaw University, protesting against the expulsion of the activists from the university. My son, Henryk, was among them.

The Arab–Israeli War of 1967

And amid all this turmoil, the Six Day Arab Israeli War of 1967 came onto the scene. Israel was maligned by the Party and the press as the aggressor, and the one-eyed Israeli General Dayan, his face contorted, as the arch-monster, the chief villain, was suddenly all over the papers and magazines. But the reaction of many Poles was not what was expected by the Party, many were laughing that "our" Jews beat "their," the Soviets', Arabs. Gomułka was furious, and in June 1967, speaking to the Congress of the Labor Unions, he accused "Jewish citizens of Poland who applauded Israeli aggression" of acting as "Israel's Fifth Column." Poland would not stop Polish citizens of "Jewish origin" from leaving Poland, if they wished to do so, he added, but no Polish citizen could have more than one motherland, which is People's Poland. This was like a bad dream! "They" would drag people to the party meetings, demanding declarations: Which is your motherland? One, only one, you cannot have two! Declare yourselves! You support the Israeli aggressors? Condemn them! *Apage, Satanas*![113] *Israel, Apage Dayan*!!! And I saw the prewar slogan of the nationalists, "Jews to Palestine" unfurling before my eyes. I was perhaps not thinking clear, to react like that, I told myself finally coming back to reality. But this was reality, and it was a nightmare. A few days later, a panel started working in the party organization of the Department of Philosophy, dragging people for "friendly individual discussions" of the political situation. I was called, but I "declined the invitation."

Gabriel was in Moscow then, on a leave of absence, researching and collecting material for a three-volume anthology of the *Planning Debates of the 1920s*. I was home, recuperating after thyroid surgery and a rather lengthy stay in hospital, when Henryk, who was listening to the radio, suddenly called to me, "We were just declared to be Israel's Fifth Column!" I could not believe it and started nervously pushing the radio buttons back and forth, as if it were possible to get back to that passage of Gomułka's speech. The expression "fifth column" was removed from the text of the speech when it was published the next day, presumably as a result of the intervention of Ochab, as well-informed people had maintained.[114] But the rest of the speech

113 Latin for "Begone, Satan!"

114 Edward Ochab (1906–1989) joined the Communist Party as a young man and rose in its ranks, working on behalf of Communism in Poland during World War II in the USSR and afterward in the People's Polish Republic. He held many important

was not retracted, and it became a clear signal to open the so-called "anti-Zionist," antisemitic campaign of 1967–1968. During the rest of 1967, party activists, we called them *hui-ven-bins* after the bloodthirsty activists of the Chinese "Cultural Revolution," went to work with great enthusiasm calling for special meetings, criticizing people for sins never committed, provoking and demanding Jews to declare themselves, to declare which one was their motherland, Poland or Israel. Thus, our own "cultural revolution," if not yet in full swing, had already started in earnest, and since it was in Poland, this Polish Cultural Revolution came with a twist, an antisemitic twist. At the same time, the infighting between the two strongest factions, Moczar and Gomułka, for leadership, for control of the Party, and subsequently the country, became almost open and for all to see, but it also became clear that it did not matter who won. Ominous forces had already been set in motion. Whichever of those factions would come out with the upper hand, a reactionary setback would result, whatever freedoms from the Polish October were still there would be erased, and both factions would use the antisemitic or "anti-Zionist card" as they called it, in their political game.

The So-called March Events

New Year's Eve of 1967 was to become our last in Poland. My family and I were watching a traditional puppet TV show in which Moczar's character sang to Shakespeare's words, "We do not sleep, so someone else could." I knew this was a portentous "watch," and it would bring nothing but disaster.

The "volcano" had erupted, and the expected "earthquake" culminated in what is in the newest history of Poland confusingly called the March Events. It was an upheaval that brought grave consequences to the lives of many people, to the intelligentsia, to

roles, including a brief stint as first secretary of the PZPR in 1956. Ochab, whose wife was Jewish, protested against Gomułka's turn to state-sponsored antisemitism and resigned from the government in 1968.

Poland's cultural life, and to the remnants of the Polish Jews, as well as to my family.

There is by now a rather vast literature concerning that period of Poland's postwar history, and there is no need to elaborate on it here, so just a few observations from my own perspective. I was on a short winter vacation for health reasons in the Tatras, when I read a small note in the daily *Trybuna Ludu* saying that an antigovernment "student demonstration" was held at Warsaw University. This was strange, to say the least. Whatever demonstration may have happened there, it was not in the normal order of things to report it in the press. The press was tightly controlled, and unless the authorities on the highest level had decided to inform the public that a demonstration had been held and broken up, nobody would have informed about it. I took the next train home, worried about where Henryk was at the time of the demonstration and about the situation in general.

A Sit-in at the Department of Philosophy

The Department of Philosophy at the university looked like a camp ground when I saw it the next day upon returning home; the students and many of my colleagues—professors—were sleeping in the seminar rooms. The March 8 demonstration at the university yard, which had started as a peaceful protest against the threatened expulsion of some students from the university for "activities not becoming of students," was brutally broken up, the demonstrators beaten by the police, and the yard cleared by force. And what did the authorities consider an activity "unbecoming" of students? They demanded a greater measure of autonomy for the youth organization affiliated with the Party, a rather modest demand. With the demonstration broken up, the students turned to sit-ins in the lecture and seminar halls, which lasted a few days. Now the events moved with enormous speed. Disciplinary actions from the authorities followed and then more student protests, which were again answered with more drastic disciplinary measures. Then came arrests and a punitive draft was attempted.

Disciplinary Draft

Despite everything, we were unprepared for such severe repercussions. When one evening, out of the blue, our Henryk was notified over the phone that he was hereby drafted into the army and was to arrive the next morning at the university to be sent off to a military camp, we were startled. I remember Gabriel running down a flight of steps to see a colleague, a neighbor of ours, perhaps he would know something more, and returning pale shortly thereafter. Our neighbor and colleague, a Warsaw University history professor, did not forgo the opportunity to give Gabriel a piece of his mind; those students, those good-for-nothing hooligans, he foamed, deserved a lesson and it was finally coming, and it was high time for it, and so on. Some fifty students were called up, even though students were exempted from military service by fulfilling their military obligation during the due course of their studies and by participating in military camps during the summer. The "draft" was so obviously illegal that it was called off before it had even started. I breathed a little easier, but not for long. Tensions in the city ran high, the papers were full of invectives against "Zionists" inciting all imaginable evil, and there were many arrests of young people. Some were arrested just in the streets when leaving the Polytechnic or the university buildings, and one might say there were regular roundups going on through the city, roundups not unlike those the Nazis had practiced during the occupation. Others were taken away from their homes.

Roundups and Arrests

One morning, Gabriel and Henryk had already left home, Helenka had gone to school as usual, and I too was ready to leave, when someone rang the doorbell. Two men stood outside, one was young, stocky, exuding brute force, the other, older and very thin, almost emaciated but so obviously a plainclothes policeman, with the wide brim of his hat shadowing his face that I did not have to ask who they were or what they wanted. "Was Henryk home?" they wanted to know, and when I nevertheless asked who they were, the younger one said with a smirk, "Colleagues." "Henryk does not have such colleagues," I retorted and pushed the door to close it. He pushed it back, but after I repeated that Henryk was not home, they left. I phoned Gabriel and he went immediately to the Physics Institute, fetched Henryk and kept him in his office until the end of the day. With the help of one of his colleagues at the vice premier's office, he arranged tickets for me and Henryk to go to Zakopane and secured a place to stay for us there in a vacation home administered by that office. Henryk could not come home that evening as they might be waiting for him, and the very thought of him in the clutches of that brute who came calling in the morning made me shudder. I met Henryk at the train station, and we left Warsaw. For the time being, I got him out of harm's way.

What Did They Yell at the Grand Party Meeting?

Zakopane was peaceful and serene, as usual at this time of the year, but I was hardly able to appreciate it. I had left here less than two weeks earlier, but a whole epoch had passed by since. My world had changed and would never be the same. On one of the walks through the valleys, I met Stanisław Wroński, the editor-in-chief of the Książka i Wiedza Publishing House. He winked at seeing Henryk with me, "Keeping him out of mischief, eh?" I would not explain, but he was not waiting for it either, he had something else on his mind, "What did they yell the other day at the Grand Meeting?" (at the Palace of Culture on March 19) he asked. He had watched it on TV, but the old set was no good and he was not sure. They yelled "faster, faster," I said, but no, they were calling a name, he said, and he wanted to know what name they had shouted. Sure, they yelled "Gierek, Gierek"[115] this was what they had yelled, I informed him, and it made a great impression on him because he took

115 Edward Gierek (1913–2001), while not a leader of one of the main factions vying for power in Poland at this point, was nonetheless popular and seen as a progressive. He served as first secretary of the PZPR after Gomułka's fall in 1970.

leave right away, adding that it was time to return to Warsaw, this was no time for vacationing.

Soon, our "vacation" was also cut short. Two days later Gabriel called, saying we must return home, the military was still claiming our son; the punitive action had been modified but not recalled. The same fifty young men were called up for one month of punitive military training, even though nobody would say what their "sin" was. This time, however, the authorities tried at least to give it the appearance of legality and a date for the service was set from April 1 until the end of the month, so we hoped that it would indeed be for one month only.

What Will Those Fired Professors Do?

The next day we took the train to Warsaw, but before leaving I still had time to read the morning paper. On the front page of the party daily, *Trybuna Ludu,* was the announcement that six professors of Warsaw University—Kolakowski, Baczko, Morawski (of my own Philosophy Department), Bauman, Maria Bielińska-Hirszowicz (of the Sociology Department), and Brus (of the Economics Department)—were fired from their posts. The announcement was set in very big, bold letters as if this were the greatest and most important recent achievement Poland could boast about. It was also announced that the Department of Philosophy of Warsaw University was dismantled, as well as the third year of the Department of Physics, Mathematics, and Economics.

"And what would the professors fired from their posts be doing now?" I overheard two "concerned" party members of "good standing" gossiping. "We'll send them packing, they'll go abroad, and their teaching careers will be finished," they resolved with obvious glee. They certainly were well informed; just a few days earlier, we ourselves watched, on our East-German TV set, the meeting of the party activists transmitted from the Grand Hall of the Palace of Culture. Gomułka promised in his speech that all the Jews of Poland would be made to emigrate, to leave Poland, and his oratory was interrupted by enthusiastic prompting from the floor, "Let them go, faster, faster!" "Them" were the Jews, "Zionists" or in the adopted then parlance, people of "Jewish origin." The atmosphere in the hall was palpably hot, the faces of the "comrades" were dripping with zeal and readiness for "action," and it was all coming through the TV set with such clarity that I, moved by an impulse, went to the front door of our apartment and double-locked it. As I was later told by others, I was not the only one that reacted in such a way. There was danger in the air; a pogrom was on many of our friends' minds.

Punitive Military Training Camp

Henryk and the group of students called up for punitive military service were all mostly from Warsaw University and they were almost exclusively Jewish. At first, they were dispatched to Hrubieszów. A week later, Gabriel went there to see our son. Hrubieszów had a special meaning for Gabriel because nearby was Komarów, his father's hometown, and the place to which he returned after he had tried unsuccessfully to reach Łódź and his wife and sons in the Łódź ghetto. Now, beset by a host of painful memories, Gabriel would see more clearly that to continue living in Poland as second-class citizens would become increasingly difficult, that to condemn the children to the indignities they did not deserve would be wrong. As he told me, this helped him make up his mind and decide to emigrate.

From Hrubieszów, for the remaining two weeks, the whole group was transferred to another camp, on the opposite side of Poland, in Lower Silesia. I went to see Henryk there. I traveled with two other women, mothers, also visiting their sons at the same military camp. I remember one of them, Mrs. Yaszunska, the wife of a known journalist of the party daily, *Trybuna Ludu*.

It was early spring, the nights were still chilly, and the boys were camping out, which was against the regulations, and wearing the light summer uniforms, was also against the regulations. Henio was brave and smart, as he tried to put on layers of clothing under the uniform, whatever he could find to keep himself warmer, using the experience from his Boy-Scout days. Now, it came in handy. He knew how to start a fire, and he was smart about knowing what to tell the investigators and especially what not to tell them. I was quite proud of him and admired his ability to cope with the spartan conditions they were put in. He told me that to talk openly we should go outside. "They have good listening devices," he explained when we went for a walk. I told him that Gabriel had turned in his party card, and his face lit up. "That's good," he said. "But we will have to leave the country," I said. "That's very good, too," he answered. I felt relieved. I knew that families were breaking up on that account: parents wanting to leave, but the children for a variety of reasons not wanting to, or vice versa, the children would push to go, while the parents, too old or perhaps too inert, or too afraid to face an unknown world, would not. At least we would not have any trouble of this kind, and we would stay united as a family.

Henryk Applied for an Exit Visa

Henryk returned home on May 1, and two days later he applied for an exit visa. After renouncing his party membership, Gabriel was out of work. He was fired from the office of the vice premier for whom he had worked for a decade and from the Party School where he held a teaching position. Suddenly unemployed and unable to keep his mind busy on problems and questions that were his usual fodder, he seemed particularly miserable, but so were we all. I was still formally employed, but the Department of Philosophy had been dismantled, and everything seemed to be in disarray. Of our family, only Helenka was still following her regular schedule of going to school. She was in tenth grade and next year would be her last year of high school, and I thought with special sadness of the very difficult task that would await her wherever we might finally end up. To complete the last grade, which leads to college, in a strange country, in a strange language, would be very difficult. And she would lose all the friends she had acquired during her happy childhood!

The Anti-Zionist Campaign in Schools

Her school was, of course, not immune to what was going on in the country in general, to the barking, foaming press, the daily triumphant reports about "Zionists" being fired from various places and positions, about people being forced to apply for exit visas. Helenka, who was always a good student, suddenly fell to the level of barely adequate. As it happened, on one of the last tests in physics, her close friend Ewa Borkowska, a good student, got so mixed up that she had to ask Helenka for help, and as a result, their answers were identical, but Ewa got a "very good" mark while Helenka got only "passed." Both girls were flabbergasted, and Ewa bravely confronted the teacher, "Why did Helena get a lower mark if our answers were the same?" "Because she cheated," the teacher said. Ewa was really brave, "No," she said, "I copied it from her, I cheated, and I do not deserve that high mark." "This can not be," the teacher answered, "she got all she deserved!" My poor child! And poor, brave Ewa! What were they doing to the children? What did they teach them? Hard to imagine the moral impact of a statement like this, "She got all she deserved!" This brought back the memory of those faraway times in Łódź, at the very beginning of the Nazi occupation when my brother-in-law was told by some scum, "I don't have to pay you, Jew, go complain if you want." Was the teacher's statement not akin to that? Did this teacher act according to an instruction, or was she acting on her own, just expressing her own suppressed hatred, I wondered. Helena and Ewa remained friends and kept in touch for years. A year later, Helenka enrolled in the twelfth grade at George Washington High School in New York, to join, still one year later, the class of 1974 at Smith College, from where she graduated four years later Magna Cum Laude, Phi Beta Kappa, and whatever other honors there were there. She would go on from there to receive her doctorate in anthropology from the University of Massachusetts and on to a successful academic career.

They Want to Make Poland Judenfrei

The authorities went about the task of making Poland *Judenfrei* with great energy. Jews were fired en masse from high or even quite ordinary positions, from various central institutions and ministries, from educational institutions around the country, as well as from factories. No Jew was indispensable, no matter what his/her qualifications. The only two people with a working knowledge of Greek and Latin employed by PWN, the largest Polish State Publishing House, the department publishing philosophical literature, were fired. To the remark of someone who tried to persuade Gomułka that their replacement would be almost impossible, he supposedly replied, "They [Jews] all know languages, why didn't you take care to prepare 'ours?'" And the press around us was barking, spewing hate that was flowing freely, and we had the feeling that it would engulf us. The Party's propaganda machine was throwing mind-boggling accusations, dirt, mud, it warned of the danger of "Zionism" which was suddenly promoted to be Poland's most menacing enemy. The inventiveness of those wild denunciations collected into a book and published on the thirtieth anniversary of those shameful events, fills one with dread even today.

We Will Go, But Where to?

Emigration was high on the day's agenda. But where to? And how? Into the unknown? Again? Begin anew when you are almost at the peak of your professional career? When you are well over forty?

We could apply to immigrate to Israel, formalities were kept very simple, but the more we were pushed into that direction by the invisible and the not-so-invisible forces, the stronger our will became to resist. The old slogans, "Jews to Palestine," "Let them go to Palestine," or sometimes "Jews to Madagascar," "Let them go to Madagascar" were now replaced by "Jews to Israel," "Let the Jews go to Israel," let them go, faster, faster. The Polish Government stripped us of citizenship and provided us with a temporary "travel document," valid only for crossing the border. Luckily, other avenues opened up; we were not defenseless in the world, and there were possibilities of moving to some countries of Western Europe and even to Canada and the United States. It was, however, a very hard decision to make and we hesitated, but when we finally decided to go, we acted very fast. First, not certain that our exit visas, especially Gabriel's, would be granted by the government as promptly as it soon became customary—four weeks from the moment of applying—we decided that Henryk would go first. He would go to Brussels, where he could stay with my family for a while. Summer was approaching, and we wanted him to leave as soon as possible, to be there in time to resume his studies at the Brussels Free University in the fall. "Brussels has a very good Physics Department," his Warsaw professor told him. "Everything will turn out for the best for you," he kindly tried to console him.

On a beautiful June day, a group of young people, students of Warsaw University, Henryk's classmates, and the three of us, Gabriel, Helenka, and I, saw him off at the Gdańsk train station. It was a sunny summer day, the group of young people looked happy, as if on a vacation outing, and nothing betrayed their tension and anxiety. I looked at my son and his group of friends, and the bitter thought would not leave me: *natsionalnoe menshinstvo*, again a national minority, always a national minority, pushed, hated, unwanted. Shouldn't we rather go to Israel?

Soon most of those present at the train station would take the same road our son had taken and they would go abroad. Some would leave with their parents, others would go alone, leaving their elderly parents behind, unable to undertake the trip into the unknown. Families were broken up again, like the first time, when we were escaping the Nazis, alone, never to see our loved ones again. We too thought for a moment about letting our son go alone, but the very thought made me shudder. As the political situation looked then, this might have been parting for many years if not forever. And indeed, it took many years until it was even possible to visit Poland again.

The American Consul

There was no more hesitation, no, we were going, no matter where. But before leaving, I had one more thing to do. I had to see the U.S. consul in Warsaw; I wanted to inquire about the prospects of obtaining entrance visas to the United States. Would we be allowed to settle there? Henryk called me from Vienna almost daily urging me to see the consul. We had to register our desire to go to America with the consul while we were still in Warsaw, he told me. He kept telling me that this was imperative if we wanted to receive those entrance visas to the United States in Vienna, after our arrival there. I could not understand the connection but promised to do as he said. There was such anxiety in his voice; he found himself suddenly alone in a strange country, a strange city, feeling like some character out of a movie or a book, an escapee from the Nazis, and I could feel that he was scared. I promised to go, and one day I did.

The Polish policeman at the entrance to the American embassy did not pay any attention to me. People were coming out and going in, and in a moment, I was in the huge waiting room, and after presenting my university ID to the receptionist, I was immediately shown to the consul's office. The consul was young, spoke adequate Polish, and was interested to talk with a Warsaw University professor. He had graduated in political science and my field, especially my writings on Bakunin, had captured his attention. I told him that I was a member of the Party and wondered if I would receive an American visa. He immediately said, more stating than asking, "Of course, you had to join [the Party] to obtain a university job?" I was taken a bit aback by his point of view. He considered it natural to join a political party to get a job. But to me, this seemed opportunistic and therefore not flawless, and I would not like to admit it, even if it was the full truth, and it was not. It was not that simple! I tried to explain myself, saying something about beliefs, ideals, and disillusionment. He listened, shook his head disapprovingly, and finally said, "I understand you, you are sincere," but then added, "Never say things like that to any other American consul!" He repeated that we would get visas to the United States and wished me good luck, adding, "Why are they pushing people like you to leave?"

I went home, glad that I had done what Henryk insisted I should do. I was, of course, still thinking about my talk with that nice American consul and could not stop thinking about it, about the idealistic versus pragmatic motives of our actions and about the pragmatist's definition of truth as that which has fruitful consequences. It was no doubt interesting, but this was no time for analyzing the meaning and practical implications of pragmatism. For now, I certainly had to attend to a multitude of nagging, mundane, practical problems. Preparing to emigrate requires a lot of work; there were errands to run, and hurdles to overcome, and it was time to get started. Wherever it would lead us now, the way for us seemed open, the way for the second emigration in our lifetime.

A New Life

An Italian charter plane took us from the Leonardo de Vinci airport in Rome to New York where HIAS volunteers received us with friendly smiles and efficient instructions. The good organization sent us to Baltimore. We thought we may settle there or eventually move to another place in the United States, but from that point, we were destined to start our American odyssey. It was a short trip and American Airlines would take us there, and indeed in no time we were in the air again, and a smiling, young, perfumed girl, a movie star, the stewardess, asked what we would have to drink, and I timidly declined, no, nothing, thank you, not only because my English was so limited, but first of all because I was certain that something to drink in a plane, so high in the air, must cost a fortune, and we were penniless newcomers.

The trip was short, as promised, and again a very friendly HIAS volunteer, a Baltimore dentist, picked us up at the airport. He took us to a motel for an overnight stay, and tomorrow, he said…, but I did not know what was going to happen tomorrow, and I did not care, either. He was a nice man, polite and smiling and very helpful with loading our belongings into his enormous car, and when we settled in that big wide car, he turned to me and asked, "Mrs. Temkin are you happy to have arrived in America?" And I did not know what to say to this nice

American; happy is such a big word, was I happy? My father, had he known, would have been happy for me and my family, but was I happy? Not at that moment, certainly. At that moment, all I knew was that I was too tired to think or feel. I do not remember if I answered the question. Perhaps I just nodded, yes, yes, because of my limited English, and I was not able to say much more. And did I really arrive? Will I ever?

What I can say now, looking back on those early moments, is that America was good to us, better than I had dared to expect. Our stay in Baltimore was short; soon we went back to New York, the place where perhaps most newcomers to the United States start their journey in the new country. A semester of English at Columbia University was more than beneficial: it gave us some time to look around, to regain a certain measure of equilibrium.

Hanna and Gabriel with Henryk, 1950.

Hanna and Gabriel with Henryk and Helena, on vacation in Zakopane, Poland, 1955.

Hanna with Henryk and Helena, Warsaw, 1959.

Hanna's during her sabbatical at the Sorbonne University, Paris, 1966.

Hanna and Gabriel at the Niagara Falls,
Canada, ca. 1975.

Hanna and Gabriel celebrating New Year's in Sarasota FL, 1998/99.